RESEARCH GUIDE
TO AMERICAN LITERATURE

American Modernism
1914–1945

RESEARCH GUIDE
TO AMERICAN LITERATURE

RESEARCH GUIDE
TO AMERICAN LITERATURE

American Modernism
1914–1945

George Parker Anderson
Bruccoli Clark Layman, Inc.

A BRUCCOLI CLARK LAYMAN BOOK

Facts On File
An imprint of Infobase Publishing

Research Guide to American Literature: American Modernism, 1914–1945
Copyright © 2010 by George Parker Anderson

Facts On File, Inc.
An imprint of Infobase Publishing
132 West 31st Street
New York NY 10001

Library of Congress Cataloging-in-Publication Data
Research guide to American literature. — New ed.
    p. cm.
"A Bruccoli Clark Layman book."
Includes bibliographical references and index.
ISBN 978-0-8160-7861-5 (v. 1 : acid-free paper)—ISBN 978-0-8160-7862-2
(v. 2 : acid-free paper)—ISBN 978-0-8160-7863-9 (v. 3 : acid-free paper)—ISBN
978-0-8160-7864-6 (v. 4 : acid-free paper)—ISBN 978-0-8160-7865-3 (v. 5 :
acid-free paper)—ISBN 978-0-8160-7866-0 (v. 6 : acid-free paper)—ISBN 978-
0-8160-7867-7 (v. 7 : acid-free paper) 1. American literature—Research—Methodology—Handbooks, manuals, etc. 2. American literature—History and criticism.
3. Canon (Literature) I. Franklin, Benjamin, 1939– II. Vietto, Angela III. Habich,
Robert D., 1951– IV. Quirk, Tom, 1946– V. Scharnhorst, Gary. VI. Anderson,
George Parker, 1957– VII. Cusatis, John. VIII. Moser, Linda Trinh, 1964– IX.
West, Kathryn, 1962– X. Facts on File, Inc.
PS51.R47 2010
810.7′2—dc22
                                    2009047815

Facts On File books are available at special discounts when purchased in bulk quantities for businesses, associations, institutions, or sales promotions. Please call our Special Sales Department in New York at (212) 967-8800 or (800) 322-8755.

You can find Facts On File on the World Wide Web at http://www.factsonfile.com

Text design by Erika K. Arroyo
Composition by Bruccoli Clark Layman
Cover printed by Art Print, Taylor, PA
Book printed and bound by Maple Press, York, PA
Date printed: May 2010
Printed in the United States of America

10 9 8 7 6 5 4 3 2 1

This book is printed on acid-free paper.

For Julie and the pack and in memory of M.J.B.

Contents

Acknowledgments

The person I would like to thank, first and last, is my wife, Julie, who is my reason for everything. My greatest debt is to Rick Layman, who gave me the opportunity to take on this project, wrote splendid essays, and was always admirably patient and professional. I am also grateful to the scholars who contributed essays. A few other friends deserve special thanks for their different ways of encouragement and support: my sister Cynthia for our Saturday-morning phone conversations; Carolyn Sigler for not letting me write anything too ignorant about children's literature; Janet Hill for just the right way of shaking her head; and Phil Dematteis, an editor dedicated to putting out the best-quality book he can.

Contributors

Series Introduction

Research Guide to American Literature is a series of handbooks for students and teachers that recommends strategies for studying literary topics and frequently taught literary works and authors. The rationale for the series is that successful study is predicated on asking the right questions and then devising a logical strategy for addressing them. The process of responsible literary investigation begins with facts and usually ends with opinions. The value of those opinions depends on the ability of the reader to gather useful information, to consider it in context, to interpret it logically, and finally to decide what the interpretation means outside the confines of the literary work. Often the answers to questions a sophisticated reader asks about a literary topic are subjective, involving a reader's perception of an author's or a character's motive; always the search for the answer to a meaningful question involves a process of self-education and, in the best of circumstances, self-awareness.

RGAL is intended as a resource to assist readers in identifying questions to ask about literature. The seven volumes in this series are organized chronologically, corresponding to generally accepted literary periods. Each volume follows this general pattern:

Part I provides the social and historical context for a literary period, explaining its historical boundaries, describing the nature of the literary output of the time, placing the literature in its social and historical contexts, identifying literary influences, and tracing the evolution of critical approaches.

Part II comprises ten study guides on general themes or topics related to the period, organized alphabetically. Each guide first provides necessary background information, then suggests questions or research topics that might be fruitfully considered, along with specific primary and secondary works that students will find useful. Each guide also includes an annotated checklist of recommended secondary works and capsule identifications of people mentioned.

Part III comprises some thirty study guides for particular literary works or authors, organized alphabetically by the author's name. Each guide begins with a brief overview of the author's career to provide context, and then suggests some half a dozen topics for discussion and research, with advice about how to begin investigating the topic. These topics are meant to facilitate classroom discussion as well as to suggest interesting ideas for research papers. Each guide includes an annotated checklist of recommended secondary works.

Part IV is an annotated general bibliography recommending the most useful general works of literary history, literary criticism, and literary reference pertinent to the period.

Part V is a glossary of terms used in the volume.

A keyword index is included in each volume.

The purpose of *RGAL* is not to tell students what literature means but to help them determine the meaning for themselves by asking significant questions and seeking answers diligently and thoughtfully. That is how learning that matters takes place. The method is as old as Socrates.

—Richard Layman

Part I
Overview

Boundaries of the Period

The period covered by this volume is defined by the two most destructive wars in human history. The year 1914 marks the beginning of World War I; the conflict resulted from entangling international alliances in Europe, with the precipitating cause being the assassination of the Austrian archduke Franz Ferdinand in Sarajevo on 28 June. The guns began to sound in August as Germany, Austria-Hungary, and the Ottoman Empire (the Central Powers) sided against Britain, France, and Russia (the Allies). The year the war began, America was little involved with world affairs. Although the opening of the Panama Canal that year demonstrated that the United States was interested in trade, President Woodrow Wilson declared America's neutrality in what was seen as a wholly European conflict. The new books Americans were reading in that first year of the Great War included Edgar Rice Burroughs's *Tarzan of the Apes,* a wild tale of the son of an English lord being adopted and raised by giant apes in Africa, and Booth Tarkington's novel *Penrod,* about the misadventures of a mischievous eleven-year-old boy. Much less read was *North of Boston,* the second book by the obscure poet Robert Frost. The first poem in this collection, "Mending Wall," spoke to American ambivalence about neighbors: "Something there is that doesn't love a wall, / That wants it down," one neighbor tells the other; he is dismayed when the man he wants to befriend continues mending the stone wall that uselessly separates their properties:

> . . . I see him there
> Bringing a stone grasped firmly by the top
> In each hand, like an old-stone savage armed.
> He moves in darkness as it seems to me,
> Not of woods only and the shade of trees.
> He will not go behind his father's saying,
> And he likes having thought of it so well
> He says again, "Good fences make good neighbors."

Many Americans wanted to be left alone, to cling to the nineteenth century and its values, but the world and the relentless pace of change would not allow the nation to wall itself off from its future. In the next thirty-one years the United States experienced tumultuous social upheavals: it went through a period of unprecedented economic growth, followed by the longest and deepest depression in its history, and it fought at terrible cost in both world wars. The last year this volume covers is 1945—the year in which World War II ended in Europe with Germany's capitulation on 8 May and in the Pacific with Japan's surrender on 10 August, days after the United States dropped atomic bombs on Hiroshima and Nagasaki. An era of unprecedented carnage had ended with the prospect of human self-annihilation.

Through the study of the period from 1914 to 1945—years that many people still alive remember—the concerns that beset contemporary society are not-so-distantly mirrored. After World War I, the United States was entering the modern era. It is significant that this period was defined in large measure by world events—not only the world wars but also the Great Depression, which affected all industrialized economies and played a major role in the rise of fascism in Europe. Although removed by oceans from Europe, Africa, and Asia, the United States was becoming a leader on the global stage; consequently, its own destiny was being shaped more and more by its interaction with other nations. At home, Americans worried about such issues as the new prominence of the youth culture, signifying a gap between the values of the generations that had been sharpened in the wake of the war; the rise of crime in the cities, intensified by Prohibition, bootlegging, and gangsters; the effects of immigration and the fear that outsiders—Communists ("Reds") or anarchists—wanted to destroy the country; and the continuing problem of race relations, so evident in the 1920s with public parades of the Ku Klux Klan, race riots, and lynchings. On a deeper level, though, Americans may have been just as apprehensive about the signs of progress, for the 1920s, with its movies and radio, its automobiles and airplanes, had been unimaginable at the beginning of the century. The great of mark of living in the modern world is the accelerated, unpredictable pace of change. Unlike the parents of children born in the year 1800, parents in the years 1900 or 2000 could have little idea of the future their children would face.

From the perspective of the twenty-first century, the iconic images that define the 1920s and 1930s—flappers dancing and smoking cigarettes, Norman Rockwell covers for *The Saturday Evening Post,* the "strange fruit" of a lynched corpse pictured on a postcard, gangsters warring with Thompson submachine guns from the running boards of sedans, American citizens standing in bread lines during the Depression—seem distant and yet still resonate. Having been winnowed by time, they reach deeply into the national psyche, telling us not only who we were but who we are. Trying to understand Americans living in the interwar period, then, allows us to gain perspective on ourselves and our own culture.

Directly or indirectly, a work of literature opens a window on the culture in which it is produced. Whether the work is T. S. Eliot's *The Waste Land* (1922) or Laura Ingalls Wilder's *Little House on the Prairie* (1935), the study of its author, of the circumstances of its composition, of the work itself, of its audiences, and of its reception and critical interpretation allows the student to see more deeply into the cultural moment in which it was written. For some authors, of course, the direct revelation of the experience of living within their culture is their main purpose for writing. In a letter to his daughter, who was attempting to begin a writing career, F. Scott Fitzgerald advised, "But when in a freak moment you will want to give the low-down, not the scandal, not the merely *reported* but the *profound* essence of what happened at a prom or after it, perhaps that honesty will come to you—and then you will understand how it is possible to make even a forlorn Laplander *feel* the importance of a trip to Cartier's!" Twenty-first-century readers may often feel themselves to be akin to Fitzgerald's Laplander when they pick up a work of literature from earlier times, but such is the skill of many of the writers discussed in this volume that they may yet come to appreciate the experience.

The best reason for studying the writers of this period, or any other, is that they provide pleasure as well as offer insight. The years between the wars produced some of America's greatest authors, and they created enduring works of art. In *Reading Lolita in Tehran: A Memoir in Books* (2003), Azar Nafisi recounts beginning her teaching career in 1979 at the University of Tehran during the Iranian Revolution and struggling to introduce her Iranian students to Fitzgerald's *The Great Gatsby* (1925). "The idea or ideas behind the story must come to you through the experience of the novel," she told them, "and not as something tacked on to it." She had a student read aloud the scene in which Tom Buchanan realizes that his wife, Daisy, is in love with Jay Gatsby; Nafisi then commented, "Fitzgerald does not tell you—he takes you inside the room and re-creates the sensual experience of that hot summer day so many decades ago, and we, the readers, draw our breath along with Tom as we realize what has just happened between Gatsby and Daisy." In a recollection that suggests how far Nafisi's students had to travel to Fitzgerald, she describes the ending of that class meeting:

> In retrospect it appears strange to me only now, as I write about it, that as I was standing there in that classroom talking about the American dream, we could hear from outside, beneath the window, the loudspeakers broadcasting songs whose refrain was *"Marg bar Amrika!"*—"Death to America!"
>
> A novel is not an allegory, I said as the period was about to come to an end. It is the sensual experience of another world. If you don't enter that world, hold your breath with the characters and become involved in their destiny, you won't be able to empathize, and empathy is at the heart of the novel. This is how you read a novel: you inhale the experience. So start breathing.

If, like Nafisi's students, we open our hearts, our senses, and our minds and breathe in the world an author presents in a poem, play, or novel, we are enriched in our own world.

Dominant Genres and Literary Forms

All literary genres thrived during the years between the world wars, but the achievements of the novelists were, arguably, the most impressive. Novelists who had established themselves before World War I continued to produce important works. Edith Wharton, who had achieved her first real success with *The House of Mirth* (1905), brought out her most acclaimed novel of manners, *The Age of Innocence*, in 1920. The great Naturalist Theodore Dreiser, whose first novel, *Sister Carrie,* had been published in 1900, enhanced his reputation with his masterpiece, *An American Tragedy,* in 1925. Willa Cather, who had brought the Great Plains to vivid life in *O Pioneers!* (1913), explored the same landscape in *My Ántonia* (1919) before turning to Southwestern settings in *The Professor's House* (1925) and *Death Comes for the Archbishop* (1927). In the 1920s younger generations of authors infused the American novel with new vigor: Sinclair Lewis with his satirical examinations of society in *Main Street* (1920), *Babbitt* (1922), and *Elmer Gantry* (1927); F. Scott Fitzgerald with his quintessential novel of the Jazz Age, *The Great Gatsby* (1925); John Dos Passos with the boldly experimental *Manhattan Transfer* (1925); Ernest Hemingway with his terse, innovative style in *The Sun Also Rises* (1926) and *A Farewell to Arms* (1929); Thomas Wolfe with *Look Homeward, Angel* (1929); and Dashiell Hammett with his hard-boiled detective novel *The Maltese Falcon* (1929). In the 1930s and 1940s these authors produced more exciting novels—notably, Fitzgerald's most profound work, *Tender Is the Night* (1934); Lewis's *It Can't Happen Here* (1935); Dos Passos's *U.S.A.* trilogy (1928–1936); and Hemingway's *For Whom the Bell Tolls* (1940)—and were joined by novelists whose works added to the distinction of the American canon: John O'Hara's *Appointment in Samarra* (1934), Zora Neale Hurston's *Their Eyes Were Watching God* (1937), John Steinbeck's *Of Mice and Men* (1937) and *The Grapes of Wrath* (1939), Nathanael West's *The Day of the Locust* (1939), and Richard Wright's *Native Son* (1940). The greatest and most prolific novelist of this remarkable period was William Faulkner, a writer who did not achieve widespread recognition until after World War II. He followed *The Sound and the Fury* (1929), a novel merging Regionalist and Modernist sensibilities, with a succession of books that continued the exploration of his mythical "postage stamp of native soil," Yoknapatawpha County, Mississippi, including *As I Lay Dying* (1930), *Sanctuary* (1931), *Light in August* (1932), *Absalom, Absalom!* (1936), *The Unvanquished* (1938), *The Hamlet* (1940), and *Go Down, Moses* (1942).

Although considered novels by many critics, *The Unvanquished* and *Go Down, Moses* can also be read as short-story cycles (collections of closely linked stories)—a form that was most famously practiced by Sherwood Anderson in *Winesburg, Ohio* (1919). Other admired cycles include Jean Toomer's *Cane* (1923), a work made up of poetry and drama, as well as stories, and John Steinbeck's novella *The Red Pony* (1945). The fact that Faulkner first wrote the chapters of *The Unvanquished* and *Go Down, Moses* as short stories he tried to sell commercially before revising them into episodic novels suggests how the lucrative magazine market for short stories played an important role in the careers of some authors. The outstanding example of a career shaped, for good and ill, by the necessity of writing stories for the commercial market was Fitzgerald, who relied on the money he earned from selling pieces to *The Saturday Evening Post* to fund his work as a novelist. But in addition to the high-paying "slicks"—so called for their glossy, high-quality paper—such as *The Saturday Evening Post, Collier's Weekly, Cosmopolitan,* and *Ladies' Home Journal,* in which the short story was a commodity, the literary marketplace for short fiction was diversified by literary magazines such as *The American Mercury, Harper's Magazine,* and *Scribner's Magazine.* Writers could also publish their stories in the many smaller magazines—low-budget, noncommercial periodicals with small circulations that proliferated after the Great War—such as *The Little Review, The Transatlantic Review, This Quarter,* and *Transition* in the expatriate community in Paris and stateside journals such as *The Dial, The Double Dealer, The Southern Review,* and *Story.* Another market for short stories was provided by the many "pulps"—so called because of the cheap paper on which they were printed—that catered to genre fiction, including *Black Mask, Amazing Stories,* and *Weird Tales.* With such a wide-open market, the short story flourished. A few of the other writers who made notable contributions to the short story were Ring Lardner, Hemingway, Dorothy Parker, Langston Hughes, John O'Hara, Katherine Anne Porter, and Eudora Welty.

Like the novel and the short story, American poetry was invigorated after World War I. Frost and Edwin Arlington Robinson—two poets who, in Frost's phrase, were "content with the old way to be new"—continued to write in established forms such as the sonnet and used rhyme and traditional meters. Other major figures in American poetry were more willing to experiment. Ezra Pound's *Hugh Selwyn Mauberly* (1920) and Eliot's *The Waste Land* were landmarks of the post–World War I world, for in form and content they showed a new sensibility that signified a profound break with the past. In their own ways such poets as Wallace Stevens, William Carlos Williams, and Marianne Moore were able—in Pound's phrase—to "make it new." In a related art, songwriting, the lyricists of Tin Pan Alley—Irving Berlin, Lorenz Hart, Ira Gershwin, Cole Porter, Oscar Hammerstein II, Howard Dietz, Yip Harburg, Dorothy Fields, Leo Robin, Johnny Mercer, and many more—made the years between the wars a golden era for the popular song.

In drama the towering figure who transformed a moribund American theater was Eugene O'Neill. From his early one-act plays, such as *Bound East for Cardiff* (1916), to his provocative and innovative full-length plays of the 1920s and 1930s, such as *The Emperor Jones* (1920), *Desire Under the Elms* (1924), and *Mourning Becomes Electra* (1931), to his posthumously produced masterpiece *Long Day's Journey into Night* (1956), O'Neill brought an energy and lyricism to the stage that captured the attention of the world and made him the first American playwright to win the Nobel Prize in literature. O'Neill's groundbreaking efforts prepared the way for the achievements of playwrights such as Lillian Hellman, Thornton Wilder, and Tennessee Williams.

With the advent of the talking motion picture and the success of *The Jazz Singer* in 1927, Hollywood began to recruit playwrights to provide dialogue for its movies. In the 1930s screenwriters—most of whom continued to come to the movies from a theater background—began to come to grips with their new medium. Hollywood money also attracted novelists such as Faulkner, Fitzgerald, and Raymond Chandler, who attempted to adapt to a system of collaboration imposed by the studios even as they struggled with the screenplay as a new literary genre.

MOVEMENTS AND SCHOOLS

The major movement associated with the years 1914 to 1945 was Modernism—a term associated with innovative or experimental authors intent on breaking sharply with the past in form, substance, or both. Eliot's *The Waste Land*—with its incorporation of fragments from many languages and times, its various voices and use of slang, its mix of allusions to myth and contemporary imagery—is regarded as the signature text of American Modernism. *Modernism* is also more broadly used to label the sensibility of the era between the world wars and to encompass all literary authors writing during these years. Within this so-called Modernist era, however, there are writers who might better be described as adherents of earlier movements. Realism, which developed as a literary movement in the latter half of the nineteenth century in the United States, was an approach adopted by writers who sought to portray in a straightforward way recognizable, representative characters, situations, and settings. Social Realists were concerned with the behaviors of characters interacting within a closely observed society, while psychological Realists were primarily interested in describing the interior experience of a particular individual. Naturalism, in which writers depicted characters whose fates were determined by genetic, social, and economic forces beyond their control, was another important nineteenth-century movement that continued as a strong current in twentieth-century literature. The influence of these earlier movements is particularly notable in certain kinds of writing, as Realism is dominant in war fiction, Regionalist works, and novels of manners, and Naturalism is evident in hard-boiled and proletarian writing. But none of these larger movements in literature are exclusive terms when they are used in describing particular works. Faulkner's *The Sound and the Fury,* for example, is considered a Modernist work because of its structure and stream-of-consciousness technique, but it also might be called a work of psychological Realism and certainly has a Naturalistic theme, as it seems that Caddy's illegitimate daughter, Miss Quentin, is fated to follow in her mother's footsteps.

Many other labels have been used to classify writers between the wars. Some are associated with particular aesthetic practices. The "School of Imagism," a descriptive phrase coined by Pound, referred to a significant approach to poetry that flourished through the World War I years. Seeking a break with the past, Pound in a 1913 article in *Poetry: A Magazine of Verse* called for the "direct treatment of the 'thing,'" suggesting that the focus of poems should be concrete images, rendered in common language rather than in the flowery diction of Romantic poetry and in the natural rhythms of speech rather than in the strict meters of traditional verse—or, as he called it, "the sequence of a metronome." Poets such as H.D. (Hilda Doolittle), Amy Lowell, and William Carlos Williams adopted these aims. In the 1930s Williams developed an approach to poetry he called objectivism, in which the poem itself was viewed as an object and its formal structure became as important as the images it presented. The objectivist poets included Louis Zukofsky, George Oppen, and Charles Reznikoff.

Some schools and movements were associated with particular magazines, frequently one of the little magazines, in which an editor was able to create a niche for a recognizable style or type of writing. One notable little magazine that subscribed to an identifiable artistic agenda was Alfred Kreymborg's *Others: A Magazine of the New Verse* (1915–1919). Publishing such poets as Eliot, Williams, Marianne Moore, Mina Loy, and Conrad Aiken, as well as many lesser-known writers, *Others* encouraged experiments in free verse. A Nashville-based group of poets calling themselves the Fugitives, including John Crowe Ransom, Donald Davidson, Allen Tate, Robert Penn Warren, and Laura Riding, created their own forum, *The Fugitive* (1922–1925), a magazine of poetry and criticism, which Warren described as providing "a battleground for debating modernism and traditionalism." In the late 1920s and early 1930s *The New Masses* (1926–1948) attempted to shape the development of what editor Michael Gold called "proletarian literature"—writing that gave voice to the concerns and aspirations of the working classes. A mainstream magazine that was associated with a particular brand of fiction was *The New Yorker,* founded in 1925 by Harold Ross. Writers for the magazine include James Thurber, S. J. Perelman, Dorothy Parker, and E. B. White. John O'Hara and Irwin Shaw, among others, developed a style of fiction known as "the *New Yorker* story," which focused on character and the establishment of mood, not on heavy plotting. The pulp magazine *Black Mask,* edited by Joseph T. Shaw, played an important role in the development of the so-called hard-boiled school of fiction practiced by writers such as Hammett and Chandler.

The little theater movement, inspired by the European free-theater movement, promoted noncommercial drama in regional theater groups, including the Chicago Little Theatre, the Arts and Crafts Theatre in Detroit, the Washington Square Players and the Neighborhood Playhouse in New York City, and the Carolina Playhouse at the University of North Carolina. One of the most important groups associated with the little theater movement was the Provincetown Players (1915–1929), founded by George Cram Cook and his wife, Susan Glaspell. This group performed Glaspell's feminist play *Trifles* (1916) and many early works by O'Neill. New York audiences were introduced to such O'Neill plays as *The Emperor Jones, The Hairy Ape* (1922), and *All God's Chillun Got Wings* (1924) at a Greenwich Village brownstone the group renovated into a theater. Other writers whose work the Provincetown Players performed included Djuna Barnes, Paul Green, Edna St. Vincent Millay, Edna Ferber, and Floyd Dell. *Theatre Arts Magazine* was the main periodical associated with the movement. A later organization that exerted a powerful influence on American drama was The Group Theatre (1931–1941), founded in New York by Harold Clurman, Lee Strasberg, and Cheryl Crawford. Inspired in part by the ideas of Konstantin Stanislavsky, this avant-garde company advocated ensemble productions of socially progressive dramas. Clifford Odets wrote such plays as *Waiting for Lefty* (1935) and *Awake and Sing!* (1935) for the Group. Other works performed by the company included

Paul Green's *The House of Connelly* (1931), Sidney Kingsley's *Men in White* (1933), Irwin Shaw's *The Gentle People* (1939), and William Saroyan's *My Heart's in the Highlands* (1939).

Certainly one of the most important movements of the era was the Harlem Renaissance, also known as the Negro Renaissance and the New Negro Movement. With the Great Migration of African Americans from the rural South to Northern cities in the wake of World War I, the Harlem section of New York City became what James Weldon Johnson called a "city within a city, the greatest Negro city in the world." The creation of journals such as *The Crisis* (1910–), *The Messenger* (1917–1928), and *Opportunity: A Journal of Negro Life* (1923–1949), and the generally increased interest by publishers in the African American experience during the boom times of the 1920s, afforded new writers unprecedented opportunities to make their voices heard. Such authors as Claude McKay, Jean Toomer, Countee Cullen, Langston Hughes, Arna Bontemps, Nella Larsen, Wallace Thurman, and Zora Neale Hurston made Harlem a vibrant literary community in the 1920s and into the 1930s.

Historical and Social Context

THE GREAT WAR YEARS

In February 1915, as the Great War was being fought in Europe, Americans in Los Angeles were going to see *The Clansman,* a movie adapted by director D. W. Griffith from Thomas Dixon's drama set in the South during Reconstruction that glorified the Ku Klux Klan and vilified African Americans. Three months later, retitled *The Birth of a Nation,* Griffith's three-hour movie premiered in New York and proved the commercial viability of the feature-length motion picture. Despite protests from the newly formed National Association for Advancement of Colored People (NAACP), race riots in some major cites, being banned in eight states, and an unprecedented $2.00 admission charge, *The Birth of a Nation* became the first movie blockbuster, grossing more than $10 million in 1915 (the equivalent of $200 million today) and becoming the most profitable movie of the silent-film era. *The Birth of a Nation* is cited by historians for increasing the visibility and growth of the NAACP, as well as for the resurgence of the Klan. The controversy the movie entailed—which occurred during the early stages of the so-called Great Migration of millions of African Africans from the oppressiveness of the Jim Crow South to the perceived opportunity of a better life in the urban North—suggests something of the swirling tensions that existed beneath the surface in America before the country became involved in World War I.

Although President Woodrow Wilson had vowed to keep the United States out of war, the country entered the conflict on the side of the Allies on 2 April 1917, after several American ships had been sunk by German submarines and the deciphering of a coded German telegram—the "Zimmerman telegram," from the German Foreign Minister Arthur Zimmermann to the German Minister to Mexico—revealed that Germany wanted to offer United States territory to Mexico in return for joining the German cause. Wilson characterized U.S. involvement as making "the world safe for democracy," and his administration portrayed the Germans as barbarous "Huns" out to destroy civilization. With volunteers and the institution of a draft, the U.S. Army reached a peak of four million soldiers; two million went overseas in the American Expeditionary Forces before the Armistice on 11 November 1918. More than half of the estimated 116,000 Americans who died in the war succumbed to disease. Many American authors who wrote of the war disparaged the idealism that had been used to promote what was recognized in retrospect as an unnecessary tragedy. In *1919* (1932), the second volume of his *U.S.A.* trilogy, John Dos Passos, who had earlier written of the devastating effects of the war experience on individuals in *Three Soldiers* (1921), uses newspaper headlines, song lyrics, biographical notes, and stream-of-consciousness passages to evoke the atmosphere of wartime America. Other important works about the war include e. e. cummings's *The Enormous Room* (1922), Thomas Boyd's *Through the Wheat* (1923), and Ernest Hemingway's *A Farewell to Arms.* More-ambivalent views of the conflict are offered in Willa Cather's *One of*

Ours (1922), Laurence Stallings and Maxwell Anderson's play *What Price Glory?* (1924), and Hervy Allen's memoir *Toward the Flame* (1926).

THE RED SCARE AND THE PALMER RAIDS

During the war the United States government, empowered by the Espionage Act of 15 June 1917, had stifled its critics by suppressing dozens of publications. For example, because of its strong opposition to American involvement in the war, the little magazine *The Masses* was banned by postal authorities in New York. The government became increasingly concerned with the perceived threat of Communism as the Bolshevik Revolution progressed and ultimately led to the creation of the Soviet Union. Anxiety about the "Reds" reached a peak after the night of 2 June 1919, when a group of anarchists, in a series of coordinated attacks, set off nine bombs within a couple of hours at the homes of U.S. Attorney General A. Mitchell Palmer and others considered hostile to labor interests or immigrants in Washington, D.C.; Boston; Paterson, New Jersey; New York City; Philadelphia; Pittsburgh; and Cleveland. Two people, including one of the bombers, died in the attacks. Palmer subsequently began a series of warrantless raids on radicals of all types, especially foreigners. His most notorious action was the roundup of 249 resident aliens, including the anarchist Emma Goldman, who were shipped off to Russia on 21 December 1919. In an essay titled "The Case against the 'Reds,'" published in *Forum* the following year, Palmer explained the need for his raids and revealed the paranoia that gripped many Americans:

> Like a prairie-fire, the blaze of revolution was sweeping over every American institution of law and order a year ago. It was eating its way into the homes of the American workmen, its sharp tongues of revolutionary heat were licking the altars of the churches, leaping into the belfry of the school bell, crawling into the sacred corners of American homes, seeking to replace marriage vows with libertine laws, burning up the foundations of society.

In the context of the panic over "Reds" the Italian anarchists Nicola Sacco and Bartolomeo Vanzetti, self-described as "a good shoemaker and a poor fish-peddler," were arrested, on little evidence, in May 1920 for a robbery and murder in Braintree, Massachusetts. Their trial became a cause célèbre that galvanized the literary Left and played a role in the evolution of proletarian literature. Another act of terrorism, the explosion of a huge bomb on Wall Street on 16 September 1920 that killed more than thirty people and injured hundreds, was quickly linked to the same anarchist group responsible for the June 1919 bombings. The Red Scare and terrorist acts were important factors in the movement to restrict immigration that culminated in the Johnson-Reed Act of 1924, effectively shutting the door on immigrants from southern and eastern Europe.

AMENDING THE CONSTITUTION

In the late 1910s the Eighteenth and Nineteenth Amendments to the U.S. Constitution wrought profound changes to American society. Passed by Congress at the end of 1917 and ratified by the required three-fourths of the state legislatures by January 1919, the Eighteenth Amendment prohibited "the manufacture, sale, or transportation of intoxicating liquors within, the importation thereof into, or the exportation thereof from the United States and all territory subject to the jurisdiction thereof for beverage purposes." It was enforced by the National Prohibition Act, popularly known as the Volstead Act, and put into effect on 17 January 1920. It was the only amendment ever to be repealed: the Twenty-First Amendment brought the "Noble Experiment" to an end on 5 December 1933. During its nearly fourteen years of existence, Prohibition did not create the "dry" society its supporters envisioned; as one can see by reading John O'Hara's *Appointment in Samarra*, drinking continued as a ritual of social interaction among every class. The widely flaunted law led to the proliferation of clandestine saloons, known as speakeasies, some of which became literary hangouts. Organized crime, exemplified by gangsters such as Al Capone in Chicago, profited enormously from bootlegging (the illegal sale of alcohol). Local bootleggers became part of the fabric of society in cities big and small. In the 1920s literary culture was so connected to drinking that some expatriate writers claimed that Prohibition played a role in their decision to leave the United States.

The Nineteenth Amendment, stating that "the right of the citizens of the United States to vote shall not be denied or abridged by the United States or by any State on account of sex," was passed by Congress on 4 June 1919 and ratified on 18 August 1920. The guarantee of the right to vote was symptomatic of an increasing acceptance of women's roles outside the home. The emerging "new woman" was associated with the iconic image of the flapper, a figure ridiculed by conservative critics as frivolous but that suggested the enlarged cultural possibilities that women were beginning to claim. The August 1922 issue of the Chicago-based magazine *The Flapper* announced an agenda that spoke to this new freedom: "What the FLAPPER stands for: short skirts, rolled sox, bobbed hair, powder and rouge, no corsets, one-piece bathing suits, deportation of reformers, nonenforcement of Blue Laws, no censorship of movies, stage or the press, vacations with full pay, no chaperons, attractive clothes, the inalienable right to make dates, good times, honor between both sexes." F. Scott Fitzgerald, whose first volume of stories was *Flappers and Philosophers* (1920), was the recognized spokesman for the concerns of youth and was typed as a "flapper writer" because of such stories as "Bernice Bobs Her Hair." The unconventional Lady Brett Ashley in Hemingway's *The Sun Also Rises* is regarded by some critics as an exemplum of a new woman.

THE TWENTIES

The "Jazz Age," "The Roaring Twenties," "The Era of Wonderful Nonsense"— these names suggest a sense of excitement and pleasure, feelings no doubt shared by the middle and upper classes who enjoyed increasing prosperity during its long economic boom. President Calvin Coolidge's famous assertion—"the chief business of the American people is business"—certainly had some validity, for U.S. industrial production rose 50 percent during the decade, and the consumer culture thrived as the sale of durable goods, especially electrical appliances, radios, and refrigerators, skyrocketed. New products were introduced: Trojan condoms; Baby Ruth, Mounds, and Butterfinger candy bars; the Hertz Drive-Ur-Self System; Drano drain cleaner; Wise Potato Chips; canned tomato juice and Hormel canned ham; Schick electric shavers; Kellogg's Rice Krispies cereal; and Wonder Bread. Coca-Cola sales rose from $4 million in 1920 to $39 million in 1929. Running for president in 1928, Herbert Hoover called for "a chicken in every pot and two cars in every garage." By the end of the decade twenty million telephones were in use, and one in five Americans owned an automobile.

The 1920 census showed that some fifty-four million Americans—more than half of the population—lived and worked in cities, where the forty-eight-hour workweek became standard. With their greater leisure time Americans played mah-jongg and flocked to sporting events and to the movies that were soon transformed by color and sound. Their heroes became athletes—Babe Ruth, Red Grange, Jack Dempsey—and they adored movie stars such as Jean Harlow, Mae West, Clara Bow, and Greta Garbo. Each year brought new developments, new marvels. Charles Lindberg's nonstop thirty-three-hour flight from New York to Paris in the *Spirit of St. Louis* seemed a symbol of the age, and Irving Berlin wrote the lyrics that many sang to themselves, for all of the blue days had been left behind:

> Nothing but blue skies
> From now on.

But while the rich got richer—the share of disposable income enjoyed by the top 5 percent of the population rose from about one-quarter to one-third—those at the bottom of the economic scale, including workers in textiles and coal, unorganized labor, Southern farmers, the elderly, single women, and most African Americans, enjoyed little benefit from the general rise in prosperity. And when billions of dollars in capital disappeared in the stock-market crashes of Black Thursday, 24 October 1929, and Black Tuesday, 29 October, formerly wealthy Americans, like the character Charlie Wales in Fitzgerald's story "Babylon Revisited" (1931), "suddenly realized the meaning of the word 'dissipate'—to dissipate into thin air; to make nothing out of something."

THE THIRTIES AND THE NEW DEAL

The dominant American figure of the 1930s was Franklin Delano Roosevelt, elected president for the first of his unprecedented four terms in 1932, as the Great Depression was at its deepest. In May of that year a "Bonus Expeditionary Force" of some eleven thousand impoverished World War I veterans and their families had marched on Washington, D.C., to petition for a second loan on the bonus that Congress had voted in 1924 to give them but that was not due to be paid until 1945. Most of the protesters, who were living in shacks below the Capitol and in shanties and tents along the Anacostia River, returned home when Congress failed to act, but a few thousand remained and continued to engage in protests. On 28 July President Herbert Hoover ordered that the men be dispersed. General Douglas MacArthur and his second in command, Major Dwight D. Eisenhower, used troops, tanks, and tear gas to drive the veterans from the city and destroy their encampments. The spectacle of the army routing former soldiers further damaged the reputation of the already unpopular Hoover. When a second "Bonus Army" arrived in Washington, D.C. in May 1933, the new president sent his wife, Eleanor Roosevelt, to meet with its leaders. Although no specific legislation was enacted for the veterans, many of them found employment in the Civilian Conservation Corps, one of several major "New Deal" programs—including the Federal Emergency Relief Administration, the Reconstruction Finance Corporation, and the Tennessee Valley Authority—passed in the first one hundred days of the Roosevelt administration to provide immediate relief to those in need.

Roosevelt's policies did not end the misery of the Depression, and the country suffered through bank failures, railway insolvencies, and closed factories throughout the decade. Rural America, plagued by low agricultural prices, floods, and droughts, had already been experiencing depression conditions in the 1920s. By 1932 farm prices had fallen to 40 percent of their 1929 levels, and a drought in 1934 reduced the corn crop by nearly 1 billion bushels. The production of durable goods plunged and did not recover its 1929 peak until 1940. Unemployment rose from four million in 1930 to eight million in 1931, and the rate of unemployment reached 25 percent in 1932. In November 1936 the Commerce Department was pleased to report that unemployment was only nine million, down from eleven million at the beginning of the year. The sense of betrayal of the American dream of hard work earning rewards was evident in the "proletarian" literature that protested the plight of workers and even in popular songs. In his lyrics for one of the seminal songs of the decade, Yip Harburg wrote of the iconic American worker who had built the railroad and "made it race against time":

> Once I built a railroad; now it's done.
> Brother, can you spare a dime?

Perhaps more than the works of any other author, John Steinbeck's novels, including *Of Mice and Men* (1937) and *The Grapes of Wrath* (1939), provide enduring images of Depression America.

THE SPANISH CIVIL WAR AND WORLD WAR II

In what was recognized by many as a likely precursor to a wider conflict, the Spanish Civil War began in 1936 when the Spanish Republic was attacked by the Nationalist forces led by General Francisco Franco, backed by the fascist dictators Adolf Hitler of Germany and Benito Mussolini of Italy. The Republicans, or Loyalists, were backed by the Communist dictator Joseph Stalin of the Soviet Union. While the United States remained neutral, a few thousand American Leftists volunteered for the Abraham Lincoln Brigade in the losing Republican cause. American writers, including Dos Passos and Hemingway, wrote anti-Franco books. Robert Jordan, the protagonist of Hemingway's *For Whom the Bell Tolls*, is an idealistic American who fights for the Republic.

World War II began when Germany invaded Poland on 1 September 1939. For more than two years the United States remained officially neutral, though its Lend-Lease program and other policies supported Britain and France, and later the Soviet Union, in their conflict with Germany and Italy, as well as China in its struggle against Japan. The United States entered the war after the 7 December 1941 Japanese surprise attack on Pearl Harbor in Hawaii. In the European theater American and Allied forces fought in North Africa and Italy before invading German-occupied France at Normandy on D day, 6 June 1944. Paris was liberated on 25 August. After a fierce German counteroffensive was overcome in the Battle of the Bulge in Belgium in December 1944, American, British, French, Canadian and Polish troops entered Germany from the west while the Soviets were invading from the east; Germany surrendered on 8 May 1945. In the Pacific the United States suffered early defeats, losing the Philippines before beginning an offensive against Japan in the summer of 1942. That year more than one hundred thousand Japanese Americans, principally on the West Coast and in Hawaii, were rounded up and placed in internment camps on the mistaken belief that they were a security threat. American soldiers fought the Japanese on a series of islands—Guadalcanal, Saipan, Guam, and Iwo Jima—leading toward the Japanese mainland; the campaign culminated in the taking of Okinawa in June 1945. General Douglas MacArthur, true to his famous pledge to return to the Philippines, led the invasion there in January 1945. The conflict with Japan concluded shortly after the United States dropped atomic bombs on Hiroshima on 6 August 1945 and on Nagasaki three days later.

Depression conditions continued into the 1940s. The unemployment rate was 14.6 percent in 1940, a year in which the government allocated $1.8 billion of its total budget of $8.4 billion for defense. As the country gained its war footing—rationing tires and gasoline and converting the automobile industry to military purposes—government expenditures increased dramatically, and unemployment all but disappeared, even as women entered the workforce in unprecedented numbers and African Americans were enlisted in the war effort. In 1943 Roosevelt earmarked for defense $100 billion of his $109 billion budget. By 1945, the final year of the war, twelve million American men and women were in uniform. Most of the literature to emerge from the war was written after 1945, but important reporting was done by such war correspondents as Martha Gellhorn, John Hersey, A. J. Liebling, and Ernie Pyle.

Literary Influences

Notable developments in American literature as a cultural endeavor occurred as publishing, book buying, and the recognition of American literary achievement became more diversified. While American writers continued to be inspired by European authors, thinkers, and artists, they also began to be recognized by Europeans for their contributions to literature. Five American authors who established their reputations in the 1920s and 1930s were awarded the Nobel Prize in literature: Sinclair Lewis in 1930, Pearl S. Buck in 1938, Eugene O'Neill in 1936, William Faulkner in 1950, and Ernest Hemingway in 1954.

NEW PUBLISHING HOUSES

Significant literary publishing houses were established in the years following World War I and in the 1920s and 1930s. The Alfred A. Knopf firm (1915–), founded by husband and wife Alfred and Blanche Wolf Knopf, published the works of such authors as Willa Cather, Langston Hughes, and H. L. Mencken; it also published Mencken's literary magazine *The American Mercury* from 1924 to 1934. Blanche Knopf was responsible for developing a list of crime and detective authors that included Dashiell Hammett and Raymond Chandler. The house of Boni & Liveright (1917–1933) produced the Modern Library series, reprinting classic works of literature in attractive, inexpensive editions. In the 1920s the firm, under the direction of Horace Liveright, also made its name by publishing new authors and experimental or controversial works. It published T. S. Eliot's *The Waste Land*, Dreiser's *An American Tragedy*, Hemingway's first American book, *In Our Time* (1925), and Faulkner's first novel, *Soldiers' Pay* (1926), in addition to works by O'Neill, Ezra Pound, Djuna Barnes, e. e. cummings, Hart Crane, and Sherwood Anderson. Harcourt, Brace (1919–) enjoyed its first major success with Lewis's *Main Street* and later brought out works by John O'Hara, John Dos Passos, James Gould Cozzens, Carl Sandburg, and Robert Penn Warren. Random House (1927–), using the purchase of the Modern Library series from Liveright as its foundation, became a powerful publisher and made history by defeating censors and winning the legal battle to have James Joyce's *Ulysses* (1922) declared publishable in the United States. New Directions (1936–), founded by James Laughlin, promoted the reputations of many noncommercial authors and published such writers as Pound, William Carlos Williams, Tennessee Williams, Henry Miller, and Dylan Thomas. Viking Press (1925–), which included John Steinbeck, Dorothy Parker, and Ernest Caldwell on its list, launched the Viking Portable Library series in 1943. These single volumes, which were made up of a generous selection of an author's best work, advanced the reputations of writers such as F. Scott Fitzgerald and Faulkner.

BOOK CLUBS AND THE PAPERBACK REVOLUTION

Book clubs developed into an important factor influencing how Americans bought and read books. Founded by Harry Scherman in 1926, the Book-of-the-Month Club sent a book chosen by its board of literary judges to its members through the mail. By the end of the 1920s the club had more than a million members and had spawned similar enterprises, including the Literary Guild and clubs sponsored by publishers such as Doubleday. Membership in book clubs increased to such a degree that in the 1950s they may have accounted for nearly one-third of all book sales in the United States. American reading habits were also affected by the so-called paperback revolution, pioneered in the United States by Pocket Books in 1939. Priced at only twenty-five cents and marketed at nontraditional venues such as drugstores, cheap paperbacks changed the way Americans regarded book buying. Other paperback publishers, including Avon (1941), Popular Library (1942), Dell (1943), and Bantam (1945), soon copied the successful Pocket Books model.

THE RECOGNITION OF THE AMERICAN WRITER

The growing recognition of American writing was shown by the increasing attention paid to American books by reviewers in newspapers. *The New York Times Book Review,* which began as a Saturday supplement to the newspaper in 1896 and became a section in the Sunday paper in 1911, developed into the most influential newspaper review section in the country, often setting the tone for the national response to a book. A prominent positive review in *The New York Times Book Review* could increase the sales of a book, while a negative review or lack of coverage could undermine a book's appeal.

Beginning in 1917 Pulitzer Prizes, established by newspaper publisher Joseph Pulitzer through the Columbia School of Journalism, were awarded annually to outstanding works of American literature. The following year the Yale University Press began awarding a prize to encourage achievement by a poet under forty by publishing his or her first book in its Yale Series of Younger Poets. In 1922 the Newbery Medal was established to recognize and encourage authors writing for children.

The practice of American academic institutions offering support to writers began in 1917, when Robert Frost accepted an appointment at Amherst College; he later held appointments at the University of Michigan, Harvard University, and Dartmouth College before returning to Amherst in 1949. In 1936 the University of Iowa, which in 1922 had become the first major school to establish a creative-writing program, created the Writers' Workshop, in which distinguished visiting authors worked with selected students. After World War II, universities became much more widely involved with the support of professional writers through writers-in-residence programs. In the late 1920s the teaching of classic nineteenth-century American literature was becoming established in universities. The scholarly journal *American Literature* began publication in 1929. The academic study of contemporary American literature did not become widespread until the 1950s.

AMERICANS IN PARIS

By the twentieth century American literature had matured to the point that writers were looking to American predecessors as well as to European authors as influences. Edith Wharton, for example, following the example of her good friend Henry James, explored the clash of American and European attitudes and cultures in her novels. Wharton's *The Age of Innocence* (1920) can be read as something of a literary rejoinder to James's *The Portrait of a Lady* (1881). At the beginning of his career Faulkner sought out Sherwood Anderson as a mentor. Walt Whitman was clearly an influence on poets as different as Sandburg and Robinson Jeffers, for both used long, irregular Whitmanesque lines. Hemingway looked back to Mark Twain in his suggestion that all of American literature flowed from *The Adventures of Huckleberry Finn* (1884).

While many European authors might also be cited as necessary predecessors of individual American writers, the most important foreign influence on American literature in the post–World War I years was not a person but a place: Paris, the center of the literary and artistic world in the 1920s. Some American writers may have traveled to Europe to escape the perceived puritanism and commercialism of American culture. Many were no doubt drawn by the favorable exchange rates that made living in France—even in Paris—comparatively cheap. But the most important reason for American writers and artists to flock to Paris was the sense that the city, with its mix of established and young artists, musicians, and writers, afforded opportunities for rich, meaningful experiences in a community that placed art and expression at the center of existence.

Matthew J. Bruccoli and Robert W. Trogdon describe the lure in *American Expatriate Writers: Paris in the Twenties* (1997):

> Paris was the center of the literary and artistic world during the Twenties. In addition to the French, there were notable figures from all over Europe—including those who had left Russia after the Revolution. The assemblage of these geniuses attracted and stimulated American writers, painters, composers, dancers, and musicians. Writers: Tristan Tzara, André Breton, Jean Cocteau, Paul Morand, Blaise Cendrars, Jules Romains, Louis Aragon, Philippe Soupault. Artists: Pablo Picasso, Francis Picabia, Fernand Léger, Jules Pascin, Joan Miró, Georges Braque, André Derain, Henri Matisse, Constantin Brancusi, Juan Gris, Natalia Gontcharova. Composers: Erik Satie, Darius Milhaud, Francis Poulenc, Igor Stravinsky, Nadia Boulanger. Diaghilev's Ballets Russes and the Ballets Suèdois were based in Paris. The Exposition des Arts Décoratifs et Industriels Modernes (which provided the name for Art Deco) opened in Paris in July 1925.

For many American writers, the presence of James Joyce may have been reason enough to travel to the French capital.

The expatriate experience in Paris was particularly important to the development of Modernism, for the time and place encouraged experimentation in technique and form and for many writers provided a necessary distance to achieve perspective on the American experience. Among the many American writers for whom their Paris sojourn was decisive in one way or another were Fitzgerald, Hemingway, Pound, Barnes, cummings, H.D. (Hilda Doolittle), Kay Boyle, Robert McAlmon, Henry Miller, Anaïs Nin, and Gertrude Stein.

Evolution of Critical Opinion

Many of those who contributed to the development of literary criticism in America after World War I did not restrict themselves to literature but ranged more broadly as cultural critics, delving into considerations of society, politics, history, language, philosophy, and other arts. The period after the war was a time of reevaluation, and a general dissatisfaction with post–World War I American culture is evident in *Civilization in the United States: An Inquiry by Thirty Americans* (1922), edited by Harold E. Stearns, which includes his essay "The Intellectual Life," as well as H. L. Mencken's "Politics," Conrad Aiken's "Poetry," Ring Lardner's "Sport and Play," George Jean Nathan's "The Theatre," and Lewis Mumford's "The City."

Some critics were considering fundamental questions about the purpose of literature, especially as the Great Depression shook society to its foundations. Marxist critics such as Mike Gold and Granville Hicks were trying to define what "proletarian literature" should become. The question of the purpose of literature was also considered by African American writers, as when Zora Neale Hurston's *Their Eyes Were Watching God* was attacked by Richard Wright for its depiction of African American folk culture. At the same time that independent critics such as Mencken, Mumford, Kenneth Burke, and Edmund Wilson were examining the relationship of literature to culture, a new and narrower focus on the work itself, which came to be known as New Criticism, was attracting adherents.

LITERARY JOURNALISTS

The most influential critic of contemporary literature after the war and through the 1920s was Henry Louis (H. L.) Mencken. Although his formal education ended with his graduation from high school, Mencken distinguished himself as a journalist, philologist, political commentator, and literary critic and came to be regarded as the country's greatest man of letters. In his newspaper columns for *The Baltimore Sun* he wrote for what he called the "civilized minority," satirizing everything from the hysteria surrounding World War I and the resurgence of the Ku Klux Klan to the Scopes "Monkey" Trial in Tennessee and the residual puritanism he believed infected American life. In all of his writing Mencken enjoyed "stirring up the animals."

Mencken began to make his name as a literary critic before World War I. His early books include *George Bernard Shaw: His Plays* (1905) and *The Philosophy of Friedrich Nietzsche* (1908), the first studies on these authors to be published in America. He also edited and wrote introductions for Henrik Ibsen's *A Doll's House* and *Little Eyolf* in 1909 and was an early champion of the work of Joseph Conrad. In 1908 Mencken began to review books for *The Smart Set: A Magazine of Cleverness,* which he edited with George Jean Nathan from 1914 to 1923. From November 1908 to December 1923 he wrote 182 monthly articles on all manner of books, American and foreign—some 2,000 in all. Although for most of his years as a reviewer Mencken generally regarded American literature as inferior to European literature—an argument he makes in his 1920 essay "The National Letters"—he had begun to see signs of hope for advancement when he wrote his last essay for *The Smart Set*. In 1923 Mencken and Nathan left that magazine to found *The American Mercury,* which they edited together for two years before Mencken became the sole editor from 1925 to 1933. At *The Smart Set* Mencken and Nathan promoted Realism in fiction and drama, publishing work by Eugene O'Neill, Dorothy Parker, Theodore Dreiser, and Willa Cather; the first commercial story by F. Scott Fitzgerald; and the first publication in the United States by James Joyce. Authors whose work appeared in *The American Mercury* included Dreiser, Sinclair Lewis, Sherwood Anderson, William Faulkner, and Carl Sandburg.

A much less combative literary journalist, Henry Seidel Canby, began his professional career as a professor of English at Yale University. He served as an assistant editor at the *Yale Review* from 1911 until becoming the editor of the *Literary Review,* a weekly supplement to the *New York Evening Post,* in 1920; in 1924 he founded *The Saturday Review of Literature,* which he edited until 1936. As the guiding hand of what became the most influential literary weekly in the United States and as the first chairman of the editorial board for the Book-of-the-Month Club, Canby exercised enormous influence on the American reading public. He was criticized both as too much of an elitist and as too much of a panderer to bourgeois tastes. Malcolm Cowley's parody in the journal *Aesthete 1925*—"Editor Outlines Middle Course between Heaven and Hell. Solution Deemed Acceptable to Both Modernists and Fundamentalists"—suggests Canby's difficult position in negotiating between his audiences while certainly overstating his success in pleasing everyone. Canby strove to broaden as well as deepen the discussion of American literature, writing in his *American Memoir* (1947) of "the Jeffersonian belief in the necessity of education for a successful democracy" that animated his career: "I wanted to go in for adult education in the value of books—all kinds of books, foreign as well as native, but particularly the current books of our own country. I wished to make criticism first of all a teaching job, backed up by explorations and estimates of new ideas."

AFRICAN AMERICAN LITERATURE

Two critics who brought attention to the cultural contributions by African Americans were Alain Locke and Sterling Brown; the latter was also a respected poet. Locke edited *The New Negro: An Interpretation* (1925), the anthology that initiated the movement that became known as the Harlem Renaissance. Locke also edited *Four Negro Poets* (1927), which brought attention to the work of Claude McKay, Jean Toomer, Countee Cullen, and Langston Hughes. In *Negro Art: Past and Present* (1936) and *The Negro and His Music* (1936) Locke provided more support for his belief that African Americans were making a distinctive contribution to American culture. Brown's criticism included *The Negro in American Fiction* (1937) and *Negro Poetry and Drama* (1937). He also edited the anthology *The Negro Caravan: Writings by American Negroes* (1941).

A USABLE PAST

Some of the most influential literary criticism published between the wars focused on the American literary past, including Van Wyck Brooks's *America's Coming of Age* (1915), F. O. Matthiessen's *American Renaissance: Art and Expression in the Age of Emerson and Whitman* (1941), and Perry Miller's *The New England Mind: The Seventeenth Century* (1939). In his three-volume *Main Currents in American Thought* (1927–1930) Vernon L. Parrington offered an overarching interpretation of American literature as the expression or representation of political, social, and economic forces. His concentration on historical background and the material conditions of society and lack of concern for aesthetics were faulted by the New Critics.

T. S. ELIOT AND THE NEW CRITICISM

The New Criticism, which became the dominant school of literary criticism in the United States in the 1940s and 1950s, was influenced by Eliot, the formidable American poet living in England who was also one of the most important literary theorists of the twentieth century. In *The Sacred Wood: Essays on Poetry and Criticism* (1920), which includes book reviews as well as several longer essays, Eliot discusses the work of Algernon Swinburne, William Blake, Dante, Philip Massinger, Ben Jonson, and William Shakespeare, and defines terms and concepts that have entered into critical discourse. In his essay "Hamlet and His Problems," for example, Eliot provides a famous formulation for how poetry communicates emotion to the reader or listener: "The only way of expressing emotion in the form of art is by finding an 'objective correlative'; in other words, a set of objects, a situation, a chain of events which shall be the formula of that particular emotion; such that when the external facts, which must terminate in sensory experience, are given, the emotion is immediately evoked." As this rather abstract description suggests, Eliot was interested in moving beyond "aesthetic" or "impressionistic" criticism that depended on the interpretations of "a sensitive and cultivated mind" toward a surer, less subjective footing for criticism. In the preface to the 1928 edition of *The Sacred Wood* he articulated the idea that unified his collection of essays: "It is an artificial simplification, and to be taken only with caution, when I say that the problem appearing in these essays, which gives them what coherence they have, is the problem of the integrity of poetry, with the repeated assertion that when we are considering poetry we must consider it primarily as poetry and not another thing."

In the United States such critics as John Crowe Ransom, Allen Tate, Robert Penn Warren, and Cleanth Brooks agreed with Eliot that literary criticism should be a largely autonomous endeavor, distinct from biography, psychology, philosophy, and other disciplines. Brooks described this critical approach as "formalist" because it was centered on a close reading and an analysis of the elements—metaphor, imagery, symbolism, and so forth—of a poem or other piece of literature and not on its cultural context. The emphasis of this approach was well tailored to the complexity of Modernist literature, particularly poetry, which seemed to require literary critics to explain the work to the reader. Brooks and Warren spread the methodology of New Criticism through their textbooks *Understanding Poetry* (1938) and *Understanding Fiction* (1943), in which they stressed that a great work of literature has multiple meanings. While not denying the importance of social, moral, cultural, or religious contexts in the study of literature, they believed that such considerations were subordinate to the study of the organic nature of a poem or novel: the way the elements combine to produce a living work of art.

CRITICISM TODAY OF THE 1914–1945 PERIOD

To indulge in gross oversimplification, in the first half of the twentieth century the focus of literary criticism generally shifted from the author's biography and supposed intention in writing a work—an approach that might be suggested by the question "What did the author mean to communicate?"—to the formal aspects of the literary object in the New Criticism, an approach perhaps best suggested by the question "How does the text work?" After the crest of the influence of the New Critics in the post–World War II years, the focus shifted again in the latter half of the twentieth century, toward the critic and the meaning he or she could find in—or make out of—the literature examined: "What is the significance of this literary work?" A variety of reader- or critic-oriented theories—from psychoanalytic, feminist, and reader-response to deconstruction, new historicist, and cultural or Marxist approaches—have flourished since the 1960s.

Literary fashions and opinions change. Contemporary judgments of the most important or the best writers are often reversed by later generations. While Eugene O'Neill was recognized as a towering figure in the American theater by his contemporaries—a judgment time has not changed— many of the novelists and poets who were regarded as major figures in their own time have faded from memory, and writers who were ignored then have come to be regarded as significant only in retrospect. In the 1920s, for example, many critics might have chosen Joseph Hergesheimer—a largely forgotten novelist whose name appears only a few times in this volume—as among the first rank of American writers. And many of the novelists who are now regarded as major figures of the interwar years—F. Scott Fitzgerald, William Faulkner, Zora Neale Hurston, to name only a few—were, for different reasons, undervalued by their contemporaries.

In the twenty-first century readers and critics have a rich variety of ways to approach literary texts. As Lois Tyson suggests in her readable introduction, *Critical Theory Today* (1998), "theory can help us learn to see ourselves and our world in valuable new ways"; but no single critical approach can exhaust the meaning of a literary text, particularly when that text is an enduring work of art. The greatest of the novels, stories, plays, and poems of the interwar years continue to speak to us as readers and to provide a not-so-distant mirror in which to contemplate our reflection.

—George Parker Anderson

Part II
Study Guides
on General Topics

African American Literature and the Harlem Renaissance

The early post–Civil War promise of equal protection and increased civil rights for African Americans was eviscerated by decades of Jim Crow laws, culminating in the 1896 Supreme Court decision in *Plessy v. Ferguson* that sanctioned legalized racial segregation. This "separate but equal" doctrine—which was used to make African Americans second-class citizens—remained America's governing policy until the 1954 decision in *Brown v. Board of Education*. Spanning the years of the two world wars, African American writers, working within an already complex formative literary tradition, continued to respond to the daunting inequities of their times in voices that were defiant and conciliatory, political and personal, measured, celebratory, and transcendent. The works of the Harlem Renaissance, varied and numerous, reflect the suffering provoked by the lingering status quo, pose disparate social and moral solutions to the cruelties of systemic injustice, and demonstrate a historically aware, conscious movement toward aesthetic vitality and freedom. Social reform leaders such as Frederick Douglass (1818–1895) and Progressive Era writer Frances Ellen Watkins Harper (1825–1911), who came of age during the Civil War and its aftermath, established protocols for public action and autobiographical frankness that served as models for a new politically vigilant generation of artists and activists, many of whom joined the burgeoning black populations that reshaped urban areas during the years of the Great Migration (roughly 1910–1940 or beyond). The uptown section of New York City called Harlem became an artists' mecca, a vibrant, thrilling "race capital" in the words of philosopher Alain Locke. As rapturously expressed by James Weldon Johnson in his essay, "Harlem: The Culture Capital," in the "New Scene" section of Locke's landmark 1925 anthology, *The New Negro*, Harlem was a "city within a city, the greatest Negro city in the world."

The cultural renaissance of the 1920s and 1930s was predicated on the work of artists and activists who broke new ground in previous generations. The last decade of the nineteenth century through to America's entrance into World War I (1917) is often characterized as the Progressive Era when social reform movements helped set new standards for labor, education, public safety, and women's rights. Black writers were acutely concerned with problems of "uplifting" the race, with exposing the exclusionary hypocrisy of the ethical ideals of the supposedly *United* States, and with offering platforms for integration or rebellion. Though writers, intent on offering correctives to derogatory, degrading images of black life presented to the white reading public, disagreed on what constituted appropriate subjects, language, politics, and the fundamental relevance of color was an inescapable constant in the literary mix. A Harlem Renaissance writer such as Nella Larsen found a literary grandmother in the prolific Harper, whose popular 1892 novel, *Iola LeRoy*, provided a counterpoint to the then-stock image of the tragic mulatta and depicted an array of characters engaged in the formation of the rising black middle class. Larsen's work is also thematically centered on middle class aspirations and values, on "passing" and racial identity. Charles W. Chesnutt turned the reductive stereotypes of white-supplied plantation literature into an affirmation of black culture, individual resolve, and community survival and triumph. His dialect tales, collected in *The Conjure Woman* (1899), anticipate Zora Neale Hurston's collections of folklore and her fictional dignifying of the multidimensionality of African American life. Paul Lawrence Dunbar (1872–1906), called "the Poet Laureate of the Negro race" by educational reformer Booker T. Washington, wrote poems in both dialect and standard English, auguring the work of Jamaican sonneteer, Claude McKay.

The debate on what constituted the best path to racial equity continued unabated into the "Renaissance" years. Artists were as often combative as they were collaborative, but the intellectual excitement of hashing out different perspectives characterized the debate. How equal rights were to be achieved was a serious, often contentious, matter of much spirited and public literary wrangling. The lines were drawn in the previous century, after the gross inequities of the Reconstruction era provoked the need for systemic reform. The key factions were divided along the opposing philosophies of the conservative Booker T. Washington (1856–1915), founder of the black-run Tuskegee Normal and Industrial Institute (1881), and the radical W. E. B. Du Bois, organizer of the Niagara Movement, which, in 1910, developed into the National Association for the Advancement of Colored People (NAACP).

Washington, who supported black economic independence through commitment to labor and self-sufficient community-building, argued that accommodation to separatist attitudes and policies, along with patience, diligence, and industry would permit African Americans to prosper and eventually integrate into the mainstream. He directly appealed to the white, moneyed readership who might help finance his school and other ventures. Black artists necessarily relied upon white producers, publishers, critics, and patrons for support and the dicey problem of negotiating and appeasing white benefactors vexed later writers such as Langston Hughes and Hurston.

Vehemently opposed to Washington's platform of patient acceptance and compromise, Du Bois advocated more deliberate, immediate action. His emphasis on intellectual achievement and racial pride helped set the standard for the writers and artists who flourished in what would be termed the New Negro Renaissance, centered in New York's Harlem. His long career extended through and beyond the years between the world wars, and he edited the NAACP's journal, *The Crisis*, which published and encouraged such writers as Hughes, Jean Toomer, Countee Cullen, and Arna Bontemps.

What is commonly referred to as the "Harlem Renaissance" of the 1920s and 1930s was part of a larger cultural emergence of writers, musicians, painters, dancers, publishers, and scholars from newly formed urban black communities in Chicago, Washington, D.C., Cleveland, Detroit, Philadelphia, and, notably, New York. The Great Migration of Southern blacks to the urban north was instigated by untenable living conditions, Jim Crow laws and lynchings, mechanization and decreased need for agricultural labor, along with increased need for labor in northern manufacturing centers after the U.S. entry into World War I. Blacks in

America struggled with problems of poverty, literacy, and self-definition in the urge toward fully realized citizenship and fully respected humanity; the writers of the Renaissance chronicled and debated the progress and setbacks in this ongoing struggle.

In 1925 Locke edited a special issue of the national magazine *Survey Graphic,* expressly devoted to showcasing "the progressive spirit of contemporary Negro life" and subtitled, "Harlem: Mecca of the New Negro." Included in the issue were writers such as Du Bois and the multifaceted James Weldon Johnson. There were poems by Anne Spencer, Jamaican-born poet Claude McKay, *Cane* (1923) author Jean Toomer, Angelina Grimke, Countee Cullen, and Langston Hughes. There were articles on jazz, the visual arts, race relations, religion, spirituality, and heritage, including the "The Negro Digs Up His Past" by Arthur (Arturo) Schomburg. In the same year, Locke anthologized most of the work in this landmark publication with additional material—including Hurston's story, "Spunk"—in *The New Negro,* often considered the manifesto of the New Negro movement.

Black-run magazines, notably *The Crisis* and the National Urban League's *Opportunity,* supported the work of young artists and helped rally the black community around urgent political issues. In 1921 *The Crisis* published the hauntingly powerful poem—dedicated to Du Bois—"The Negro Speaks of Rivers," by the gifted young, blues-inspired Hughes, who became one of the leading figures of the Renaissance era and one of the most innovative, versatile writers in American letters. His gifts were recognized by the literary editor of *The Crisis,* Jessie Redmon Fauset, a novelist as well as a mentor to younger artists, such as Hughes and Nella Larsen, author of the novels *Quicksand* (1928) and *Passing* (1929). Washington, D.C.–based poet, playwright, and short-story writer Georgia Douglas Johnson fostered community among artists by holding literary salons at her home. Visitors to what became known as the S Street Salon included Fauset, Du Bois, Locke, Grimke, Hughes, Spencer, Toomer, Cullen, Marita Bonner, Gwendolyn B. Bennett, and the formidable anthropologist/author Hurston, whom Alice Walker reveres as a literary mother. Hurston's work—most notably, her novel *Their Eyes Were Watching God* (1937)—ranks among the most significant achievements in American literature.

Of continuing concern was the incendiary issue of how black writers represented black life to the eager, often appreciative, but jaundiced and possibly patronizing eye of the white reading public. A writer such as Hurston, who was in many ways ahead of her times, was controversial within the circle of her artist peers, in part because of her shifting ideas on social reform but also because of her expansive and challenging views on identity politics. In the 1940s the harsh urban realism of Richard Wright (1908–1960) and his graphic literature of social protest anticipated the postwar work of Ralph Ellison, James Baldwin, and the militant writers of the Black Arts Movement. Wright's substantial body of work includes novels, poems, stories, essays, and his 1945 autobiography, *Black Boy.* The impact of his signal 1940 novel *Native Son* resonated with a new generation of writers whose work both reflected the immediate need for civil rights and helped foment the long-awaited reforms.

TOPICS FOR DISCUSSION AND RESEARCH

1. A focus on children was essential to the creation of a black national identity, therefore many prominent Harlem Renaissance figures, including Jessie Fauset, Countee Cullen, Nella Larsen, Arna Bontemps and Langston Hughes, wrote expressly for African American children. Fauset and W. E. B. Du Bois published a children's magazine called *The Brownies' Book,* copies of which can be found online in the Library of Congress's rare book digital collection (<http://lcweb2. loc.gov/cgi-bin/ampage?collId=rbc3&fileName=rbc0001_2004ser01351page. db> [accessed 8 September 2009]). The second inside page of the magazine announces: "Designed for all children, but especially for Ours." Read through the material included in *The Brownies' Book* and consider how African American culture is presented to its audience of children. As a starting point, read Annette Browne's poem, "The Wishing Game" and Annie Virginia Culbertson's dialect poem, "The Origin of White Folks" on page 7 in the January 1920 issue and discuss how each work presents positive images of black identity. See Katharine Capshaw Smith's *Children's Literature of the Harlem Renaissance* for help in contextualizing the thematic emphases of African American children's literature.

2. Jazz Age musical innovations influenced many African American poets, including Helene Johnson, Sterling Brown, Langston Hughes, and Gwendolyn B. Bennett. Research the ways that jazz and blues rhythms and the images of Harlem's nightlife were used by one or more of these poets. You might start by reading aloud Brown's "Ma Rainey" (1932), Johnson's "Poem" (1927), and Hughes's "Jazzonia" (1926), all of which can be found in Venetria K. Patton and Maureen Honey's *Double-Take: A Revisionist Harlem Renaissance Anthology* (2001). How do the poems celebrate and rhythmically replicate the intensity and improvisational spirit of jazz? Focus on identifying the subjects of each poem and the effects of each poet's use of slang or colloquial language and rhythmic repetitions. See also Hurston's essay "How It Feels to Be Colored Me," available online at <http://mapsites.net/gotham/Docs/Hurston.htm> [accessed 8 September 2009] for her descriptive response to a Harlem cabaret jazz band.

3. Much of the work of the Harlem Renaissance is directly concerned with protesting racial oppression and countering dehumanizing images of African Americans that pervaded popular culture. Compare Claude McKay's 1919 "If We Must Die" with Countee Cullen's 1927 "From the Dark Tower" and/or Langston Hughes's 1922 "The Negro Speaks of Rivers." How do these poems express racial pride and resistance to oppression? For social and historical context, see Alain Locke's 1925 essay "The New Negro" in his classic anthology of the same title.

4. Many women writers of the period were deeply concerned about the double oppression of racism and sexism. Compare the presentation of African American women's lives in Marita Bonner's "To Be Young—a Woman—and Colored" (1925) and Marion Vera Cuthbert's "Problems Facing Negro Young Women" (1936), both available in Patton and Honey's *Double-Take.*

5. Jessie Fauset's *The Plum Bun* (1929) and Nella Larsen's *Passing* (1929) are both thematically centered on "passing" for white. What social constraints and internal conflicts do the protagonists of these novels experience in their quests

and struggles for selfhood? See Cheryl Wall's *Women of the Harlem Renaissance* (1995) and Sharon L. Jones's *Rereading the Harlem Renaissance: Race, Class, and Gender in the Fiction of Jessie Fauset, Zora Neale Hurston, and Dorothy West* (2002) for background on race and gender, and James Weldon Johnson's novel from an earlier period, *The Autobiography of an Ex-Colored Man* (1912), for another literary treatment of this subject.

RESOURCES

Criticism

Arna Bontemps, ed., *The Harlem Renaissance Remembered* (New York: Dodd, Mead, 1972).

Twelve critical essays on key Harlem Renaissance literary figures such as Langston Hughes, Jean Toomer, Zora Neale Hurston, and Jessie Redmon Fauset and a memoir of the period by poet and novelist Arna Bontemps.

Dickson D. Bruce Jr., *Black American Writing from the Nadir: The Evolution of a Literary Tradition, 1877–1915* (Baton Rouge: Louisiana State University Press, 1989).

Comprehensive study of African American literature from the end of Reconstruction to World War I, the era preceding the Harlem Renaissance.

Ann Douglas, *Terrible Honesty: Mongrel Manhattan in the 1920s* (New York: Farrar, Straus & Giroux, 1995).

Argues that post–World War I New York became the epicenter of historical change as black and white artists and intellectuals defined a new, non-Eurocentric American culture.

Ann duCille, *The Coupling Convention: Sex, Text, and Tradition in Black Women's Fiction* (New York: Oxford University Press, 1993).

Discusses the subversive use of the marriage plot in works such as Nella Larsen's *Quicksand* and Hurston's *Their Eyes Were Watching God* and explores the multidimensionality of black women's fiction from 1853 to 1948, and its thematic preoccupation with race and identity.

Henry Louis Gates Jr. and Gene Andrew Jarrett, eds., *The New Negro: Readings on Race, Representation, and African American Culture, 1892–1938* (Princeton: Princeton University Press, 2007).

Collects one hundred essays on art, music, politics, and literature from the period 1892 through 1938 by such writers as W. E. B. Du Bois, Alain Locke, Hurston, and Richard Wright, focusing on the crucial issues of race and representation as epitomized in the conception of the "New Negro."

George Hutchinson, *The Harlem Renaissance in Black and White* (Cambridge, Mass.: Belknap Press of Harvard University Press, 1995).

Contextualizes the Harlem Renaissance within a broader, pluralistic cultural context, focusing on interracial exchange, nationalism, and the genesis of literary Modernism.

Sharon L. Jones, *Rereading the Harlem Renaissance: Race, Class, and Gender in the Fiction of Jessie Fauset, Zora Neale Hurston, and Dorothy West* (Westport, Conn.: Greenwood Press, 2002).
A comprehensive overview of Harlem Renaissance history and aesthetics focusing on how Fauset, Hurston, and Dorothy West resist race, class, and gender oppression and how their work defies reductive categorizations.

Alain Locke, ed., *The New Negro* (New York: A. & C. Boni, 1925).
One of the signal texts of the Harlem Renaissance. Locke collects fiction, poetry, and critical essays about art, literature, and culture by such prominent voices as Hurston, Hughes, Toomer, James Weldon Johnson, and Locke himself.

Venetria K. Patton and Maureen Honey, eds., *Double-Take: A Revisionist Harlem Renaissance Anthology* (Livingston, N.J.: Rutgers University Press, 2001).
An expansive collection of essays, literature, and period artwork with inclusiveness as its goal. The book features a balanced selection of work by men and women and by well-known and lesser-known writers and focuses attention on themes related to gender and sexual orientation.

Katharine Capshaw Smith, *Children's Literature of the Harlem Renaissance* (Bloomington: Indiana University Press, 2004).
A critical analysis of the essential place of black children in the formation of a new black national identity. The writers, educators, and activists, including Du Bois, Bontemps, and Hughes, who made children a prime concern, created a new tradition of African American children's literature.

Cheryl Wall, *Women of the Harlem Renaissance* (Bloomington: Indiana University Press, 1995).
An intellectual history that traces the devaluation of women artists within the "New Negro" ranks, focusing on Fauset, Larsen, and Hurston; including discussions of Anne Spencer, Marita Bonner, and Georgia Douglas Johnson; and making connections to musical artists Bessie Smith and Josephine Baker.

PEOPLE OF INTEREST

Gwendolyn B. Bennett (1902–1981)
Poet, journalist, fiction writer, graphic artist, and teacher. Her work was widely published in journals and anthologies such as *The Crisis, Opportunity,* and Countee Cullen's *Caroling Dusk* (1927).

Marita Bonner (1899–1971)
Author of the 1925 essay, "On Being Young—a Woman—and Colored," that won a literary contest sponsored by *The Crisis.* Bonner was a playwright and short-story writer as well as an essayist.

Sterling A. Brown (1901–1989)
Poet, literary critic, and—like his father—a professor at Howard University. Brown specialized in African American folklore and literature.

Charles W. Chesnutt (1858–1932)
Became the nation's first widely read African American author with such works as *The Conjure Woman* (1899) and *The Marrow of Tradition* (1901) and continued to publish into the 1920s. In 1928 he was awarded the Spingarn Medal by the NAACP for his literary exploration of racial issues in America.

Countee Cullen (1903–1946)
Known primarily as a poet but was also a teacher, playwright, novelist, essayist, and author of children's books. Following his first three volumes of poetry— *Color* (1925), *Copper Sun* (1927), and *The Ballad of the Brown Girl* (1927)—his works included a satiric novel, *One Way to Heaven (*1932), and fanciful works for children, *The Lost Zoo* (1940) and *My Lives and How I Lost Them* (1942).

W. E. B. Du Bois (1868–1963)
A brilliant intellectual who is often credited with initiating African American studies as an academic discipline. In his groundbreaking masterpiece *The Souls of Black Folk* (1903), Du Bois explained to his primarily white audience what it felt like to be black in a racist society, using the term "double-consciousness" to describe the twin and "warring" allegiances to race and country that comprised the black man's psychology; he also prophetically declared "the color line" to be the major problem of the new century.

Jessie Redmon Fauset (1882–1961)
Literary editor of *The Crisis* from 1919 to 1926. She was respected for her novels, which include *Plum Bun: A Novel without a Moral* (1928)—often considered her finest work—and *The Chinaberry Tree: A Novel of American Life* (1931). Her thematic focus is on the black family and she explores the tensions, psychosocial constraints, and responses to racism—including the choice to "pass" as white—that undermine and determine individual identity.

Rudolph Fisher (1897–1934)
Novelist, short-story writer, playwright, musician, and physician who wrote what is considered the first black detective novel: *The Conjure-Man Dies: A Mystery Tale of Dark Harlem* (1932). Fisher was known especially for his artistry as a short-story writer with such works as "City of Refuge" (1925), which was published in the mainstream *Atlantic Monthly*.

Angelina Weld Grimke (1880–1958)
Poet, prose writer, and playwright, a great-niece of well-known white abolitionists Sarah and Angelina Grimke. Her three-act play *Rachel* (1916) overtly protested violent racial injustice and lynching; her letters reveal her lesbian sexual orientation.

Charles S. Johnson (1893–1956)
Sociologist, scholar, the first black president of Fisk University, national research director of the Urban League and the editor of the League's magazine, *Opportunity: A Journal of Negro Life*. His books include *The Negro in Chicago* (1922) and *The Negro in American Civilization* (1930). He edited the 1927 anthology *Ebony and Topaz*, which included work by Hughes, Hurston, Bontemps, Fauset, and Locke.

Georgia Douglas Johnson (1880?–1966)
Acclaimed Washington, D.C.–based poet and influential literary salon host. Her collections of poetry are *The Heart of a Woman* (1918), *Bronze* (1922), *An Autumn Love Cycle* (1928), and *Share My World* (1962).

Helene Johnson (1906–1995)
Lyric poet published in journals and anthologies of the era. Poems such as "Sonnet to a Negro in Harlem" and the jazz-inspired "Poem," both published in Countee Cullen's *Caroling Dusk* (1927), celebrate Harlem street life. Johnson was a cousin of the novelist Dorothy West.

James Weldon Johnson (1871–1938)
One of the most significant figures of the day, author of *The Autobiography of an Ex-Colored Man* (1912) and coauthor with his brother, J. Rosamond Johnson, of "the black national anthem" "Lift Every Voice and Sing"; also a poet, critic, journalist, activist, lawyer, and professor; and secretary and organizer for the NAACP.

Nella Larsen (1891–1964)
Best remembered as the author of the autobiographical novels *Quicksand* (1928) and *Passing* (1929), which centered on racial identity, family dynamics, and crossing the color line and were championed by Du Bois and literary peers such as Georgia Douglas Johnson. Born in Chicago to a Danish mother and a West Indian father, Larsen in adulthood was repudiated by her white half sister.

Alain Locke (1886–1954)
Harvard- and Oxford-trained Howard University philosopher who played a crucial role in initiating what became known as the Harlem Renaissance by promoting the work of African-American writers.

Charlotte Osgood Mason (1854–1946)
White philanthropist and patron of writers, notably Hughes and Hurston. Mason liked to be called "Godmother," and, though generous, was also deemed too controlling by the beneficiaries of her largesse.

Claude McKay (1889–1948)
Jamaica-born poet, novelist, essayist, memoirist, and social chronicler who first came to Harlem in 1914. Du Bois, whose *The Souls of Black Folk* had a major impact on radicalizing McKay's outlook, condemned the overt sexuality in McKay's award-winning 1928 novel, *Home to Harlem*, believing that the work pandered to the white audience's stereotypes of black amorality.

Arthur (Arturo) Schomburg (1874–1938)
Librarian, archivist, and historian whose initial collection of manuscripts and artwork formed the New York Public Library's Schomburg Center for Research in Black Culture.

Anne Spencer (1882–1975)
Poet and activist who lived and worked in Lynchburg, Virginia, but was intellectually engaged with the Harlem literary community. Her work was included in

the most notable anthologies of her time, including James Weldon Johnson's *The Book of American Negro Poetry* (1922), Louis Untermeyer's *American Poetry Since 1900* (1923), Alain Locke's *The New Negro* (1925), Countee Cullen's *Caroling Dusk* (1927), Charles Johnson's *Ebony and Topaz* (1927), Sterling Brown's *The Negro Caravan* (1941), and Langston Hughes and Arna Bontemps's *The Poetry of the Negro, 1746–1949* (1949).

Wallace Thurman (1902–1934)
Novelist, journalist, editor, and playwright whose *The Blacker the Berry: A Novel of Negro Life* (1929) exposes bias within the African American community against darker-skinned blacks.

Carl Van Vechten (1880–1964)
White novelist, music and drama critic, essayist, photographer, and arts patron whose controversial roman à clef, *Nigger Heaven* (1926), depicted Harlem life. A later edition contained blues lyrics written expressly for the novel by Langston Hughes.

Eric Walrond (1898–1966)
Caribbean short-story writer, essayist, journalist, and Guggenheim Fellowship recipient whose 1926 collection of stories, *Tropic Death,* has been favorably compared to Jean Toomer's *Cane.*

Dorothy West (1907?–1998)
Novelist, short-story writer, and founder/editor of the journals *Challenge* and *New Challenge.* Her novel *The Living is Easy* (1948) deals with race, class, and family dynamics.

Walter White (1893–1955)
Essayist, novelist, civil-rights leader, arts patron, and executive secretary of the NAACP from 1931 until his death. *Rope and Faggot: The Biography of Judge Lynch* (1929) is a potent study of the psychosocial and economic bases of lynching.

—Kate Falvey

"The Essence of a Continent": The Lyricists of Tin Pan Alley

In F. Scott Fitzgerald's *Tender Is the Night* (1934) Nicole Warren, a young, beautiful recovering mental patient, plays records on her phonograph for Dr. Richard Diver. The year is 1919, when phonographs had become an affordable luxury for Americans. Even though they are sitting "behind a low wall, facing miles and miles of rolling night," near her Swiss clinic, the couple is transported far away, to America, by listening to the "thin tunes, holding lost times and future hopes in liaison." Fitzgerald combines the lyrics from then-popular songs to suggest the music:

> They were so sorry, dear; they went down to meet each other in a taxi, honey; they had preferences in smiles and had met in Hindustan, and shortly afterward they must have quarreled, for nobody knew and nobody seemed to care—yet finally one of them had gone and left the other crying, only to feel blue, to feel sad.

The jumble of lines—including a phrase from Shelton Brooks's "The Dark Town Strutters Ball" and an allusion to Oliver G. Wallace and Harold Weeks's "Hindustan"—anticipates the plot of the novel, for Nicole and Dick will marry, break apart, and divorce, leaving Dick "to feel blue." But in this early moment with Nicole, he is borne back by the music and the lyrics to memories before the war. For Dick Diver, Nicole seems a "scarcely saved waif of disaster bringing him the essence of a continent."

Many Americans of the period between the world wars believed that popular songs, more intimately than any other form of entertainment, captured something of the essence of their culture. The growing popularity of American music after World War I had its roots in the latter years of the nineteenth century. In the 1890s New York City had become the center of the music industry in the production of pianos and sheet music. West Twenty-eighth Street became popularly known as "Tin Pan Alley"—the name deriving from the tinny sound of pianos being played as songsmiths plied their trade. In the early 1900s the tempo of the country was changing, becoming more urban, and the syncopated rhythms of piano rags were the rage. Irving Berlin, whose "Alexander's Ragtime Band" (1911) was one of the most popular songs before World War I, was quoted in an article in the 17 August 1924 issue of *The New York Times* as associating the change in American music with the advent of the automobile: "All the old rhythm was gone, and in its place was heard the hum of an engine, the whirr of wheels, the explosion of an exhaust. The leisurely songs that men hummed to the clatter of horses' hoofs did not fit into this new rhythm—the new age demanded new music for new action. The country speeded up."

The boom of popular music between the wars that brought about a golden era for lyricists was the product of many and varied forces. With the end of World War I, the Broadway musical broke away from the Viennese operetta that had dominated the prewar stage, and a new market for American songs was created.

At the same time that the influences of blues and jazz were transforming ragtime, Victorian domestic culture was being replaced by a culture of consumerism, as performing music on the piano in the home began to give way to listening to music on player pianos in movie theaters, on 78-rpm records on phonographs, and, as the 1920s progressed, on the ever-more ubiquitous radio. While the demand for new songs was increasing, the newspapers that often published witty, light verse in their columns—most notably "The Conning Tower" column by F.P.A. (Franklin P. Adams)—encouraged a ready pool of would-be lyricists. With the maturation of Broadway and movie musicals and the success of integrated productions such as *Show Boat* (1927)—in which songs were written to be performed by a character in a dramatic situation to advance the plot—lyricists faced new challenges and opportunities. As Philip Furia notes in *The Poets of Tin Pan Alley*, Berlin, along with wordsmiths such as Lorenz Hart, Ira Gershwin, Cole Porter, Oscar Hammerstein II, Howard Dietz, Yip Harburg, Dorothy Fields, Leo Robin, and Johnny Mercer, "took the American vernacular and made it sing."

Far more than the poets of the little magazines, the lyricists of Tin Pan Alley wrote the words that echoed in the minds of Americans. One reason, then, for studying the lyrics of popular songs is to gain a better understanding of a significant cultural expression of the era. Yet, it is also important to recognize the art involved in the task of the lyricist. In a postscript to the foreword to his collection *Lyrics on Several Occasions* (1959) Ira Gershwin, perhaps only half facetiously, denied that his work should be treated as poetry: "Since most of the lyrics in this lodgement were arrived at by fitting words mosaically to music already composed, any resemblance to actual poetry, living or dead, is highly improbable." He also, however, makes an observation in his commentary on "I Got Plenty o' Nuthin'" that suggests that the lyricist encounters challenges the poet does not: "It takes years and years of experience to know that such a note cannot take such a syllable, that many a poetic line can be unsingable, that many an ordinary line fitted into the proper musical phrase can sound like a million."

Furia provides an overview of the development of popular songs in his introduction to *American Song Lyricists, 1920–1960* (2002), and the biographical essays included in the book are good starting points for studying major lyricists. Robert Kimball and Robert Gottlieb's *Reading Lyrics* (2000) is a reliable source for the lyrics of many standard songs from the interwar period. Students with access to the Internet will be able to listen to various recordings of many songs through the *Internet Archive* site.

TOPICS FOR DISCUSSION AND RESEARCH

1. In *American Popular Song: The Great Innovators, 1900–1950* (1972) Alec Wilder asserts that music and words "cannot be separated. One may talk about *words,* or one may talk about *music,* but one cannot talk about *song* and mean anything less that the combination of the two." Like many critics, though, Wilder maintains that song lyrics "are not poems and are not intended to be." For Philip Furia in *The Poets of Tin Pan Alley: A History of America's Great Lyricists* (1990), however, the distinction is much less clear. Read Furia's first

chapter, "Blah, Blah, Blah Love: Alley Standards," and consider the examples he cites from such lyricists as Lorenz Hart, Leo Robin, and Cole Porter. Is there a distinction you would draw between song lyrics, without the music, and poetry? What would make a song lyric a poem?

2. The great majority of the popular songs produced by Tin Pan Alley lyricists concerned love. Furia suggests that to appreciate the artistry of these word-smiths "we must listen, not for new ideas or deep emotion, but for the deft-ness with which the lyricist solves the problem posed by a song of the 1930s, 'What Can You Say in a Love Song That Hasn't Been Said Before?'" Do some research into the songs by some of the lyricists listed in "People of Interest" and pick out three songs that you think are the most inventive answer to this question. What are the reasons for your choices? Can you identify particular words or phrases that seem to you to be an especially appropriate fit for the music? Wilder's *American Popular Song,* which focuses on musical innovations, might be a valuable source to consult.

3. Popular songs—music and words—sometimes provide a way to enter into the culture of a time. Irving Berlin's "Blue Skies" (1927), for example, is often cited as an iconic song of the 1920s, and "Brother, Can You Spare a Dime?" (1931), with lyrics by Yip Harburg and music by Jay Gorney, is regarded as emblematic of the 1930s. What is it about each of these songs that makes them memo-rable? Why do you think each became so associated with the decade in which it was written? Create a portfolio of five other songs for each decade that seem to you representative of that period.

4. The best way to appreciate the work of a lyricist is by a close study of his or her development. Looking through the biographical essays in *American Song Lyricists, 1920–1960* may help you decide on a lyricist who interests you. These essays also present a list of selected songs and a bibliography of secondary sources to consult. What do you see as the strengths and weaknesses of your lyricist? What are his or her best songs?

RESOURCES

Primary Works
Ira Gershwin, *Lyrics on Several Occasions* (New York: Knopf, 1959).
A selection of Gershwin's lyrics, with commentary by the writer.

Internet Archive <http://www.archive.org/index.php> [accessed 1 November 2009].
A website through which audio recordings of many songs can be accessed.

Bibliography
Edward Foote Gardner, *Popular Songs of the Twentieth Century,* volume 1: *Chart Detail & Encyclopedia 1900–1949* (St. Paul, Minn.: Paragon House, 2000).
Six hundred monthly charts of the era, each listing the top twenty songs, created by the author. No actual surveys were made of the most popular songs in America until the 1940s.

Biography

Will Friedwald, *Stardust Melodies: A Biography of Twelve of America's Most Popular Songs* (New York: Pantheon, 2002).
Covers songs written between 1914 and 1938: "St. Louis Blues," "Stardust," "Mack the Knife," "Ol' Man River," "Body and Soul," "I Got Rhythm," "As Time Goes By," "Night and Day," "Stormy Weather," "Summertime," "My Funny Valentine," and "Lush Life."

Philip Furia, *The Poets of Tin Pan Alley: A History of America's Great Lyricists* (New York: Oxford University Press, 1990).
An examination of the genius of major lyricists that makes a compelling argument for the author's assertion that there "is simply no simple distinction between lyrics and poetry."

Furia, ed., *Dictionary of Literary Biography*, volume 265: *American Song Lyricists, 1920–1960* (Detroit: Bruccoli Clark Layman/Gale, 2002).
A survey of the lives and careers of thirty-seven major popular lyricists with an informative general introduction to the period.

Thomas S. Hischak, *Word Crazy: Broadway Lyricists from Cohan to Sondheim* (New York: Praeger, 1991).
Sketches the careers and distinctive characteristics of some of the greatest American theater lyricists. Hischak asserts that the belief in Broadway musicals is that the words should "serve the music."

Robert Kimball and Robert Gottlieb, eds., *Reading Lyrics* (New York: Pantheon, 2000).
A chronological presentation of outstanding lyricists from 1900 to 1975. Each writer is introduced with a headnote and a selection of his or her work.

Criticism

Kenneth J. Bindas, ed., *America's Musical Pulse: Popular Music in Twentieth-Century Society* (Westport, Conn.: Praeger, 1992).
A collection of twenty-eight essays by various contributors intended "to nudge readers to think of the more complex issues behind the popular sound." The book includes several essays that touch on the era between the wars.

Arnold Shaw, *The Jazz Age: Popular Music in the 1920s* (New York & Oxford: Oxford University Press, 1987).
A readable history that treats the 1920s as a "crucial period in the history of popular music," mixing ragtime, jazz, and blues. Shaw contends that in these years "elements of black and white music first achieved a rich and permanent fusion."

Alec Wilder, *American Popular Song: The Great Innovators, 1900–1950* (New York: Oxford University Press, 1972).
Argues that popular music became truly American at about the turn of the century and that during this fifty-year period it was greatly influenced by a few

outstanding song composers. Wilder believes that music and words cannot be separated, but his "analytical emphasis . . . is on the work of the composers."

PEOPLE OF INTEREST

Irving Berlin (1888–1989)
Established himself as a songwriter on Tin Pan Alley before World War I and wrote for stage musicals on Broadway after 1914 and for Hollywood musicals in the late 1920s and 1930s. His 899 published songs include such hits as "Blue Skies," "Cheek to Cheek," "White Christmas," "Steppin' Out with My Baby," "God Bless America," and "There's No Business Like Show Business." He is considered the greatest American songwriter of the twentieth century.

George M. Cohan (1878–1942)
A composer, director, producer, playwright, librettist, and actor, as well as America's first influential theater lyricist. Cohan was instrumental in establishing a genuine American musical theater and breaking Broadway away from imitation European operettas. The majority of his most original work was done before World War I, but also he wrote "Over There" (1917), the most memorable song from that war.

Buddy DeSylva (1895–1950)
A lyricist who wrote for Broadway musicals and the early movies. He collaborated on many hit songs of the 1920s, including "Look for the Silver Lining" (1920), "April Showers" (1921), "I'll Build a Stairway to Paradise" (1922), "The Best Things in Life Are Free" (1927), and "Button Up Your Overcoat" (1929).

Howard Dietz (1896–1983)
A lyricist best known for his collaborations with composer Arthur Schwartz: "I Guess I'll Have to Change My Plan" (1929), "Dancing in the Dark" (1931), "Alone Together" (1932), "You and the Night and the Music" (1934), and "By Myself" (1937).

Al Dubin (1891–1945)
A successful lyricist on Tin Pan Alley, where he collaborated on hits such as "Tip Toe through the Tulips" (1929) and "Dancing with Tears in My Eyes" (1930). In Hollywood he worked with composer Harry Warren on such songs as "You're Getting to Be a Habit with Me" (1933), "I Only Have Eyes for You" (1934), and "Lullaby of Broadway" (1935).

Dorothy Fields (1905–1974)
A successful female lyricist in a field dominated by men. She collaborated on such songs as "I Can't Give You Anything but Love" (1928), "On the Sunny Side of the Street" (1930), "I'm in the Mood for Love" (1935) and "A Fine Romance" (1936).

Ira Gershwin (1886–1984)
Collaborated with his composer brother, George, to produce many hit songs in the 1920s and 1930s, including "Fascinating Rhythm" (1924), "The Man I Love"

(1924), "Someone to Watch over Me" (1926), "'S Wonderful" (1927), "Embraceable You" (1930), "I Got Rhythm" (1930), "Let's Call the Whole Thing Off" (1937), and "They Can't Take That Away from Me" (1937). The brothers' *Of Thee I Sing* (1931) was the first musical to win the Pulitzer Prize for drama. Ira also worked with George and DuBose Heyward on the folk opera *Porgy and Bess* (1935).

Mack Gordon (1904–1959)
Wrote the lyrics for hits such as "Time on My Hands, You in My Arms" (1930), "With My Eyes Wide Open I'm Dreaming" (1934), "Chattanooga Choo-Choo" (1941), "I've Got a Gal in Kalamazoo" (1942), and "You Make Me Feel So Young" (1946).

Oscar Hammerstein II (1895–1960)
An early proponent of writing songs that were integrated into the action of musicals. Hammerstein collaborated with Jerome Kern on songs for *Show Boat* (1927) and with Richard Rodgers on *Oklahoma!* (1943), *Carousel* (1945), *South Pacific* (1949), and *The King and I* (1951).

Otto Harbach (1873–1963)
A mentor to Oscar Hammerstein II. Harbach believed that songs should be written to fit the action of a dramatic work. One of his most famous songs is "Smoke Gets in Your Eyes" (1933).

E. Y. "Yip" Harburg (1896–1981)
Turned to songwriting after his business failed after the stock-market crash of 1929. Harburg wrote the lyrics for "Brother, Can You Spare a Dime?" (1932), the emblematic song of the Great Depression, as well as for "April in Paris" (1932), "It's Only a Paper Moon" (1932), "Lydia, the Tattooed Lady" (1939), and the songs for *The Wizard of Oz* (1939).

Lorenz Hart (1895–1943)
Contributed witty, acerbic lyrics to Richard Rodgers's romantic melodies, producing the sweet-sour mix that made the partners famous. Hart's credits include "Manhattan" (1925), "My Heart Stood Still" (1927), "Ten Cents a Dance," "I Wish I Were in Love Again" (1937), "My Funny Valentine" (1937), "This Can't Be Love" (1938), "Bewitched, Bothered and Bewildered" (1940), and "Wait Till You See Her" (1942).

DuBose Heyward (1885–1940)
South Carolina poet, novelist, and playwright. Heyward wrote the novel *Porgy* (1925), about the love of a crippled black beggar for a faithless woman. In 1927 he adapted the story as a play and won a Pulitzer Prize. He then collaborated with Ira and George Gershwin to turn the play into the classic American folk opera *Porgy and Bess* (1935).

Gus Kahn (1886–1941)
A German-born lyricist who collaborated on "Toot, Toot, Tootsie! (Goodbye)" (1921), "Ain't We Got Fun?" (1921), "It Had to Be You" (1924), "Yes, Sir, That's My Baby" (1925), "Makin' Whoopee" (1927), and "Love Me or Leave Me."

Burt Kalmar (1884–1947)
Wrote the lyrics for songs such as "Who's Sorry Now?" (1923), "I Wanna Be Loved By You" (1928), "Three Little Words" (1930).

Ted Koehler (1894–1973)
Worked with composer Harold Arlen to produce such songs as "Get Happy" (1930), "Between the Devil and the Deep Blue Sea" (1931), "I've Got the World on a String" (1932), "I Gotta Right to Sing the Blues" (1932), and "Stormy Weather" (1933).

Frank Loesser (1910–1969)
Collaborated with composer Hoagy Carmichael in 1938 on "Small Fry," "Heart and Soul," and "Two Sleepy People." His greatest successes came later in the songs he wrote for Broadway musicals, including *Guys and Dolls* (1950), *Most Happy Fella* (1956), and *How to Succeed in Business without Really Trying* (1961).

Johnny Mercer (1909–1976)
Born to wealth in Georgia and became a singer-songwriter. Mercer's songwriting credits include "I'm an Old Cowhand from the Rio Grande" (1936), "Too Marvelous for Words" (1937), "Hooray for Hollywood" (1938), "Jeepers Creepers" (1938), "You Must Have Been a Beautiful Baby" (1938), "Blues in the Night" (1941), and "Ac-cent-tchu-ate the Positive" (1944)..

Mitchell Parish (1900–1993)
Wrote the lyrics for Hoagy Carmichael's "Star Dust" and Duke Ellington's "Mood Indigo" (1931) and "Sophisticated Lady" (1933). Parish also supplied lyrics for "Stars Fell on Alabama" (1934) and "Moonlight Serenade" (1939).

Cole Porter (1891–1964)
A lyricist who wrote his own music. Porter had many hits, including "Let's Do It" (1928), "What Is This Thing Called Love?" (1929), "Night and Day" (1932), "You're the Top" (1934), "Just One of Those Things" (1935), "I've Got You under My Skin" (1936), and "You'd Be So Nice to Come Home To" (1943).

Andy Razaf (1895–1973)
African American lyricist, collaborated with Fats Waller on such songs as "Honeysuckle Rose" (1929), "Ain't Misbehavin'" (1929), and "(What Did I Do to Be So) Black and Blue" (1929).

Leo Robin (1895–1984)
Wrote the lyrics for songs that include "Thanks for the Memory" for the movie *The Big Broadcast of 1938* and "Diamonds are a Girl's Best Friend" for the play *Gentlemen Prefer Blondes* (1949).

—*George Parker Anderson*

Family Stories and the Stratemeyer Syndicate

In the 1920s children's literature began to be viewed more seriously, and children's writers approached their work more professionally than in the past. The Newbery Medal was established in 1922 to promote literary merit in the field, and *Horn Book Magazine,* which provided reviews of children's books, was founded in 1924. Between the world wars, authors with established reputations writing for adults such as Dorothy Canfield Fisher, Booth Tarkington, Vachel Lindsay, and Carl Sandburg chose to write for young readers, as well. Writing for children became a particular concern for African American authors who wanted to remake the image of their race as they contended with what Katharine Capshaw Smith describes in *Children's Literature of the Harlem Renaissance* (2004) as "the legacy of minstrelsy and its pickaninny image, a degradation codified in all forms of white media, from books to songs to postcards to motion pictures." W. E. B. Du Bois devoted an annual issue of the National Association for the Advancement of Colored People (NAACP) magazine *The Crisis* to children's literature from 1911 to 1934, and he published the magazine *The Brownies' Book* (1920–1921) to promote positive literature for African American children. The Harlem Renaissance writers Langston Hughes and Arna Bontemps, who collaborated on *Popo and Fifina: Children of Haiti* (1932), also wrote separately for children.

As a subject for serious academic study, children's literature has received increasing attention since the 1970s. Sophisticated research and criticism have demonstrated that books for children, apart from their often considerable literary merit, provide a fascinating lens through which to view culture. As Anne Scott MacLeod observes in the preface to her *American Childhood: Essays on Children's Literature of the Nineteenth and Twentieth Centuries* (1994), however, the idea that children's literature "reflects" culture is an oversimplification:

> No metaphor as direct as 'reflection' can convey the subtleties of the connections between children's books and culture. Writing for children, adults bring to bear their own experience of childhood, their ideas of what childhood is or ought to be, their commitment to the conventions of their own time, and their concerns for their own society's problems and progress. In other words, authors of children's books consciously take into account myriad extrinsic considerations that they might or might not bring to writing for adults. Indeed, most writers for children practice some degree of self-censorship. They often tell children the truth, but it is seldom the whole truth.

"Not telling the whole truth" is, perhaps, a good way to characterize many of the children's books centered on family life prevalent in the 1920s and 1930s. In her *American Children's Literature and the Construction of Childhood* (1998) Gail Schmunk Murray asserts that "childhood, and particularly the nuclear family that nurtured children, was idealized and modeled with unceasing repetition. . . . It was almost as if authors consciously sought to remove any unpleasantness of real life—whether discrimination against minorities, suffering and death, the consumerism of the twenties, or the effects of the Great Depression. In the face of an increasingly pluralistic culture, authors of children's books emphasized nostalgia and dominant-culture, middle-class themes." Authors such as Elizabeth Coatsworth, Eleanor Estes, Elizabeth Enright, Rachel Field, and Doris Gates presented family stories in which children were allowed to enjoy childhood while learning basic values from responsible adults. Although sometimes poor, the families depicted do not experience real suffering, and the dangers of the outside world do not undermine family unity. Two of the most popular children's writers of the 1930s, Laura Ingalls Wilder in *The Little House in the Big Woods* (1932) and the subsequent books in her Little House series and Carol Ryrie Brink in *Caddie Woodlawn* (1935), set their narratives of strong, supportive families in the nineteenth century. Even writers depicting other cultures, such as Kate Seredy's Hungarian family in *The Good Master* (1935) and Hilda Van Stockum's Irish family in *The Cottage at Bantry Bay* (1938), present much the same vision of the protective family in which emotionally supported children show curiosity, honesty, and bravery while meeting and overcoming challenges. Lois Lenski, who often focused on poor, white, uneducated families in her regional series, and Florence Crannell Means, a white woman who wrote sensitively of African, Asian, Jewish, Native, and Mexican Americans, were authors who ranged beyond the dominant culture in their family stories.

A second notable trend of the years between the wars was the continued success of Edward Stratemeyer and what he called his "Syndicate," which he began in 1906 with the Bobbsey Twins series. The Henry Ford of children's literature, Stratemeyer provided a writer with a two-page outline for a particular volume, paid a flat fee ranging from $75 to $125, and contractually required the writer not to use elsewhere or even claim connection with the pseudonym assigned to the book. In *Edward Stratemeyer and the Stratemeyer Syndicate* (1993) Deidre Johnson details the numbers that define his legacy:

> In his 47-year career, Stratemeyer used 83 pseudonyms. He authored approximately 275 stories and outlined roughly 690 others, hiring writers to complete the latter. After his death, his daughters assumed control of his empire, the Stratemeyer Syndicate, publishing over 480 more books. When they died, the publisher Simon & Schuster purchased the Syndicate, publishing over 290 more titles. The fiction factory Stratemeyer built grinds on. He began in obscurity and went on to become a major force in twentieth-century series; although his name has returned to obscurity, his creations have not. The older ones live on in readers' memories; undated versions delight a new generation today.

Stratemeyer responded to the popularity of adult mysteries by creating his two most successful series for juveniles: the Hardy Boys mysteries, written under the pseudonym Franklin M. Dixon, in 1927; and the Nancy Drew mysteries, written under the pseudonym Carolyn Keene, in 1930.

TOPICS FOR DISCUSSION AND RESEARCH

1. In a 1932 essay, "Books and the Negro Child," Langston Hughes suggested that overcoming what he called a "racial inferiority complex" was one of the most important challenges facing parents and educators of African American

children. "Only when one is no longer ashamed of one's self," Hughes argued, "can one feel fully American, and capable of contributing proudly to the progress of America. . . . The need today is for books that Negro parents and teachers can read to their children without hesitancy. . . . books whose dark characters are not all clowns, and whose illustrations are not all caricatures." In what ways does Hughes and Arna Bontemps's *Popo and Fifina: Children of Haiti* (1932) help to meet this need? Compare the depictions of children and families in *Popo and Fifina* with those depicted in some of the other family stories that were popular in the same decade. How is the ideology of race expressed in each? What distinctly American cultural values does each book express?

2. In a 1937 *Bookweek* address Laura Ingalls Wilder commented on why she began her Little House series: "I wanted the children now to understand more about the beginning of things, to know what is behind the things they see—what it is that made America as they know it. . . . I realized that I had seen and lived it all—all the successive phases of the frontier, first the frontiersman, then the pioneer, then the farmers, and the towns." Although Wilder claimed to have presented the truth in her Little House series, critics have investigated how she fictionalized her experience, emphasizing the values that she wanted to communicate to children. Does reading about Wilder and her working relationship with her daughter Rose Wilder Lane in Anita Clair Fellman's essay and William Holtz's biography of Lane change the way you view the Little House books? Should it?

3. Like Wilder's Little House books and Carol Ryrie Brink's *Caddie Woodlawn*, Marjorie Kinnan Rawlings's *The Yearling* (1938) was a novel about a youngster's experience on the frontier in the nineteenth century; but, in contrast to Wilder and Brink, Rawlings was adamant that her book was not intended primarily for children. She wrote her editor, Maxwell Perkins, that it was "*not* a story for boys, though some of them might enjoy it. It will be a story *about* a boy—a brief and tragic idyll of boyhood. . . . it is important that no announcement ever be made, anywhere, that the book is a 'juvenile.'" Yet, since its publication *The Yearling* has been regarded as a classic novel for youth. Is *The Yearling* different from Wilder's and Brink's books? Is it a book for children or adults?

4. The early Hardy Boys and Nancy Drew books were shortened and thoroughly revised in 1959, in part to remove racist stereotypes. Many readers, including Phil Zuckerman of Applewood Books, believed that the revisions did damage to the originals. In the essay collection *Rediscovering Nancy Drew* (1995) Zuckerman comments on his fear that he would be accused of reprinting racist books: "When you reissue books from the past you have to live with what existed back then. . . . You must understand that this is the way it was and that there were good things and there were bad things and that you can at least talk to your children about the bad things and explain them." *Rediscovering Nancy Drew* includes essays that discuss the racism in the originals, particularly the first book in the series. Because both reprints of original volumes and the revised editions are accessible in libraries, it will probably be possible for students to do their own comparisons for other books in the series. Are the originals superior to the revisions? Is Zuckerman right that it is worthwhile

to reprint the originals? What does the marketing of these books in three eras—the 1930s, late 1950s, and early 1990s—reveal about society in these different times?

RESOURCES

John Cech, ed., *Dictionary of Literary Biography,* volume 22: *American Writers for Children, 1900-1960* (Detroit: Bruccoli Clark Layman/Gale, 1983).
Provides bibliographies and biographical and career information for many of the writers prominent from 1914 to 1945.

Beverly Lyon Clark, *Kiddie Lit: The Cultural Construction of Children's Literature in America* (Baltimore: Johns Hopkins University Press, 2003).
A provocative introduction that explores "changing attitudes toward children's literature in the last century and a half, changes that allowed *kiddie lit* to emerge as a derogatory term and changes that allow us, now, to revalue, to ironize, it."

Carolyn Stewart Dyer and Nancy Tillman Romalov, eds., *Rediscovering Nancy Drew* (Iowa City: University of Iowa Press, 1995).
Twenty-seven essays treating all aspects of the series from its creation, publication, and collection to the responses of fans and critics.

Anita Clair Fellman, "Laura Ingalls Wilder and Rose Wilder Lane: The Politics of a Mother-Daughter Relationship," *Signs: Journal of Women in Culture and Society,* 15, 3 (1990): 535–561.
A close examination of "an intense and troubled relationship."

Marilyn S. Greenwald, *The Secret of the Hardy Boys: Leslie McFarlane and the Stratemeyer Syndicate* (Athens: Ohio University Press, 2004).
A biography of the author of the first sixteen Hardy Boys mysteries.

William Holtz, *The Ghost in the Little House: A Life of Rose Wilder Lane* (Columbia: University of Missouri Press, 1993).
A biography of the daughter of Laura Ingalls Wilder.

Deidre Johnson, *Edward Stratemeyer and the Stratemeyer Syndicate* (New York: Twayne, 1993).
Looks "at the early works that launched Stratemeyer's career, the rapid development of stories and series in different genres, and the prevalent traits and themes in the works." Johnson is also the author of the 1982 bibliographic study *Stratemeyer Pseudonyms and Series Books: An Annotated Checklist of Stratemeyer and Stratemeyer Syndicate Publications.*

The Lion and the Unicorn, special Nancy Drew issue, edited by Nancy Tillman Romalov, 18 (June 1994).
Special issue of the magazine, devoted to essays on Nancy Drew.

Anne Scott MacLeod, "Family Stories, 1920–1940," in her *American Childhood: Essays on Children's Literature of the Nineteenth and Twentieth Centuries* (Athens: University of Georgia Press, 1994), pp. 157–172.

Draws a distinction between stories of the 1920s, in which she sees a "preoccupation with striving and achieving," and those of the 1930s, in which the fiction centers "on the plainer comforts of home and family."

Gail Schmunk Murray, "Idealized Realism, 1920–1950," in her *American Children's Literature and the Construction of Childhood* (New York: Twayne, 1998), pp. 145–174.
Examines the strategies children's authors employed to create more-realistic children and settings than in the past, within an idealized conception of the family.

Melanie Rehak, *Girl Sleuth: Nancy Drew and the Women Who Created Her* (Orlando: Harcourt, 2005).
Explores the origin and development of the series, principally through biographies of Mildred Wirt Benson and Harriet Stratemeyer Adams.

Katharine Capshaw Smith, *Children's Literature of the Harlem Renaissance* (Bloomington & Indianapolis: Indiana University Press, 2004).
A chronological examination, beginning with the influence of W. E. B. Du Bois and proceeding through the publishing house of Carter G. Woodson to the collaborative work of Langston Hughes and Arna Bontemps.

PEOPLE OF INTEREST

Mildred Wirt Benson (1905–2002)
Journalist and author of many books for children and young adults. Benson wrote twenty-three of the first thirty Nancy Drew novels.

Arna Bontemps (1902–1973)
Wrote and edited nonfiction and fiction for children and adolescents. His books include *You Can't Pet a Possum* (1934) and *We Have Tomorrow* (1945), a collection of career stories of successful blacks for older girls and boys.

Carol Ryrie Brink (1895–1981)
Author of works for adults as well as juveniles. Brink is best known for *Caddie Woodlawn* (1935), a Newbery Medal–winning novel set in her native Idaho.

Elizabeth Coatsworth (1893–1986)
Author of more than eighty books for children. Coatsworth won a Newbery Medal for *The Cat Who Went to Heaven* (1930).

Elizabeth Enright (1909–1968)
Short-story writer for adults, as well as a children's author and illustrator. Enright wrote four books about the Melendy family—*The Saturdays* (1941), *The Four-Story Mistake* (1942), *Then There Were Five* (1944), and *Spiderweb for Two* (1951)—showing family life in the 1940s.

Eleanor Estes (1906–1988)
Author whose best-known books were about the Moffats, a family living in the New England town of Cranbury in the years before World War I.

Rachel Field (1894–1942)
Novelist as well as a children's author. Field was the first woman to win a Newbery Medal with *Hitty, Her First Hundred Years* (1929), about the history of a carved doll.

Doris Gates (1901–1987)
California-born author who wrote about a family of migrant farmworkers in the San Joaquin Valley in *Blue Willow* (1936).

Langston Hughes (1902–1967)
Author of a short play, *The Gold Piece* (1921), published in the children's magazine *The Brownies' Book* when he was nineteen. Hughes continued to write for children throughout his career, including collaborations with Arna Bontemps and the poetry collection *The Dream Keeper* (1932).

Rose Wilder Lane (1887–1968)
Journalist and novelist who assisted her mother, Laura Ingalls Wilder, in writing the Little House series. Her own novels about the life of pioneers in South Dakota are *Let the Hurricane Roar* (1933) and *Free Land* (1938).

Lois Lenski (1893–1974)
A prolific author and illustrator of children's books whose career stretched from the 1920s to the 1970s. Lenski made her reputation with *Phebe Fairchild: Her Book* (1936), the first of a series of historical books for preteens. She is also known for her pioneering series of seventeen books exploring various regions of the country, beginning with *Bayou Suzette* (1943), set in Louisiana.

Leslie McFarlane (1902–1977)
Canadian journalist and author. McFarlane wrote for the Stratemeyer Syndicate for twenty-one years; his works include the first Hardy Boys mysteries.

Florence Crannell Means (1891–1980)
A white woman who wrote books for girls that feature African American, Chicana, Hopi, Navajo, and Japanese American heroines. Her 1945 novel *The Moved-Outers* treats the incarceration of Japanese Americans during World War II.

Kate Seredy (1899–1975)
Born in Hungary, immigrated to the United States in 1922, and wrote about her homeland in *The Good Master* (1935) and other books.

Hilda Van Stockum (1908–2006)
Born in the Netherlands and raised in part in Ireland, the setting for her novel *The Cottage at Bantry Bay* (1938). Her books usually feature families and have a variety of settings.

Edward Stratemeyer (1862–1930)
Author of juvenile literature and entrepreneur who established the Stratemeyer Syndicate in 1906. Between 1910 and 1930 Stratemeyer created eighty-two series featuring many of the most popular characters in children's fiction, including the

Rover Boys, the Bobbsey Twins, Tom Swift, Dorothy Dale, and Ruth Fielding. His most successful creations were Nancy Drew and the Hardy Boys.

Laura Ingalls Wilder (1867–1957)

Began in her early sixties to write historical fiction drawing on her childhood experiences of traveling in a covered wagon and growing up on the frontier. Wilder's readers follow a fictionalized version of her family in *Little House in the Big Woods* (1932), *Little House on the Prairie* (1935), *On the Banks of Plum Creek* (1937), *By the Shores of Silver Lake* (1939), *The Long Winter* (1940), *Little Town on the Prairie* (1941), and *These Happy Golden Years* (1943).

—George Parker Anderson

The Great Depression and Proletarian Literature

The Great Depression had a profound psychological effect on many Americans, shaking their faith in capitalist ideology. The notions that opportunity was equal and unlimited and that success was assured for energetic, hardworking, talented individuals no longer seemed valid. In *The Great Depression: America, 1929–1941* (1993) historian Robert S. McElvaine writes, "Perhaps the chief impact of the Great Depression was that it . . . took away, at least temporarily, the easy assumptions of expansion and mobility that had decisively influenced so much of past American thinking."

In his groundbreaking study *Writers on the Left: Episodes in American Literary Communism* (1961) Daniel Aaron asserts that "American literature, for all of its affirmative spirit, is the most searching and unabashed criticism of our national limitations that exists." Homegrown socialist critiques of American capitalism from the early years of the twentieth century include Upton Sinclair in *The Jungle* (1906), Jack London in *Iron Heel* (1908), and Max Eastman and Floyd Dell in the journal *The Masses*, which was suppressed for its opposition to the involvement of the United States in World War I. In the wake of the Bolshevik Revolution in Russia, Eastman founded *The Liberator* (1918–1924), a more radical successor to *The Masses*. In 1919 John Reed, a former writer for *The Masses*, published his admiring account of the revolution, *Ten Days That Shook the World*.

The influence of Marxist ideas and language among the American Left increased with the establishment of the Soviet Union. In "Towards a Proletarian Art," an editorial in the February 1921 issue of *The Liberator*, Michael Gold invoked Walt Whitman as well as the Russian proletariat, arguing against the leisured intellectuals centered in magazines such as *The Little Review* and *Seven Arts*:

> It is not in that hot-house air that the lusty great tree will grow. Its roots must be in the fields, factories and workshops of America—in the American life.
>
> When there is singing and music rising in every American street, when in every American factory there is a drama group of the workers, when mechanics paint in their leisure, and farmers write sonnets, the greater art will grow and only then.
>
> Only a creative nation understands creation. Only an artist understands art.

Gold concludes that a proletarian art must come "from the deepest depths upward."

In the latter half of the 1920s, before the stock-market crash, the deepening radicalism of many American writers was evident in organized support for Nicola Sacco and Bartolomeo Vanzetti, Italian-born anarchists whose 1921 trial and conviction and 1927 executions became a cause célèbre for the literary Left, as well as in the founding of the New Playwrights Theater (1926–1929) and *The New Masses* (1926–1948), a literary journal that under Gold's editorship became a vehicle for the promotion of proletarian culture by the Communist Party, including the creation of John Reed Clubs across the country. Writers such as Nelson Algren, Langston

Hughes, Meridel Le Sueur, Tillie Olsen, and Richard Wright were members of the clubs. In "Go Left, Young Writers?" an editorial in the January 1929 issue, Gold wrote, "In the past eight months the *New Masses* has been slowly finding its path toward the goal of a proletarian literature in America." But despite the theoretical pronouncements of Gold and a continuing debate about the definition of *proletarian literature* by other writers, including Eastman, V. F. Calverton, Joseph Freeman, and Granville Hicks, the term in practice, especially as the economic crisis deepened in the early 1930s, was used loosely to describe any work that showed sympathy with the poor and working classes or that was critical of capitalism.

A means of criticizing the deficiencies, failures, and brutalities of American capitalism, proletarian literature flourished during the Great Depression. Poets treating proletarian themes included Kenneth Fearing, Kenneth Patchen, Muriel Rukeyser, Genevieve Taggard, and Carl Sandburg. Playwrights such as Clifford Odets in *Waiting for Lefty* (1935) and John Howard Lawson in *Marching Song* (1937) explored strained labor relations. Some of the most notable novels of the 1930s, including Gold's *Jews without Money* (1930), Henry Roth's *Call It Sleep* (1934), Nelson Algren's *Somebody in Boots* (1935), John Steinbeck's *The Grapes of Wrath* (1939), and Richard Wright's *Native Son* (1940), depicted the desperate conditions of the underclass. Other outstanding achievements of the decade included novel trilogies by John Dos Passos, James T. Farrell, Daniel Fuchs, and Josephine Herbst.

Reading *Proletarian Literature in the United States: An Anthology* (1935), edited by Hicks and others, is an excellent way for students to gain insight into the spirit of this literature. *Writing Red: An Anthology of American Women Writers, 1930–1940* (1987), edited by Charlotte Nekola and Paula Rabinowitz, is also recommended. Jon Christian Suggs's *American Proletarian Culture: The Twenties and Thirties* (1993), *Dictionary of Literary Biography Documentary Series*, volume 11, a copiously illustrated history of the era, provides context for understanding the literature in its evolving culture.

TOPICS FOR DISCUSSION AND RESEARCH

1. In the introduction to his *Proletarian Writers of the Thirties* (1968) David Madden acknowledges the problems inherent in the label *proletarian* and cites a letter he received from an indignant Herbst, a novelist who believed that her work had been "considerably damaged" by being categorized as such: "Who thinks up these things and makes the selections? Who says what is what? There were actually arguments about the word 'proletarian' when it was pitched in, during the thirties. I thought of the writing as 'revolutionary' in the sense that the whole century was going to be involved, in one way or another, with revolution, and I think this is quite right. But proletarian was a narrow word, and part of the jargon."

   After you read a particular "proletarian" work—say, Herbst's *The Executioner Waits* (1934)—research the background of the writer and the way the work was received. Was the word *proletarian* used in reviews? Was the writer's background mentioned, and did it seem to be a factor in how the work was evaluated? Is the label *proletarian* appropriate for the work?

2. In "Notes of the Month," an editorial published in the September 1930 issue of *The New Masses* and reprinted in part in Suggs's *American Proletarian Culture,* Gold lists nine elements of what he calls "Proletarian Realism." Among other claims, he contends that a work of this kind must deal "with *real conflicts* of men and women who work for a living" and must never be "pointless": "Every poem, every novel and drama, must have a social theme." One of the more interesting elements he elaborates has to do with the writer's attitude toward his or her material: "Away with drabness, the bourgeois notion that the Worker's life is sordid, the slummer's disgust and feeling of futility. There *is* horror and drabness in the Worker's life; and we will portray it; but we know this is not the last word; we know that this manure heap is the hope of the future; we know that not pessimism, but revolutionary élan will sweep this mess out of the world forever." Do you think these considerations are important for evaluating a literary work of art? Does the work you have read meet Gold's criteria?

3. The first American Writers' Congress was held in New York City in 1935 in response to a call from *The New Masses* for a gathering to discuss the writing craft and the responsibilities of the community of writers. Wright was the keynote speaker. While the Communist Party USA sponsored the congress, it was attended by leftists of various stripes, many of whom loudly resisted the attempt by the Communists to dictate how writers should respond to current social and political issues. By the time of the second American Writers' Congress in 1937, the Communist Party had declared the Popular Front, which involved a less polarizing approach to writers' concerns. Papers delivered at both congresses have been published in collections edited by Henry Hart. Read a selection of essays from the 1935 congress and consider what the responsibility of the writer at such a time might have been and what degree of control the Communist Party sought to exercise over writers. Are there similarly politicized groups today? Do they have a legitimate function? Read a selection of essays from the 1937 congress. What are the differences in political philosophy between the two congresses?

RESOURCES

Primary Works

Jack Conroy and Curt Johnson, eds., *Writers in Revolt: The Anvil Anthology* (New York & Westport, Conn.: Lawrence Hill, 1973).

Includes work by such writers as Nelson Algren, Erskine Caldwell, Langston Hughes, Meridel Le Sueur, Frank Yerby, and Kenneth Patchen. Conroy's introduction gives a brief history of *The Anvil* (1932–1935) and *The New Anvil* (1939–1940); he asserts that *The Anvil* was "the pioneer of proletarian magazines devoted solely to creative work—fiction and verse—and lasted through more issues than any of the rest."

Henry Hart, ed., *American Writers' Congress* (New York: International Publishers, 1935).

A collection of twenty-eight papers delivered at the first congress of the League of American Writers. In his introduction Hart writes of the class struggle in which the interests of writers are inseparable from those of "the propertyless and oppressed."

Hart, ed., *The Writer in a Changing World* (New York: Equinox Cooperative Press, 1937).
Papers delivered at the second American Writers' Congress, with an introduction by Joseph Freeman.

Granville Hicks, Joseph North, Michael Gold, Paul Peters, Isidor Schneider, and Alan Calmer, eds., *Proletarian Literature in the United States: An Anthology*, introduction by Joseph Freeman (New York: International Publishers, 1935).
Valuable both as a historical document and as an interesting collection; includes the writings of more than fifty authors divided into five sections: "Fiction," "Poetry," "Reportage," "Drama," and "Literary Criticism."

Charlotte Nekola and Paula Rabinowitz, eds., *Writing Red: An Anthology of American Women Writers, 1930–1940* (New York: Feminist Press of The City University of New York, 1987).
Focuses on neglected women writers who "contributed to and were themselves moved by the intellectual, literary, and political energy of the left." This anthology presents writings of more than thirty authors, divided into three sections: "Fiction," "Poetry," and "Reportage, Theory, and Analysis."

Joseph North, ed., New Masses: *An Anthology of the Rebel Thirties* (New York: International Publishers, 1969).
Edited by the principal founder of the weekly *New Masses*, which began publication in January 1934. The anthology is divided into five sections: "Poetry," "Short Stories and Sketches," "Reportage," "The Writer and Society," and "Essays and Comment." An appendix reprints the 22 January 1935 "Call for an American Writers' Congress."

Harvey Swados, ed., *The American Writer and the Great Depression* (Indianapolis, Ind.: Bobbs-Merrill, 1966).
An anthology designed to convey the impact of the Depression and to offer "a cross section of good writing of the period."

Bibliography

David R. Peck, *American Marxist Literary Criticism, 1926–1941: A Bibliography* (New York: American Institute for Marxist Studies, 1975).
Includes a list of Marxist periodicals and of "critics and criticism in books and periodicals buried in the records of Depression radicalism."

Criticism

Daniel Aaron, *Writers on the Left: Episodes in American Literary Communism* (New York: Harcourt, Brace & World, 1961).
A chronicle of the involvement of American writers with the Far Left in the first half of the twentieth century. Mixing group narratives, representative figures, and interchapters in a manner inspired by John Dos Passos's *U.S.A.* (1938), Aaron creates a reliable and readable work of literary and cultural history. It is,

however, limited by his neglect of women, minorities, and drama and his focus on New York writers.

James D. Bloom, *Left Letters: The Culture Wars of Mike Gold and Joseph Freeman* (New York: Columbia University Press, 1992).
A study of "perhaps the most prominent literary Communists" of the 1920s and 1930s that examines "what they accomplished and what they set out to achieve."

Franklin Folsom, *Days of Anger, Days of Hope* (Niwot: University Press of Colorado, 1994).
Memoir of the man who was the executive secretary of the League of American Writers from 1937 to 1942. An excellent account of the inner workings of the most active Communist writers' organization of the time, the book includes a good bibliography of other works related to proletarian literature.

David Madden, ed., *Proletarian Writers of the Thirties* (Carbondale & Edwardsville: Southern Illinois Press / London & Amsterdam: Feffer & Simons, 1968).
A collection of essays by various critics. Writers discussed include John Dos Passos, Edward Dahlberg, Robert Cantwell, Jack Conroy, and Daniel Fuchs.

Bill Mullen and Sherry Lee Linkon, eds., *Radical Revisions: Rereading 1930s Culture* (Urbana: University of Illinois Press, 1996).
Essay collection that poses "a new set of questions about the 1930s," showing particular interest in issues of gender and race.

Walter B. Rideout, *The Radical Novel in the United States, 1900–1954* (Cambridge, Mass.: Harvard University Press, 1956).
Attempts a "reasonable" discussion "of a body of fiction which once was exaltedly praised in some quarters and now in most quarters is categorically condemned."

Jon Christian Suggs, ed., *Dictionary of Literary Biography Documentary Series,* volume 11: *American Proletarian Culture: The Twenties and Thirties* (Detroit: Bruccoli Clark Layman/Gale Research, 1993).
Following a useful historical overview, presents revealing letters, articles, reports, and essays arranged chronologically to raise "representative issues and theories of working-class, proletarian, and revolutionary literature and culture."

PEOPLE OF INTEREST

Nelson Algren (1909–1981)

Grew up in Chicago and earned a journalism degree at the University of Illinois. Arrested for vagrancy and theft as he lived as a vagabond in the early 1930s, Algren drew on his experiences in *Somebody in Boots* (1935), a novel that, like all of his fiction, portrays the American underclass. His third novel, *The Man with the Golden Arm* (1949), depicts the life of a morphine addict.

William Attaway (1911–1986)
Born in Greenville, Mississippi, and moved with his family to Chicago—thus participating in the Great Migration, the subject of Attaway's novel *Blood on the Forge* (1941).

Erskine Caldwell (1903–1987)
A prolific novelist and short-story writer whose tall tales of the rural South defined the region for many readers, Caldwell made his reputation with his novels *Tobacco Road* (1932) and *God's Little Acre* (1933).

Abraham Cahan (1860–1951)
A Lithuanian Jew who immigrated to the United States in 1882, a socialist, a labor organizer, the longtime editor of the Yiddish newspaper *Jewish Daily Forward,* and a fiction writer. Cahan's most admired work was *The Rise of David Levinsky* (1917), about a man whose quest for an American identity results in his isolation and alienation.

V. F. Calverton (1900–1940)
Pen name of George Goetz. Calverton was the founder and editor of *Modern Quarterly,* a journal of radical social thought.

Robert Cantwell (1908–1978)
Drew on his experiences working in a wood-veneer factory for four years in writing *The Land of Plenty* (1934), a novel about a strike at a wood-products plant in the Pacific Northwest.

Jack Conroy (1899–1990)
Best known for his proletarian novel *The Disinherited* (1933). Conroy also collaborated with Arna Bontemps on a study of African American migration to the North, *They Seek a City* (1945), which was expanded as *Anyplace but Here* (1966).

Edward Dahlberg (1900–1977)
Drew on his experiences in a Jewish orphanage in Cleveland and as a slum dweller and hobo for his novel *Bottom Dogs* (1929). He also wrote poetry, criticism, and the autobiography *Because I Was Flesh* (1964).

Floyd Dell (1887–1969)
Socialist and important figure in the Chicago Renaissance. Dell moved to Greenwich Village and joined the staff of *The Masses* and then *The Liberator.* His first novel was *Moon-Calf* (1920), a best-selling bildungsroman about a Midwesterner who leaves his small town for Chicago.

John Dos Passos (1896–1970)
A fellow traveler but never a member of the Communist Party; involved with his friend John Howard Lawson in the New Playwrights Theater. Dos Passos was admired by leftist literary critics until he became critical of Communist involvement in the Spanish Civil War.

Max Eastman (1883–1969)
Editor of *The Masses*, a socialist magazine of art and politics, from 1912 until it folded in 1917. Eastman also founded and edited *The Liberator*. He later became a critic of the control Soviet Communists wielded over literary and artistic expression.

James T. Farrell (1904–1979)
Prolific Chicago-born short-story writer and novelist most noted for his gritty portrait of his native city as seen through the eyes of the title character in his Studs Lonigan trilogy: *Young Lonigan* (1932), *The Young Manhood of Studs Lonigan* (1934), and *Judgment Day* (1935).

Kenneth Fearing (1902–1961)
Proletarian poet whose collections include *Angel Arms* (1929), *Dead Reckoning* (1938), and *Collected Poems* (1940). Also a novelist, Fearing often employed multiple narrators, as in *The Big Clock* (1946), a thriller in which a murderer pursues a witness to his crime.

Joseph Freeman (1897–1965)
One of the original editors of *The New Masses* and an editor and translator of Soviet literature. In *An American Testament: A Narrative of Rebels and Romantics* (1936) he provides a personal view of the development of the radical movement in the 1920s and 1930s.

Daniel Fuchs (1909–1993)
Author of the "Williamsburg trilogy" of novels that depict the lives of poor Jews in Brooklyn: *Summer in Williamsburg* (1934), *Homage to Blenholt* (1936), and *Low Company* (1937).

Michael Gold (1893–1967)
Committed Communist Party member and an early advocate for proletarian literature. Gold's most famous work was *Jews without Money* (1930), a novel based on his experiences growing up in a poor family on the Lower East Side of Manhattan.

Albert Halper (1904–1984)
Wrote about the people he knew growing up as the son of Lithuanian Jewish immigrants and working in Chicago. His novels include *Union Square* (1933), *The Foundry* (1934), *The Chute* (1937), and *Little People* (1942).

Josephine Herbst (1897–1969)
A committed Marxist whose novels treated the lives of the laboring poor. Herbst is best known for a trilogy based on the history of her own family: *Pity Is Not Enough* (1933), *The Executioner Waits* (1934), and *Rope of Gold* (1939) follow the Trexler-Wendel family from the late nineteenth century through the boom of the 1920s and the economic collapse of the 1930s.

Granville Hicks (1901–1982)
Literary critic, Communist Party member, and editor of *The New Masses*. Hicks was the author of *The Great Tradition* (1933), a Marxist interpretation of American literature.

Langston Hughes (1902–1967)
Major figure of the Harlem Renaissance. Hughes was deeply involved in the politics of the 1930s, traveling to the Soviet Union in 1932 and reporting on the Spanish Civil War for the *Baltimore Afro-American.*

John Howard Lawson (1894–1977)
Playwright and screenwriter. Lawson became involved in labor politics and wrote the play *Marching Song* (1937), based on a sit-down strike. He was one of the Hollywood Ten, spending a year in prison when he refused to inform on fellow radicals.

Meridel Le Sueur (1900–1996)
Communist Party member who wrote for the *Daily Worker* and *The New Masses.* Le Sueur was the author of *Salute to Spring* (1940), a story collection that depicts the hardships of women during the Depression.

Albert Maltz (1908–1985)
Radical and pacifist who began his career collaborating with Yale classmate George Sklar on the plays *Merry Go Round* (1932) and *Peace on Earth* (1933). His story collection *The Way Things Are* (1938) was followed by his first novel, *The Underground Stream* (1940), about an effort to unionize autoworkers. Maltz became a successful screenwriter in the 1940s and was one of the Hollywood Ten.

Clifford Odets (1906–1963)
Playwright and screenwriter who became involved with the ensemble Group Theatre, first as an actor and then as its most celebrated writer. Odets established his reputation with *Awake and Sing!* (1934), *Waiting for Lefty* (1935), and *Paradise Lost* (1935), all of which treated the struggles of ordinary people during the Depression.

Tillie Olsen (1913–2007)
Activist and feminist of the 1930s and the author of the story collection *Tell Me a Riddle* (1961) and the novel *Yonnondio: From the Thirties* (1974).

Kenneth Patchen (1911–1972)
Raised in a working-class Ohio family. Patchen's first collection of poetry, *Before the Brave* (1936), was notable for its proletarian sympathies. The prolific Patchen became an important voice in the San Francisco Poetry Renaissance and was an inspiration for the Beat writers.

Philip Rahv (1908–1973)
Cofounder with William Phillips of *Partisan Review,* a magazine begun as the organ of the John Reed Club in New York City. Rahv became an influential literary critic.

John Reed (1887–1920)
Best known for his account of the Bolshevik Revolution, *Ten Days That Shook the World* (1919). Reed is the only American buried at the foot of the Kremlin wall in Moscow.

Henry Roth (1906–1995)
Immigrant who grew up on the Lower East Side of New York City and wrote the semiautobiographical *Call It Sleep* (1934), a Modernist novel with proletarian sympathies.

Muriel Rukeyser (1913–1980)
Poet who was sympathetic to the Communist Party. Rukeyser won the Yale Series of Younger Poets Prize for her first collection, *Theory of Flight* (1935), and went on to have a productive career.

Carl Sandburg (1878–1967)
A central figure in the so-called Chicago Renaissance, the author of *Chicago Poems* (1916) and the prose poem *The People, Yes* (1936), the latter celebrating the American spirit in the midst of the Depression. He also wrote a six-volume biography of Abraham Lincoln (1926–1939).

Genevieve Taggard (1894–1948)
Poet who edited *May Days,* a 1925 collection of more than two hundred poems drawn from *The Masses* and *The Liberator.* Her most political collection, *Calling Western Union* (1936), was inspired by her observations of a Vermont quarry workers' strike.

Mary Heaton Vorse (1874–1966)
Journalist who covered labor issues. Vorse's novel *Strike!* (1930) was inspired by a violent textile strike in Gastonia, North Carolina. She described her association with the Provincetown Players in *Time and the Town: A Provincetown Chronicle* (1942).

Clara Weatherwax (1905–1958)
Author of a single novel, *Marching! Marching!* (1935), which was inspired in part by the general strike of 1934–1935 in San Francisco and won a contest sponsored by *The New Masses* for the best new novel "on an American proletarian theme."

Richard Wright (1908–1960)
Author of *Native Son* (1940). Wright described his experience with the Communist Party in "I Tried to Be a Communist"; it was included in *The God That Failed* (1950), edited by Richard Crossman.

Leane Zugsmith (1903–1969)
Journalist who became a fiction writer. Zugsmith made her reputation as a proletarian novelist with novels such as *The Reckoning* (1934), about the life of a boy of the slums, and *A Time to Remember* (1936), an account of the unionization of a department store.

—*George Parker Anderson*

The Hard-Boiled Detective and the Pulps

Hard-boiled crime fiction developed in the early 1920s in pulp magazines that flourished in the period between the world wars. The pulps, so called because of the cheap paper on which they were printed, were marketed without pretense of literary sophistication to a blue-collar, mostly male audience. Some 120 pulp magazines were available on newsstands in the 1920s and 1930s. They were typically published biweekly or monthly, priced at ten or twenty cents each for 128 pages of stories on a general theme—love stories, adventure stories, Westerns, and detective fiction, among other topics. *Black Mask Magazine* (1920–1951) was the most successful of the detective-fiction pulps, and most of the first-generation pulp detective fiction known to readers in the twenty-first century was published there, including stories and serialized novels by Dashiell Hammett, Raymond Chandler, Horace McCoy, Erle Stanley Gardner, and Cornell Woolrich.

The earliest pulp detective fiction is characterized by five elements: it features a tough, independent hero who is master of his environment; it is violent, often gratuitously so; the setting is the lower rungs of a society marred by corruption; the language is colloquial; and the emphasis is on action, often at the expense of plot development. Its purpose is unapologetically to entertain rather than to instruct. Little claim can be made that most early hard-boiled detective fiction had enduring literary qualities. Usually it was limited to the short-story form, and until the late 1920s it appeared exclusively in pulp magazines, which usually paid authors about a penny a word.

In the late 1920s Hammett explicitly proposed to "make literature" from the detective story, and he set the standard for enduring works in the form by adapting techniques from both mainstream literature and earlier forms of crime fiction, placing an emphasis on structure, character development, dramatic presentation, and literary resonance. His third novel, *The Maltese Falcon* (serialized in *Black Mask,* then published by Knopf in 1930), is regarded as having set the literary standard for the hard-boiled crime novel. Hammett was the first of the three great early hard-boiled writers, each offering new perspectives on the treatment of crime and criminals in literature. Chandler brought a sophisticated literary style and further character development with his first two novels, *The Big Sleep* (1939) and *Farewell, My Lovely* (1940). Ross Macdonald, freely acknowledging the influence of Hammett and Chandler, introduced psychologically complex characters and intricate plots in his novels, reaffirming the literary qualities of the form in his best works, *The Galton Case* (1959), *The Far Side of the Dollar* (1965), and *The Underground Man* (1971) among them. Mickey Spillane was the most popular of the mid-century hard-boiled detective writers, though he cannot be accused of literary excellence, nor did he pretend that his work was anything other than low-brow entertainment.

The roll of hard-boiled detective writers is a long one that includes John D. MacDonald, Cornell Woolrich, Charles Willeford, Jim Thompson, and Chester Himes. Among contemporary writers Joe Gores stands out. Michael Connelly, Elmore Leonard, Walter Moseley, Donald Westlake (writing as Richard Stark), Laurence Block, Dennis Lehane, George Pelicanos, and Loren Estleman are among the most respected practitioners of this increasingly popular literary genre, which also includes women such as Marcia Muller, Sue Grafton, and Sara Paretsky.

The reader seeking to familiarize him or herself with early pulp detective fiction is well served by three anthologies. Otto Penzler's *The Black Lizard Big Book of Pulps* (2007), a massive compilation, provides a good sense of the development of the pulp crime story. William F. Nolan's *The Black Mask Boys* (1985) offers an excellent selection of stories from the most important of the detective-fiction pulps, along with a brief history of the magazine and short biographies of the *Black Mask* writers that often provide the best information available about lesser-known figures. Herbert Ruhm's *The Hard-Boiled Detective* (1977) also draws its contents from *Black Mask*. Web resources for hard-boiled detective fiction are risky for the most part: they tend to be compiled by well-meaning fans who often lack the training to identify reliable sources. Students are well advised to begin with the recommended print resources. Movies—film noir in particular—draw heavily on hard-boiled fiction. The works edited by Ian Cameron, Lee Server, and Alain Silver are excellent sources of movie criticism that discuss both the sources and the cinematic results.

TOPICS FOR DISCUSSION AND RESEARCH

1. The dime novels of the late nineteenth century were pulp paperbacks named for their price that were published for unsophisticated readers. They were the precursors of the pulps of the early twentieth century. In the introduction to his collection *The Dime Novel Detective* (Bowling Green, Ohio: Bowling Green University Popular Press, 1982) Gary Hoppenstand claims that what he calls the Avenger detective stories that appeared in the dime novels are an unrecognized category of detective fiction. Read sample Avenger stories in Hoppenstand's book and compare them to sample stories in Nolan's *The Black Mask Boys*. On the basis of that comparison, describe the characteristics of hard-boiled fiction as represented in Nolan's books.

2. Pulp magazines had essentially died out by the time of World War II. Why? What replaced them? Is there a contemporary source of entertainment equivalent to the pulp magazine? How is the audience the pulps addressed catered to now? Erin Smith's *Hard-Boiled: Working Class Readers and Pulp* (2000) provides an important analysis of the pulp readership and is a useful starting point.

3. Hard-boiled detective fiction, though most often regarded as a subgenre of mystery fiction, had a clear relationship with so-called mainstream writing. Ernest Hemingway (notably in *To Have and Have Not* [1937]), William Faulkner (in *Sanctuary* [1931]) and John O'Hara (in *Appointment in Samarra* [1934]) wrote hard-boiled fiction, for example. Who influenced whom? How did mainstream writers influence hard-boiled detective writers and vice versa?

4. Hard-boiled fiction is more highly respected in France than in the United States, presumably because influential thinkers after World War II found in that work an expression of existentialist philosophy. Catherine Savage Brosman's *Existential Fiction* (Detroit: Gale Group, 2000) is an excellent

introduction to the subject, though it deals primarily with French writers. Read Brosman's introduction and discuss the existential elements of key hard-boiled crime novels, such as Hammett's *The Maltese Falcon* or McCoy's *They Shoot Horses, Don't They?* (1935).

5. Hard-boiled crime fiction is regarded by some critics as a reaction against the Golden Age mystery. To address such a topic, one must first define the qualities of both literary types and then measure examples against those definitions. Find Golden Age writer S. S. Van Dine's "Twenty Rules for Writing Detective Fiction" (available at <http://gaslight.mtroyal.ca/vandine.htm> [accessed 13 November 2009]) and measure the literary technique of a hard-boiled crime novel, perhaps James M. Cain's *The Postman Always Rings Twice* (1934), against those rules.

RESOURCES

Primary Works

William F. Nolan, ed., *The* Black Mask *Boys: Masters in the Hard-Boiled School of Detective Fiction* (New York: Morrow, 1985).
Includes an overview of the magazine, which was edited by Joseph T. Shaw, and stories by Dashiell Hammett, Raymond Chandler, Erle Stanley Gardner, Horace McCoy, Carroll John Daly, Frederick Nebel, Raoul Whitfield, and Paul Cain.

Otto Penzler, ed., *The Black Lizard Big Book of Pulps* (New York: Vintage Crime/Black Lizard Original, 2007).
More than 1,100 pages, comprising stories and two serialized novels. The collection is divided into three sections: "The Crimefighters," "The Villains," and "The Dames." Each story is introduced by Penzler.

Herbert Ruhm, ed., *The Hard-Boiled Detective: Stories from* Black Mask *Magazine, 1920–1951* (New York: Vintage, 1977).
Offers sixteen stories from *Black Mask* and a useful introduction.

Joseph T. Shaw, ed., *The Hard-Boiled Omnibus: Early Stories from* Black Mask (New York: Simon & Schuster, 1946).
The earliest anthology of *Black Mask* stories, compiled by the magazine's most highly regarded editor.

Criticism

George Parker Anderson and Julie B. Anderson, eds., *Dictionary of Literary Biography*, volume 226: *American Hard-Boiled Crime Writers* (Detroit: Gale, 2000).
Biographical and critical assessments of thirty-one writers active between 1922 and 2000, as well as a general introduction.

Rara Avis: Bibliographies <http://www.miskatonic.org/rara-avis/biblio/> [accessed 13 November 2009].
Provides full checklists of key figures' works.

Lee Server, Martin H. Greenberg, and Ed Gorman, eds., *The Big Book of Noir* (New York: Carroll & Graf, 1998).
A good collection of critical articles about different iterations of noir: movies, fiction, comic books, and radio and television.

Alain Silver, Elizabeth Ward, and others, eds., *Film Noir: An Encyclopedic Reference to the American Style,* third edition (Woodstock, N.Y.: Overlook Press, 1992).
An excellent source of information about movies from the 1930s to the 1960s that show the influence of the hard-boiled sensibility. Some three hundred movies are identified and analyzed.

Erin Smith, *Hard-Boiled: Working Class Readers and Pulp Magazines* (Philadelphia: Temple University Press, 2000).
A sociological study of the pulps, their editors, marketing strategies, advertisers, and readership. Smith's book is the most reliable study of its kind.

Ralph Willett, "Hard-Boiled Detective Fiction," *British Association for American Studies* <http://www.baas.ac.uk/resources/pamphlets/pamphdets.asp?id=23#ch2> [accessed 13 November 2009].
A brief general overview that may be useful to students seeking a quick orientation to the field.

Edmund Wilson, "The Boys in the Back Room: Notes on California Novelists," in his *Classics and Commercials: A Literary Chronicle of the Forties* (New York: Farrar, Straus, 1950).
An article by the respected literary and cultural critic that denies the importance of hard-boiled fiction, claiming that it was minimalist and relatively meaningless.

PEOPLE OF INTEREST

James M. Cain (1892–1977)
One of the American hard-boiled writers who was admired by the French. Cain's first novel, *The Postman Always Rings Twice* (1934), was an inspiration for Albert Camus's *L'Etranger* (1942; translated as *The Stranger,* 1946). Cain's other novels include *Serenade* (1937), *Mildred Pierce* (1941), and *Double Indemnity* (1943).

Paul Cain (1902–1966)
An author about whom little is known. Cain wrote *Fast One* (1933), regarded as one of the best examples of the hard-boiled crime novel.

Raymond Chandler (1888–1959)
The author of seven novels featuring detective Philip Marlowe, beginning with *The Big Sleep* (1939). He is the hard-boiled writer who has been most admired by literary critics.

Erle Stanley Gardner (1889–1970)
Created the mystery-solving defense attorney Perry Mason, who appeared in more than eighty novels beginning with *The Case of the Velvet Claws* (1933).

Dashiell Hammett (1894–1961)
The leader of the hard-boiled school. Hammett's writing career is defined by five novels published in a five-year span: *Red Harvest* (1929), *The Dain Curse* (1930), *The Maltese Falcon* (1930), *The Glass Key* (1931), and *The Thin Man* (1934).

Horace McCoy (1897–1955)
Best known for his first novel, *They Shoot Horses, Don't They?* (1935). McCoy was admired in France as an existentialist. His other works include *No Pockets in a Shroud* (1937), *I Should Have Stayed Home* (1938), and *Kiss Tomorrow Good-Bye* (1948).

Joseph T. Shaw (1874–1952)
The editor of *Black Mask* from 1926 to 1936. "Cap" Shaw was instrumental in the creation of hard-boiled fiction.

Raoul Whitfield (1898–1945)
A hard-boiled pioneer who contributed scores of stories to *Black Mask,* Whitfield published his first novel, *Green Ice,* in 1930.

Cornell Woolrich (1903–1968)
A prolific writer who created a psychologically menacing noir world in his fiction. His first crime novel, *The Bride Wore Black* (1940), began a six-novel sequence known as the Black series.

—*Richard Layman*

Modernism and the Changing American Vision

Modernism as a term and as a literary movement defies a consensus definition, particularly when it comes to its beginning and ending. In *Axel's Castle* (1931), the first major study of what Edmund Wilson called a "distinct movement" that later came to be called Modernism, the American critic saw its origins in 1870s French literature. While some critics have used the end of World War II as a line to divide Modernism from Postmodernism, for others the spirit that prompted Modernism did not end with the war and indeed continues to shape the literature of the present. For many, Modernism is timeless, not limited by a span of years but instead denotes an aesthetic—the qualities and sensibility inherent in a particular work. In this sense, critics will cite as "Modernist" or even "Postmodernist" works written much earlier than anyone would argue Modernism as a movement existed—Laurence Sterne's quirky masterpiece *The Life and Opinions of Tristram Shandy, Gentleman* (1760–1767), for example, is often so labeled.

Few if any critics, however, would disagree with the proposition that the beginnings of a worldwide cultural change had its roots in the nineteenth century and blossomed in the early twentieth century—in American literature, especially after World War I. The ideas that contributed to changing the ways human beings viewed themselves and their place in the world certainly included those of Karl Marx and Friedrich Engels in the treatise generally known as *The Communist Manifesto* (1848), Charles Darwin in *On the Origin of Species* (1859), and Sigmund Freud in *The Interpretation of Dreams* (1899). In *The First Moderns: Profiles in the Origins of Twentieth-Century Thought*, William R. Everdell traces the story of Modernism through mathematicians, physicists, painters, politicians, biologists, logicians, filmmakers, musicians, and architects, as well as through poets, playwrights, and novelists. Everdell writes that the intellectual origins of Modernism "lie in an often profound rethinking of the whole mind set of the nineteenth century." In the modern world, thinkers were giving up "the old belief that things could be seen 'steadily and whole' from some privileged viewpoint at a particular moment" and embracing a "nonlogical, nonobjective, and essentially causeless mental universe." Writers who sought to find ways to explore this evolving sensibility pioneered the experimental literary approaches associated with literary Modernism—ambiguity and multiple interpretations of events; the use of myth as a structural device; the sophisticated probing of the unconscious and subconscious of the individual psyche; the incorporation of dreamlike or surreal sequences; experimentation with forms, styles, voices, and the use of language; and techniques such as interior monologues, stream of consciousness, fragmentation, flashbacks, and other manipulations of time.

In the early years of the twentieth century, with the wisespread acceptance of culture-changing inventions such as electric lighting, movies, automobiles, telephones, and radios, the pace of change was bending upward along an ever-steepening, unpredictable curve. Americans and others living in industrial economies felt themselves in the grip of a palpable transformation. In 1893 at the Chicago World's Fair, the American historian Henry Adams recognized what he felt was a fundamental shift in the organization of the world. In *The Educa-*

tion of Henry Adams (1907) he wrote of seeing massive dynamos featured in an exhibit as a symbol of the future. Adams "began to feel the forty-foot dynamos as a moral force, much as the early Christians felt the Cross"—but with no clear idea of its portent. The British novelist Virginia Woolf, looking back from 1924, famously suggested a rather precise moment of transformation: "On or about December 1910 human character changed. All human relations shifted—those between masters and servants, husbands and wives, parents and children. And when human relations shift there is at the same time a change in religion, conduct, politics and literature."

Most critics recognize European writers as the leaders in developing new ways to explore the human condition as the nineteenth turned to the twentieth century. Nine of the ten major Modernist writers Malcolm Bradbury treats in *The Modern World,* —Fyodor Dostoevsky, Henrik Ibsen, Joseph Conrad, Thomas Mann, Marcel Proust, James Joyce, Luigi Pirandello, Woolf, and Franz Kafka— are European. But American authors such as Gertrude Stein, T. S. Eliot, and Ezra Pound—all expatriates living in Europe—also played major roles in pioneering new approaches and techniques. Pound was something of an entrepreneur of Modernism, not only in his own poetry but also as a catalyst and guide to others striving to, in his words, "make it new." He was involved in the Modernist movements Imagism and Vorticism, served as the foreign editor for Harriet Monroe's Chicago-based *Poetry: A Magazine of Verse,* and aided in the publication and promotion of the two greatest landmarks of literary Modernism in English, Eliot's *The Waste Land* (1922), which he helped to write and edited, and Joyce's *Ulysses* (1922).

In the United States, Americans were exposed to modern European art and sculpture and avant-garde movements such as Cubism, Futurism, Fauvism, and Expressionism in the 1913 Armory Show, so called because it was held at the Sixty-Ninth Regiment Armory in New York City. The proliferation of little magazines such as *The Little Review* (1914–1929), which attempted to serialize *Ulysses* and was fined $100 for publishing obscenity in 1920, and *The Fugitive* (1922–1925), published in Nashville, which Robert Penn Warren called "a battleground for debating Modernism and traditionalism," was another indication of the growing momentum of the movement.

Social changes were also significant in creating the conditions in which American Modernism thrived. The country experienced great waves of immigration in the first decades of the century; entered a period of economic expansion in the 1920s; became unsettled by the Red Scare, precipitated by the Bolshevik revolution; intensified urbanization, both as a result of demobilization after the war and the migration of African Americans from the rural South to northern cities; and coped with the enormous cultural changes promised by constitutional amendments making Prohibition the law of the land and permitting women the right to vote. Many writers in the U.S. were critical of the developing consumerist culture and its materialistic values as well as its repressive tendencies. In *Beyond Culture: Essays on Literature and Learning* (1965), critic Lionel Trilling notes "the disenchantment of our culture with culture itself" and suggested that "the characteristic element of modern literature, or at least of the most highly developed modern literature, is the bitter line of hostility to civilization which runs through it."

Within American Modernism, there are different strains. Although writers such as Robert Frost, F. Scott Fitzgerald, and Ernest Hemingway were thoroughly modern in their sensibility, aware of the complexity of their culture and its intellectual trends, they generally did not write works that made extraordinary demands upon their readers. On the other hand, such writers as Stein, Pound, Eliot, Hart Crane, Marianne Moore, Wallace Stevens, Eugene O'Neill, John Dos Passos, and William Faulkner often experimented and produced works readers found difficult to understand. An incomplete list of works of so-called High Modernism that were published between the wars would include Stein's *The Making of Americans* (1925); Pound's *Hugh Selwyn Mauberly* (1920) and *The Cantos* (1917-1973); Eliot's *Four Quartets* (1943); Crane's *The Bridge* (1931); Moore's *Selected Poems* (1935); Stevens's *Harmonium* (1923; revised and enlarged, 1931) and *Ideas of Order* (1935; enlarged 1936); O'Neill's *The Emperor Jones* (produced 1920), *Strange Interlude* (produced 1928), and *Mourning Becomes Electra* (produced 1931); Dos Passos's *Manhattan Transfer* (1925) and his *U.S.A.* trilogy (1938); and Faulkner's *The Sound and the Fury* (1929), *As I Lay Dying* (1930), and *Absalom, Absalom!* (1936).

Especially in the last three decades, critics have sought to expand the idea of Modernism, the canon of Modernist texts, and the way in which the movement is conceived. Increasingly, critics see Modernism not as a single movement but as a field of intersecting subtraditions and movements. The titles of a few of the scores of studies of Modernism—these all published since the year 2000—are suggestive of some of the ways the field is being reconceived and reinterpreted: *New Deal Modernism: American Literature and the Invention of the Welfare State* (2001) by Michael Szalay; *Making Something Happen: American Political Poetry between the Wars* (2001) by Michael Thurston; *Black and White and Noir: America's Pulp Modernism* (2002) by Paula Rabinowitz; *Crossroads Modernism: Descent and Emergence in African-American Literary Culture* (2002) by Edward M. Pavlic; *Cruising Modernism: Class and Sexuality in American Literature and Social Thought* (2003) by Michael Trask; *Strangers at Home: American Ethnic Modernism between the World Wars* (2005) by Rita Keresztesi; *Sensational Modernism: Experimental Fiction and Photography in Thirties America* (2007) by Joseph B. Entin; and *Modernism on File: Writers, Artists, and the FBI, 1920–1950* (2008) edited by Claire A. Culleton and Karen Leick. A profound movement inspired by momentous intellectual and social changes, Modernism as a concept is changing still.

TOPICS FOR DISCUSSION AND RESEARCH

1. Examine the contemporary reviews for a particular Modernist text. Did reviewers note the use of what would now be considered Modernist techniques—the use of an achronological structure or of interior monologues, for example—or were the use of such techniques seemingly accepted without comment? What does the contemporary reaction to the text show about how

the author and her or his text were regarded? Compare your own reactions to those of the reviewers. Extend your research by finding subsequent criticism that treats the author's experimentalism. How has the appreciation of what the author achieved changed?

2. In one traditional understanding of literary Modernism, critics have seen the writer as seeking to transcend the realities of modern society by creating works that stand apart from that world in their imaginative complexity and aesthetic integrity. Some critics and authors believe that works of art are—or should be—beyond politics. Asked the question, "How would you describe the political tendency of American writing since 1930," Stein in a 1939 symposium in *Partisan Review*, "The Situation in American Writing," answered: "Writers only think that they are interested in politics, they are not really, it gives them a chance to talk and writers like to talk but really no real writer is interested in politics." Respond to Stein's assertion by examining a work of High Modernism that you've read. What, if anything, does it have to say about the political reality of its time or our own?

3. The perception that modern writers were apolitical was not a view shared by J. Edgar Hoover and the Federal Bureau of Investigation, who regarded many writers as possible dangers to domestic tranquility. Files were kept on African American writers such as Langston Hughes, Claude McKay, and Richard Wright, and other writers associated with political radicalism, including Edna St. Vincent Millay, Henry Roth, Muriel Rukeyser, Hemingway, and John Steinbeck. As Culleton and Leick write in the introduction to *Modernism on File*, the authorities identified writers as legitimate targets of investigation when they transgressed "the boundaries between art and obscenity, or art and political insurgency." Find out what you can about the reasons for the investigation of any of these authors. Was the investigation warranted? Is government investigation of an author ever appropriate?

4. As Modernism is reconsidered and reconceived, the question of who and what should be assigned reading in order to define the movement arises as often as the subject is taught. In many of the studies of American Modernism published in recent years, neglected writers and works are often suggested as being worthy of study. Find and read an often ignored work deemed important by one or more critics—Nella Larsen's *Quicksand* (1928) or *Passing* (1929), or Pietro di Donato's *Christ in Concrete* (1939), or perhaps one of the writers listed in "People of Interest" below—and then consider the argument of the critic. Would the work you read be worth the attention of others in a discussion of American literary Modernism?

RESOURCES

Houston A. Baker Jr., *Modernism and the Harlem Renaissance* (Chicago: University of Chicago Press, 1987).

A provocative and personal study of African American culture on its own terms, in which Baker discusses strategies he designates as "*the mastery of form* and *the deformation of mastery*" to discuss "Afro-American modernism." He takes Booker

T. Washington's emergence in 1895 as a national leader as a marker for the beginning of the change he describes.

Malcolm Bradbury, *The Modern World* (London & New York: Viking Penguin, 1988).
Bradbury's accessible study, written to accompany a major BBC television series on Modernism, explores the richness of his multifaceted subject through consideration of ten writers.

Claire A. Culleton and Karen Leick, eds., *Modernism on File: Writers, Artists and the FBI, 1920–1950* (New York: Palgrave Macmillan, 2008).
A collection of twelve essays showing that J. Edgar Hoover's "investigative practices had considerable effect on the lives and creative activities of writers and artists . . . and as often as his efforts curtailed their work and artistic license, their counterefforts to stave off or circumvent government interventions shaped and affected the burgeoning modern arts movement consequently making it a self-conscious movement fed on and not starved by the twentieth century federal gaze."

Joseph B. Entin, *Sensational Modernism: Experimental Fiction and Photography in Thirties America* (Chapel Hill: University of North Carolina Press, 2007).
Defines "sensational modernism" as a mode of aesthetics that "blends a sensational focus on the body, shock, and social extremes with a modernist emphasis on formal innovation and aesthetic self-consciousness."

William R. Everdell, *The First Moderns: Profiles in the Origins of Twentieth-Century Thought* (Chicago & London: University of Chicago Press, 1997).
A wide-ranging survey of a variety of important figures with a personal touch: "Where Modernism began may have more to do, as we shall see, with a couple of mathematicians in Germany and a cabaret in Paris than with novels and buildings."

Hugh Kenner, *A Homemade World: The American Modernist Writers* (New York: Knopf, 1975).
Kenner, who states that his topic is a fifty-year reshaping of the American language, focuses on six writers—the poets William Carlos Williams, Wallace Stevens, and Marianne Moore, and the novelists F. Scott Fitzgerald, Ernest Hemingway, and William Faulkner—as the creators of an American "homemade" Modernism.

Pericles Lewis, *The Cambridge Introduction to Modernism* (Cambridge, England & New York: Cambridge University Press, 2007).
A readable general introduction, relevant to an understanding of American Modernism though the focus is on English literature.

Michael Soto, *The Modernist Nation: Generation, Renaissance, and Twentieth-Century American Literature* (Tuscaloosa: University of Alabama Press, 2004).
Focuses on Modernist movements of the United States. Soto claims that "The Lost Generation and Harlem Renaissance (or the 'Negro Renaissance,' as it was called at the time) clearly represent the two most significant movements associated with American literary modernism."

Edmund Wilson, *Axel's Castle: A Study in the Imaginative Literature of 1870–1930* (New York & London: Scribners, 1931).
Called the "first major study of international literary modernism" by Malcolm Bradbury, Wilson's readable work presents the new movement in literature as "the development of Symbolism and of its fusion or conflict with Naturalism." It includes chapters on T. S. Eliot and Gertrude Stein as well as W. B. Yeats, Paul Valery, Marcel Proust, and James Joyce.

PEOPLE OF INTEREST

Conrad Aiken (1889–1973)
A poet, essayist, and fiction writer, Aiken was particularly interested in psychological themes. As a child he discovered the bodies of his parents, after his mother was murdered by his father, who then committed suicide. His work was acclaimed by many Beat writers.

Margaret Anderson (1886–1973)
Founded and edited *The Little Review,* which serialized installments of James Joyce's *Ulysses* (1922) and published such writers as Sherwood Anderson, Vachel Lindsay, and William Carlos Williams.

Djuna Barnes (1892–1982)
An avant-garde poet, playwright, and prose writer, Barnes is best known for her novel *Nightwood* (1936), a fragmented narrative based on the experience of expatriation in Paris.

Hart Crane (1899–1932)
A difficult, allusive poet who is best known for *The Bridge* (1930), an epic poem that uses the Brooklyn Bridge as its setting and organizing symbol to examine American culture. Like Walt Whitman, Crane attempted to offer a vision of the American experience that offered promise and hope.

Hilda Doolittle (1886–1961)
Known as H.D., Doolittle was a major contributor to the Imagist movement whose poetry collections include *Sea Gardens* (1916).

Robinson Jeffers (1887–1962)
Robinson, who lived in a primitive granite cottage he helped build on the Monterey coast with his wife and twin sons, wrote from a perspective he called "Inhumanism," which considered humankind as only a part of larger, more important whole. He is known for short lyrics such as "To the Stone Cutters," "Boats in a Fog," and "Hurt Hawks" and longer narrative poems such as *Roan Stallion* (1925).

Amy Lowell (1874–1925)
Became an important and flamboyant promoter of Imagism and modern poetry. Her collections include *Men, Women and Ghosts* (1916) and *What's O'clock* (1925).

Harriet Monroe (1860–1936)
The founder of *Poetry: A Magazine of Verse* in 1912, Monroe edited the journal until her death. Providing a platform for experimental work as well as for traditional forms, *Poetry* published work by such writers as T. S. Eliot, Carl Sandburg, Ezra Pound, and Robert Frost.

Marianne Moore (1887–1972)
The editor of *The Dial* from 1925 to 1929, Moore established herself as an important Modernist poet with *Selected Poems* (1935).

Merrill Moore (1903–1957)
A member of the Fugitives, Moore was a practicing psychiatrist as well as a prolific poet. He was especially known for his experimentations with the sonnet form.

George Oppen (1908-1984)
Oppen was an important member of the Objectivist school of poets. His first collection, *Discrete Series* (1934), was introduced by Ezra Pound and praised by William Carlos Williams. He did not publish more poetry until the 1960s, when his collection *Of Being Numerous* (1968) won a Pulitzer Prize.

Ezra Pound (1885–1972)
One of the central figures of literary Modernism, Pound encouraged many other writers, including T. S. Eliot, Robert Frost, James Joyce, and Ernest Hemingway. Eliot dedicated *The Waste Land* (1922) to "Ezra Pound, *il miglior fabbro*" (the superior maker). His own writing included *Hugh Selwyn Mauberly* (1920) and *The Cantos*, a poetic project he worked on from the 1920s to his death.

John Crowe Ransom (1888–1974)
A notable poet and critic, Ransom was one of the editors of *The Fugitive* and founded the *Kenyon Review*. He is the author of *The New Criticism* (1941).

Laura Riding (1901–1991)
The only woman to be a member of the Fugitives, Riding published her first collection, *The Closed Chaplet* in 1926. With Robert Graves, she wrote *A Survey of Modernist Poetry* (1927). She stopped writing poetry after the publication of *Collected Poems* (1938).

Gertrude Stein (1874–1946)
A major Modernist writer who lived most of her adult life as an expatriate in Paris, Stein and her companion, Alice B. Toklas, established their residence at 27 rue de Fleurus, as a gathering place for the avant-garde literary and artistic community. Her works include *Three Lives* (1909), a collection of novellas that explore the consciousness of three women, the experimental *The Making of Americans* (1925), a nonnarrative family saga, and her memoir *The Autobiography of Alice B. Toklas* (1934), perhaps her most accessible work.

Allen Tate (1899–1979)
A Southern poet, critic, biographer, and novelist, Tate attended Vanderbilt University, where he was a Fugitive as well as an Agrarian. His poetry collections

include *Poems: 1928–1931* (1932), *The Mediterranean and Other Poems* (1936), and *Selected Poems* (1937).

Robert Penn Warren (1905–1989)

The Kentucky-born Warren attended Vanderbilt University and was a member of the Fugitives. He had a distinguished career as a critic, collaborating with Cleanth Brooks on textbooks such as *Understanding Poetry* (1938) that promoted the principles of New Criticism; a fiction writer, whose most acclaimed novel was *All the King's Men* (1946), inspired by the career of Huey Long; and a poet who published fifteen collections, including *Brother to Dragons: A Tale in Verse and Voices* (1953; revised 1979), which explores the murder of a slave by Thomas Jefferson's nephew.

Edmund Wilson (1895–1972)

A novelist and a diarist as well as one of the great literary critics of his era, Wilson stood apart from other critics and schools in his individual blending of biographical and literary criticism. His notable works in addition to *Axel's Castle* include *The Wound and the Bow: Seven Studies in Literature* (1941), *The Boys in the Back Room: Notes on California Novelists* (1941), and *The Shores of Light: A Literary Chronicle of the Twenties and Thirties* (1952).

Anzia Yezierska (1880–1970)

Immigrating with her family from the Russian-Polish town of Plinsk to New York City's Lower East Side, Yezierska graduated from Columbia University and achieved notoriety as an author with the story collection *Hungry Hearts* (1920) and *Salome of the Tenements* (1923).

Louis Zukofsky (1904–1978)

Introduced to William Carlos Williams by Ezra Pound, Zukofsky with Williams promoted Objectivism. He edited a 1931 issue of *Poetry* that featured the work of Williams, Carl Rokosi, Charles Reznikoff, and George Oppen as well as *An "Objectivists" Anthology* (1932). His lifelong project was *"A"* (1978), a poem in twenty-four movements.

—*George Parker Anderson*

The New Deal and Writers: American Guides and Living Newspapers

Created as a response to the Great Depression, the Works Progress Administration (WPA) of President Franklin D. Roosevelt gave jobs on public-works projects to millions of unemployed Americans and also included a small component devoted to the arts. Initiated in the spring of 1935, the WPA's first program, known as Federal One, included the Federal Art Project, the Federal Music Project, the Federal Writers Project, and the Federal Theatre Project—the latter two directly employing writers and playwrights. Within a year of its launch, Federal One was employing some forty thousand people throughout the United States. From its inception Federal One was attacked by critics who believed that supporting the arts was not the proper role of the federal government; Harry Hopkins, director of the WPA, responded that writers, actors, artists, and musicians, like everyone else, needed to eat.

The Federal Writers Project, directed in its first four years by Henry G. Alsberg, existed until 1943; after July 1939 it was administered by the states as the WPA's Writers Program. In *The Dream and the Deal: The Federal Writers' Project, 1935–1943* (1972) Jerre Mangione writes that the project reached its peak employment of 6,686 in April 1936 and was represented in every state and the District of Columbia. The final count for publications by the project was at least "276 volumes, 701 pamphlets, and 340 issuances (leaflets, articles, radio scripts)." This total included "guidebooks for each of the forty-eight states, Washington, D.C., Puerto Rico and Alaska; about thirty guides to cities such as New York, New Orleans, San Francisco, Los Angeles; more than a score of other book-length guides such as *U.S. One, The Ocean Highway, The Oregon Trail, Skiing in the East, Here's New England, Death Valley Guide;* and approximately one hundred and fifty volumes in the project's highly varied Life in America Series, which ranged in titles from *Hands that Built New Hampshire* to *The Albanian Struggle in the Old World and New.*" The most famous productions of the project were the acclaimed state guides, which, with the exception of the Idaho guide edited by Vardis Fisher, followed the same organization:

> Part One contains essays on the history, setting, people, commerce, art, literature, recreation, and educational facilities of the state. The second part deals with a state's cities in terms of general information, history, and major points of interest. The longest section, part three, which often takes up half the volume, consists of tours that follow the highways into every corner of the state, illuminating each mile of the way with historical information and Americana which is often amusing. In addition to the three major segments, each state guide is prefaced by information useful to travelers . . . and a calendar of annual events. A historical chronology of significant developments, a bibliography, as many as one hundred photographs, and about a dozen maps (one of them a map of the entire state in color) complete the contents. The longest of the state guides is New York, with 782 pages; the shortest North Dakota, with 371 pages.

Although most of those hired for the Federal Writers Project had little or no formal experience, the long list of those who participated includes Conrad Aiken, Nelson Algren, Saul Bellow, Arna Bontemps, John Cheever, Jack Conroy, Kenneth Fearing, Dorothy Canfield Fisher, Ralph Ellison, Zora Neale Hurston, Norman Macleod, Claude McKay, Willard Motley, Kenneth Rexroth, May Swenson, Studs Terkel, Jim Thompson, Margaret Walker, Eudora Welty, Richard Wright, Anzia Yezierska, and Frank Yerby.

The Federal Theatre Project, directed by Hallie Flanagan, at its peak employed nearly thirteen thousand theatre workers—playwrights, journalists, writers, actors, directors, designers, dancers, musicians, and technicians—many of whom had lost employment before the Great Depression took hold, because audiences for theatrical productions had declined with the rising popularity of radio and movies. In its four-year history, the theatre project introduced some one hundred new playwrights and produced more that 1,200 plays, bringing the experience of live theatre, often at little or no charge, to many Americans who had never seen a play before. The major radio networks carried the *Federal Theatre of the Air* to an estimated ten million listeners.

In her introduction to *Federal Theatre Plays* (1938), a collection of three scripts edited by Pierre de Rohan, Flanagan describes the scope of the program, then in its third year. Calling the Federal Theatre Project an attempt to "supplement and stimulate commercial theatre enterprise," she outlines eight major lines of activities that received government support:

> *classics,* produced not as academic exercises, but as plays for a modern audience; *theatre of entertainment,* including circus, vaudeville, variety, musical comedy; *children's theatre,* including marionettes, planned in cooperation with psychologists and boards of education; *dance drama,* such as *How Long Brethren,* and *American Exodus;* an *American drama series,* which by this time includes the work of practically every American writer from Clyde Fitch to Irwin Shaw, Clifford Odets, Paul Green, Rachel Crothers, John Howard Lawson, Sidney Howard; *Living Newspaper,* creating drama out of everyday factual material; *radio drama,* and the *Negro theatre.* . . .

The most famous—and controversial—productions of the federal stage were the Living Newspaper plays. Vehicles for large-scale employment, the plays made use of large production crews and casts, as well as staffs of journalists to do research. Although WPA director Hopkins had promised a "free, adult, uncensored" theatre, the first Living Newspaper project developed by the New York City unit, *Ethiopia,* which focused on the Italian Fascist invasion of the African nation, was cancelled because of State Department concerns about the portrayal of Italian dictator Benito Mussolini. Some of the Living Newspaper projects, though, mixed imaginative staging with social consciousness in acclaimed productions. Notable Living Newspapers included *Triple-A Plowed Under,* which treated the politics of farming; *Power,* which advocated public ownership of utilities; and *One Third of a Nation,* which engaged the problem of hunger and poverty. As all of these productions advocated positions favored by the Roosevelt administration, they were attacked as propaganda.

In a November 1938 article in *Theatre Arts*, "The Technique of the Living Newspaper," Arthur Arent, the "Managing Editor" of several productions, described the intent: "The Living Newspaper is a dramatization of a problem—composed in greater or lesser extent of many news events, all bearing on the one subject and interlarded with typical but non-factual representations of the effect of these news events on the people to whom the problem is of great importance." The characters were not fully developed, psychologically convincing individuals but types depicted as subject to social forces. An important feature of the plays was the "Voice of the Living Newspaper," an amplified, disembodied voice that set scenes, provided context and explanation, and sometimes spoke up for the disadvantaged. In his introduction to *Liberty Deferred and Other Living Newspapers of the 1930s Federal Theatre Project* (1989), edited by Lorraine Brown, Tamara Liller, and Barbara Jones Smith, scholar Stuart Cosgrove describes the varied devices employed: "Satire, puppetry, visual projection, shadow-graphic acting, crowd scenes, and a fluid style of space-staging, in which characters were isolated by precise lighting plots, were all brought together within a single production."

The Federal Theatre Project, more than any other part of the WPA, was the target of conservative critics, who succeeded in ending its funding in June 1939. It and the other Federal One projects raised questions about the appropriateness of government funding for the arts that continue to be debated. As you learn more about the Federal One projects and their legacy, consider the issue for yourself. What judgment can be made on the New Deal projects that were instituted to help writers during tough economic times? Is such a program warranted under pressing economic conditions? Should the government have a role in supporting the arts?

TOPICS FOR DISCUSSION AND RESEARCH

1. The American Guide series was generally praised by critics for its unexpected revelations about the culture. In *The Saturday Review of Literature* (14 June 1941) Frederick Gutheim remarked: "This is not the well selected, carefully sculptured mosaic of formal history of geographical description; it is the profuse disorder of nature and life, the dadaist jumble of the daily newspaper. It gets in your blood and sends you crowing from oddity to anecdote, from curiosity to dazzling illumination of single fact." Mangione quotes Robert Cantwell's suggestion that the guidebooks revealed a side of the country that was not usually acknowledged: "None of the common generalizations about America and the American temperament seem to fit it, least of all those attributing to Americans qualities of thrift, sobriety, calculation of commercial acumen. On the contrary, it is doubtful if there has ever been assembled anywhere such a portrait, so laboriously and carefully documented, of such a fanciful, impulsive, childlike, absent-minded, capricious and ingenious people." Many of the WPA guides have been republished; try to obtain the one for your home state. Do you find support for the critics' praise? What is your review of the guide? Are the essays at all relevant to the state that you know today?

2. One of the projects that evolved from the Federal Writers Project was the collection of the stories of former slaves. Students can access this material through the *Born in Slavery* website. The introductory essay by Norman Y. Yetman describes the collection and how it came about, while also assessing its importance and its problems. Explore the site and read some of the slave narratives. The second appendix in the Yetman article, which identifies the race of some of the interviewers, allows you to choose a particular interviewer to follow. Do you see problems with the interviews? Do you think the interviews are worth studying? Based on your initial foray into the collection, what is your preliminary assessment of this WPA project?

3. An illustrated script for *Power: A Living Newspaper*, which was first performed at the Ritz Theatre in New York City on 23 February 1937, is accessible on the Web. As this vignette from act 1, scene 8 suggests, the play promotes the idea that the government should be involved in the business of supplying electric power to the citizens:

GIRL: What would happen if the company wouldn't give us electricity any more?

FATHER: We'd be in a hell of a fix.

GIRL: Then why doesn't the Government give us electricity?

FATHER: Because it would be competing with private business, and, besides, everybody knows that the Government wouldn't be efficient.

GIRL (pauses, apparently thinking): Daddy, who runs the Post Office?

FATHER: The Government runs the Post Office.

GIRL: Why does the Government run the Post Office?

FATHER: Because it's too important to us to permit anybody else to run it.

GIRL: Well, Daddy, don't you think electricity is important? You said we'd be in a hell of a fix if the company quit giving it to us.

FATHER: Watch your language, young lady!

When she was questioned about the Federal Theatre Project before the House Un-American Activities Committee, Hallie Flanagan asserted that the Living Newspaper was propaganda for democracy. Committee member J. Parnell Thomas then asked her: "What do you mean by that? Propaganda for what forms of democracy and what particular things?" What do you make of her statement? Is it fair to characterize this play as only propaganda? Students might want to investigate other Living Newspaper scripts, even those that were prepared but never performed, such as *Liberty Deferred*.

RESOURCES

Primary Works

Born in Slavery: Slave Narratives from the Federal Writers' Project, 1936–1938
   <http://lcweb2.loc.gov/ammem/snhtml/snhome.html> [accessed 5 November 2009].

The result of employing out-of-work writers to conduct interviews with former slaves. The collection "offers more than 2,300 typewritten narratives comprising over 9,500 page images with searchable text and bibliographic records, and more than 500 photographs of former slaves with links to their corresponding narratives."

Lorraine Brown, Tamara Liller, and Barbara Jones Smith, eds., *Liberty Deferred and Other Living Newspapers of the 1930s Federal Theatre Project,* introduction by Stuart Cosgrove (Fairfax, Va.: George Mason University Press, 1989).
Presents two plays—*1935* and *Injunction Granted*—that were produced by the Federal Theatre. A third play, *Medicine Show,* calling for the socialization of health services, had an unsuccessful commercial run. The final play, *Liberty Deferred,* treating race relations, was developed by two black playwrights, Abram Hill and John Silvera, for the Federal Theatre but was not performed.

Power: A Living Newspaper <http://newdeal.feri.org/power/contents.htm> [accessed 6 November 2009].
The script for one of the most successful Living Newspaper presentations. The essay "Electricity in the Limelight: The Federal Theatre Project Takes on the Power Industry," reached by a link from this site, provides useful context for the production.

Pierre de Rohan, ed., *Federal Theatre Plays,* introduction by Hallie Flanagan (New York: Random House, 1938).
A collection of scripts that Flanagan suggests in her introduction are representative of three lines of activity of the Federal Theatre. Included are E. P. Conkle's *Prologue to Glory,* a play about Abraham Lincoln and an example of the American historical series; Arthur Arent's *One-Third of a Nation,* which is "perhaps the most mature and objective of the Living Newspapers; and W.E.B. Dubois's *Haiti,* showcasing "the Negro branch" of the project.

Criticism

Christine Bold, *The WPA Guides: Mapping America* (Jackson: University Press of Mississippi, 1999).
Examines "the mapping of American identities—national, regional, local—onto the landscape; the struggles over cultural ownership, dispossession, and citizenship provoked by that process; and the federal government's role in brokering the politics of representation." Bold includes chapters on the Idaho, North Carolina, and Missouri guides and the Highway Route series.

Hallie Flanagan, *Arena: The History of the Federal Theatre* (New York: Duell, Sloan & Pearce, 1940).
The story of the project as told by its director, a passionate advocate for government-supported theater.

Jerre Mangione, *The Dream and the Deal: The Federal Writers' Project, 1935–1943* (New York: Avon, 1972).

A comprehensive history of "an extraordinary governmental enterprise" by the coordinating editor of the project under Henry G. Alsberg.

The New Deal Stage: Selections from The Federal Theatre Project, 1935–1939 <http://memory.loc.gov/ammem/fedtp/fthome.html> [accessed 5 November 2009].
An excellent site for exploring documents related to the Federal Theatre Project.

John O'Connor and Lorraine Brown, *The Living History of the Federal Theatre Project: Free, Adult, Uncensored* (London: Eyre Methuen, 1986).
A well-illustrated history of notable productions.

Susan Quinn, *Furious Improvisation: How the WPA and a Cast of Thousands Made High Art out of Desperate Times* (New York: Walker, 2008).
A sympathetic history of the Federal Theatre Project.

PEOPLE OF INTEREST

Henry G. Alsberg (1881–1970)
Director of the Federal Writers Project from 1935 to 1939. Alsberg was the driving force behind the cultural essays that were included in the state guides.

Arthur Arent (1904–1972)
Author of the five Living Newspaper projects produced in New York: *Triple-A Plowed Under, 1935, Injunction Granted, Power,* and *One-Third of a Nation.* He also edited and assisted in the writing of the script for *Ethiopia,* which was not performed.

Martin Dies (1900–1972)
Texas congressman who became the first chairman of the House Un-American Activities Committee in 1938. A Democrat, Dies was an early supporter of Roosevelt's New Deal but turned against the policies by 1937. He investigated what he believed was Communist infiltration into Federal One programs.

Hallie Flanagan (1890–1969)
Director of experimental drama at Vassar College who was chosen to lead the Federal Theatre Project.

Harry Hopkins (1890–1946)
Chief architect of the New Deal programs; a close friend of Franklin and Eleanor Roosevelt.

Elmer Rice (1892–1967)
Instrumental in the early planning for the Federal Theatre Project. Trained as a lawyer, Rice began his career as a playwright with courtroom dramas; his first play, *On Trial* (1914), introduced the flashback structure to American theater. His most enduring works were *The Adding Machine* (1922), an expressionist drama, and *Street Scene* (1929), a realistic drama set in New York City.

—George Parker Anderson

On Trial: American Justice and "A Good Shoemaker and a Poor Fish-Peddler"

Several "Trials of the Century" in the years from 1914 through 1945 revealed deep divisions and anxieties within American society. The 1924 Chicago trial of Richard Loeb and Nathan Leopold, in which the two privileged young men were found guilty of the thrill killing of a fourteen-year-old boy, contributed to the growing concern about the morality of the younger generation. The 1925 trial of John Scopes in Dayton, Tennessee, for teaching the theory of evolution—the so-called Monkey Trial—brought to the fore the conflict between traditional religious values and science. The 1931 trial of the "Scottsboro boys"—nine African American youths aged thirteen to nineteen who were falsely accused of raping two white women in Alabama—was the most notorious of many cases that made manifest the ongoing racial oppression in the South. Such trials raised issues writers cared about as citizens. Writers also knew that the American system of justice and the inherent drama of a trial provided good material, as was proved by Theodore Dreiser's masterpiece *An American Tragedy* (1925), which was based on the 1906 trial of Chester Gillette for murdering Grace Brown in a rowboat on Big Moose Lake in the Adirondack Mountains in New York. Similarly, the Scopes trial, the first to be broadcast nationwide on the radio, inspired some of the finest newspaper columns by the Baltimore journalist and literary critic H. L. Mencken. And the plight of the Scottsboro boys, whom Langston Hughes visited in Kilby State Penitentiary near Montgomery, led to the production of his first play, *Scottsboro Limited*, in 1932, and John Wexley's *They Shall Not Die*, produced in 1934.

The legal case that most deeply involved American writers—and, indeed, became a worldwide cause célèbre—was the murder trial of Nicola Sacco and Bartolomeo Vanzetti. The crime that began a seven-year chain of events ending in their execution on 23 August 1927 was a brutal robbery and murder in Braintree, Massachusetts, a few miles south of Boston. At about three o'clock in the afternoon of 15 April 1920 Frederick Parmenter, the paymaster for the Slater & Morrill Shoe Factory, and Alessandro Berardelli, his bodyguard, were walking down Pearl Street carrying two heavy steel boxes filled with $15,776.51 in five hundred pay envelopes for the factory workers. They were accosted by two men wearing dark clothes, one of whom pulled a pistol and began shooting. Berardelli was shot four times and Parmenter twice; both died. Another man joined the two assailants, and the three carried the payroll boxes to a nearby car, an elegant Buick with two occupants. Two days later, the abandoned getaway car was found. Some witnesses said that the criminals were "dagos."

Acting on a tip about suspicious-looking Italians, police on 5 May 1920 arrested Sacco and Vanzetti, workingmen who had never before been in trouble with the law. At the time of their arrest, however, Vanzetti was carrying a loaded .38 caliber Harrington and Richardson revolver, and Sacco had a loaded .32 caliber Colt automatic. In one of Sacco's pockets was a note in Vanzetti's handwriting, apparently ready for the printer:

Workers, you have fought all the wars. You have worked for all the bosses. You have wandered over all the countries. Have you harvested the fruit of your labors, the price of your victories? Does the past comfort you? Does the present smile on you? Does the future promise you anything? Have you found a piece of land where you can live like a human being and die like a human being? On these questions, on this argument, and on this theme, the struggle for existence, Bartolomeo Vanzetti will speak. Hour—Day— Hall—. Admission free. Free discussion. Bring the ladies with you.

The Italian immigrants—described by Vanzetti as "a good shoemaker and a poor fish-peddler" on receiving their death sentences—were also World War I draft dodgers, atheists, and anarchists. Any one of these attributes would have been enough to arouse the antipathy of authorities and jurors.

As the tortuous legal proceedings against the men progressed—Vanzetti was convicted of an earlier attempted robbery in Bridgewater before being tried with Sacco for the Braintree murders—the tactics of the prosecutor, District Attorney Frederick G. Katzmann, and the evident bias against the men shown by the presiding judge, Webster Thayer, were such that growing numbers of the public came to believe that the accused, if not innocent, were not receiving a fair trial. In *The Best Times: An Informal Memoir* (1966) John Dos Passos remembered the strong feelings the trial stirred:

> It is hard to explain to people who never lived through the early twenties the violence of the revulsion against foreigners and radicals that went through the United States after the first world war. To young men who had come home from Europe convinced that militarism was the enemy of civilization this reaction seemed to embody all the evil passions that militarism fed on. When we took up for Sacco and Vanzetti we were taking up for freedom of speech and for an even-handed judicial system which would give the same treatment to poor men as to rich men, to greasy foreigners as to redblooded Americans.

The protests gained strength and, fueled by the involvement of Dos Passos and other writers such as Edna St. Vincent Millay and Katherine Anne Porter, became international. In *The Sacco-Vanzetti Affair* (2009) Moshik Temkin suggests that international interest in the case may have worked against the defendants:

> The Sacco-Vanzetti affair emerged as a major international concern at the height of one of the most sensitive and tumultuous periods in the history of America's interaction with the world, and particularly Europe, a period that, in a number of ways, resembles our own. The affair was generated not only by the widespread notion that Sacco and Vanzetti were punished purely for their politics and ethnicity but also by the potent reaction to the post–World War I rise of American global supremacy and, concomitantly, American isolationism. The result of this protest, both national and foreign, was complex and paradoxical. It turned Sacco and Vanzetti into famous men, put tremendous pressure on American authorities, created a raucous controversy in the United States over the intervention of foreigners in American matters, and led to a

backlash that sealed Sacco and Vanzetti's fate: the two men were executed not *despite* the international campaign on their behalf but rather *because* of it.

Judge Thayer imposed death sentences on the two men on 9 April 1927. Their executions on 23 August sparked protests—even riots and attacks on American embassies and businesses—around the world. Tanks protected the American embassy in Paris, three died in clashes in Germany, and thousands protested in Geneva, Amsterdam, Tokyo, Johannesburg, and across South America.

Dozens of books have examined the case of Sacco and Vanzetti, some proclaiming their innocence and others their guilt, and no definitive answer can now be drawn as to the men's culpability. As the literary critic Edmund Wilson wrote in 1928, the case of the two Italian immigrants "revealed the whole anatomy of American life, with all its classes, professions, and points of view and all their relations, and it raised almost every fundamental question of our political and social system." Students interested in the literary response to the Sacco and Vanzetti case should begin with history. Bruce Watson's *Sacco and Vanzetti: The Men, the Murders, and the Judgment of Mankind* (2007) is a solid work on which to build a thesis. From there one can move to assessments of specific literary works.

TOPICS FOR DISCUSSION AND RESEARCH

1. The "Verse Index" section of the bibliography in Louis Joughin and Edmund Morgan's *The Legacy of Sacco and Vanzetti* (1948) lists 144 poems; Joughin notes that "not one poem has been discovered which supports the authorities and condemns the men." Given that the public was divided about the guilt or innocence of the accused, why do you think this would be the case? Joughin identifies and briefly discusses a dozen poems of literary merit, including Witter Bynner's "The Condemned," Countee Cullen's "Not Sacco and Vanzetti," E. Merrill Root's "Flames," Malcolm Cowley's "For St. Bartholomew's Day," Arthur Davison Ficke's "Prayer in Massachusetts" and "Massachusetts Thanksgiving 1927," James Rorty's "Gentlemen of Massachusetts," and Brent Dow Allinson's "For the Honor of Massachusetts." Many of these poems are in *America Arraigned!* (1928), an anthology edited by Lucia Trent and Ralph Cheyney, but that book can be hard to find. Locate in the collections of the individual poets as many of the twelve poems singled out by Joughin as you can. Do you agree with Joughin's judgments? What makes each poem effective—or not, if you disagree?

2. Louis Joughin singles out Lola Ridge—a largely forgotten poet who led an extraordinary life and was deeply involved in the protests over Sacco and Vanzetti—as having written the most interesting poems about the executed men. Her "Two in the Death House" appeared in Trent and Cheyney's *America Arraigned!*; her "Three Men Die" was included in her last collection, *Dance of Fire* (1935), and is discussed by Nancy Berke. Peter Quartermain calls her long allegorical poem *Firehead* (1929) "her response to the Sacco and Vanzetti affair." Read what you can find about Ridge and read her poems about the Italian anarchists. Do they offer a perspective that requires consideration? Do

you agree with Joughin's claim that "Ridge's verses almost certainly deserve a permanent place among the chief American poems"?

3. The most accessible of the contemporary poems about Sacco and Vanzetti were by Edna St. Vincent Millay, a poet with an established reputation in the mid 1920s. "Justice Denied in Massachusetts," collected in her *The Buck in the Snow, & Other Poems* (1928), was first published in the *New York World* two days before the execution. The *Modern American Poetry* website (<http://www.english.illinois.edu/maps/poets/m_r/millay/millay.htm>) includes a section on the poem, a selection from an essay by John Timberman Newcomb, and remarks on the poem by Elizabeth Majerus. Despite the clear allusion to the case in the title, there is no reference in the poem to the fate of the men. What do you think of this approach? Is the poem more powerful or less so for not directly addressing the controversy?

4. Among the novels that have drawn on the Sacco and Vanzetti case, the two most distinguished efforts are Upton Sinclair's *Boston* (1928) and John Dos Passos's *U.S.A.* trilogy (1928–1936). The approaches in these works offer a strong contrast: while Sinclair provides a detailed narrative incorporating many of the social and legal details of the case, Dos Passos only refers explicitly to the two men briefly, though powerfully, in a Newsreel and Camera Eye near the end of the third volume of the trilogy and in the narrative of the radicalized secretary Mary French, though the case implicitly carries much greater weight in the novel. Studying either of these works would be worthwhile. Why was the fate of Sacco and Vanzetti so important to these authors? What effect do they suggest the case had on American society in the late 1920s and 1930s. Do you think the use each author made of the case was appropriate in the context of his novel?

RESOURCES

Primary Works

Maxwell Anderson, *Winterset* (Washington, D.C.: Anderson House, 1935); republished in *Eleven Verse Plays, 1929–1939* (New York: Harcourt, Brace, 1940). Originally produced in New York's Martin Beck Theatre on 25 September 1935. After first trying a straightforward approach to the Sacco-Vanzetti material in the unsuccessful drama *Gods of the Lightning* (1928), which he wrote with Harold Hickerson, Anderson shifted his focus in *Winterset* to the survivors of the immigrants he thought were wrongly accused and executed.

Nathan Asch, *Pay Day* (New York: Brewer & Warren, 1930).
Novel, set on the night of Sacco's and Vanzetti's executions, that contrasts a young New Yorker's night of pleasure seeking against the momentous event in Boston.

John Dos Passos, *The Big Money* (New York: Harcourt, Brace, 1936).
The culminating volume of Dos Passos's panoramic *U.S.A.* trilogy (1928–1936). The trial and execution of Sacco and Vanzetti are referred to specifically in the sections "Newsreel LXVI" and "The Camera Eye 50" and provide the occasion for Dos Passos's declaration "all right we are two nations" and, responding to the execution, "we stand defeated America."

Dos Passos, *Facing the Chair: Story of the Americanization of Two Foreignborn Workmen* (Boston: Sacco-Vanzetti Defense Committee, 1927).
A 128-page account in which Dos Passos discusses the flaws he sees in the case against Sacco and Vanzetti. It was published after the men had been condemned but before their executions.

Henry Harrison, ed., *The Sacco-Vanzetti Anthology of Verse* (New York: Harrison, 1927).
A thirty-two-page collection that includes Root's "Flames."

Edna St.Vincent Millay, *The Buck in the Snow, & Other Poems* (New York: Harper, 1928).
Slender collection divided into four sections. "Justice Denied in Massachusetts" is the second of five poems in section 2.

Upton Sinclair, *Boston* (New York: Boni, 1928).
Well-researched historical novel in which "the characters who are real persons bear real names, while those who bear fictitious names are fictitious characters."

Lucia Trent and Ralph Cheyney, eds., *America Arraigned!* (New York: Dean, 1928).
Ninety-five-page poetry collection that includes Bynner's "The Condemned," Cullen's "Not Sacco and Vanzetti," Ficke's "Prayer in Massachusetts," Rorty's "Gentlemen of Massachusetts," and Ridge's "Two in the Death House."

Criticism

Nancy Berke, *Women Poets on the Left: Lola Ridge, Genevieve Taggard, Margaret Walker* (Gainesville: University Press of Florida, 2001), pp. 52–60.
Includes a discussion of Ridge's Sacco and Vanzetti poems.

"Edna St. Vincent Millay," *Modern American Poetry*, <http://www.english.illinois.edu/maps/poets/s_z/williams/williams.htm> [accessed 20 November 2009].
Provides background on the Sacco and Vanzetti case and critical readings of "Justice Denied in Massachusetts."

Felix Frankfurter, *The Case of Sacco and Vanzetti: A Critical Analysis for Lawyers and Laymen* (Boston: Little, Brown, 1927).
Analysis of the trial that is severely critical of Judge Webster Thayer and the prosecution. Frankfurter served as an associate justice of the United States Supreme Court from 1939 to 1962.

Louis Joughin and Edmund Morgan, *The Legacy of Sacco and Vanzetti* (New York: Harcourt, Brace, 1948).
Study of the impact of the case on American law, society, and literature.

"Lola Ridge," *Modern American Poetry* <http://www.english.illinois.edu/maps/poets/m_r/ridge/ridge.htm> [accessed 20 November 2009].

Biography of Ridge and excerpts from discussions of her work by several critics. The "Poetry and Politics" link leads to Lucia Trent and Ralph Cheyney's introduction to *An Anthology of Revolutionary Poetry* (1929), edited by Marcus Graham, which provides a useful context for reading Ridge's poems.

Donald Pizer, ed., *Dictionary of Literary Biography*, volume 274: *John Dos Passos's U.S.A.: A Documentary Volume* (Detroit: Bruccoli Clark Layman/Thompson Gale, 2003).
Reference work with full, well-illustrated sections on the backgrounds, writing, publication and reception, and reputation of the novel.

Peter Quartermain, "Lola Ridge," in the *Dictionary of Literary Biography*, volume 54: *American Poets, 1880–1945, Third Series*, Part 2: N–Z, edited by Quartermain (Detroit: Bruccoli Clark Layman/Gale Research, 1987), pp. 353–361.
Illustrated biography of Ridge with discussions of her important works, including *Firehead* (1929), her response to the Sacco and Vanzetti case.

Moshik Temkin, *The Sacco-Vanzetti Affair: America on Trial* (New Haven, Conn.: Yale University Press, 2009).
Analyzes the reasons for the national and international attention to the case and the result on the outcome of the trial.

Bruce Watson, *Sacco and Vanzetti: The Men, the Murders, and the Judgment of Mankind* (New York: Viking, 2007).
The recommended general history of the case.

PEOPLE OF INTEREST

Maxwell Anderson (1888–1959)
Playwright and poet whose most famous work was the World War I drama *What Price Glory?* (1924), coauthored with Laurence Stallings. His other notable plays include the political satire *Both Your Houses* (1933) and *Winterset* (1935), about the survivors of Sacco and Vanzetti.

Nathan Asch (1902–1964)
Son of Yiddish writer Sholem Asch. In the early 1920s he lived as an expatriate in Paris, where he wrote his first novel, *The Office* (1925). *Pay Day* (1927), his novel set on the night of the executions of Sacco and Vanzetti, was his third book.

John Dos Passos (1896–1970)
Author of the novel *Manhattan Transfer* (1925) and the *U.S.A.* trilogy (1928–1936). Dos Passos was deeply involved in the protests against the Sacco and Vanzetti trial.

Theodore Dreiser (1871–1945)
The most important Naturalist in American literature. Dreiser is best known for *Sister Carrie* (1900) and his masterpiece, *An American Tragedy* (1925), an indictment of the justice system that is based on a real murder case.

James T. Farrell (1904–1979)
Best known as the author of the Studs Lonigan trilogy (1932–1935). Farrell wrote about the Sacco and Vanzetti case in *Bernard Clare* (1946), the first novel in a trilogy about struggling artists and political activists in New York City during the Depression. The other works in the trilogy are *The Road Between* (1949) and *Yet Other Waters* (1952).

Langston Hughes (1902–1967)
African American author who was deeply involved in the case of the Scottsboro boys. It is referenced in his short-story collection *The Ways of White Folks* (1934), and his wider concern with the lynching of African Americans is evident in his poems.

H. L. Mencken (1880–1956)
The most celebrated journalist and critic of his era. Mencken was long associated with *The Baltimore Sun* and also edited the influential magazines *The Smart Set* and *The American Mercury*. He championed Realism in fiction, especially the works of Dreiser and Lewis. His reporting on the Scopes trial has been collected in *A Religious Orgy in Tennessee: A Reporter's Account of the Scopes Monkey Trial* (2006).

Edna St. Vincent Millay (1892–1950)
Poet who excelled at writing sonnets. With *The Harp-Weaver and Other Poems* (1923) Millay became the first woman to win a Pulitzer Prize for poetry. She wrote of the Sacco and Vanzetti Case in her poems "Justice Denied in Massachusetts," "Hangman's Oak," "The Anguish," "To Those without Pity," and "Wine from These Grapes."

Katherine Anne Porter (1890–1980)
Published *The Never Ending Wrong* (1977) on the fiftieth anniversary of the executions of Sacco and Vanzetti. The memoir is based on notes she took in the 1920s about her involvement in the protests against the executions.

Lola Ridge (1873–1941)
Proletarian poet associated with the little magazines such as *Others, Broom,* and *New Masses*. Ridge was known for her intense empathy for the poor. Her collections include *The Ghetto, and Other Poems* (1918), *Sun-Up, and Other Poems* (1920), and *Red Flag* (1927). She wrote about Sacco and Vanzetti in "Two in the Death House," "Three Men Die," and *Firehead* (1929).

Upton Sinclair (1875–1968)
Famous for his novel *The Jungle* (1906). Sinclair was a prolific writer who treated social problems in his fiction and nonfiction. His novel about the Sacco and Vanzetti case, *Boston* (1928), is regarded as one of his best works.

John Wexley (1907–1985)
Dramatist and liberal social critic. Wexley wrote about the Scottsboro boys case in his play *They Shall Not Die* (1934).

—George Parker Anderson

"That Ain't the Way the Chinese Behave": American Identity and the Literature of Place

Asked by a student at the University of Virginia whether his characters were "regional" or "universal," William Faulkner responded:

> I feel that the verities these people suffer are universal verities—that is, that man, whether he's black or white or red or yellow still suffers the same anguishes, he has the same aspirations, his follies are the same follies, his triumphs are the same triumphs. That is, his struggle is against his own heart, against—with the hearts of his fellows, and with his background. And in that sense there's no such thing as a regional writer, the writer simply uses the terms he is familiar with best because it saves him having to do research. That he might write a book about the Chinese but if he does that, he's got to do some research or somebody'll say "Ah! you're wrong there, that ain't the way the Chinese behave." But if he uses his own region, which he is familiar with, it saves him that trouble.

For reasons that are cultural, historical, and personal, many Americans are profoundly influenced, if not shaped, by their identification with a particular region of the country and often a more localized sense of belonging to a particular place. Faulkner, one suspects, would have had trouble indeed had he chosen to ignore Sherwood Anderson's advice to write about what he knew and instead decided to place Yoknapatawpha County, his fictional "postage stamp of native soil," in China rather than Mississippi.

Faulkner's Yoknapatawpha, Thomas Wolfe's Altamont, and John O'Hara's Gibbsville are the most notable examples of fictional milieus that writers between the world wars created and then explored over the course of their careers. Many other authors, while not thought of as "regional" in any limiting sense, became associated with certain places: Edwin Arlington Robinson's Tilbury Town, Maine; Robert Frost's New England farm; Edith Wharton's high-society New York; William Carlos Williams's Paterson, New Jersey; Edgar Lee Masters's Spoon River, Illinois; Sherwood Anderson's Winesburg, Ohio; Willa Cather's Great Plains and desert Southwest; Zora Neale Hurston's Florida; Wallace Stegner's Rocky Mountain West; John Steinbeck's Salinas Valley, California; Raymond Chandler's Los Angeles; and Robinson Jeffers's California coastline are vivid fictional worlds realized by writers who were connected to their settings in deeply personal ways. By creating convincing fictions and poems set in specific places and times, these writers and others reveal the complexity of the larger American experience.

Beyond locating their writings in places they know well, authors make use of attitudes their readers have about these settings—generalized notions about farms, small towns, cities, or regions—by choosing to defy or resist or fulfill the readers' expectations. The power of attitudes many readers have about regional differences is well illustrated by David Marion Holman in *A Certain Slant of Light: Regionalism and the Form of Southern and Midwestern Fiction* (1995).

Holman begins his study by recalling General Robert E. Lee's meeting with General Ulysses S. Grant at Appomattox Court House to discuss the surrender of the Army of Northern Virginia. Quoting Shelby Foote's contrast in *The Civil War: A Narrative* (1974) of the brown-haired, somewhat awkward, "rumpled and dusty" Grant and the silver-haired, "tall and patrician-looking, immaculately groomed and clad" Lee, Holman writes that the meeting in retrospect has come to seem an emblem signifying "the final surrender of the southern patrician to the midwestern commoner, the subjection of manners to methods, the victory of pragmatism over romanticism, the final triumph of democracy over aristocracy and slavery." Holman argues that in the meeting of Grant and Lee, Americans also see regions:

> A southerner or a midwesterner sees what other Americans see, but also attaches a regional importance to the event; and all of us, whatever our allegiance, can see other Americans as southerners and midwesterners, and so can participate in their regional evaluations. We expect the southerner to see in the Appomattox meeting the fall of discrete culture and its eventual replacement by industrial conformity. In the victory of the northern armies, we expect him to see the irresistible but deplorable defeat of gentlemen by a mob of commoners. Likewise, we expect the midwesterner to see Lee's surrender as a moral judgment on the degenerate aristocratic South, and the triumph of Grant's and Sherman's Army of the West, where the eastern Army of the Potomac had for so long failed to overcome its enemy, as proof that the true strength of American character and democracy resides not in the East but in the farms and small towns of the Midwest. We expect this response from the southerner and the midwesterner because all of us, whether southerner, midwesterner, New Englander, or westerner, participate in a commonly held idea of region.

Americans have many shared beliefs, or myths, about what their country is or should be—the land of opportunity, of equality and justice, where the dream of a better life is always possible—and also many myths that are based on regional identities. Holman maintains "that what is not factual, but rather what is believed without prior regard for any facts, is at the core of what informs regional mythologies and the literature of region."

As readers explore the localized fictional worlds created by the writers of the interwar period—worlds separated from their own by time if not distance—they are afforded the opportunity to think more deeply about a central issue: How important is a sense of place to one's conception of self? It is a question worth asking about literature and about life.

TOPICS FOR DISCUSSION AND RESEARCH

1. Choose a work by one of the authors who is closely associated with a region or locale. Examine closely how the writer uses or creates a sense of place in the work. Pick out scenes or passages in which you think the author makes the best use of the physical and/or psychological environment. Is the setting just a

backdrop—that is, would another setting work just as well—or is it integral to the effect of the work? In what ways is the evocation of place relevant to the meaning and power of the work?

2. Examine works by two or more writers who treat the same region. For example, compare the visions of Florida in the novels and stories of Zora Neale Hurston and Marjorie Kinnan Rawlings or the visions of New England in the poems of Edwin Arlington Robinson and Robert Frost. Are their views in agreement, opposed, or complementary? Does setting play the same role in the works of both writers? Does one writer provide a more convincing or complete view of the land and its people than the other?

3. Knowledge of an author's personal circumstances may deepen your appreciation of the meaning or importance of setting in his or her work. For example, Edith Wharton wrote about her contemporary New York society in her first major novel, *The House of Mirth* (1905). After she had seen some of the horrors of World War I at first hand, she wrote again of New York society in *The Age of Innocence* (1920); but in this work she chose to depict the 1870s, and she characterized the writing of the novel as a "momentary escape." What differences do you see in Wharton's attitude toward New York society in the two novels? What does she show her readers about New York in *The Age of Innocence* that she did not reveal in *The House of Mirth*?

4. *American Diversity, American Identity: The Lives and Works of 145 Writers Who Define the American Experience* (1995), edited by John K. Roth, presents brief discussions of the myths that define American attitudes about the four major regions of the country: for the Northeast the myth is the belief in "a city set upon a hill," encompassing ideas of American newness, destiny, and exceptionalism; for the South it is "the presence of the past," defining the region by its historical legacy and especially the lost Civil War; for the Midwest it is "the heart of the country," a phrase that indicates the region's reverence for "American values" such as "honesty, generosity, love of land, and devotion to family"; and for the West it is "the geography of hope," a picture of a land providing "a solace of wide-open spaces that we can come home to, a frontier of second chances where we can start over as the person we were meant to be." As you read the literature of a region, explore the myths that inform American attitudes about it. Does the author you are reading make use of one of these myths? How?

RESOURCES

Criticism

John Gordon Burke, ed., *Regional Perspectives: An Examination of America's Literary Heritage* (Chicago: American Library Association, 1973).

A collection of five assessments "of writers by writers consciously trying to outline a regional tradition": Hayden Carruth on New England, George Garrett on the South, John Knoepfle on the Midwest, Larry Goodwyn on the Southwest, and William Everson on the West.

Jean Carol Griffith, *The Color of Democracy in Women's Regional Writing* (Tuscaloosa: University of Alabama Press, 2009).
A study of Edith Wharton, Ellen Glasgow, and Willa Cather that examines each writer's "interest in regional contributions to American origins and scrutinizes these writers' explorations of the fate of those origins once democracy expands beyond the boundaries they associate with the nineteenth century."

David Marion Holman, *A Certain Slant of Light: Regionalism and the Form of Southern and Midwestern Fiction,* Southern Literary Studies (Baton Rouge: Louisiana State University Press, 1995).
Argues that "all of us, whether southerner, midwesterner, New Englander, or westerner, participates in a commonly held idea of region." Holman discusses "selected midwestern and southern writers whose works appeared between 1832 and 1925," including Ellen Glasgow, Willa Cather, William Faulkner, and Ernest Hemingway.

Sherrie A. Inness and Diana Royer, eds., *Breaking Boundaries: New Perspectives on Women's Regional Writing* (Iowa City: University of Iowa Press, 1997).
Essay collection that "explores the multiplicity of connections between women and regional writing" in "an attempt to chart some of the major ways that U.S. regional writing has changed and why it is still a literary genre of particular importance to today's women writers." The volume includes pieces that discuss the works of Mary Hunter Austin and Meridel Le Sueur.

Philip Joseph, *American Literary Realism in a Global Age* (Baton Rouge: Louisiana State University Press, 2007).
Discusses Mary Hunter Austin, Willa Cather, Abraham Cahan, William Faulkner, and Zora Neale Hurston.

Diane Dufva Quantic, *The Nature of the Place: A Study of Great Plains Fiction* (Lincoln: University of Nebraska Press, 1995).
Explores "the various manifestations of the myths of westward expansion in Great Plains fiction and the transformation of the assumptions implicit in the mythic images that became necessary when the land was claimed, communities were formed and life began in real time." Writers discussed include Willa Cather, F. Scott Fitzgerald, O. E. Rölvaag, Mari Sandoz, Wallace Stegner, and Laura Ingalls Wilder.

John K. Roth, ed., *American Diversity, American Identity: The Lives and Works of 145 Writers Who Define the American Experience* (New York: Holt, 1995).
Includes essays on many writers from the years between the world wars. Writers are categorized in thirteen ways, with four regional categories. For example, Robert Frost, John O'Hara, Eugene O'Neill, and Edith Wharton are assessed in the section "A City upon a Hill: *American Identities in the Northeast.*"

Melanie Louise Simo, *Literature of Place: Dwelling on the Land before Earth Day 1970* (Charlottesville: University of Virginia Press, 2005).
Examines writers who have "some kind of attachment to a place" and "tried to communicate that experience through the written word" by considering "selected

American works from about 1890 to 1970." Among the writers discussed are Wallace Stegner, Willa Cather, Mary Hunter Austin, Robert Frost, Marjorie Kinnan Rawlings, and John Steinbeck.

Frederick W. Turner, *Spirit of Place: The Making of an American Literary Landscape* (San Francisco: Sierra Club Books, 1989).
Celebrates writers "who learned in loneliness and silence and deprivation how truly to see where on the American earth they were." The book includes chapters on Willa Cather, Mari Sandoz, William Faulkner, John Steinbeck, and William Carlos Williams.

Floyd C. Watkins, *In Time and Place: Some Origins of American Fiction* (Athens: University of Georgia Press, 1977).
A study of "cultural and historical and geographical backgrounds and their effects on fiction," with chapters on John Steinbeck's *The Grapes of Wrath* (1939), Willa Cather's *My Ántonia* (1918) and *Death Comes to the Archbishop* (1927), William Faulkner's *As I Lay Dying* (1930), and Sinclair Lewis's *Main Street* (1920).

Harold L. Weatherby and George Core, eds., *Place in American Fiction: Excursions and Explorations* (Columbia: University of Missouri Press, 2004).
Includes essays on the importance of a sense of place in the work of William Faulkner, Katherine Anne Porter, Eudora Welty, F. Scott Fitzgerald, and Wallace Stegner.

Mark Royden Winchell, *Reinventing the South: Versions of a Literary Region* (Columbia: University of Missouri Press, 2006).
A collection of essays divided into two parts. In the first part Winchell treats the agrarian view of the South; in the second part he writes about the competing vision of the region that he sees being offered by such writers as William Faulkner and Tennessee Williams.

PEOPLE OF INTEREST

Sherwood Anderson (1896–1941)
Examined in his most acclaimed work, *Winesburg, Ohio* (1919), a town based on Clyde, Ohio.

Mary Hunter Austin (1868–1934)
Wrote about California's San Joaquin Valley in her earlier works and later about New Mexico in such books as *The Land of Journey's Ending* (1924) and *Starry Adventure* (1931).

Abraham Cahan (1860–1951)
Wrote about the Jewish immigrant experience on New York's Lower East Side in *The Rise of David Levinsky* (1917).

Erskine Caldwell (1903–1987)
Depicted rural Georgia in his best-known novels, *Tobacco Road* (1932) and *God's Little Acre* (1933).

Raymond Chandler (1888–1959)
Wrote seven novels featuring detective Philip Marlowe including *The Big Sleep* (1939) and *Farewell, My Lovely* (1940) that are set in Los Angeles.

Walter Van Tilburg Clark (1909–1971)
Wrote of Nevada in his most admired novels, *The Ox-Bow Incident* (1940) and *The Track of the Cat* (1949).

August Derleth (1909–1971)
Examined the history of Wisconsin from the early 1800s through twenty-eight volumes of fiction and poetry he called the Sac Prairie Saga, beginning with *Still Is the Summer Night* (1937).

J. Frank Dobie (1888–1964)
A Texas-born writer and historian who strove to present realistic stories of life in the Texas brush country and northern Mexico. His many works include *Corona-do's Children: Tales of Lost Mines and Buried Treasures of the Southwest* (1930) and *Guide to Life and Literature of the Southwest* (1943).

William Faulkner (1897–1962)
Wrote of the fictional Yoknapatawpha County, which was based on Lafayette County, Mississippi, in many of his novels, including *The Sound and the Fury* (1929), *Absalom, Absalom!* (1936), and *The Hamlet* (1940).

Robert Frost (1874–1963)
One of the major poets of the twentieth century, deeply associated with the land-scape of New England. His many collections include *North of Boston* (1914), *New Hampshire* (1923), *West-Running Brook* (1928), and *A Masque of Reason* (1945).

Zona Gale (1874–1938)
Set her stories, novels, and plays mainly in her native Wisconsin. After World War I, she became more critical of small-town life. Her most acclaimed novel, *Miss Lulu Bett* (1920), is about a woman who works as a domestic servant in the home of her married sister. Gale's dramatization of the novel won a Pulitzer Prize.

Ellen Glasgow (1873–1945)
Virginia-born novelist who wrote of Southern manners in the trilogy *The Romantic Comedians* (1926), *They Stooped to Folly* (1929), and *The Sheltered Life* (1932). *Barren Ground* (1925), considered by many to be her best work, features a strong woman who overcomes betrayal to become a successful farmer.

Paul Green (1894–1981)
North Carolina playwright who began his career writing one-act folk dramas such as those collected in *The Lord's Will and Other Plays* (1925) and *Lonesome Road: Six Plays for the Negro Theater* (1926) and later was known for his series of "symphonic dramas," beginning with *The Lost Colony: A Symphonic Drama of Sir Walter Raleigh's Ill-Fated Colony on Roanoke Island in the Late Sixteenth Century* (1937), which combined music, drama, and dance in outdoor celebrations of historic events.

Zane Grey (1872–1939)
Popular and prolific writer of Westerns who achieved his first popular success with *Riders of the Purple Sage* (1912).

Paul Horgan (1903–1995)
Novelist, short-story writer, and historian who often wrote of the West. His works include the story collection *The Return of the Weed* (1936), set in New Mexico.

Zora Neale Hurston (1891–1960)
Wrote of her native Florida in much of her work, including the novels *Jonah's Gourd Vine* (1934) and *Their Eyes Were Watching God* (1937).

Robinson Jeffers (1887–1962)
Born in the East but deeply affected by and associated with the rugged California coastline where he built his home, Tor House, and wrote his poems. A good collection is *Robinson Jeffers: Selected Poems* (1965).

Josephine Johnson (1910–1990)
Wrote of life in the Midwest in her first novel, *Now in November* (1934), which was set on a farm and won a Pulitzer Prize; in her story collection *Winter Orchard* (1935); and in her novel *Jordanstown* (1937), which centers on a newspaperman.

Meridel Le Sueur (1900–1996)
Radical and early feminist author. Le Sueur wrote of the Midwest in *Salute to Spring* (1940) and *North Star Country* (1945).

Percy MacKaye (1875–1956)
Playwright who championed community-based pageant dramas. MacKaye wrote folk plays such as *This Fine-Pretty World* (1923) and *Kentucky Mountain Fantasies: Three Short Plays for an Appalachian Theatre* (1928).

John P. Marquand (1893–1960)
Popular novelist and short-story author who wrote satirical novels of manners set in New England, including *The Late George Apley* (1937), *Wickford Point* (1939), and *H. M. Pulham, Esquire* (1941).

Edgar Lee Masters (1868–1950)
Poet who based his fictional community Spoon River—explored in his most famous work, *Spoon River Anthology* (1915)—on the small Illinois towns of his youth, Petersburg and Lewistown.

William Maxwell (1908–2000)
Longtime fiction editor at *The New Yorker*, novelist, and short-story writer who wrote mainly about life in the Midwest in the early twentieth century. His novels include *They Came Like Swallows* (1937) and *The Folded Leaf* (1945).

John O'Hara (1905–1970)
Wrote of the fictional Gibbsville, Pennsylvania—based on his native Pottsville—in his first novel, *Appointment in Samarra* (1934), and many subsequent stories and novels.

Marjorie Kinnan Rawlings (1896–1953)
Wrote of Florida in her novel *The Yearling* (1938) and her collection of autobiographical essays *Cross Creek* (1942).

Eugene Manlove Rhodes (1869–1934)
Self-educated writer who drew on his experiences as a cowboy in Westerns such as *The Desire of the Moth* (1916), *Copper Streak Trail* (1922), and *The Proud Sheriff* (1935).

Conrad Richter (1890–1968)
Novelist and short-story writer who often wrote of two frontiers: the Ohio River Valley between the Revolutionary and Civil Wars and the Southwest at the close of the nineteenth century. His best-known work is the Ohio trilogy, comprising *The Trees* (1940), *The Fields* (1946), and *The Town* (1950).

Lynn Riggs (1899–1954)
The son of a Cherokee farmer, a poet and dramatist whose plays include *Green Grow the Lilacs* (1931), the basis for the musical *Oklahoma!* (1943); *The Cherokee Night* (1936); and *Russet Mantle* (1936).

Elizabeth Madox Roberts (1881–1941)
Respected regionalist poet and novelist who captured the speech and manners of her native Kentucky in her first novel, *The Time of Man* (1926), about the struggles of tenant farmer Ellen Chesser.

Edwin Arlington Robinson (1869–1935)
Major poet who set many of his poems in Tilbury Town, which was inspired by Gardner, Maine.

O. E. Rölvaag (1876–1931)
Norwegian who immigrated to Minnesota in 1896 and wrote novels in his native language, including an admired trilogy about Norwegian immigrants on the Northwest frontier that was translated and published in the United States as *Giants in the Earth* (1927), *Peder Victorious* (1929), and *Their Father's God* (1929).

Mari Sandoz (1896–1966)
Wrote nonfiction works as well as novels about the trans-Missouri region. Her first book, *Old Jules* (1935), treats the Nebraska landscape, her frontier community, and her Swiss-immigrant father.

Winfield Townley Scott (1910–1968)
Journalist and poet who was influenced by Edward Arlington Robinson and Robert Frost. Scott wrote poetry inspired by New England in works such as *Elegy for Robinson* (1936) and *Wind the Clock* (1941).

Virginia Sorensen (1912–1991)
Wrote of the West and the Mormon experience. In her first novel, *A Little Lower than the Angels* (1942), a non-Mormon woman marries a Mormon man.

Wallace Stegner (1909–1993)
Wrote of the Rocky Mountains in novels such as *On a Darkling Plain* (1940) and *The Big Rock Candy Mountain* (1943).

John Steinbeck (1902–1968)
Wrote of California's Salinas Valley in his most important works of fiction, including the novels *Of Mice and Men* (1937) and *The Grapes of Wrath* (1939).

Jesse Stuart (1907–1984)
A child of Kentucky sharecroppers and a versatile author who wrote of his native region in more than fifty books, including *Man with a Bull-Tongue Plow* (1934; revised, 1954), a collection of some seven hundred sonnets; the short-story collection *O'W-Hollow* (1936); the autobiographical *Beyond Dark Hills* (1938); and the comic novel *Taps for Private Tussie* (1943).

Ruth Suckow (1892–1960)
Novelist and short-story writer who often wrote of the small towns of Iowa she knew growing up as the daughter of a Congregationalist minister. Her works include the novels *Country People* (1924), about three generations of a German American family, and *The Odyssey of a Nice Girl* (1925), which treats the provinciality of small town life, and the story collection *Children and Older People* (1931).

Frank Waters (1902–1995)
Novelist, historian, and biographer who explored the history and culture of the Southwest in his many books, including his fictionalized treatment of the history of his family in his Colorado trilogy: *Wild Earth's Nobility* (1935), *Below Grass Roots* (1937), and *Dust within the Rock* (1940).

Eudora Welty (1909–2001)
Wrote of her native Mississippi in stories and novels including *A Curtain of Green and Other Stories* (1941) and *The Golden Apples* (1949).

Glenway Wescott (1901–1987)
Wisconsin-born author who lived as an expatriate in France in the 1920s and into the 1930s. He wrote of his native state in novels such as *The Apple of the Eye* (1924), about a boy who rebels against the Puritanism of his upbringing, and *The Grandmothers* (1927), which began as a memoir.

Edith Wharton (1862–1937)
Wrote of the customs and manners of New York society in such novels as *The House of Mirth* (1905), *The Age of Innocence* (1922), and *The Buccaneers* (1938) and of rural New England in *Ethan Frome* (1911) and *Summer* (1917).

Laura Ingalls Wilder (1867–1957)
Wrote of the pioneer experience in the Midwest in her "Little House" series that began with *Little House in the Big Woods* (1932), set in her native Pepin, Wisconsin.

Tennessee Williams (1911–1983)
Wrote of the South in many of his plays, including *A Streetcar Named Desire* (1947), set in New Orleans.

William Carlos Williams (1883–1963)
Poet born in Rutherford, New Jersey, where he had a long career as a physician. Williams was inspired by his experiences in his community, which is the focus of his epic five-volume poem *Paterson* (1946–1958).

Thomas Wolfe (1900–1938)
Wrote of Altamont, based on his native Asheville, North Carolina, in his first two novels, *Look Homeward, Angel* (1929) and *Of Time and the River* (1935).

—George Parker Anderson

Writing for Money: *The Saturday Evening Post* and the Literary Marketplace

Between the world wars the marketplace for fiction was dominated by the "slicks"—magazines printed on smooth, glossy paper to accommodate the color advertisements that reached audiences numbering in the millions. Magazines such as *Collier's Weekly, Cosmopolitan, Ladies' Home Journal, Red Book Magazine, Woman's Home Companion,* and the most successful of the slicks, *The Saturday Evening Post,* published hundreds of short stories and serialized novels every year by well-known writers as well as by newcomers, thus helping to create a market that made it possible to prosper as a professional author.

F. Scott Fitzgerald was the most prominent "literary" writer of the time who wrote often for the slicks. Over the course of his twenty-year career (1920 to 1940) Fitzgerald sold more than ninety stories to the high-paying magazines—sixty-five of them to *The Saturday Evening Post.* After 1922 Fitzgerald made more than $5,000 annually from his novels only in 1923, 1927, and 1934, and those sums derived mainly from advances rather than from sales. For the last thirteen years of his life—except for 1934, when *Tender Is the Night* was published—Fitzgerald realized less than $100 per year from sales of his novels. Only his ability to sell stories to the slicks enabled him to write for a living, especially during the nine-year gap between *The Great Gatsby* and *Tender Is the Night.* In the years following *The Great Gatsby* and the bonanza he realized from its sale to stage and screen, Fitzgerald relied heavily on the *Post* for his income, averaging more than $22,000 a year from 1927 through 1932. He became one of the magazine's best-paid authors, reaching a peak of $4,000 per story in 1929—a year when most Americans earned less than half that sum annually. For good or ill, the market of *The Saturday Evening Post* and the other slicks strongly influenced Fitzgerald's career.

Although many authors claimed to disdain writing for the slicks, Bernard DeVoto, himself a *Saturday Evening Post* contributor, declared, "There are two classes of writers who do not write for *The Saturday Evening Post:* those who have independent means or make satisfactory incomes from their other writing, and those who can't make the grade. Many of the former and practically all of the latter try to write for the *Post.*" Whether for the money or for the immense audience the magazines reached, many of the most important writers of the time sold—or tried to sell—to *The Saturday Evening Post* and its siblings. Ernest Hemingway's submissions to *The Saturday Evening Post* were rejected, but Willa Cather, James Gould Cozzens, Ellen Glasgow, E. W. Howe, Gertrude Stein, Edith Wharton, and Thomas Wolfe appeared there. Sinclair Lewis, Ring Lardner, and Booth Tarkington wrote often for the magazine. John P. Marquand became a household name through his writing for *The Saturday Evening Post,* publishing both short stories and serialized novels, including *The Late George Apley* (1937). In the 1930s and early 1940s William Faulkner placed seventeen stories in the magazine, including "Red Leaves" (1930), "Mountain Victory" (1932), and "The Bear" (1942).

While the slick magazines made writing for a living a possibility for many otherwise struggling authors, contemporary critics believed that the powerful financial lure of the big magazines had a deleterious effect on the writers and their work. The slicks, the critics charged, encouraged writing as mere entertainment and published only formulaic fiction. *The Saturday Evening Post* and its famous editor, the politically conservative George Horace Lorimer, symbolized the dominance of the slick magazines and became the target of those who believed that the commercial short story was the antithesis of literature.

In his annual *Best Short Stories* volumes Edward O'Brien routinely inveighed against the "commercialization" of literature and championed "little" magazines, though he sometimes chose stories from the slicks as among the year's best. In "Merchant in Letters: Portrait of George Horace Lorimer" in the 21 May 1930 issue of *Outlook and Independent,* Benjamin Stolberg disparaged the "manufactured" characters and "stencilled plots" of the stories in *The Saturday Evening Post,* asserting that the magazine had "done more to develop the technique of the short story as good composition and second-rate literature than any other periodical." The socialist author Upton Sinclair argued in *Money Writes!* (1927) that the slicks skewed the values of a generation of writers who sought publication there: "They read your manuscripts promptly, and pay the very highest price upon acceptance. So they are the goal of every young writer's ambition, and the most corrupting force in American letters. Their stuff is as standardized as soda crackers; originality is taboo, new ideas are treason, social sympathy is a crime, and the one virtue of man is to produce larger and larger quantities of material things. They have raised up a school of writers, panoplied in prejudice, a lynching squad to deal with every sign of protest against the ideals of plutocracy." For Sinclair, Lorimer was the "great literary fascist" who was destroying American literature.

Fitzgerald lost his ability to write for the slicks in the mid 1930s. "Trouble," his last story published in *The Saturday Evening Post,* appeared in the 6 March 1937 issue; he was paid $2,000 for it. In the late 1930s Fitzgerald's main market for fiction was *Esquire,* which accepted shorter, less conventional work but paid a top price of only $250. Along with many other Depression-era literary authors, including Faulkner, Fitzgerald was drawn to the money available in Hollywood and tried his hand at screenwriting for the movies—another much-criticized market believed to corrupt literary talent and stall the advancement of literature.

TOPICS FOR DISCUSSION AND RESEARCH

1. In *George Horace Lorimer and* The Saturday Evening Post (1948) John Tebbel asserts that "Lorimer's criterion for acceptance was simple: 'Will the *Post* audience like it?'" He goes on to quote Lorimer: "A magazine like the *Post* has to be like a full meal, beginning with soup, going on to the most important course, which is roast beef, then maybe a salad, and it must have dessert." Tebbel claims that Lorimer sometimes "deliberately published stories he knew would appeal only to about ten per cent of the audience." Read some of the fiction in a few issues of *The Saturday Evening Post* from the post–World War I period of Lorimer's editorship, 1918 to 1936. Do you see the "full meal"

Lorimer described? What conclusions can be drawn about the audience(s) this meal is supposed to feed? What are the values, tastes, and prejudices that are being served? Is Sinclair's criticism—that its fiction lacks social sympathy and is bourgeois and unoriginal—justified?

2. Tebbel lists several popular authors among Lorimer's "inner circle," including Mary Roberts Rinehart, Irvin S. Cobb, Kenneth Roberts, Joseph Hergesheimer, and Harry Leon Wilson. Investigate the career of one of these writers, or some other regular contributor to the *Post*. What does the author's work show about the values and tastes of contemporary readers?

3. In his preface to *The Short Stories of F. Scott Fitzgerald* (1989) Matthew J. Bruccoli asserts that Fitzgerald's stories "have been dismissed as hackwork and condemned for impeding his serious work." Assess some of the stories Fitzgerald wrote for *The Saturday Evening Post,* such as "Bernice Bobs Her Hair" (1920), "The Ice Palace" (1920), "The Offshore Pirate" (1920), "Jacob's Ladder" (1927), "A Short Trip Home" (1927), "Two Wrongs" (1930), and "Babylon Revisited" (1931). Are all of them hackwork? Are any of them?

4. Read Faulkner's stories "Red Leaves" and "Mountain Victory" and Hans H. Skei's chapters on them in *Reading Faulkner's Best Short Stories* (1999). Do you agree with Skei's assessment? What qualities in these stories allowed them to succeed as commercial works and, according to Skei, to endure as literature?

RESOURCES

Jan Cohn, *Creating America: George Horace Lorimer and the Saturday Evening Post* (Pittsburgh, Pa.: University of Pittsburgh Press, 1989).
Argues that studying the magazine during the thirty-eight years of Lorimer's editorship (1899 to 1936) reveals the inception of mass culture and entertainment as shaped by Lorimer's conception of America.

Tom Dardis, *Some Time in the Sun* (New York: Scribners, 1976).
A study of writers in Hollywood that focuses on Fitzgerald, Faulkner, Nathanael West, Aldous Huxley, and James Agee. While Fitzgerald and Faulkner were attracted to Hollywood for the money, Dardis argues that the charge that these authors did hackwork is a simplistic and false assessment of the effect of the movies on their careers.

William Faulkner, *Selected Short Stories of William Faulkner* (New York: Modern Library, 1955).
An accessible collection of thirteen stories, including "Red Leaves" and "Mountain Victory."

Richard Fine, *West of Eden: Hollywood and the Profession of Authorship* (Washington, D.C.: Smithsonian Institution Press, 1993).
Examines "the 'Hollywood as destroyer' legend," arguing that writers "crossed a professional—indeed cultural—divide" by choosing to work in the film industry, because Hollywood practices in regard to the writer's independence and creative autonomy were antithetical to what they had known.

F. Scott Fitzgerald, *The Short Stories of F. Scott Fitzgerald,* edited by Matthew J. Bruccoli (New York: Scribners, 1989).
A generous selection of Fitzgerald's stories, with a preface by the editor and informative headnotes that identify where each story was first published.

Hans H. Skei, *Reading Faulkner's Best Short Stories* (Columbia: University of South Carolina Press, 1999).
Includes chapters that discuss the marketing of Faulkner's stories "Mountain Victory" and "Red Leaves" to *The Saturday Evening Post.*

John Tebbel, *George Horace Lorimer and The Saturday Evening Post* (Garden City, N.Y.: Doubleday, 1948).
A friendly assessment of Lorimer that includes two lengthy chapters on the *Post* school of fiction, describing the editor's personal relationships with many authors.

PEOPLE OF INTEREST

Robert W. Chambers (1865–1933)
One of the most prolific and popular writers of the early decades of the twentieth century. Chambers published at least one book, and as many as four, every year from 1894 to 1938.

Irvin S. Cobb (1876–1944)
Humorist, journalist, short-story writer, and novelist. Cobb was a prolific author and a national celebrity in his day.

Bernard DeVoto (1897–1955)
Editor of the *Saturday Review of Literature* (1936 to 1938) and *Harper's* (1935 to 1955). His works include *Mark Twain's America* (1932), *Mark Twain at Work* (1942), and a Pulitzer Prize–winning history of the Rocky Mountain fur trade, *Across the Wide Missouri* (1947).

Joseph Hergesheimer (1880–1954)
Popular novelist whose work was often serialized in *The Saturday Evening Post* before being published in book form. His novel *Linda Condon* (1919) shows his disenchantment with contemporary American culture.

Mary Roberts Rinehart (1876–1958)
Novelist and playwright who blended romance with mystery fiction to become one of the highest-paid writers in the first half of the twentieth century. One of her most popular characters was Tish, a spinster who was an amateur detective.

Kenneth Roberts (1885–1957)
Began his career as a writer for *The Saturday Evening Post* and became a novelist who explored American history, including Benedict Arnold's exploits in the Revolutionary War in *Arundel* (1930) and *Rabble in Arms* (1933).

Upton Sinclair (1875–1968)
Journalist associated with the muckraking movement who became famous for *The Jungle* (1906), a novel about the plight of workers in the Chicago meatpacking industry that led to the passage of the Pure Food and Drug Act and the Meat Inspection Act. He also addressed social problems in his novels *Oil!* (1927), about scandals in the administration of President Warren G. Harding, and *Boston* (1928), which treats the trial of Nicola Sacco and Bartolomeo Vanzetti, as well as in his nonfiction.

Ben Ames Williams (1889–1953)
Popular writer who, beginning in 1917, published 135 stories, 35 serials, and 7 articles in *The Saturday Evening Post*.

Harry Leon Wilson (1867–1939)
Humorist, novelist, and short-story writer whose writing was regularly featured in *The Saturday Evening Post*. His best-known works include *Ruggles of Red Gap* (1915), a novel about an English valet in a cattle town that was originally serialized in the magazine, and the stories that feature the ranch owner and tale-teller Ma Pettengill, collected in *Somewhere in Red Gap* (1916), *Ma Pettengill* (1919), and *Ma Pettengill Talks* (1923).

—George Parker Anderson

Part III
Study Guides
on Works and Writers

Sherwood Anderson, *Winesburg, Ohio*

(New York: Huebsch, 1919)

For Sherwood Anderson (1876–1941) writing was a second career. He was a successful business owner in Elyria, Ohio, in 1912 when, after a nervous breakdown, he decided he could no longer reconcile his creative ambitions with the demands of a materialistic life. Consequently, he abandoned his business and family to pursue a literary calling. He published his first novel, *Windy McPherson's Son* (1916), at age forty, and his most famous work, *Winesburg, Ohio,* three years later. As if to make up for lost time, Anderson wrote prolifically, and several of his novels, such as *Poor White* (1920) and *Dark Laughter* (1925), were positively reviewed and sold well. In his lifetime he published twenty-six books, including thirteen novels, several volumes of memoirs, collections of essays and short stories, a biography of fellow Midwestern novelist Theodore Dreiser, and a stage adaptation of *Winesburg, Ohio.* None of his other work, however, has had the lasting significance of the Winesburg stories. Because of that collection, Anderson was influential on the generation of writers that followed him, particularly Ernest Hemingway, William Faulkner, and Thomas Wolfe. He was a friend of all of these men, although he eventually had fallings-out with them.

Anderson led a peripatetic life, traveling restlessly and settling for a time in Chicago, New Orleans, and rural Virginia, where he bought two small-town weekly newspapers, the Republican *Smyth County News* and the *Marion Democrat.* He married three more times after his first failed union; his second wife, Tennessee Mitchell, a Chicago bohemian whom he married in 1916, had previously had an affair with the poet Edgar Lee Masters. Anderson was setting out on another endeavor, an extended tour of Central and South America, when he died from a perforated intestine after swallowing a piece of a toothpick embedded in a martini olive.

Winesburg, Ohio was written mostly in 1915–1916. Around this time he read Masters's poetry collection *Spoon River Anthology* (1915), in which the inhabitants of a small-town cemetery soliloquize about their humble lives from beyond the grave. Biographer Kim Townsend observes that Anderson stayed up all night reading Masters's work, which "crystallized" Anderson's idea for his own collection. Masters's work resonated with Anderson's Whitmanesque desire to give voice to the ordinary people around him, who were often overlooked as subjects for fiction. (Anderson always chafed when his work was compared to Masters's, probably in large part because of his personal antipathy toward the poet related to Mitchell.) Although some of the stories were published separately in periodicals such as *The Masses* and *The Seven Arts,* Anderson intended all along for them to be part of the same work.

Winesburg, Ohio is about the stifled dreams and secret miseries of the inhabitants of the titular small Midwestern town. The stories are linked by the impressions of young George Willard, a newspaper reporter who comes to understand that he must leave his hometown if he hopes to realize his literary ambitions. *Winesburg, Ohio* opens with an introductory piece, "The Book of the Grotesque" (originally Anderson's title for the whole collection), which lays out the concept of "the grotesque" that the subsequent stories illustrate: as a person embraces a particular truth and tries to live solely by it, that single-mindedness distorts the person's life and makes of the truth a falsehood.

Examples of these grotesques among the inhabitants of Winesburg are Wing Biddlebaum, the subject of the story "Hands," a recluse with compulsively restless hands who had once, in another town and under another name, been a schoolteacher, until his overly familiar way with his students nearly led to accusations of improper behavior and his being lynched; George Willard's mother, Elizabeth, a beaten-down figure who fervently, jealously hopes for a more fulfilling life for her son; Alice Hindman, the subject of the story "Adventure," who gives her virginity to a young suitor on the night before he leaves to find his fortune in Chicago, then spends the rest of her life succumbing to an increasingly desperate spinsterhood; and Curtis Hartman, the local Presbyterian minister, who in "The Strength of God" is driven to distraction by lonely schoolteacher Kate Swift—herself a grotesque, revealed in "The Teacher" to be fixated on her student George.

Other stories concern particular milestones in George's life. "Nobody Knows," "An Awakening," and "Sophistication" describe his tentative explorations of sexuality and the mysteries of male-female relationships. In "Death" he must cope with the passing of his mother. And in "Departure," the last story in the collection, he boards the train that will take him into the larger world. His hometown becomes "a backdrop on which to paint the dreams of his manhood." George is generally understood to be a stand-in for the author, who shared his protagonist's small-town Midwestern origins and his desire to escape, but at the same time to memorialize, the scene of his youth. Anderson thought of himself as perpetually immature, as his biographers have noted, and saw George's steps toward maturity as analogous to his own artistic coming-of-age.

Winesburg, Ohio met with mostly positive reviews upon publication, with some of the most enthusiastic notices coming from important sources. H. L. Mencken—at the time probably the most influential voice on cultural matters in the nation—called the collection "a truly extraordinary book." Some reviewers objected to the portrayal of sexuality, judging the characters' behavior to be neurotic and perverted. Later, in retrospect, Anderson tended to exaggerate the negative response to *Winesburg, Ohio* to make the work seem more controversial than it was. Some small-town Ohioans no doubt were displeased to imagine themselves fictionalized as the people of Winesburg, but generally the collection was hailed as a step forward for American literature: for the first time an American writer had depicted the lives of ordinary people with the compassionate insight of European short-story masters such as Anton Chekhov.

TOPICS FOR DISCUSSION AND RESEARCH

1. To understand *Winesburg, Ohio* one must understand Anderson's attitude toward "the grotesque," since this idea, more than any other, connects the people of Winesburg. As is made clear in "The Book of the Grotesque," Anderson did not necessarily consider the term pejorative: "Some were

amusing, some almost beautiful," thinks the old writer about the procession of grotesques that appears before him in a dream. In the story "Paper Pills," the narrator implicitly likens the grotesques to gnarled apples left behind by the pickers: "Only the few know the sweetness of the twisted apples." The metaphor is generally taken to express Anderson's interest in those whose stories were typically overlooked as literary subjects; according to David D. Anderson, the author "approaches the people in his stories as he does the apples, secure in his knowledge that the sources or natures of their deformities are unimportant when compared to their intrinsic worth as human beings." At the same time, one might consider whether the narrator's word *delicious*—used in the same paragraph to describe the story of a man's life as well as twisted apples—might also suggest a condescending attitude, as though both were to be consumed. Does the notion of the grotesque bring readers closer to or distance them from Anderson's subjects?

2. As opposed to portrayals of small-town life that depict a close-knit community, Winesburg is populated with lonely, isolated individuals who, usually because of some earlier disappointment or trauma, are unable to connect with the people around them. The psychological toll of this isolation is one of the overarching themes of *Winesburg, Ohio*. When characters do reach out, they find that they cannot express coherently the truth that has rendered them grotesque, however urgently they might want to. The lesson they try to impart is frequently incomprehensible and frightening—even repellent—to the hearer. As Thomas Yingling notes, many of the social institutions that tend to bring people together are apparently absent in Winesburg: religion seems to have little influence, and politics, as evidenced by Tom Willard's lonely status as a Democratic campaigner in the Republican town, is also isolating. David D. Anderson contends that in the Winesburg stories Anderson "determined to treat isolation as a phenomenon of the individual in an individual sense rather than as a manifestation of a social evil," but other critics, such as Yingling and J. Gerald Kennedy, look at the work in a historically specific context, one in which the community-based agrarian life is being supplanted by ever-encroaching industrialization. What was Anderson attempting to convey by filling his town with such alienated individuals?

3. In many cases the event that made these characters into grotesques has to do with sexuality and male-female relationships, which the stories in *Winesburg, Ohio* portray mostly pessimistically. Elizabeth Willard, Curtis Hartman, and Ray Pearson are disappointed and resentful in their marriages. The story "Respectability" describes how town telegraph operator Wash Williams's experience with an unfaithful wife, and his mother-in-law's terribly misguided attempt to reconcile the couple, instilled in him a pathological hatred of women. For Alice Hindman, one act of sexual congress condemns her to a life of solitude. Readers might consider whether the prospects are better for the generation represented by George Willard. The book chronicles his fumbling attempts at connecting with several young women, but an evening he spends with Helen White in the penultimate story, "Sophistication"—during which the two young people experience "a brief hour of absolute awareness,"

as Walter B. Rideout describes it—suggests that he might have a capacity for mature intimacy. A very different view of the relationship between George and Helen is provided by Marilyn Judith Atlas in her gender-based analysis of the collection.

4. Another important type of relationship in *Winesburg, Ohio* is that between parents and children, which Anderson also portrays as prone to misunderstanding and resentment. His portrayal of George Willard's parents—his mother fiercely devoted to her son and his father a braggart with limited ability as a provider—seems based on Anderson's own upbringing. In her essay Marcia Jacobson explains how, through his autobiographical protagonist, Anderson portrayed his "ongoing struggle with his father" but also implicitly acknowledged "how much he was his father's son." Other relationships between parents and children, such as those in "'Queer'" and "The Untold Lie," are also fraught with complications and ambivalent attitudes. What insights into the roles and responsibilities of parents and children can one draw from the collection?

5. As signaled in "The Book of the Grotesque," which gives "the old writer" a sort of controlling presence of the overall work, the life of the artist and the role of art in a community are significant themes. One of the reasons that the grotesques of Winesburg are drawn to George is his facility with words; as Malcolm Cowley writes in his introduction to the 1960 Viking edition of the work, they believe "that he alone in Winesburg has an instinct for finding the right words and using them honestly." At the same time, however, the artist's life can be isolating, as is shown by Enoch Robinson in "Loneliness." David Stouck suggests that artists like "the old writer" and Enoch Robinson "are among the least capable of expressing themselves to others." Do you agree with this judgment? Is George Willard potentially different from the other artists depicted in the collection?

RESOURCES

Biography

Walter B. Rideout, *Sherwood Anderson: A Writer in America*, volume 1 (Madison: University of Wisconsin Press, 2006).
The first volume of Rideout's authoritative biography, published posthumously. It covers Anderson's life until 1927, including the period during which his most significant work was published.

Kim Townsend, *Sherwood Anderson* (Boston: Houghton Mifflin, 1987).
The most detailed full-length account of the writer's life.

Criticism

David D. Anderson, "Sherwood Anderson's Moments of Insight," in *Critical Essays on Sherwood Anderson,* edited by Anderson (Boston: G. K. Hall, 1981), pp. 155–171.
Considers Anderson's achievement in *Winesburg, Ohio* in terms of the collection's representation of "the wonder of human life, a compassionate regard for it, and a compelling sense of discovering significance in the commonplace."

Marilyn Judith Atlas, "Sherwood Anderson and the Women of Winesburg," in *Critical Essays on Sherwood Anderson,* edited by David D. Anderson (Boston: G. K. Hall, 1981), pp. 250–266.
Looks at the female characters in *Winesburg, Ohio,* considering particularly why none of them are allowed the possibility of escape from small-town life that is accorded George Willard and some of the other male characters.

Marc C. Conner, "Fathers and Sons: *Winesburg, Ohio* and the Revision of Modernism," *Studies in American Fiction,* 29 (2001): 209–238.
Argues that the father-son relationship is at the heart of *Winesburg, Ohio* rather than that between mother and son. To become fulfilled as an artist, George must seek reconciliation with his father.

Malcolm Cowley, introduction to *Winesburg, Ohio,* by Sherwood Anderson (New York: Viking, 1960).
Sketches the genesis of *Winesburg, Ohio* and describes it as "a work of love, an attempt to break down the walls that divide one person from another."

Philip Gerber, "*Winesburg, Ohio:* Serendipities of Form," *Old Northwest,* 15 (1992): 233–243.
Discusses how in *Winesburg, Ohio* Anderson anticipated important twentieth-century American themes and literary approaches, including colloquial language and the belief that everyone is a victim of social forces.

Marcia Jacobson, "*Winesburg, Ohio* and the Autobiographical Moment," in *New Essays on* Winesburg, Ohio, edited by John W. Crowley (Cambridge, England: Cambridge University Press, 1990), pp. 53–72.
Focuses on the character of George Willard to consider *Winesburg, Ohio* in the context of "the American boy-story," a genre of coming-of-age stories that includes Mark Twain's *The Adventures of Tom Sawyer,* Thomas Bailey Aldrich's *The Story of a Bad Boy,* and Booth Tarkington's *Penrod.*

J. Gerald Kennedy, "From Anderson's *Winesburg* to Carver's *Cathedral:* The Short Story Sequence and the Semblance of Community," in *Modern American Short Story Sequences: Composite Fictions and Fictive Communities,* edited by Kennedy (New York: Cambridge University Press, 1995), pp. 194–215.
Contextualizes *Winesburg, Ohio* in its historic setting, the 1890s, to consider how the multiple, communal perspectives of the stories illustrate the end of collective life in the United States.

Clarence Lindsay, *Such a Rare Thing: The Art of Sherwood Anderson's "Winesburg, Ohio"* (Kent, Ohio: Kent State University Press, 2009).
Focuses on four stories from *Winesburg, Ohio*—"Hands," "Respectability," "The Strength of God," and "Loneliness"—to examine both Anderson's artistic innovation and the critical neglect he has faced.

Kim Moreland, "Just the Tip of the Iceberg Theory: Ernest Hemingway and Sherwood Anderson's 'Loneliness,'" *Hemingway Review,* 19 (2000): 47–56.

Analyzes Anderson's portrayal of the artist Enoch Robinson, and how that portrayal might have influenced Hemingway's conception of writing.

Walter B. Rideout, "The Simplicity of *Winesburg, Ohio,*" in *Critical Essays on Sherwood Anderson,* edited by David D. Anderson (Boston: G. K. Hall, 1981), pp. 146–154.
Considers the combination of realistic description and abstract concepts that gives *Winesburg, Ohio* a "simplicity—paradox or not—of a complicated kind."

David Stouck, *"Winesburg, Ohio* as a Dance of Death," in *Critical Essays on Sherwood Anderson,* edited by David D. Anderson (Boston: G. K. Hall, 1981), pp. 181–195.
Discusses the medieval concept of life as a "Dance of Death" as a central theme and structuring principle of the collection.

William A. Sutton, *The Road to Winesburg: A Mosaic of the Imaginative Life of Sherwood Anderson* (Metuchen, N.J.: Scarecrow Press, 1972).
Describes Anderson's process of writing *Winesburg, Ohio,* with special attention to the work's real-life inspirations in the author's family and his boyhood home of Clyde, Ohio.

Thomas Yingling, "*Winesburg, Ohio* and the End of Collective Experience," in *New Essays on* Winesburg, Ohio, edited by John W. Crowley (New York: Cambridge University Press, 1990), pp. 99–128.
Reads *Winesburg, Ohio* as an "elegy" for an age of community based on oral tradition. Yingling argues that newspaperman and writer George Willard represents the coming-of-age of print culture.

—Charles Brower

Willa Cather, *My Ántonia*
(Boston & New York: Houghton Mifflin, 1918)

Willa Cather (1873–1947) was born in Back Creek Valley (now Gore), Virginia, to a farming family; the increasing difficulties of sustaining a family and livelihood through farming in the postbellum South led her parents to move the family to a ranch near Red Cloud, Nebraska, when Cather was nine. That endeavor too proved unsuccessful, and the family moved a year later into Red Cloud itself, where Cather's father opened an insurance business and she was educated, first at home and then at Red Cloud High School. She then moved to Lincoln, the capital, where she attended the University of Nebraska and began publishing both short fiction and journalism during her undergraduate years. She subsequently moved to Pittsburgh, where she lived from 1895 to 1905, and then to New York City, where she lived most of the rest of her life, working in both places as a schoolteacher and journalist, including serving as managing editor for *McClure's* magazine during her early years in New York. Her own creative writing became increasingly important to her, and she left *McClure's* in 1912 to devote herself to her writing career. All twelve of her novels were published after 1912, including the three novels in what is often called her "prairie trilogy": *O Pioneers!* (1913), *The Song of the Lark* (1915), and *My Ántonia* (1918). She won the Pulitzer Prize for her novel of World War I, *One of Ours* (1922); her deepening dissatisfaction with postwar values is evident in later novels such as *The Professor's House* (1925), a Modernist work set in the 1920s that in part focuses on the despoilment of Anasazi relics, and *Death Comes for the Archbishop* (1927), which treats the friendship of two French priests who administer Catholic holdings in the New Mexico Territory in the mid nineteenth century. Her last novel, *Sapphira and the Slave* (1940), was also the first set in her native Virginia. She died of a cerebral hemorrhage in 1947 in the New York home she had shared for more than forty years with her friend and companion Edith Lewis.

For two main reasons, *My Ántonia* stands as a particularly significant work in Cather's career: as the culmination of her prairie trilogy, it was the last work in which she focused on the Great Plains of her own era, the world she had experienced and with which she is most often associated; and as perhaps her most autobiographical novel, given the many parallels between the life of Jim Burden, the narrator, and her own, particularly his life of movement away from the land and life of Nebraska while maintaining emotional ties to the country that shaped him and cherishing the memories of his youth. Yet, while those biographical contexts are relevant to and enhance any reading of the novel, there is more than enough within its pages on which to focus, not only in its presentation of pioneer life and the Great Plains between the end of the nineteenth and beginning of the twentieth century but also in its complex engagement with themes of immigration and gender, class and sexuality, memory and storytelling, nostalgia and change.

Traces of all of these themes—as well, perhaps, as of Cather herself—are present in the brief but important "Introduction," in which an unnamed old friend of Jim Burden explains how he or she came to be given Burden's memoir of Ántonia Shimerdas, the Bohemian girl both had known growing up: "More than any other person we remembered, this girl seemed to mean to us the country, the conditions, the whole adventure of our childhood." The introduction provides a frame by which Burden's friend—Cather herself?—describes the circumstances that produced the narrative that follows: Burden's explanation that he had written down his memories of Ántonia to amuse himself on long trips across the country, that he had not taken the time to arrange his account so it "hasn't any form." The introduction concludes with a description of how Burden at the last moment decided to give a title to the manuscript he brought to his friend's apartment: "He went into the next room, sat down at my desk and wrote across the face of the portfolio 'Ántonia.' He frowned at this moment, then prefixed another word, making it 'My Ántonia.' That seemed to satisfy him."

The novel is divided into five sections—Book I, "The Shimerdas"; Book II, "The Hired Girls"; Book III, "Lena Lingard"; Book IV, "The Pioneer Woman's Story"; and Book V, "Cuzak's Boys"—each centered on a different stage in, and setting for, the interconnected but quite different lives of Jim and Ántonia. Just as the title of the novel both suggests Ántonia as its main subject but makes clear with the use of the word *My* the importance of Jim's perspective in the telling of the story, so too does the title of each book focus on other characters—from Ántonia's family in Book I, to other immigrant girls and women in Books II through IV, to Ántonia's husband and sons in Book V—of whom readers learn only through Jim's point of view. While Jim and Ántonia move further apart geographically and socially as time passes, Books IV and V end with deeply moving sections in which they reconnect and recognize their abiding friendship and profound tie to the land.

Readers of *My Ántonia* would benefit from a familiarity with her earlier works—particularly the other two prairie novels, which are entirely separate from *My Ántonia* and each other in characters and plot but treat similar themes—and her biography as traced and analyzed most recently and thoroughly in David Porter's *On the Divide*. To gain insight into the historical, cultural, biographical, and literary contexts, Sheryl Meyering's *Understanding* O Pioneers! *and* My Ántonia, and the collection of essays edited by John Murphy and Merrill Skaggs are recommended. Marilyn Arnold's *Reference Guide* is a useful starting point for investigating Cather scholarship before 1984; the Rosowski, O'Brien, and Bloom collections help frame the many directions that scholarship has taken since then.

TOPICS FOR DISCUSSION AND RESEARCH

1. Given its status as the third of Cather's prairie novels, *My Ántonia* can be productively analyzed in relationship to the West, the setting for those works that are considered Cather's most important contributions. Such analyses could focus on the changing realities of pioneer life in that region: changes due partly to the three decades or more that pass from Books I to V, partly to shifts in Jim's own perspective as he matures from a young boy just arrived in Nebraska, to a college student returning to it, to a married New Yorker traveling through, and partly to the multiple Western settings of the novel—including prairie farms and homesteads, the town of Black Hawk, Lincoln and the university there, and even stories of Alaska and San Francisco in the later books. But equally worthy of analysis are the novel's engagements with mythic versions of the West, as the opening pages' references to Jesse James, Indians, and desperadoes make clear. For a recent analysis of these multiple Wests, see Diana H. Polley's essay, "Americanizing Cather: Myth and Fiction in *My Ántonia*," in Bloom's collection; for an argument that the South from which Jim emigrates is an equally important region in the text, see Anne Goodwyn Jones's essay, "Displacing Dixie: The Southern Subtext in *My Ántonia*," in O'Brien's collection.
2. As a new arrival to the West in Book I, Jim shares with Ántonia, and likewise with the Shimerdas, the hired girls, Lena Lingard, and Ántonia's husband, Cuzak, the transforming experience of immigration. Cather uses these characters and others—including the Russian brothers Pavel and Peter, whose story is important in Book I—to present a complex vision of immigration and ethnicity, raising the issue of the Old World past and New World/Western present as expressed in changing customs, languages, and religious practices.

Cather explores the benefits and losses entailed in the immigration experience, especially the possibilities and difficulties of Americanization/assimilation. Sally Allen McNall's "Immigrant Backgrounds to *My Ántonia*" and Michael Gorman's "Jim Burden and the White Man's Burden," both in the Bloom collection, provide insights into these topics. Elizabeth Ammons's essay, "*My Ántonia* and African American Art," in the O'Brien collection considers African American identity in the novel, particularly through the pianist "Blind" d'Arnault on whom Jim focuses for almost a full chapter in Book II.

3. Ántonia and the other hired girls are likewise defined explicitly and implicitly through their identities as women—another worthwhile area for discussion and analysis. Ántonia's experiences and the stages of her life—from family farmhand in Book I to hired girl in Book II, to single mother in Book IV, to matriarch in Book V—follow from her destiny as a woman with limited choices within her culture. A related topic is Jim's perspective on gender and sexuality, which is influenced by his ongoing relationship with Lena Lingard but, as with everything in his memoir, is shaped by his relationship with Ántonia, who is successively a childhood playmate, the object of his adolescent crush, a sibling, and a role model. Blanche H. Gelfant's "The Forgotten Reaping-Hook: Sex in *My Ántonia*" and Deborah G. Lambert's "The Defeat of a Hero: Autonomy and Sexuality in *My Ántonia*," both in the Bloom collection, and Marilee Lindemann's "'It Ain't My Prairie': Gender, Power, and Narrative in *My Ántonia*," in the O'Brien collection, investigate questions of gender and sexuality in the novel.

4. No topic of discussion relevant to *My Ántonia* is separate from the issue of narration and perspective, as the title of the book and the introduction highlight the centrality of Jim's particular voice and point of view. How to view Jim and whether or not to accept his presentation of himself at face value are crucial questions for any analysis. Moreover, significant portions of each book are devoted to stories told by other characters, from Otto and the Russian brothers in Book I to Mrs. Stevens in Book IV, and each such story raises similar questions about the motivations of the storytellers, along with the inseparable issue of audience (also a concern for Jim, since he shares his memoir with his unnamed friend). Recommended essays for beginning research are Annette McElhiney's essay on point of view and Paula Woolley's essay, "'Fire and Wit': Storytelling and the American Artist in Cather's *My Ántonia*," in the Bloom collection.

5. On one level Jim's narrative seems to be a relatively straightforward chronology, beginning with his youthful experiences in Nebraska and proceeding through events in his life to his reconnection with Ántonia and her family. Yet, the time frame of the introduction immediately complicates that chronology, making clear that it is being actively constructed through Jim's present perspective and memories, and throughout the text Jim's present voice intercedes in the historical narration; the storytelling moments and the gaps in time between books similarly complicate the text's chronology and highlight the need for analysis of time in the novel. Loretta Wasserman's essay uses Henri Bergson's philosophies of time—viewing time as more circular and cyclical than linear—to frame some of these questions, while Miles Orvell's essay, "Time, Change, and

the Burden of Revision in *My Ántonia*," in the O'Brien collection relies on nostalgic visions of history and time to contextualize the novel.

RESOURCES

Biography

David Porter, *On the Divide: The Many Lives of Willa Cather* (Lincoln: University of Nebraska Press, 2008).

The most recent and thorough biography of Cather, moving smoothly between biography, historical and cultural contexts, and textual readings and analyses. Porter is guided throughout by an argument that Cather's life and work focused on not only "the divide" of the high prairie (as she and others called that area between the East and far West) but on other divisions, as well.

Bibliography

Marilyn Arnold, *Willa Cather: A Reference Guide* (Boston: G. K. Hall, 1986).

Particularly valuable for its thorough bibliography of Cather criticism and scholarship between 1895 and 1984. Each entry includes a brief but clear annotation that highlights focal points and unique contributions to the scholarship.

Murphy Skaggs and Merrill Maguire Skaggs, eds., *Willa Cather: New Facts, New Glimpses, Revisions* (Madison, N.J.: Fairleigh Dickinson University Press, 2008).

A valuable update on trends and discoveries in Cather studies since Arnold's book. The biography and bibliography sections—including the exhaustive "Willa Cather Collection Finding Aid," which documents all of the archival and electronic holdings of Cather materials around the country and world—are particularly useful.

Criticism

Harold Bloom, ed., *Willa Cather's My Ántonia* (New York: Bloom's Literary Criticism, 2008).

A new edition in the Modern Critical Interpretations series. This collection is an excellent introduction to recent scholarship on the novel; its eleven essays, many referenced above, cover topics from sex and medicine to storytelling and the process and meanings of rereading the novel.

Annette Bennington McElhiney, "Willa Cather's Use of a Tripartite Point of View in *My Ántonia*," *CEA Critic*, 56 (Fall 1993): 65–76.

An exemplary analysis of narration and perspective in the novel. McElhiney focuses on how Jim's narration is contextualized both in time (his present adult voice and past maturing one) and by the outside narrator with whose voice the novel opens.

Sheryl L. Meyering, *Understanding* O Pioneers! *and* My Ántonia: *A Student Casebook to Issues, Sources, and Historical Documents* (Westport, Conn.: Greenwood Press, 2002).

Geared specifically for student reference and work, with a variety of important texts and contexts, especially on historical, economic, and cultural issues related to the prairie and the West, through which to analyze the novel.

John J. Murphy, My Ántonia: *The Road Home* (Boston: Twayne, 1989).
An entry in the Twayne's Modern Classics series, including an extended analysis of the novel and many other helpful historical, biographical, and bibliographic materials. Murphy's analysis focuses on Cather's creation of a heroic image of her pioneer characters.

Sharon O'Brien, ed., *New Essays on* My Ántonia (Cambridge, England: Cambridge University Press, 1999).
Features four compelling analyses of the novel, each focused closely on one of the themes and topics as above; O'Brien's introduction effectively highlights the novel's overall effectiveness and enduring relevance to American literature and identity.

Susan J. Rosowski, ed., *Approaches to Teaching Willa Cather's* My Ántonia (New York: Modern Language Association, 1989).
Despite the title, useful for students as well as teachers. The book features essays on all five themes and topics, especially the West and gender.

Loretta Wasserman, "The Music of Time: Henri Bergson and Willa Cather," *American Literature*, 57 (May 1985): 226–239.
Philosophical and textual analyses of time and chronology in Cather's work, with a particular emphasis on *My Ántonia*.

Willa Cather Archive, Center for Digital Research in the Humanities, University of Nebraska-Lincoln <http://cather.unl.edu/> [accessed 10 November 2009].
An Internet database that includes not only links to particular texts by and related to Cather but also galleries and multimedia collections that contextualize her works and life.

—*Ben Railton*

John Dos Passos, *Manhattan Transfer*
(New York: Harper, 1925)

John Dos Passos (1896–1970) was regarded as one of the most important writers in America during the 1920s and 1930s, rivaling Ernest Hemingway and F. Scott Fitzgerald for critical acclaim. The future author was born in a Chicago hotel room where John R. Dos Passos, a wealthy lawyer from Washington, D.C., took his mistress, Lucy Addison Sprigg Madison, to deliver their son in secret. He was called John Madison, taking his mother's last name. Dos Passos sent John and his mother to Europe, where the boy spent most of his early life. They returned to the United States when John was ten, and he entered Choate School. In 1910 his father's wife died; his parents married three months later, and John took his father's last name. When the circumstances of his birth were discovered by the Choate headmaster, Dos Passos was denied a diploma. He earned early admission to Harvard University, entering at the age of sixteen. He graduated in 1916 and studied art and architecture in Spain for a year.

Dos Passos joined a gentleman's volunteer ambulance corps at the beginning of U.S. participation in World War I and spent most of the war in France and Italy. He began his first published novel, *One Man's Initiation—1917* (1920), in the trenches, and in the next fifty years he wrote fifteen novels, three plays, one volume of poetry, and nineteen nonfiction books, including his autobiography. His *U.S.A.* trilogy—*The 42nd Parallel* (1930), *1919* (1932), and *The Big Money* (1936)—was considered the most significant fiction work of the period. After observing the abuses of the Russian Communists during the Spanish Civil War in 1937, Dos Passos abandoned his radicalism and became one of the chief opponents in the literary community of the Communist Party. His reputation suffered among liberal critics as a result.

Though *Manhattan Transfer* was John Dos Passos's fourth novel, it was his first fully successful work. At the time Dos Passos wrote the novel, he was heavily influenced by the various currents of Modernism that had been developing in Europe at the end of the nineteenth century and had influenced the American expatriate writers who gathered in Paris after World War I. A trained artist, Dos Passos sought to apply the concepts of impressionism, Expressionism, and collage, as well as more-modern artistic modes such as Cubism, Fauvism, and Futurism, to his writing. The cinematic technique of abruptly shifting scenes clearly influenced him. He adapted the discordant tones and surprising rhythms of Igor Fyodorovich Stravinsky's music and the performances of the Ballets Russes to literary applications in his novel.

Manhattan Transfer, which takes its title from the station in the Meadowlands of New Jersey where passengers caught the train to Manhattan, is set in the first quarter of the twentieth century—from 1896 to 1923 or 1924. It attempts a panoramic view of the people in the city, the first great metropolis in the United States, the second in the world after London. The cast of characters is large and eclectic. It includes bootleggers, chorus girls, and petty thieves; blue-collar workers, newspapermen, and shopkeepers; socialites, stockbrokers, and wealthy businessmen. The setting is the streets of Manhattan, from the Bowery at the southern tip to 125th Street, then at the northern limit of urban development. The overriding theme is the comparison of Manhattan with the great biblical cities of Babylon and Nineveh destroyed by God because of the immorality of their people.

Dos Passos uses real places, real events, newspaper accounts, contemporary songs, and other elements of contemporary culture to draw his portrayal of New York. He develops the stories of two featured characters, the earnest newspaperman Jimmy Herf and the opportunistic actress Ellen Thatcher (whose name changes as she remakes her identity) over the period of the novel to demonstrate the destructive effect of the city on its inhabitants and their moral direction.

Some one hundred lesser characters from various walks of life are introduced to reinforce his point.

When Dos Passos wrote *Manhattan Transfer*, he was an admitted fellow traveler, meaning that he endorsed the aims of the Communist Party but was not a member. Party membership in the 1920s was reserved for the most radical adherents of Marxist philosophy, and Dos Passos maintained a healthy skepticism, though he felt that what he called "monopoly capitalism" was a corrupt economic system. That philosophy pervades his novel. But, as Sinclair Lewis points out in his long critique published as a review in 1925, despite the strong influence of artistic, social, and economic philosophies, Dos Passos wrote a novel that is interesting, alive with accurate depictions of the character and of the contemporary environment. Lewis argues that for that reason *Manhattan Transfer* is superior to the efforts of other modernist writers, whether American, British, or European. Though Dos Passos was a committed leftist, who enthusiastically embraced modern literary and artistic theories, he was first of all a novelist, meaning that his first concern was to write a readable novel that captured what he called the voice of the people.

The study of *Manhattan Transfer* is enhanced by a reading of Dos Passos's earlier work—particularly his nonfiction, in which he expresses his social and political concerns. David Sanders's *John Dos Passos: A Comprehensive Bibliography* (1987) lists those early books, and the previously uncollected shorter pieces are republished in *John Dos Passos: The Major Nonfictional Prose* (1988), edited by Donald Pizer, one of the most dependable Dos Passos scholars. Townsend Ludington has published two key works necessary to anyone seeking a sense of the circumstances of Dos Passos's life at the time of his novel. The most reliable biography is his *John Dos Passos: A Twentieth-Century Odyssey* (1984). It was preceded by *The Fourteenth Chronicle* (1973), a collection of Dos Passos's letters and journals with biographical interludes—a particularly useful book. Ludington's biography may be supplemented by Virginia Spencer Carr's *John Dos Passos: A Life* (1984). Melvin Landsberg, always trustworthy on Dos Passos, published two useful books: *Dos Passos' Path to U.S.A.* (1972) and *John Dos Passos's Correspondence with Arthur K. McComb* (1991).

Though the MLA index lists more than fifty critical articles about *Manhattan Transfer* between 1964 and 2009, students are well advised to begin with Michael Clark's excellent chapter on the novel in *Dos Passos's Early Fiction, 1912–1938* (1987) and with the chapter in Lisa Nanney's *John Dos Passos* (1998). Janet Galligani Casey offers an informed feminist reading in her chapter on the novel in *Dos Passos and the Ideology of the Feminine* (1998). From there, students can profitably proceed to the articles.

TOPICS FOR DISCUSSION AND RESEARCH

1. *Manhattan Transfer* can be fruitfully studied from several perspectives. Perhaps most important is the consideration of the novel as social history. Throughout the work, Dos Passos sprinkles hundreds of references to song lyrics, newspaper articles, and contemporary stage presentations. A key to the early segment

about Ellen Thatcher, for example, is her seeing a performance of *Peter Pan*, starring Maude Adams, that played on Broadway at the Empire Theatre in 1905. These allusions suggest the manner in which popular culture of the period was expressed. One of the main characters of the book is a newspaperman; the other is an actress. The implications of those choices deserve careful consideration. Students should read the novel along with a good social history of the period or along with a history of New York in the early twentieth century to identify Dos Passos's many contemporary references.

2. Similarly, Dos Passos uses national and world events to mark time in the novel. It opens in 1896 with the announcement by New York governor Levi P. Morton of the consolidation of the five boroughs into the metropolis of New York City. There are references to the Russo-Japanese War in 1906, to various labor disputes, and to events leading to American involvement in World War I. The manner in which these allusions work to establish the historical environment for the novel is a study valuable to students of both literature and history. One might pick a year between 1900 and 1920, read newspaper headlines from a national newspaper from that year, and identify sections in the novel where Dos Passos treats important events.

3. Geography, particularly social geography, is a key element of *Manhattan Transfer*. Demographics are central to Dos Passos's message. The tenements on the Lower and Upper East Side, the social setting in Midtown, where restaurants based on Sherry's and Delmonico's are significant, the Clairmont Inn in what was at the beginning of the novel the farmland setting at 125th Street and Broadway, the residential expansion of the Upper West Side along the Hudson, all are integral to the novel. The opening chapter with vignettes set at the 125th Street ferry dock, bringing in people from upstate New York; Lennox Hill Hospital at Seventy-seventh and Lexington, serving the German community and inhabitants of the Upper East Side tenements; and the Jewish neighborhood in Lower East Side provide the boundaries of Dos Passos's novel: it is all of Manhattan. Modes of transportation are equally important. As the novel opens, passenger access to Manhattan is chiefly by ferry. The island was served by seven bridges carrying primarily freight trains. By the end of the novel, Penn Station has been built, providing passenger train access. The effect of the resultant burgeoning population growth is one of Dos Passos's primary concerns. A useful exercise is to chart the action of the novel as it focuses on different parts of the city and to identify the real places, many now gone, that Dos Passos uses as social landmarks.

4. Biblical references, particularly to the books of Nahum and Jonah, provide a major strain of allusion, particularly in the last sections of the novel. The figure of Jonah, the prophet who ignored God's command to warn the people of Nineveh of the consequences of their sinful ways, is central to Dos Passos's message. The examination of biblical imagery, coupled with the strain throughout the novel of destruction by fire, is especially rewarding. What parallels did Dos Passos see between Nineveh and New York City?

5. *Manhattan Transfer* was daring in 1925 for its frank treatment of sexuality and sexual relations. Homosexuality, abortion, marital discord, and divorce

are all depicted candidly, and Dos Passos fought with his publishers to avoid censorship. Consideration of the significance of sexuality in Dos Passos's novel is recommended.

RESOURCES

Primary Works

The Fourteenth Chronicle: Letters and Diaries of John Dos Passos, edited by Townsend Ludington (Boston: Gambit, 1973).
Selections from Dos Passos's letters and diaries, with useful biographical interchapters.

John Dos Passos: The Major Nonfictional Prose, edited by Donald Pizer (Detroit: Wayne State University Press, 1988).
A comprehensive collection of Dos Passos's previously uncollected journalism that provides a reliable record of the evolution of his social and political thought.

John Dos Passos's Correspondence with Arthur K. McComb; or, "Learn to Sing the Carmagnole," edited by Melvin Landsberg (Niwot: University Press of Colorado, 1991).
Dos Passos's letters to his Harvard classmate, with whom he shared an interest in literature.

Bibliography

David Rohrkemper, *John Dos Passos: A Reference Guide* (Boston: G. K. Hall, 1980).
An annotated bibliography of articles about Dos Passos. It must be supplemented with the MLA index for articles and books after 1980.

David Sanders, *John Dos Passos: A Comprehensive Bibliography* (New York: Garland, 1987).
A good bibliography of primary and secondary sources. Particularly useful for the study of *Manhattan Transfer* is Sanders's annotated checklist of critical articles and his list of reviews. This work must be supplemented with the MLA bibliography for works after 1987.

Biography

Virginia Spencer Carr, *John Dos Passos: A Life* (Garden City, N.Y.: Doubleday, 1984).
A good full-length biography that serves as an excellent supplement to Ludington.

John Dos Passos, *The Best Times* (New York: New American Library, 1966).
The author's highly recommended autobiography, with much useful information about his life up to and at the time of composition of *Manhattan Transfer.*

Melvin Landsberg, *Dos Passos' Path to U.S.A.: A Political Biography 1912–1936* (Boulder: Colorado Associated University Press, 1972).
Biography by a highly respected Dos Passos scholar concentrating on the author's political education up to the time of his *U.S.A.* trilogy.

Townsend Ludington, *John Dos Passos: A Twentieth-Century Odyssey* (New York: Dutton, 1984).
The first full biography of Dos Passos and recommended as the biographical source of first reference. Ludington worked closely with Dos Passos's wife and daughter and made excellent use of the Dos Passos archive at the University of Virginia.

Criticism

Janet Galligani Casey, *Dos Passos and the Ideology of the Feminine* (New York: Cambridge University Press, 1998).
Interesting study of Dos Passos's use of gender in his fiction. Chapter 3 (pp. 99–130) treats *Manhattan Transfer*.

Michael Clark, *Dos Passos's Early Fiction, 1912–1938* (Selingsgrove, Pa.: Susquehanna University Press, 1987).
An excellent study that considers the intellectual background and social traditions that inform Dos Passos fiction. Chapter 8 (pp. 97–122) treats *Manhattan Transfer*.

Lisa Nanney, *John Dos Passos* (New York: Twayne, 1998).
A reliable general study of the author's work.

—Richard Layman

T. S. Eliot, *The Waste Land*

(New York: Boni & Liveright, 1922)

Although his career as a writer spanned more than fifty years and was dedicated even more to drama and literary criticism than to poetry, T. S. Eliot (1888–1965) is still most often identified as the poet of *The Waste Land*, the defining work of literary modernism. Born in St. Louis, Missouri, to Henry Ware Eliot, a businessman and son of a Unitarian minister, and Charlotte Champe Eliot, a social worker and poet, Thomas Stearns Eliot was the last of seven children. His formal education began at the private Smith Academy in St. Louis and then continued at Milton Academy near Boston. In 1906 he enrolled at Harvard, where he began to immerse himself in the two pursuits that occupied the rest of his life: philosophy and literature. He spent the year 1910–1911 studying in Paris, encountering firsthand some of the premier French writers and intellectuals of the day. Although he retained an American outlook, Eliot came increasingly to think in European terms, identifying himself as an artist and critic within the broader tradition of Western civilization. In Paris, Eliot became close friends with Jean Verdenal, a French medical student who was killed in World War I; Eliot's first published collection, *Prufrock and Other Observations* (1917), was dedicated to Verdenal.

Eliot returned to Harvard to pursue a doctorate in philosophy, but his studies took him to Germany and then to Oxford, where he met and immediately impressed fellow American poet Ezra Pound. Through Pound's advocacy Eliot was able to publish his first major poem, "The Love Song of J. Alfred Prufrock," in *Poetry* magazine in 1915. That same year Eliot met and married Vivien Haigh-Wood, a young Englishwoman who, along with Pound and even more than Verdenal, exerted a profound influence on Eliot's work for the next decade.

Eliot relocated to England permanently and over the next few years worked as a teacher and then at Lloyd's Bank, meanwhile continuing to write poems and doing editorial work for the literary magazine *The Egoist*. During this period Eliot began to cement his place as an important poet and critic—publishing new volumes of poems and the hugely influential critical volume *The Sacred Wood* (1920)—but his personal life was becoming acutely difficult. In addition to financial strain, his and Vivien's physical and mental ailments caused disquiet in their marriage. In 1921 Eliot underwent psychological treatment in England and then in Switzerland. This combination of circumstances, Eliot later acknowledged, created the emotional atmosphere out of which came *The Waste Land.*

An examination of Eliot's drafts shows that Pound played a pivotal role in editing and revising *The Waste Land* into the fragmented tour de force that has become the archetype of Modernist poetry. The publication of the poem in 1922 sparked an unprecedented level of response in the literary world, both positive and negative. Nothing like this cacophonic, disjointed poem had been seen before. Its fractured aesthetic and strange modern rhythms proved incomprehensible to some but appealed immediately to a segment of the public desperate for a new literary representation of the disorienting experiences of modern urbanized life. Eliot, however, consistently downplayed the idea of *The Waste Land* as the statement of a generation.

After his recovery from his psychological problems and the publication of *The Waste Land,* Eliot began a period of new cultural and literary influence. In 1922 he founded the *Criterion,* which quickly became one of the most important journals of literature, culture, and politics in Europe, and in 1925 he accepted a position as literary editor at the Faber and Gwyer publishing house. In these positions he presided for years over the formation of literary sensibility in Britain and America with a level of influence enjoyed by few individuals before or since.

In 1927 Eliot became a British citizen and shocked the public by being confirmed into the Church of England, a decision wholly incompatible with the iconoclastic image maintained by admirers and detractors alike. The combination of new commitments signaled his entrenchment, surprising to many but demonstrably in keeping with his cultural theorizations over the preceding decade, as a man of order and tradition. The new stability in his life was aided by his separation from Vivien, formalized in 1932.

In 1930 Eliot published the religious poem "Ash Wednesday." Another poem from this decade, "Burnt Norton" (1936), also featuring strong metaphysical elements, became the cornerstone of the poetic masterpiece of the latter half of Eliot's career, *Four Quartets* (1943). The 1930s, however, marked a shift in Eliot's creative work from poetry to drama. His verse play *Murder in the Cathedral,* which remains his best-known dramatic work, opened in 1935, and *The Family Reunion* premiered in 1939.

Four Quartets was Eliot's last major work of poetry. For the remaining two decades of his life he focused his efforts on verse plays, critical writing, and his work at Faber, nurturing the talents of a new generation of poets, including W. H. Auden. In the late 1940s and 1950s, Eliot's public fame reached a zenith, including reception in 1948 of the Nobel Prize in literature. *The Cocktail Party,* another of his most acclaimed verse dramas, debuted in 1949.

Vivien had died in a mental hospital in 1947. Eliot spent some thirty years single and celibate before marrying Valerie Fletcher in 1957. They remained together until Eliot's death from heart failure in 1965.

TOPICS FOR DISCUSSION AND RESEARCH

1. Eliot's early working title for *The Waste Land* was "He Do the Police in Different Voices," a line taken from Charles Dickens's novel *Our Mutual Friend* (1865). Perhaps the most remarkable—and disorienting—feature of *The Waste Land* is its employment of multiple voices, languages, and linguistic registers. Among these elements are the words of several first-person speakers, some named, some unnamed; the elevated language of prophecy; the colloquial speech of working-class Londoners; a host of fragments and phrases drawn from or alluding to literature of the past, including Isaiah, St. Augustine, Ovid, Dante, Shakespeare, Webster, Marvell, Verlaine, and many others; and lines in Greek, Latin, English, French, German, and Italian. Still, many readers, following Eliot's hint in the Notes about the figure of Tiresias, see one dominant voice or consciousness uniting, or at least lending some order to, all of the rest. Nancy Gish explores this idea in The Waste Land: *A Poem of Memory and Desire* (1988), as do Jewel Spears Brooker and Joseph Bentley in *Reading* The Waste Land: *Modernism and the Limits of Interpretation* (1990). Tracing the different voices in the poem and testing the notion that one is dominant will help students experience how *The Waste Land* coheres—or does not cohere—as a whole.

2. *The Waste Land* has often been regarded as the first nearly adequate poetic representation of the chaos wrought in Europe by World War I. While on one level the poem's images of blasted, barren landscapes can be seen as an approximation of the battlefields of France, on another level its violently fractured depiction of Europe's linguistic, literary, and cultural heritage implies a state of European disunity on a broader scale. In the years preceding the composition of the poem Eliot was busily immersing himself in the possibilities of European culture and literature—reading, traveling, listening to music, and even writing some successful poems in French. At the same time disillusionment,

impatience, and mistrust regarding European traditions had already begun to characterize the thought of many young writers, Eliot included. *The Waste Land* betrays little sense of possibility for Europe, as though in the modern world the European inheritance amounts only to "A heap of broken images." It is also significant that Eliot's study of philosophy included passionate attention to the traditions of the East, and there is in the poem a turning eastward toward key texts of Buddhism and Hinduism. The title of the third section, "The Fire Sermon," refers to a sermon given by the Buddha, and the final section, "What the Thunder Said," is punctuated by words and phrases drawn from the Hindu Upanishads. If *The Waste Land* is, indeed, a poem of European dissolution, it is worth considering the ways in which Eliot's invocation of Eastern mythologies challenges, expands, or undercuts the idea of Europe itself. Christina Hauck's chapter "Not One, Not Two: Eliot and Buddhism" in David Chinitz's *Companion to T. S. Eliot* (2009) provides a useful introduction to Eliot's background in Buddhist studies; it includes A. David Moody's article "The Mind of Europe in T. S. Eliot," which examines how Eliot dealt with the difficulty of holding together an idea of Europe.

3. The textual history of *The Waste Land* adds further layers of complexity and interest to the poem. Before it fell into Pound's hands, *The Waste Land* was much longer and included a great deal more guiding connective material. Also, the poem appeared in print in three separate versions within two months in late 1922: it was published without Eliot's explanatory Notes in *The Criterion* in England and then in *The Dial* in the United States, and finally, with the Notes added, as a book by Boni and Liveright. The publication of the facsimile version, edited by Valerie Eliot, in 1971 opened up a new horizon of interpretative possibilities. Readers now have access to Eliot's original drafts, showing the many emendations and excisions the poem underwent, mostly at Pound's suggestion, before publication. Lawrence Rainey explores in detail the implications of the composition and publication history of *The Waste Land* in his companion volumes *Revisiting* The Waste Land (2005) and *The Annotated* Waste Land *with Eliot's Contemporary Prose* (2005). Students might consider the effect that Eliot's and Pound's alterations had on the overall effect of the poem, the role that the Notes have on our understanding of the poem, and the ways in which the ability to peek into the process of composition and revision of a poem affects the way we read the product we think of as the final one.

4. Like most of Eliot's other work, *The Waste Land* offers discouraging prospects for intimacy—emotional, spiritual, and physical—between men and women. Several episodes in the poem, from the strained exchanges between the two speakers in "A Game of Chess" to the crude assignation between the "young man carbuncular" and the "typist home at teatime" to the songs of the Thames daughters in "The Fire Sermon," describe unfeeling, unproductive, and abortive sexual encounters. Running through the poem, and echoing the myth of the Fisher King that is one of its sources, is the theme of sterility and the desire for the return of fecundity, but the feelings of absence are here unrelieved by any suggestion of the kind of fruitful union that might lead to regeneration. In *The Cambridge Introduction to T. S. Eliot* (2006) John Xiros Cooper analyzes

the myth of the Fisher King and Eliot's employment of it. Patrick Query explores the theme of sexuality in general in Eliot's work in his chapter in Chinitz's *Companion to T. S. Eliot*. Students may find it useful to investigate *The Waste Land* in terms of its treatment of sexuality and sexual relations and to consider how these issues are entwined with the specific features of the modern world the poem describes.

5. In 1952 the young American critic John Peter argued that *The Waste Land*, far from being a purely detached statement of the condition of a generation or a society, is in fact the record of a speaker's mourning for a lost love—specifically, for a young man. Eliot reacted swiftly and unambiguously in refuting Peter's suggestion, an unusual move from a poet who almost always preferred to remain distant from interpretations of his own work. In 1969, well after Eliot's death, Peter returned to his original claim and went on to specify that the lost male love in *The Waste Land* is Jean Verdenal, Eliot's co-boarder from his sojourn in Paris. In 1978 James E. Miller took up Peter's line of thought in *T. S. Eliot's Personal Waste Land: Exorcising the Demons*, analyzing the work as Eliot's poetic means of coming to terms with Verdenal's death. This kind of biographical criticism has always been a thorny matter among Eliot scholars, not least because Eliot's own greatest contribution to literary criticism is what is called the impersonal theory of poetry. In his famous essay "Tradition and the Individual Talent" (1919), among other places, Eliot insisted that poetry be interpreted—and, to an extent, written—on its own terms, objectively, apart from any knowledge of or interest in the facts of the poet's own life. This impersonal position, however, is complicated by other statements in which Eliot seems to acknowledge that *The Waste Land* is, indeed, the record of personal feelings and experience. Students might consider issues of impersonality in poetry and of the role of biography in criticism in the light of Eliot's statements on these matters and the increasing amount of scholarship that combines critical and biographical analysis.

RESOURCES

Primary Works

The Annotated Waste Land *with Eliot's Contemporary Prose*, edited by Lawrence Rainey (New Haven, Conn.: Yale University Press, 2005).
Pairs the editor's thorough annotations of *The Waste Land* with Eliot's critical prose, also extensively annotated by Rainey, from 1921.

The Waste Land: A Facsimile and Transcript of the Original Drafts Including the Annotations of Ezra Pound, edited by Valerie Eliot (London: Faber & Faber, 1971).
Provides the original drafts of the poem with the revised version on the facing pages, with an introduction and some important notes by Eliot's widow.

The Waste Land: Authoritative Text, Contexts, Criticism, edited by Michael North (New York: Norton, 2001).
The Norton Critical Edition. It Includes a well-annotated version of the poem, as well as many of its background sources, Eliot's statements pertaining to the

poem, and a selection of criticism from its early reception to the late twentieth century.

The Waste Land by T. S. Eliot as Hypertext <eliotswasteland.tripod.com> [accessed 5 November 2009].
Usefully indexed to Eliot's source texts and his own other works.

Biography

Lyndall Gordon, *T. S. Eliot: An Imperfect Life* (New York: Norton, 1998).
The most widely used biography. The author makes many connections between Eliot's life, interior and exterior, and his works.

Criticism

Jewel Spears Brooker and Joseph Bentley, *Reading* The Waste Land: *Modernism and the Limits of Interpretation* (Amherst: University of Massachusetts Press, 1990).
A philosophically oriented analysis.

David Chinitz, "T. S. Eliot: *The Waste Land*," in *A Companion to Modernist Literature and Culture,* edited by David Bradshaw and Kevin J. H. Dettmar (Oxford: Blackwell, 2006), pp. 324–332.
A brief but helpful introduction to the poem.

Chinitz, ed., *A Companion to T. S. Eliot* (Chichester, U.K.; Malden, Mass.: Wiley-Blackwell, 2009).
The most comprehensive and recent guide to Eliot's life, work, and ideas. The book includes essays by Michael Coyle and James Longenbach on *The Waste Land.*

John Xiros Cooper, *The Cambridge Introduction to T. S. Eliot* (New York: Cambridge University Press, 2006).
An accessible guide to Eliot with sections on his life, the contexts for his writing, explications and analyses of his major works, and a brief reception history.

Nancy Gish, The Waste Land: *A Poem of Memory and Desire,* Twayne's Masterwork Studies, no. 13 (Boston: G. K. Hall, 1988).
Provides concise analysis of all sections of *The Waste Land,* as well as brief contextual discussions.

James E. Miller, *T. S. Eliot's Personal Waste Land: Exorcism of the Demons* (University Park: Pennsylvania State University Press, 1977).
A controversial but often-cited book that was the first to make explicit arguments for the homoerotic qualities of *The Waste Land* and Verdenal's significance to Eliot.

Modern American Poetry: T. S. Eliot (1888–1965) <http://www.english.illinois.edu/maps/poets/a_f/eliot/eliot.htm> [accessed 10 November 2009].
A wealth of information on Eliot's life and works, with important essays by Eliot critics and numerous contextual links.

A. David Moody, "The Mind of Europe in T. S. Eliot," in *T. S. Eliot at the Turn of the Century,* edited by Marianne Thormahlen (Lund, Sweden: Lund University Press, 1994), pp. 13–32.
Traces the development of Eliot's idea of Europe in his poetry and criticism.

Moody, ed., *The Cambridge Companion to T.S. Eliot* (New York: Cambridge University Press, 1994).
The precursor to Chinitz's *Companion.* It includes an important essay on *The Waste Land:* Harriet Davidson's "Improper Desire: Reading *The Waste Land.*"

Lawrence Rainey, *Revisiting* The Waste Land (New Haven, Conn.: Yale University Press, 2005).
Offers detailed accounts of the writing, publication, and reception of *The Waste Land,* as well as extensive notes and synoptic tables.

W. C. Southam, ed., *A Guide to* The Selected Poems of T. S. Eliot (London: Faber & Faber, 1994).
An essential guide to Eliot's poetry through the 1920s that includes a section-by-section analysis of *The Waste Land.*

—Patrick Query

William Faulkner, *The Sound and the Fury*
(New York: Cape & Smith, 1929)

William Faulkner (1897–1962) is recognized as one of the giants of American literature; but he was not widely acclaimed in the United States until *The Portable Faulkner,* an overview collection of his work, was published in 1946—twenty years after the publication of his first novel, Soldiers' Pay. He won the Nobel Prize in literature for 1949.

Born in New Albany, Mississippi, Faulkner grew up and lived most of his life in Oxford, home of the University of Mississippi (where he attended classes but did not graduate) and seat of Lafayette County, which served as the model for his most famous creation: Yoknapatawpha County, the setting for most of his fiction. During the mid 1920s he lived for several months in New Orleans, where he met Sherwood Anderson, the author of *Winesburg, Ohio* (1919), who advised him to write about what he knew. In "A Note on Sherwood Anderson" (1953) Faulkner recalls the older author saying, "You're a country boy; all you know is that little patch up there in Mississippi where you started from." Faulkner followed Anderson's advice in writing his third novel, which he called "Flags in the Dust." It was the first of his books to be set in his apocryphal county and to feature the "residents" of that county, many of whom reappeared in later works. That novel was an ambitious endeavor for Faulkner. Clearly excited by the artistic possibilities afforded by the people and places he had introduced, he offered it to Boni and Liveright, the publisher of his first two novels, calling it in a letter to

Horace Liveright "THE book, of which those other things were but foals ... the damdest best book you'll look at this year." The publisher disagreed, but this frustrating experience led the author to a higher achievement: Faulkner responded to the rejection by writing another novel, also set mostly in Yoknapatawpha County but written, he said, with no regard for publication. That book was *The Sound and the Fury*. ("Flags in the Dust" was published by Harcourt, Brace in a severely cut form and under the title *Sartoris* in 1929, the same year Cape and Smith published *The Sound and the Fury;* the uncut version was published with Faulkner's original title in 1973.) Many readers and critics consider *The Sound and the Fury* the greatest of Faulkner's nineteen novels, though it has plenty of competition for that honor: it was the first in a string of masterpieces Faulkner wrote through the 1930s and into the 1940s, including *As I Lay Dying* (1930), a black comedy about the challenges the Bundren family face trying to get their dead matriarch, Addie, properly buried in a cemetery in Jefferson, the faraway seat of Yoknapatawpha County; *Sanctuary* (1931), a sordid tale in which a University of Mississippi coed, Temple Drake, is kidnapped by a bootlegger named Popeye and winds up in a Memphis brothel; *Light in August* (1932), Faulkner's first novel to deal closely with the issue of race and racism, especially in its central character, the racially ambiguous Joe Christmas; *Absalom, Absalom!* (1936), a multigenerational tale in which characters in 1909–1910 attempt to understand the story of the mysterious Thomas Sutpen, who showed up in Jefferson one day in the 1830s and established himself as a planter, only to have his "design" ruined by civil war, both in his family and throughout his region; *The Hamlet* (1940), the first novel in the so-called Snopes trilogy, in which a poor white son of a barn-burning father is able to insinuate himself into a more respectable position as a shopkeeper and, later, as the husband of the store owner's daughter; and *Go Down, Moses* (1942), another multigenerational study of family and race, this time of the McCaslin family, which also provides a close look at the vanishing wilderness of Mississippi in the central novella of the book, "The Bear."

The Sound and the Fury, however, remained Faulkner's own favorite novel because it was his "most splendid failure," a remark recorded in *Faulkner in the University* (1959), a collection of statements he made while writer-in-residence at the University of Virginia in the late 1950s. In two introductions, which were intended for republications of the novel but were not published until after his death, Faulkner described how writing his first three novels had helped him to improve as a writer and cited the rejection of "Flags in the Dust" as crucial to the development of his artistic vision. "One day," he wrote, "I seemed to shut a door between me and all publishers' addresses and book lists. I said to myself, Now I can write. ... So I, who had never had a sister and was fated to lose my daughter in infancy, set out to make myself a beautiful and tragic little girl."

That "little girl" was Candace "Caddy" Compson, arguably the central character in the book and definitely its most tragic figure. The story for Faulkner began with a mental picture of her muddy drawers, visible to her brothers as she climbed a tree to look on at death—literally, the funeral wake for the children's grandmother. As Faulkner recounted, he tried to tell the story four different ways in the novel, and once more years later. The first three of the four sections of the novel are each recounted by one of the Compson brothers, while the fourth is told from an omniscient point of view. Seventeen years later, Faulkner published in *The Portable Faulkner* another attempt to tell the story, this time in what he termed an "Appendix" to the novel: a chronology of the entire Compson lineage from its beginning in 1699 to the end of World War II in 1945.

The novel is notable for its highly modernistic traits, which include a psychologically rich stream-of-consciousness narration; a fragmented narrative in which snippets of text and unexplained images contribute piece by piece to the tapestry of the plot; the use of multiple points of view, each offering individual interpretations of shared events; a textual and rhetorical presentation dependent on typographic and stylistic departures from prose conventions; and the spare use of exposition, forcing the reader to discern meaning gradually. *The Sound and the Fury* affords many avenues of inquiry for readers and critics at all levels of scholarly expertise. A search of the MLA bibliography yields more than five hundred books and articles about the novel, and the number climbs each year.

TOPICS FOR DISCUSSION AND RESEARCH

1. One of the most obvious topics for discussion and research is immediately evident when one begins to read the book: the difficulty of following and making sense of the narrative, the first section of which is the most confusing. Each of the four sections of the novel is headed only with a date, indicating the principal day on which most of the action of that section takes place; the novel features frequent flashbacks, however, especially in the first two sections.

   The opening section, "April Seventh 1928," is told by the youngest brother, Benjy, a mentally challenged thirty-three-year-old with no conception of time or any real understanding of what he sees and hears; consequently, Benjy's narrative frequently and suddenly shifts from the present day to various moments in his past without explanation or even clarification of what is happening. What are the incidents Benjy remembers, and when did they occur? He often returns to the memory of Caddy climbing a tree to look at death while her brothers watch from below. Why is this memory—the earliest moment revealed in the various narrators' recollections—so important to the characters and to the novel?

   The second section, narrated by the oldest brother, Quentin, is dated "June Second 1910," and is set largely in and around Cambridge, Massachusetts, where Quentin has spent a year attending Harvard University. Quentin recounts what happens on the day he will commit suicide by drowning himself in the Charles River; but as in the Benjy narrative, much of this section consists of fragmentary flashbacks. What are the most important memories for Quentin? What are the main motivations for his act of suicide?

   The third section, "April Sixth 1928," is narrated by Jason Compson. Though much more conventional in its first-person narration and set almost entirely on the date named in the title—which is Good Friday—the section does include several key flashbacks involving Caddy, who has given her illegitimately conceived child, Miss Quentin, to be raised by Jason and their mother. What are Jason's attitudes toward his sister and his niece?

The final section, "April Eighth 1928," is commonly called "Dilsey's section" because of the prominence in it of the Compsons' African American servant, though she does not serve as narrator. It is set entirely on Easter Sunday 1928 and culminates in the discovery that Miss Quentin has run away, taking the money that Caddy had intended for her but that Jason had appropriated. The section juxtaposes Jason's attempt to intercept Quentin (and "his" money) with Dilsey's attendance at an Easter sermon. Why is Dilsey such an important character? What is her role in the novel?

Studying Faulkner's rhetorical and narrative techniques in each of the sections is one of the most useful ways of appreciating the novel, especially as his approach relates to modernism as a literary and historical movement characterized by fragmented and piecemeal ways of approaching "truth." Several formalist approaches to the novel, including those by Cleanth Brooks, Olga Vickery, and Michael Millgate, comment on the modernistic attributes of the novel, while John T. Matthews's *The Play of Faulkner's Language* (1982) serves as a good general work on Faulkner's rhetorical technique.

2. Another area worthy of investigation lies in the allusiveness and intertextuality of the novel. These features begin with its title, a reference to Macbeth's "Tomorrow and tomorrow" soliloquy in the Shakespeare play:

> Tomorrow, and tomorrow, and tomorrow,
> Creeps in this petty pace from day to day,
> To the last syllable of recorded time;
> And all our yesterdays have lighted fools
> The way to dusty death. Out, out, brief candle!
> Life's but a walking shadow, a poor player
> That struts and frets his hour upon the stage
> And then is heard no more: it is a tale
> Told by an idiot, full of sound and fury,
> Signifying nothing. (Act 5, Scene 5, ll. 19–28)

Beyond its apparent association with Benjy's narration, how does this passage relate to the novel in terms of tone and theme? Is it relevant to the depiction or interpretation of other characters? Examining Stephen M. Ross and Noel Polk's annotations to the novel will provide a good starting point for students to begin to explore specific and broader connections between the novel and other works. Are the April time settings, for example, an allusion to T. S. Eliot's *The Waste Land* (1922), in which it is described as "the cruellest month"? Or are the biblical allusions and the specifically Christian meanings of the April dates—Maundy Thursday, Good Friday, and Easter—more relevant to a deeper understanding of the novel? Perhaps the most important intertextual association is Faulkner's use of Quentin Compson as a major character in *Absalom, Absalom!* Is it appropriate to read the Quentin Compson of *The Sound and the Fury* through the lens of the character presented in the later novel? John T. Irwin's *Doubling and Incest/Repetition and Revenge* (1975;

revised, 1996) offers a psychoanalytic approach to Faulkner's use of Quentin as a major character in both *The Sound and the Fury* and *Absalom, Absalom!*

3. Students of Southern history may read the novel as a commentary on the decline of the Old South as represented by the aristocratic Compsons, whose historical prominence can be gleaned only from the Appendix. How is this history relevant to the actions and attitudes of the characters in the novel, in particular to Quentin Compson? The novel's connection to the mentality prevalent in the South decades after the end of the Civil War is significant in Matthews's The Sound and the Fury: *Faulkner and the Lost Cause* (1991).

4. Although the theme of race and racism is not as much emphasized in *The Sound and the Fury* as it is in the later *Light in August,* readers may yet want to consider the role race plays in the novel. What is the effect of the racial attitudes of the time on the characters, white and black? How do the black characters—Dilsey and the various members of her family who are tasked with taking care of Benjy—compare to the Compsons? Thadious Davis's "'Jim Crow' and *The Sound and the Fury*" and Eric J. Sundquist's "The Myth of *The Sound and the Fury,*" both of which are collected in Harold Bloom's *William Faulkner's* The Sound and the Fury (1988), offer good starting points for readers interested in exploring themes pertaining to race.

5. One especially interesting avenue for students to pursue has to do with the character of Caddy, the central figure in the book. Why does Faulkner choose not to give her a voice in the novel? What is the meaning of her disappearance as a character over the course of the novel? Caddy is always seen through the eyes of her brothers. What does she mean for each of them? How is Caddy's fate relevant to that of her daughter? Bloom's *Caddy Compson* (1990) combines many short critical extracts on Caddy, beginning with Faulkner's own reflections on writing the novel, and longer critical essays examining her from a variety of perspectives. Among these essays, Linda W. Wagner's "Language and Act: Caddy Compson" concentrates on how Faulkner actually created her, with "special attention to Caddy's role as language-creator and giver." Intertextual and archetypal readings are key in essays by Gladys Milliner and Andre Bleikasten, who demonstrate Caddy's ties to the biblical Eve and the Greek Eurydice, respectively. And family ties are the focus of essays by Cleanth Brooks, who writes about Caddy's relationship with Benjy, and John T. Irwin, who emphasizes her relationship with Quentin.

RESOURCES

Primary Works

The Sound and the Fury: An Authoritative Text, Backgrounds and Contexts, Criticism, edited by David Minter, second edition (New York: Norton, 1994).

Includes a scholarly "corrected text" of the novel, representing, as closely as possible, Faulkner's intent, as well as the 1946 "Appendix," selected letters and introductions by Faulkner, other background materials, and a collection of critical essays.

The Sound and the Fury: A Hypertext Edition, edited by R. P. Stoicheff and others, University of Saskatchewan <http://www.usask.ca/english/faulkner> [accessed 29 October 2009].
Responds to Faulkner's lament in letters to his publisher that publishing technology did not allow the opening section to be printed in different-colored ink according to when each past incident occurred. This website also includes various other critical resources for readers of the novel.

Biography

Joseph Blotner, *Faulkner: A Biography* (2 volumes, New York: Random House, 1974; revised, 1 volume, New York: Random House, 1984).
The most comprehensive biography of Faulkner.

David L. Minter, *William Faulkner: His Life and Work* (Baltimore: Johns Hopkins University Press, 1980).
A good general biography that also examines Faulkner's fiction. The commentary on *The Sound and the Fury* stresses biographical factors that played a part in Faulkner's conception, writing, and later reactions to the novel.

Jay Parini, *One Matchless Time: A Life of William Faulkner* (New York: Harper-Collins, 2004).
An excellent biography drawing on many previously unavailable sources, including letters, memoirs, and interviews.

Criticism

Harold Bloom, ed., *Caddy Compson* (New York: Chelsea House, 1990).
A collection of critical essays, most originally published in the 1970s and 1980s, examining the character from different perspectives.

Bloom, ed., *William Faulkner's* The Sound and the Fury (New York: Chelsea House, 1988).
An anthology of criticism of the novel from different theoretical approaches, including formalist, psychoanalytic, historical, and poststructuralist studies. Of particular interest for students of Modernism are Donald Kartiganer's "*The Sound and the Fury* and the Dislocation of Form" and Gary Lee Stonum's "*The Sound and the Fury:* The Search for a Narrative Method."

Cleanth Brooks, *William Faulkner: The Yoknapatawpha Country* (New Haven, Conn.: Yale University Press, 1963).
One of the early landmark studies of Faulkner's fiction. The chapter on *The Sound and the Fury* treats in particular the role of time and religion in the novel. The various obsessions the Compson brothers have with past, present, and future, and how each represents for them a "false interpretation of eternity," are juxtaposed against the outlook of Dilsey, whose "ultimate commitment," because of her simple yet heartfelt Christian faith, "is to eternity."

Frederick L. Gwynn and Joseph Blotner, eds., *Faulkner in the University: Class Conferences at the University of Virginia, 1957–1958* (Charlottesville: University of Virginia Press, 1959).
Useful for anyone interested in reading Faulkner's own commentary on his fiction. He consistently refers to *The Sound and the Fury* as his favorite among his novels. He also comments on characters in the novel, particularly Quentin and Caddy.

Stephen Hahn and Arthur F. Kinney, eds., *Approaches to Teaching Faulkner's* The Sound and the Fury (New York: Modern Language Association, 1996).
A collection of articles applying a wide variety of critical theories to the novel. Intended for teachers, it includes a chapter, "Beginnings," focused on teaching (or reading) the novel for the first time, and a concluding chapter situating the novel as part of Faulkner's larger body of fiction.

John T. Irwin, *Doubling and Incest/Repetition and Revenge: A Speculative Reading of Faulkner* (Baltimore: Johns Hopkins University Press, 1975; revised, 1996).
A psychoanalytic reading of Faulkner's fiction, focusing largely on the character of Quentin Compson.

John T. Matthews, *The Play of Faulkner's Language* (Ithaca, N.Y.: Cornell University Press, 1982).
A deconstructive study of Faulkner's rhetoric that includes a close reading of *The Sound and the Fury*.

Matthews, The Sound and the Fury: *Faulkner and the Lost Cause* (Boston: Twayne, 1991).
An accessible study focusing largely on the novel's larger context in Southern history.

Michael Millgate, *The Achievement of William Faulkner* (New York: Random House, 1966).
An early overview of Faulkner's novels, primarily from a formalist theoretical approach.

Stephen M. Ross and Noel Polk, *Reading Faulkner:* The Sound and the Fury: *Glossary and Commentary,* Reading Faulkner Series (Jackson: University Press of Mississippi, 1996).
A line-by-line interpretation of the novel and commentary on key words, phrases, and longer passages.

Olga Vickery, *The Novels of William Faulkner: A Critical Interpretation* (Baton Rouge: Louisiana State University Press, 1959; revised, 1964).
An influential formalist study of Faulkner's fiction. The chapter on *The Sound and the Fury*, titled "Worlds in Counterpoint," focuses largely on how readers must, in effect, create their own version of the story from the four points of view offered in the novel. Vickery argues that a primary theme of the novel, as suggested by the structure of the work, is "the relation between the act and man's apprehension of the act, between the event and the interpretation."

Linda Wagner-Martin, ed., *William Faulkner: Six Decades of Criticism* (East Lansing: Michigan State University Press, 2002).

Divided into four parts, one of which focuses on "the Enduring Core" of Faulkner's works: *The Sound and the Fury* and *Absalom, Absalom!*

William Faulkner on the Web, edited by John B. Padgett <http://www.mcsr.olemiss.edu/~egjbp/faulkner/> [accessed 29 October 2009].

Among other resources, features a brief commentary on *The Sound and the Fury* and a partial glossary of characters in the novel.

—*John B. Padgett*

William Faulkner, *As I Lay Dying*

(New York: Cape & Smith, 1930)

Faulkner began writing *As I Lay Dying* on 25 October 1929 and completed the manuscript just forty-seven days later. He wrote much of the novel while working nights at the University of Mississippi power plant, where he supervised the feeding of coal into the boilers. Faulkner's comments about the writing of the novel have shaped some of the critical reaction to the work. In *Faulkner in the University* he remembers his attitude at the beginning: "I set out deliberately to write a tour-de-force. Before I ever put pen to paper and set down the first word I knew what the last word would be. . . . Before I began I said, I am going to write a book by which, at a pinch, I can stand or fall if I never touch ink again." The novel is often compared to *The Sound and the Fury* in regard to form: both are, essentially, stream-of-consciousness family stories centered on a single dominant female member of the family. *As I Lay Dying* differs from the earlier novel in at least two significant ways, however. First, the Bundrens are a poor farming family living on the outskirts of Yoknapatawpha County—a sharp contrast to the affluent and socially prominent Compsons of Jefferson. Second, *As I Lay Dying* is far less limited in the number of viewpoints from which the story is presented. Instead of just three first-person narrators, as in the earlier novel, *As I Lay Dying* is told via fifty-nine monologues, including at least one by every member of the Bundren family and eight additional speakers from outside the family who offer additional perspective and commentary on the story and the social milieu.

The novel focuses on the death and (eventual) burial of Addie Bundren, a former schoolteacher from Jefferson, the county seat, who married a poor farmer from the Frenchman's Bend section of the county, which is located some distance from Jefferson. As the novel opens, she is on her deathbed; the family is preparing, as best they can, for her funeral and burial in Jefferson, which, the reader discovers later, is to fulfill a promise her husband, Anse, made to her years earlier. The novel explores both the grief and the self-interest of each member of the family, sometimes in the same breath. Cash, the eldest son, is a carpenter and shows his love for his mother by building her coffin "on the bevel" right outside her window, where she can see and hear his efforts. Jewel, her third son—and, the reader learns, the product of an affair she had with a preacher—is forced to give up his beloved horse to allow their journey to continue. Dewey Dell, the fourth child and only daughter, finds her grief over her mother's death conflicted by her own unwanted pregnancy. And the youngest child, Vardaman, enacts his anger and grief first by blaming the doctor and later, in one of the shortest monologues in the book, by equating Addie with an enormous fish he had caught: "My mother is a fish."

The second son, Darl, is in some ways the most interesting character in the book. He has the most monologues, and he knows that Jewel was begotten by someone other than Anse and that Dewey Dell is pregnant; none of the other characters (except Addie and Dewey Dell, respectively) seem aware of these circumstances. More thoughtful and reserved than the other Bundrens and regarded by people outside the family as strange, Darl was denied Addie's love as a child and now seems intent on preventing her burial in Jefferson. In the end he pays a price for his differentness: he is committed by the family to the state asylum in Jackson.

The arduous journey to Jefferson and the threats of flood and fire along the way constitute the primary plot of the novel. Over the nine days in July it takes them to reach the cemetery in Jefferson, the surviving Bundrens must also deal with the ever-increasing smell of the decaying corpse and the outrage of those they encounter along the way. At the same time, the journey motif masks other self-interested reasons the Bundrens have to travel to Jefferson, ranging from the serious (Dewey Dell's wish for an abortion) to the comical (Anse's need for false teeth and a new wife) and the mundane (Cash's longing for a "graphophone" and Vardaman's wish to see a toy train and to taste bananas for the first time). The novel is noteworthy for its technical brilliance, its acute exploration of the individual psyches of its narrators, and its masterful blending of pathos and comedy.

TOPICS FOR DISCUSSION AND RESEARCH

1. One fruitful area of research for students has to do with the form in which the novel is written: fifty-nine monologues, varying in length from one sentence to several pages, by the seven members of the Bundren family and eight outside observers: neighbors Tull, Armstid, Cora, and Samson; acquaintances Whitfield and Peabody; and strangers Mosely and Macgowan. The fragmented nature of the narrative, which is told in stop-start fashion with some scenes either not narrated (most notably, the actual burial of Addie) or related in an oblique manner, and the use of stream of consciousness, which is employed varyingly in the monologues, are emblematic modernistic techniques. One area of inquiry might be to compare Faulkner's use of such techniques in this novel to his employment of them in other works or to another author's use of multiple perspectives and stream of consciousness. One might also examine how Faulkner's techniques shape content and meaning. How do the number and nature of the monologues by each of the narrators and their placement in what is essentially a straight chronological telling of the story affect plot and character?

How do each of the family members function in the story? Why do Jewel and Addie have only a single monologue? Why are Darl and Vardaman the characters with the most monologues? Peabody's statement about death being "a function of the mind" seems significant, especially since Addie's monologue, the fortieth in the book, appears after her death. How does her monologue, with its focus on the failure of language—"that words are no good; that words don't ever fit even what they are trying to say at"—relate to the larger story?

2. The title of the novel is taken from book 11 of Homer's *Odyssey,* where Agamemnon says to Odysseus, "As I lay dying the woman with the dog's eyes would not close my eyes for me as I descended into Hades." The connection of the novel to myth in general is worth exploration, as is its connection to archetypes such as the journey/quest motif or the "madman/poet" figure exemplified by Darl. Should such connections be considered ironic? For instance, is the journey a heroic or mock-heroic quest? Cleanth Brooks suggests that one principal theme of the novel may be "the nature of the heroic deed."

3. Another area of interest for readers has to do with the comic aspects of the novel, which include both the broad farce of the journey itself as well as the more nuanced humor arising from the characters, such as how Dewey Dell came to be pregnant by allowing Lafe to pick into her cotton sack and Cash's matter-of-fact list of reasons for making Addie's coffin "on the bevel." The character of Anse is particularly open to comic exploration, with his seeming shiftlessness, his ability to get others to do things for him, and the final victory in the novel, in which he marries the woman from whom he borrowed a shovel to bury Addie. Much of the humor is decidedly black, arising from injury and mayhem, such as the decision to set Cash's broken leg with cement and the various insults to Addie's corpse: the fire and flood from which her coffin is barely saved, the increasing odor from the body's decay, Vardaman's boring of holes into the coffin (and into her face) so that she can breathe. What do you find humorous in the novel? How does the humor affect the overall mood of the work as one of grief and despair over the death of Addie?

4. As a family drama, the novel offers several possibilities for research into the interrelationships among the Bundrens—especially Addie's relationships to the others. Her single monologue, situated between monologues by Cora and Whitfield, powerfully reveals the innate aloneness that marriage and motherhood have violated. Of equal interest for research are psychoanalytic inquiries into the minds of the Bundren family—the commingling of grief over the death of Addie and their individual self-interests in continuing the journey to Jefferson. Darl, in particular, because he was denied his mother's love, is an interesting topic for such inquiry—his descent into "pure consciousness" as a way to cope with his familial situation and his rivalry with Jewel, Addie's favorite child, are good openings for more complex psychological approaches to the novel. What makes Darl insane? Why does Addie deny him her love? How does Dewey Dell's own impending motherhood affect her?

5. Faulkner began writing *As I Lay Dying* the day after the 1929 stock-market crash, which marked the beginning of the Great Depression. The contrast of the impoverished Bundrens, a farming family, with the townsfolk they encounter

raises sociological questions about class. How important are attitudes about social class in the novel? Do they figure in the relationship between Anse and Addie, who, as a schoolteacher, married beneath her class when she "took Anse" as her husband? The name of the oldest child, Cash, suggests the main thing the Bundrens lack, while that of the youngest child, Vardaman, alludes to the "redneck" Mississippi politician James K. Vardaman, who, along with Governor Theodore Bilbo, represented populist, racist forces among whites in Mississippi at the time. What are the sociological, economic, and political forces that have kept the Bundrens poor for so long? What are their prospects for the future?

RESOURCES

Criticism

André Bleikasten, *The Ink of Melancholy: Faulkner's Novels, from* The Sound and the Fury *to* Light in August (Bloomington: Indiana University Press, 1990).
A multifaceted approach to Faulkner that examines *As I Lay Dying* as a "tour de force," focusing on modernistic and postmodernistic aspects of the form of the novel, on mythical and intertextual dimensions of the plot, and on psychoanalytic aspects of characters in the novel.

Cleanth Brooks, *William Faulkner: The Yoknapatawpha Country* (New Haven, Conn.: Yale University Press, 1963).
Includes a chapter on *As I Lay Dying* that focuses largely on the mythic elements in the novel, both straight and ironic, and examines how Faulkner achieves a mingling of "the grotesque and the heroic, the comic and the pathetic, pity and terror."

Michael Millgate, *The Achievement of William Faulkner* (New York: Random House, 1966).
Includes a chapter on *As I Lay Dying* that points out formal similarities to *The Sound and the Fury* and discusses the novel as a tour de force in terms of its technical brilliance in language and in the variety of perspectives, none of them "authorial," offered by the fifteen narrators.

Daniel J. Singal, *William Faulkner: The Making of a Modernist* (Chapel Hill: University of North Carolina Press, 1997).
Includes a chapter on *As I Lay Dying* that examines how Faulkner uses Modernist techniques, motifs, and themes.

Eric J. Sundquist, *Faulkner: The House Divided* (Baltimore: Johns Hopkins University Press, 1983).
Includes a chapter on *As I Lay Dying* that focuses largely on the conjunction of form and technique in the novel, particularly as they relate to the power of words to communicate meaning.

Olga Vickery, *The Novels of William Faulkner: A Critical Interpretation* (Baton Rouge: Louisiana State University Press, 1959; revised, 1964).

Includes "The Dimensions of Consciousness," which indicates some of the similarities between *As I Lay Dying* and *The Sound and the Fury*—particularly in the creation of "private worlds," each of which "manifests a fixed and distinctive way of reacting to and ordering experience." The chapter treats each of the fifteen narrators in turn, focusing on the degree to which each character is able to encompass "words, action, and contemplation"—what Vickery refers to as "the possible modes of response" to experience—as well as "sensation, reason, and intuition," which constitute "the levels of consciousness."

Warwick Wadlington, As I Lay Dying: *Stories out of Stories* (New York: Twayne, 1992).
Examines the social milieu in which the novel is set and critics' perceptions of the novel. A chief concern is for the sociology and culture depicted in the novel: what is meant by "family," why the Bundrens' journey is such an "outrage" to the community, and how the "master cultural story" of economics influences the actions and events in the novel.

—John B. Padgett

F. Scott Fitzgerald, *The Great Gatsby*
(New York: Scribners, 1925)

In the early 1920s F. Scott Fitzgerald (1896–1940) and his young wife, Zelda Sayre Fitzgerald, became the symbolic couple of the period to which Fitzgerald gave a name in his second story collection, *Tales of the Jazz Age* (1922). Married to Sayre a week and a day after the publication of his first novel, *This Side of Paradise* (1920), Fitzgerald seemed to live his life in public: his second novel, *The Beautiful and Damned* (1922), is about the improvident life that wrecks a young married couple; two years later, he detailed how he and Zelda managed to squander his hard-earned money in the humorous essay "How to Live on $36,000 a Year"—not "yacht-and-Palm-Beach wealthy," as Fitzgerald asserted, but a staggering sum nonetheless at a time when most Americans made less than $2,000 per annum. Before and after the publication of his third novel, *The Great Gatsby* (1925), Fitzgerald was more widely known for his entertaining stories in *The Saturday Evening Post* and as a celebrity spokesman for the young generation than he was as a novelist. His public persona, almost entirely of his own making, obscured the deeper truth that Fitzgerald was a professional writer, as well as a serious literary artist.

In 1937 Fitzgerald looked back in his essay "Early Success" on the beginning of his career—the period just after he had learned that his first novel was to be published: "While I waited for the novel to appear, the metamorphosis of amateur into professional began to take place—a sort of stitching together of your whole life into a pattern of work, so that the end of one job is automatically the beginning of another." In the 1933 essay "One Hundred False Starts" he described his approach to fiction:

Mostly, we authors repeat ourselves—that's the truth. We have two or three great and moving experiences in our lives—experiences so great and so moving that it doesn't seem at the time that anyone else has been so caught up and pounded and dazzled and astonished and beaten and broken and rescued and illuminated and rewarded and humbled in just that way ever before.

Then we learn our trade, well or less well, and we tell our two or three stories—each time in a new disguise—maybe ten times, maybe a hundred, as long as people will listen.

Fitzgerald drew on his emotional experience but did not write autobiography. At his best he wrote with an awareness of history and his cultural moment, transmuting and combining his deepest feelings with social observations and psychological insights to create enduring fiction. In a literary career of twenty years he published some 160 short stories and four novels, including the masterpieces *The Great Gatsby* and *Tender Is the Night* (1934). A fifth promising novel, *The Last Tycoon* (1941), was unfinished when he died of a heart attack on 21 December 1940.

Born on 24 September 1896 in St. Paul, Minnesota, Francis Scott Key Fitzgerald was the son of Mollie McQuillian Fitzgerald, whose enterprising Irish immigrant father had made her family's fortune in the city as a grocery wholesaler, and Edward Fitzgerald, a descendant of distinguished families in Maryland, who did not succeed in any of the business ventures he attempted. Fitzgerald's ambition to write began early, and his first publication, "The Mystery of The Raymond Mortgage," appeared in *St. Paul Academy Now & Then* when he was thirteen. In 1913 he entered the socially stratified world of Princeton University, where he neglected his studies but read widely, wrote for school publications, and worked on musical comedies for the Triangle Club. He startled his friend, fellow Princetonian Edmund Wilson, with his bluff declaration and question, "I want to be one of the greatest writers who ever lived, don't you?" In his sophomore year, during a Christmas vacation in St. Paul, he met and began an epistolary romance with Ginevra King, a wealthy Chicago debutante, whose ultimate rejection of him became part of the emotional underpinning for *The Great Gatsby*. Fifteen years after writing the novel he listed "Memory of Ginevra's Wedding" as the inspiration for Daisy and Tom Buchanan's marriage in chapter four.

In October 1917, his junior year at Princeton, Fitzgerald left the university to enter the army as a second lieutenant. He began his first novel, "The Romantic Egoist," while he was stationed at Fort Leavenworth, Kansas, and submitted it to Scribners in February 1918. Although the novel was rejected in August, an editor—probably Maxwell Perkins—sent an accompanying letter suggesting that Fitzgerald revise and resubmit the work. While posted at Camp Sheridan, near Montgomery, Alabama, Fitzgerald met Zelda Sayre at a country club dance. World War I ended before Fitzgerald was shipped overseas—a circumstance he always regretted. He and Zelda were engaged in 1919, but she broke off the engagement when it appeared that his prospects for supporting her were dim. Returning to St. Paul, Fitzgerald rewrote "The Romantic Egoist"—the story of young Amory Blaine's quest to know himself—retitled it *This Side of Paradise,* and submitted it to Scribners in August 1919. In the next few months he experienced as dramatic a change in fortune as any that he ever described in his fiction: the novel was accepted; his stories began to sell; and he and Zelda resumed their engagement. No longer "Mr. Nobody from Nowhere" (as Tom Buchanan calls Gatsby), Fitzgerald had achieved his dreams of success by April 1920. At twenty-three he had a beautiful wife and had established himself as an author with a bright future.

The next five years were filled with experiences that were meaningful for Fitzgerald's later novels. On 26 October 1921 Zelda gave birth to a daughter, Scottie, the couple's only child. From October 1922 to April 1924 the Fitzgeralds rented a house in Great Neck, Long Island; the lively social scene there found its way into Fitzgerald's third novel. During this period he became friends with the writer Ring Lardner, later a model for Abe North in *Tender Is the Night,* and grew more dependent on alcohol. He gathered material that fed directly into his work on *The Great Gatsby:* he met Max Gerlach, a reputed bootlegger who used the expression "old Sport"; heard the story of Robert Kerr, a Great Neck friend whose experience with a yachtsman inspired the relationship in the novel between Jimmy Gatz/Jay Gatsby and Dan Cody; and became acquainted with the gambler Arnold Rothstein, the model for Meyer Wolfshiem. After leaving Long Island, where Fitzgerald had begun working on his novel, the family settled on the French Riviera. There Zelda had a flirtation—perhaps an affair—with a French aviator, Edouard Jozan. The couple also became close friends with Gerald and Sara Murphy, an expatriate couple who were important to the composition of *Tender Is the Night.*

In April 1924 Fitzgerald had written to Perkins, "in my new novel I'm thrown directly on purely creative work—not trashy imaginings as in my stories but the sustained imagination of a sincere and yet radiant world. . . . This book will be a consciously artistic achievement + must depend on that as the 1st books did not." In writing *The Great Gatsby* Fitzgerald showed astonishing progress as an artist: he had given *This Side of Paradise* an episodic, picaresque structure because it could contain his varied autobiographical material; the pieced-together nature of the book was so apparent that one reviewer dubbed it "the collected works of F. Scott Fitzgerald published in novel form." *The Great Gatsby* marks his maturation as a novelist—a master of form, as well as of style. In a letter to Fitzgerald, the poet T. S. Eliot asserted that "it seems to me to be the first step American fiction has taken since Henry James."

TOPICS FOR DISCUSSION AND RESEARCH

1. In writing *The Great Gatsby* Fitzgerald drew on his knowledge of contemporary culture, from stories in the news to the lyrics of popular songs. Readers interested in the background of the novel should consult *F. Scott Fitzgerald's* The Great Gatsby: *A Documentary Volume* (2000). The editor, Matthew J. Bruccoli, writes: "The more the reader knows about the author's intentions and material, the better the reader responds to the work." Do you agree? How does reading about the Fuller-McGee case, looking at the covers of the sheet music of the popular songs mentioned, or seeing pictures of the possible models for Gatsby's mansion affect your view of the novel?

2. Several of Fitzgerald's stories of the early 1920s—the so-called *Gatsby* cluster stories—were clearly connected to the novel, including "Winter Dreams" (1922), which Fitzgerald described as a "sort of 1st draft of the Gatsby idea"; "Absolution" (1924), originally written as the prologue to an early version of the novel; and "'The Sensible Thing'" (1924), in which a man tries to recapture the love of a woman who broke off their engagement. In each story Fitzgerald explores ideas and/or situations that are also treated in the novel. What connections do you see between each of these stories and the novel? What do the protagonists of the stories—Dexter Green, Rudolph Miller, and George O'Kelly, respectively—share with Jay Gatsby?

3. Fitzgerald was a saver, and as a result of this trait the student of his work has an extraordinary opportunity to "peer over his shoulder" during the creation of a masterpiece. Three versions of the novel exist at progressive stages of composition before its publication: (1) The earliest version is preserved in Bruccoli's The Great Gatsby: *A Facsimile of the Manuscript* (1973), which Fitzgerald revised through successive typescripts, probably many times, before sending it to Scribners. (2) Fitzgerald's final typescript, now lost, was set in type by the publisher and returned to the author as galley proofs for further revision; the proofs have been published as *Trimalchio: An Early Version of* The Great Gatsby (2000). (3) Finally, Fitzgerald's work on the proofs, in which he rearranged portions of the novel and returned to his original title, has been preserved and published as The Great Gatsby: *The Revised and Rewritten Galleys* (1990). Close study of these stages of composition can yield many insights into Fitzgerald's creative process, as particular passages can be traced from one version to the next. The reader might, for example, follow Nick's meditation on the "fresh, green breast of the new world" from its first appearance at the end of the first chapter in the manuscript through its revision and final placement at the end of the published novel. Another good approach would be a holistic comparison of one of the early drafts to another or to the final text. How does Fitzgerald's presentation of Gatsby, Nick, Daisy, or Tom change?

4. One of the most intriguing comments in Fitzgerald's correspondence with Maxwell Perkins during the composition of *The Great Gatsby* is his plea in a late August 1924 letter: "For Christ's sake don't give anyone that jacket you're saving for me. I've written it into the book." In his essay "Celestial Eyes—From Metamorphosis to Masterpiece," published in the *Princeton University Library Chronicle* (Winter 1992), Charles Scribner III observes: "Under normal circumstances, the artist illustrates a scene or motif conceived by the author; he lifts, as it were, his image from a page of the book. In this instance, however, the artist's image *preceded* the finished manuscript and Fitzgerald actually maintained that he had 'written it into' his book." Scribner's essay investigating the meaning of Fitzgerald's remark, along with the series of Francis Cugat's preliminary sketches and colorful final painting for the dust jacket, can be accessed through the F. Scott Fitzgerald Centenary website (<http://www.sc.edu/fitzgerald/essays/eyes/eyes.html>). What thematic connections do you see between Cugat's jacket and the novel?

5. In a May 1925 letter to Edmund Wilson, written after he had read the reviews of *The Great Gatsby*, Fitzgerald commented on what he thought was the critical weakness of his novel: "The worst fault in it, I think is a Big Fault: I gave no account (and had no feeling about or knowledge of) the emotional relations between Gatsby and Daisy from the time of their reunion to the catastrophe. However the lack is so astutely concealed by the retrospect of Gatsby's past and by blankets of excellent prose that no one has noticed it—tho everyone has felt the lack and called it by another name." Do you agree with Fitzgerald's assessment? How would you characterize the couple's feelings for each other during their brief time together? Can you trace the evolution of the relationship between the former lovers?

6. During the writing of the novel that became *The Great Gatsby* Fitzgerald considered many possible titles, including "Among Ash Heaps and Millionaires," "Trimalchio," "Trimalchio in West Egg," "On the Road to West Egg," "Gold-Hatted Gatsby," "The High-Bouncing Lover," and "Gatsby." On 19 March 1925, just three weeks and one day before publication, Fitzgerald cabled Perkins from Capri: "CRAZY ABOUT TITLE UNDER THE RED WHITE AND BLUE STOP WHART [*sic*] WOULD DELAY BE." While Scribners did not act on this last requested change, the proposed title points to a theme that has interested critics of the novel ever since: Fitzgerald had written a story that in some essential way(s) is about living in America. What does Fitzgerald's novel say about American society or the so-called American dream? If you take the American dream to signify the pursuit of happiness, what is it that the novel suggests would make Gatsby happy? What is the true desire of each of the important characters—Jay Gatsby, Nick Carraway, Daisy Fay Buchanan, Tom Buchanan, and Jordan Baker? An interesting perspective on some of these questions is provided by Azar Nafisi, who recounts her experience of teaching *The Great Gatsby* in a culture—Iran after the overthrow of the shah—that viewed the United States with hostility.

7. Fitzgerald's most famous novel has inspired voluminous and wide-ranging analyses. In *"The Great Gatsby*: A Survey of Scholarship" (2009) Jackson R. Bryer suggests good starting points for interpretations of the novel as a criticism of the American success myth; for examinations of the connections between Fitzgerald's novel and other texts, most notably Eliot's *The Waste Land* (1922); for studies of his characters, especially Nick's role as narrator; and for analyses of the motifs and symbol patterns of the novel. In her *Critical Theory Today* (1998) Lois Tyson uses *The Great Gatsby* as the illustrative text to demonstrate how ten different theories might be applied to the same work. She chose Fitzgerald's novel because it "lends itself well" to each of the approaches she discusses, though she goes on to assert that "most works lend themselves more readily to some frameworks than to others." A good way to generate ideas and insights is to compare several approaches to the novel—either essays that Bryer suggests or some of Tyson's analyses. Is there a particular approach to which the novel best lends itself? If so, why?

RESOURCES

Primary Works

The Great Gatsby: *A Facsimile of the Manuscript*, edited by Matthew J. Bruccoli (Washington: Bruccoli Clark/NCR, 1973).
Reproduction of the last draft preceding Fitzgerald's work with successive typescripts, consisting of two or more conflated layers of manuscript.

The Great Gatsby: *The Revised and Rewritten Galleys*, edited by Bruccoli, F. Scott Fitzgerald Manuscripts, no. 3 (New York: Garland, 1990).
Shows the important stylistic and structural revisions that the editor contends made the novel a masterpiece.

Trimalchio: An Early Version of The Great Gatsby, edited by James L. West III (Cambridge, England: Cambridge University Press, 2000).
Includes a comment by the editor in which he compares reading this early complete version of the novel to "listening to a well known musical composition, but played in a different key and with an alternate bridge passage."

The Short Stories of F. Scott Fitzgerald: A New Collection, edited by Bruccoli (New York: Scribners, 1989).
The key stories in which Fitzgerald experimented with ideas and situations for *The Great Gatsby* and *Tender Is the Night*. The collection includes a valuable introduction and instructive headnotes.

Biography

Matthew J. Bruccoli, *Some Sort of Epic Grandeur: The Life of F. Scott Fitzgerald*, second revised edition (Columbia: University of South Carolina Press, 2002).
The most comprehensive and fact-filled biography, indispensable for the study of Fitzgerald's professional and artistic development.

Bruccoli, Scottie Fitzgerald Smith, and Joan P. Kerr, eds., *The Romantic Egoists: A Pictorial Autobiography from the Scrapbooks and Albums of F. Scott and Zelda Fitzgerald* (New York: Scribners, 1974).
An artful collection that draws from seven scrapbooks and five photograph albums and integrates comments from Fitzgerald's self-evaluating ledger. The editors include the Fitzgeralds' only child.

F. Scott Fitzgerald: A Life in Letters, edited by Bruccoli (New York: Touchstone/Simon & Schuster, 1995).
The best collection of Fitzgerald's correspondence.

Bibliography

Matthew J. Bruccoli, *F. Scott Fitzgerald: A Descriptive Bibliography*, revised edition (Pittsburgh: University of Pittsburgh Press, 1987).
A primary bibliography that provides much useful information on the publication of all of Fitzgerald's works.

Jackson R. Bryer, "The Great Gatsby: A Survey of Scholarship and Criticism,"
in *Approaches to Teaching Fitzgerald's* The Great Gatsby, edited by Bryer and
Nancy P. VanArsdale (New York: Modern Language Association of America,
2009), pp. 3–15.
An admirable attempt to organize "the literally hundreds of essays and book sections" treating the novel.

Criticism

Matthew J. Bruccoli, ed., *Dictionary of Literary Biography*, volume 219: *F. Scott
Fitzgerald's* The Great Gatsby: *A Documentary Volume* (Detroit: Bruccoli
Clark Layman/The Gale Group, 2000); republished as *F. Scott Fitzgerald's*
The Great Gatsby: *A Literary Reference* (New York: Carroll & Graf, 2002).
A valuable "biography" of the novel, divided into sections on its background, writ-
ing, reception, and reputation. Copiously illustrated, the book includes selected
scholarly articles and criticism and covers the Fitzgerald revival as well as movie
treatments of the novel.

Bruccoli, ed., *New Essays on* The Great Gatsby (Cambridge, England: Cambridge
University Press, 1985).
A collection of five excellent pieces, including George Garrett's acute "Fire and
Freshness: A Matter of Style in *The Great Gatsby.*"

Jackson R. Bryer, ed., *F. Scott Fitzgerald: The Critical Reception* (New York: Franklin, 1978).
Provides contemporary reviews of all of Fitzgerald's major works, with a general
introduction.

Andrew T. Crosland and F. Scott Fitzgerald, *A Concordance to F. Scott Fitzgerald's*
The Great Gatsby (Detroit: Gale Research, 1975).
A useful resource for studying motifs, imagery, and style.

Scott Donaldson, ed., *Critical Essays on F. Scott Fitzgerald's* The Great Gatsby
(Boston: G. K. Hall, 1984).
Selected essays from the 1970s and 1980s, divided into four sections—"Overviews,"
"The Artist at Work," "Fresh Approaches," and "History-Myth-Making"—along
with correspondence about the novel.

The F. Scott Fitzgerald Centenary <http://www.sc.edu/fitzgerald/index.html>
[accessed 10 November 2009].
A website maintained by the University of South Carolina that provides access
to a wealth of material on Fitzgerald and his works, including images of personal
items such as the author's silver hip flask.

Roger Lathbury, *Literary Masterpieces: The Great Gatsby* (Detroit: Manly/Gale
Group, 2000).
A good introductory reference that clearly explains the evolution and themes of
the novel, while also presenting important critical responses to it and providing
useful contexts for understanding its significance.

Azar Nafisi, "Gatsby," in her *Reading Lolita in Tehran: A Memoir in Books* (New York: Random House, 2003), pp. 81–153.
A description of Nafisi's experience teaching *The Great Gatsby* at the University of Tehran during the early days of the Islamic Revolution in 1979. Her students held a mock trial: "the case of the Islamic Republic of Iran versus *The Great Gatsby.*"

Mary Jo Tate, *F. Scott Fitzgerald A to Z: The Essential Reference to His Life and Work* (New York: Facts on File, 1998).
Covers Fitzgerald's entire career, with detailed entries on all of his novels, stories, and characters.

Lois Tyson, *Critical Theory Today: A User-Friendly Guide* (New York: Garland, 1998).
A readable book aimed at introducing different critical theories. To illustrate how the theories work, Tyson offers a fully developed interpretation of *The Great Gatsby* from ten approaches: Psychoanalytic; Marxist; Feminist; New Critical; Reader-Response; Structuralist; Deconstructionist; New Historicist and Cultural; Lesbian, Gay, and Queer; and Postcolonial and African American.

—George Parker Anderson

F. Scott Fitzgerald, *Tender Is the Night*
(New York: Scribners, 1934)

The effect of the European expatriate experience on Americans is a major theme in *Tender Is the Night* (1934), F. Scott Fitzgerald's richest and most powerful novel. The Fitzgeralds, who had spent a couple of months in Europe in 1921, returned to the Continent in April 1924 so that Fitzgerald could finish work on *The Great Gatsby*. They remained in Europe, mostly in France, for two and a half years. During this period Fitzgerald did complete *The Great Gatsby*, the novel that many consider his masterpiece. He also began friendships with Ernest Hemingway and with Gerald and Sara Murphy, the charming couple who served as partial models for Dick and Nicole Diver in *Tender Is the Night*. But Fitzgerald wasted much of his time and energy in extravagance and dissipation. The Fitzgeralds' marriage was strained as the result of Zelda's romantic involvement with a French aviator and Scott's increased indulgence in alcohol. In October 1924 Fitzgerald was beaten by police in Rome, an incident that he wrote about in the earliest draft of his new novel; it ultimately became Dick Diver's experience in the concluding chapters of Book 2 of *Tender Is the Night*, signaling Diver's accelerated deterioration. As the years passed, and Fitzgerald's struggles with his novel continued—he worked on two other plots before settling on the Divers' story—Europe became entwined in his mind with his fear of his own deterioration.

When he began work on the novel that became *Tender Is the Night*, Fitzgerald was brimming with confidence and determined that it would establish him as the leading writer of his generation. He boasted in a 1 May 1925 letter to his editor at Scribners, Maxwell Perkins, three weeks after the publication of *The Great Gatsby*, that it would be "something really NEW in form, idea, structure—the model for the age that Joyce and Stien [sic] are searching for, that Conrad didn't find." As conceived in the summer of 1925 the novel was the story of Francis Melarky, a talented twenty-one-year-old Southerner with a violent temper who is reluctantly traveling with his mother in Europe. Inspired in part by a news story about Dorothy Ellingson, a sixteen-year-old San Francisco girl who had killed her mother in an argument over the daughter's wild life, Fitzgerald intended matricide to be a key element of his novel. A comic ballad that he wrote and recited for friends at the time includes the lines:

> Just a boy that killed his mother
> I was always up to tricks
> When she taunted me I shot her
> Through her chronic appendix.

Most of the author's work on the Melarky version of the novel was done from the fall of 1925 through December 1926, during which he made substantial progress on four chapters: Melarky is beaten by police in Rome; he and his mother arrive on the French Riviera, where he meets a charming couple, Seth and Dinah (the prototypes for the Divers), and an alcoholic composer modeled on Fitzgerald's friend Ring Lardner; he attends a congenial dinner party given by Seth and Dinah; and he travels with the couple to Paris, where he kisses Dinah in a taxi. Although Fitzgerald sporadically returned to this material until 1932, revising and rearranging chapters, no evidence exists to suggest that he proceeded further with the action.

The Fitzgeralds returned to America at the end of 1926. In January 1927 they traveled to Hollywood, where Scott worked on an unproduced screenplay and met the actress Lois Moran, the model for the Rosemary Hoyt character and the subject of an intense marital quarrel. That year Fitzgerald was busy writing and publishing stories for money, including "Jacob's Ladder," the ghost story "A Short Trip Home," and "Magnetism"—all of which he later "stripped" (his word for taking a phrase or passage from a story and incorporating it into a novel) for *Tender Is the Night*. The Fitzgeralds returned to Europe in April 1928, remaining until September, and in March of the following year they began their fourth and final sojourn on the Continent. Fitzgerald's story "The Rough Crossing" (1929), about a playwright's infatuation with a young admirer that sparks a marital row on a transatlantic voyage, anticipated a new approach to his novel.

In July 1929 Fitzgerald wrote to Perkins, "I am working night + day on novel from a new angle that I think will solve previous difficulties." Temporarily abandoning the Melarky material, he wrote two chapters set aboard a ship crossing to Europe. The main characters in the fragment are Lew Kelly, a movie director; his wife, Nicole; and Rosemary, an aspiring actress who is accompanied by her mother—a triangle that features the first names of the leading female characters in *Tender Is the Night*. Fitzgerald abandoned the Kelly version, however, and what work he could do on his novel during the next three years was on the Melarky version.

The event that eventually turned Fitzgerald to the Diver plot was Zelda's mental breakdown in April 1930, which was followed by a diagnosis of schizophrenia and treatment in Switzerland—principally at Les Rives de Prangins clinic in Nyon from June 1930 to September 1931; the institution served as the model for the clinic that Dick Diver and Franz Gregorovious run in *Tender Is the Night*. To pay Zelda's medical bills Fitzgerald continued to write stories, including "One Trip Abroad" (1930), about a young American couple who lose their love and promising future in Europe; it culminates in Switzerland, "a country where very few things begin, but many things end." Fitzgerald was also deeply affected by the death of his father; he made the trip home alone in January 1931 to attend the burial, just as Dick Diver does on news of his own father's death.

Returning to America in 1932, Fitzgerald planned a new version of his novel, beginning with a character sketch of his protagonist:

> The novel should do this. Show a man who is a natural idealist, a spoiled priest, giving in for various causes to the ideas of the haute Burgeoise [*sic*], and in his rise to the top of the social world losing his idealism, his talent and turning to drink and dissipation. Background one in which the leisure class is at their truly most brilliant + glamorous such as Murphys.

As the frustrating years passed, the story of a young man who killed his mother must have become increasingly remote to a writer who was trying to cope with a disintegrating marriage, his own alcoholism, and his wife's mental illness. Only when Fitzgerald turned to the Diver version, a story much closer to the events of his own life, did he achieve control of his material and technique.

TOPICS FOR DISCUSSION AND RESEARCH

1. As is the case with *The Great Gatsby*, the student of *Tender Is the Night* with access to the F. Scott Fitzgerald Manuscripts series of volumes has the opportunity to follow Fitzgerald through his long and fascinating composition process. One of the most interesting aspects of that process is how Fitzgerald repackaged his emotional experience as he abandoned the Francis Melarky and Lew Kelly drafts, salvaging material for the Dick Diver version. Some of Melarky's experiences were used for the young actress, while others were given to the character who became Dick Diver. Is it odd that Fitzgerald is able to shift experiences between characters who are quite different from one another? Do the experiences work better in the original situations, or are they just as convincing in the new context? The student interested in learning more about the composition of the novel should consult Matthew J. Bruccoli's *The Composition of* Tender Is the Night (1963) or Bruccoli and George Parker Anderson's *F. Scott Fitzgerald's* Tender Is the Night: *A Documentary Volume* (2003).

2. Between *The Great Gatsby* and *Tender Is the Night* Fitzgerald published fifty-five short stories, many of which played a role—sometimes minor, sometimes quite important—in the development of the latter novel. In stories such as "One Trip Abroad," "The Swimmers" (1920), "Babylon Revisited" (1931), and "The Hotel Child" (1931) he assesses the effect of the expatriate

experience on Americans. In "Two Wrongs" (1930) and "What a Handsome Pair!" (1932) he explores marital discord; in "Jacob's Ladder" (1927) he writes about an older man's infatuation with a young actress, and in "A New Leaf" (1931) he examines how an alcoholic acts in a relationship. Much more so than he did when he was working on *The Great Gatsby*, Fitzgerald explored ideas and/or situations in his stories that he later treated in the novel. Exploring the connections between *Tender Is the Night* and its so-called cluster stories can open new perspectives on the novel. Students might want to read the essays on cluster stories in *New Essays on F. Scott Fitzgerald's Neglected Stories* (1996). Bruccoli and Anderson's *F. Scott Fitzgerald's* Tender Is the Night: *A Documentary Volume* explores links between the stories and the Melarky and Kelly versions, as well as between the stories and the published novel.

3. Fitzgerald took his title from a line in John Keats's poem "Ode to a Nightingale." You can listen to a recording of Fitzgerald reading the first portion of the poem at the F. Scott Fitzgerald Centenary website, <http://www.sc.edu/fitzgerald/voice.html>. What connections can you draw between Keats's poem and the novel? Do you think it is an appropriate title for the novel? William E. Doherty addresses this question in an essay that is included in the collections edited by Marvin J. Lahood (1969) and Milton R. Stern (1986), as well as in *F. Scott Fitzgerald's* Tender Is the Night: *A Documentary Volume*.

4. In a 28 May 1934 letter to Fitzgerald, Hemingway criticized the characters in *Tender Is the Night:* "Goddamn it you took liberties with peoples pasts and futures that produced not people but damned marvelously faked case histories." Another writer friend, John O'Hara, was also critical of Fitzgerald's method. In a 30 July 1962 letter to Gerald Murphy, O'Hara wrote that Fitzgerald "as he moved along, got farther away from any resemblance to the real Murphys. Dick Diver ended up as a tall Fitzgerald." Nevertheless, O'Hara believed that Fitzgerald succeeded despite his failure to capture Murphy in Dick Diver: "I'm sure Scott's dissatisfaction with TITN was due to his failure to present the Murphys, but he got his novel anyhow." Is Dick Diver convincing as a character, and is his deterioration credible? Students may find it helpful to consult Bruccoli and Judith S. Baughman's *The Reader's Companion to F. Scott Fitzgerald's* Tender Is the Night (1996), which includes a chronology of events in the novel and a note on its time scheme.

5. In "Fitzgerald's Brave New World," included in Stern's collection, critic Edwin Fussell compares *Tender Is the Night* to *The Great Gatsby*: "Although the pattern is more complex than in *Gatsby*, practically the same controlling lines of theme can be observed. The man of imagination, fed on the emotions of romantic wonder, is tempted and seduced and (in this case, nearly) destroyed by that American dream which customarily takes two forms: the escape from time and materialistic pursuit of a purely hedonistic happiness. . . . Thematically the lines come together when Nicole attempts to own Dick and therefore to escape time—keeping him clear of it, too—as when Gatsby tries to buy back the past." Do you agree with Fussell's comparison? How do you view Nicole's role in the novel? Is she as responsible for Dick's destruction as Daisy is for Gatsby's?

6. Fitzgerald was disappointed with the reception of *Tender Is the Night* and came to believe that he was wrong to begin the novel with Rosemary Hoyt's view of the Divers. "Its great fault," he wrote Perkins in 1938, "is that the true beginning—the young psychiatrist in Switzerland—is tucked away in the middle of the book. If pages 151–212 were taken from their present place and put at the start the improvement in appeal would be enormous." Fitzgerald had actually begun work on such a revision by reordering a copy of the novel, writing on the inside front cover, "This is the final version of the book as I would like it." Malcolm Cowley edited this revised version in 1951, but the original 1934 flashback version is the one that has been republished most often. Read Cowley's introduction to the revised edition, which is reprinted in Stern's *Critical Essays on Fitzgerald's* Tender Is the Night, and consider his argument. Stern and Bruccoli disagree over the issue of the two editions of *Tender Is the Night* in essays included in the section of Stern's collection titled "The Text Itself." Do you agree with Cowley's decision to seek publication for Fitzgerald's partially revised personal copy of his novel?

RESOURCES

Primary Works

Tender Is the Night: *The Melarky and Kelly Versions,* 2 volumes, edited by Matthew J. Bruccoli, F. Scott Fitzgerald Manuscripts, no. 4a (New York: Garland, 1990).
Manuscript and typescript drafts for the third-person-narrated Francis Melarky version and the Francis Melarky-narrated version, as well as a manuscript for the Lew Kelly version.

Tender Is the Night: *The Diver Version,* 5 volumes, edited by Bruccoli, F. Scott Fitzgerald Manuscripts, no. 4b (New York: Garland, 1990).
The manuscript draft and two typescripts for the Diver version, as well as the setting copy for the serial; revised serial galleys and inserts; and revised book galleys. Fitzgerald incorporated and revised material conceived for the Francis Melarky and Lew Kelly versions into the Diver version.

Tender Is the Night, "With the Author's Final Revisions," edited by Malcolm Cowley (New York: Scribners, 1951).
Presents the novel in straight chronological fashion. The reorganized novel is divided into five sections according to a plan Fitzgerald had laid out: 1. Case History; 2. Rosemary's Angle; 3. Casualties; 4. Escape; and 5. The Way Home.

Biography

Matthew J. Bruccoli, *Scott and Ernest: The Authority of Failure and the Authority of Success* (New York: Random House, 1978); revised as *Fitzgerald and Hemingway: A Dangerous Friendship* (New York: Carroll & Graf, 1994).

Focuses on Fitzgerald's most important literary relationship during the time he was working on *Tender Is the Night.*

Criticism

William Blazek and Laura Rattray, *Twenty-First-Century Readings of* Tender Is the Night (Liverpool, U.K.: Liverpool University Press, 2007).
Presents twelve varied essays reassessing Fitzgerald's novel. The pieces focus on literary, historical, and social contexts, as well as on questions of narrative design, strategy, and method.

Matthew J. Bruccoli, *The Composition of* Tender Is the Night (Pittsburgh: University of Pittsburgh Press, 1963).
Analyzes the manuscripts and typescripts Fitzgerald saved from his work on his novel, identifying seventeen drafts of the Francis Melarky, Lew Kelly, and Dick Diver versions. The volume also includes a chapter on the reception and reputation of the novel.

Bruccoli and George Parker Anderson, eds., *Dictionary of Literary Biography,* volume 273: *F. Scott Fitzgerald's* Tender Is the Night: *A Documentary Volume* (Detroit: Bruccoli Clark Layman/Thompson Gale, 2003).
Includes full, well-illustrated sections on the background, writing, publication, reception, and reputation of *Tender Is the Night.* The volume also provides a useful bibliography of works about the novel.

Bruccoli and Judith S. Baughman, eds., *The Reader's Companion to F. Scott Fitzgerald's* Tender Is the Night (Columbia: University of South Carolina Press, 1996).
A valuable aide to reading and appreciating the novel, with one hundred pages of explanatory notes; chapters on the time scheme and chronology; and reproductions of Fitzgerald's plans for the Diver version.

Jackson R. Bryer, ed., *New Essays on F. Scott Fitzgerald's Neglected Stories* (Columbia: University of Missouri Press, 1996).
Includes essays that examine the connections of "One Trip Abroad," "Jacob's Ladder," and "The Swimmers" to *Tender Is the Night.*

Gerald J. Kennedy and Jackson R. Bryer, eds., *French Connections: Hemingway and Fitzgerald Abroad* (New York: St. Martin's Press, 1999).
Explores the influence of Fitzgerald and Hemingway on each other; includes six essays focusing on *Tender Is the Night.*

Marvin J. LaHood, ed., Tender Is the Night: *Essays in Criticism* (Bloomington: Indiana University Press, 1969).
The first collection of essays on *Tender Is the Night.* This volume appeared when the novel was beginning to gain traction with critics. In addition to essays focused on the novel, it includes several general assessments of Fitzgerald's work in which *Tender Is the Night* is discussed.

Milton R. Stern, ed., *Critical Essays on* Tender Is the Night (Boston: G. K. Hall, 1986).

Includes reviews and critical essays from the 1940s to the 1980s. In his introduction Stern asserts that the "central subject of *Tender Is the Night* is the moral history of the western world just before and after World War One, and most especially it is the continuing history of the American Dream."

—*George Parker Anderson*

Robert Frost, *North of Boston*

(London: David Nutt, 1914; New York: Holt, 1915)

While most people associate Robert Frost (1874–1963) with the landscape and people of twentieth-century New England, he was born in San Francisco less than ten years after the end of the Civil War. After the death of his father in 1885, Frost's mother moved the family to New Hampshire and then Massachusetts, where Frost attended high school with his future wife, Elinor Miriam White. He attended Dartmouth College for one term and Harvard University for two years; but, preferring a regimen of independent reading and needing to support his growing family, he took on odd jobs (including teacher, factory worker, cobbler, and, like his father before him, newspaperman) before settling down as a poultryman and farmer in Derry, New Hampshire. In Derry, Frost began writing many of the poems that made up his first three collections—*A Boy's Will* (1913), *North of Boston* (1914), and *Mountain Interval* (1916)—and for which he became famous.

Although Frost lived in England from 1912 to 1915 and later made temporary homes in Michigan and Florida, most of his life was spent in the countryside of New England. There he wrote his poems, raised his family (he and Elinor had six children, two of whom died in infancy), and taught at various institutions, including Amherst College and Dartmouth College. He published six more books of poetry—*New Hampshire* (1923), *West-Running Brook* (1928), *A Further Range* (1936), *A Witness Tree* (1942), *Steeple Bush* (1947), and *In the Clearing* (1962)—and two plays. While Frost never wrote prose in any sustained way, several of his short prose pieces—including "The Figure a Poem Makes," "The Constant Symbol," and "Education by Poetry"—give readers a glimpse into his ever-evolving theories and philosophies of poetry. He received many honors and awards for his poetry, including four Pulitzer Prizes. In 1961 the eighty-six-year-old author—by then the most famous living poet in America—recited his poem "The Gift Outright" at the inauguration of President John F. Kennedy. He died two years later.

North of Boston, as David Sanders points out, was Frost's "second book of poems but the first to reveal his full dramatic power and moral awareness." When it was first published in 1914 in England, the volume began with the "The Pasture" as a prologue and was followed by fifteen poems: "Mending Wall," "The Death of the Hired Man," "The Mountain," "A Hundred Collars," "Home Burial," "The Black Cottage," "Blueberries," "A Servant to Servants," "After Apple-Picking," "The Code," "The Generations of Men," "The Housekeeper," "The Fear," "The Self-Seeker," and "The Wood-Pile." The American edition, published the following year, added a final poem, "Good Hours." Frost was anxious about the critical reception of his new book, coming as it did after *A Boy's Will* had been described as "naively engaging" by a reviewer for *The Times Literary Supplement*. Frost's letters of the time show that there was nothing naive about his approach to his art. The seeming simplicity of his verse was the result of a conscious artistry, and his use of the loose iambic pentameter lines of blank verse to capture the vernacular and speech patterns of New England constituted an original contribution to prosody. Two aspects of Frost's poems—his rural themes and his emphasis on the sound of ordinary speech—make them both easily accessible and deceptively simple. His poems are some of the first that are taught to schoolchildren because they often take the details of nature as their subjects and employ rhythms and rhymes that seem natural to the ear. But while the poems are unlike the often-opaque works of his Modernist contemporaries T. S. Eliot, Ezra Pound, and Wallace Stevens, they are no less sophisticated. Indeed, Frost was highly serious about what poetry could do, how it should sound, and the kinds of knowledge (often quite grim) about people that it can convey.

TOPICS FOR DISCUSSION AND RESEARCH

1. Frost made comments, private and public, about the individual poems in *North of Boston* and about the collection as a whole; many of these statements have been gathered by Jeffrey S. Cramer in *Robert Frost among His Poems* (1996). Some of Frost's most intriguing remarks about how he selected the pieces for *North of Boston* were made in a note he wrote explaining his selection of sixteen poems for the anthology *This Is My Best* (1942). Frost suggests that he chose the poems for *North of Boston* by "looking backward over the accumulation of years to see how many poems I could find towards some one meaning it might seem absurd to have had in advance, but it would be all right to accept from fate after the fact. The interest, the pastime, was to learn if there had been any divinity shaping my ends and I had been building better than I knew." For *North of Boston*, he asserts, he chose a group of poems "to show the people and to show that I had forgiven them for being people." Who are the people featured in *North of Boston*? What sort of values do they represent? In what way might Frost be said to have "forgiven them for being people"?

2. "Mending Wall" begins as a simple observation of the elements of nature that take their toll on a stone wall ("Something there is that doesn't love a wall") and the work of neighbors to put it back together. But what looks like an act of communal and friendly labor becomes an opportunity for Frost to explore other issues. The poet Lawrence Raab suggests that "Mending Wall" is about education and cautions against choosing sides by sympathizing with either the

speaker or his neighbor. A variety of other critical views can be easily accessed at the *Modern American Poetry* website on Frost. Why do you think there are so many different ways to interpret the poem? What do you think the poem is really about?

3. In "The Death of the Hired Man" Frost captures the conversation of a married couple, Mary and Warren. That conversation is not about the death of Silas, the hired man—revealed in the title and the last line of the poem—but about his life. Mary expresses sympathy for Silas ("He's worn out, he's asleep beside the stove. / When I came up from Rowe's I found him here, / Huddled against the barn-door fast asleep, / A miserable sight, and frightening, too—"), whereas Warren harbors bad feelings about the last time Silas left ("Off he goes always when I need him most") and is not inclined toward pity or forgiveness ("But I'll not have the fellow back"). The couple goes on to talk about Silas in detail: the work he did for them in the past, his achievements, the ways in which he let them down, his family, his now broken state. Their dialogue creates a history of a character who never actually enters the poem. Is this strategy an effective one? In the end, about which character in the poem does the reader learn the most? When Warren finally goes inside to see Silas and returns to say only one word to Mary—"Dead"—what feeling has Frost evoked in his reader?

4. "Home Burial" tells the story of a couple who has lost a child. (The death of a child is also at the center of the later "Out, Out—," and both poems are often read as Frost's responses to the death of his four-year-old son, Elliot, in 1900.) A narrator sets the scene ("He saw her from the bottom of the stairs / Before she saw him"), but the poem quickly becomes a conversation between the husband and wife in which their stops and starts reveal their inability to communicate in the face of this death. How does Frost situate his reader in this scene? Do you sympathize with one character more than the other? Like "The Death of a Hired Man," as well as "A Servant to Servants" and "The Housekeeper," "Home Burial" examines how men and women relate to each other. What do Frost's poems seem to reveal about his views on marriage and more generally about relations between the sexes?

5. Many of the poems in *North of Boston* are concerned with country labor, from the daunting tasks of a farmwife in "A Servant of Servants" to the unspoken rules that seem to govern how workingmen relate to each other in "The Code." Even though the task in "After Apple-Picking" is completed ("I am done with apple-picking now"), the speaker is haunted by the day's work, still feeling it in his body ("My instep arch not only keeps the ache, / It keeps the pressure of a ladder-round"), seeing dreamlike visions of it ("Magnified apples appear and disappear"), and rehearsing the noises associated with it ("I keep hearing from the cellar bin / The rumbling sound / Of load on load of apples coming in"). The poem perfectly conjures up the ways in which manual labor lingers in the body and the mind. What do you see as Frost's attitude toward labor in the collection?

6. In many of Frost's poems, readers can follow a speaker working his or her way toward some understanding of what a scene or experience reveals. In "The

Wood-Pile" the speaker does not perform work but tromps through the snow without purpose, musing on a bird that flies ahead of him, before coming quite unexpectedly on a pile of wood that has been chopped down by unknown hands. Why does Frost focus on the details of this forgotten pile—its color, its age, the method by which it has been held in this place? What does this scene allow the speaker of the poem to think about? In a Frost poem the emphasis is on both nature and the humans who inhabit that nature, and yet it is always telling where the poem ends. In this case, the final image of the wood-pile warming the frozen swamp, "with the slow smokeless burning of decay," leaves the wood, untouched by the human who has come upon it, to perform the only function it can. What kind of relationship, then, does such a poem forge between nature and its human interloper?

7. As you read the poems of *North of Boston*, consider the book as a whole—from the implications of its title and its dedication, "To E.M.F. This Book of People," to the organization of the volume. How, for example, do "The Pasture" and "Good Hours"—poems printed in italic type in the American edition to open and close the volume—function in the design of the book? Does "The Pasture" prepare the reader for the poems that follow? Is "Good Hours" appropriate as a conclusion? What do you think is the major theme of the collection?

RESOURCES

Primary Works

The Notebooks of Robert Frost, edited by Robert Faggen (Cambridge, Mass.: Belknap Press of Harvard University Press, 2006).
Reproduces the musings, drafts, fragments, and thoughts that Frost kept in his notebooks throughout his life, giving readers access to his poetic process and philosophies.

Robert Frost on Writing, edited by Elaine Barry (New Brunswick, N.J.: Rutgers University Press, 1973).
Includes commentary by Frost relevant to *North of Boston.*

"Robert Frost: Why He Selected Sixteen Poems," in *This Is My Best: Over 150 Self-Chosen and Complete Masterpieces, Together with their Reasons for Their Selections,* edited by Whit Burnett (New York: Dial, 1942), pp. 277–292.
Includes comments on his process of gathering his poems for *A Boy's Will* and *North of Boston.*

Biography

Jay Parini, *Robert Frost: A Life* (New York: Holt, 1999).
Pays particular attention to the effect that various emotional crises—including his long battle with depression—had on Frost's poems.

John Evangelist Walsh, *Into My Own: The English Years of Robert Frost* (New York: Grove, 1988).
A detailed examination of a period that was critical to Frost's development as an artist and to *North of Boston.*

Criticism

Jeffrey S. Cramer, *Robert Frost among His Poems: A Literary Companion to the Poet's Own Biographical Contexts and Associations* (Jefferson, N.C. & London: McFarland, 1996).
A useful reference "intended to provide information crucial to an understanding of a body of work often misunderstood." Cramer provides brief notes on all of Frost's poems.

Cary Nelson and Edward Brunner, *Modern American Poetry: Robert Frost (1874–1963)* <http://www.english.illinois.edu/maps/poets/a_f/frost/frost. htm> [accessed 11 December 2009].
A useful site that presents excerpts from a variety of critical views on many poems, including four from *North of Boston:* "Mending Wall," "Home Burial," "After Apple-Picking," and "The Wood-Pile."

Robert Pack, *Belief and Uncertainty in the Poetry of Robert Frost* (Lebanon, N.H.: University Press of New England, 2003).
Places close readings of the best of Frost's poems in the context of poems by, among others, William Wordsworth, Robert Blake, Gerard Manley Hopkins, and Wallace Stevens.

Richard Poirier, *Robert Frost: The Work of Knowing* (New York: Oxford University Press, 1977).
Offers nuanced and in-depth readings of Frost's poems, highlighting the way they produce both the guise of simplicity and the seriousness of thought.

Lawrence Raab, "On 'Mending Wall' by Robert Frost," in *Touchstones: American Poets on a Favorite Poem,* edited by Robert Pack and Jay Parini (Hanover, N.H.: University Press of New England, 1996), pp. 203–208.
Argues that the poem "asks neither for advocacy nor for application, but for investigation. It is not a statement but a performance. It enacts its meanings."

David Sanders, "Frost's *North of Boston,* Its Language, Its People, and Its Poet," *Journal of Modern Literature,* 27 (Autumn 2003): 70–78.
Provides valuable context for appreciating the poems of Frost's second collection.

Peter Stanlis, *Robert Frost: The Poet as Philosopher* (Wilmington, Del.: ISI, 2007).
Argues that Frost's poems reveal his philosophical belief in the dualism of spirit and matter and tracks the influence of figures such as Charles Darwin and Albert Einstein on Frost's work.

—Alexandra Socarides

Dashiell Hammett, *The Maltese Falcon*

(New York: Knopf, 1930)

Dashiell Hammett became a writer out of necessity. Born in 1894 in rural St. Mary's County, Maryland, Hammett grew up in Baltimore, where his family moved when he was five. Hammett was forced to drop out of high school after one semester to help support his brother, sister, and tubercular mother. During his teens he held a succession of odd jobs, and in 1915, when he was twenty-one, he joined the Pinkerton's National Detective Service, then one of the most professional detective bureaus in the world. His career was interrupted when he joined the army in 1918 during World War I. He contracted Spanish influenza that year and became tubercular himself. After the war Hammett worked sporadically, mostly part-time, as a Pinkerton detective, but by November 1920 his illness was severe enough to require hospitalization, and he was more or less disabled for the next seven years. He fell in love with his nurse at a U.S. Public Health Service Hospital in Tacoma, Washington, and after she became pregnant they were married in July 1921. Their daughter Mary was born in October. In 1922, when he commenced writing, Hammett's only income was his disability payments and what he could earn writing short stories at a penny a word, primarily for the adventure-pulp magazine *Black Mask*.

Hammett drew on his experience as a detective for his realistic fiction, which distinguished him from other pulp writers, whose primary goal was to publish stories that provided uninterrupted action, gratuitous violence, and heroes able to overcome any foe. By the end of 1925 Hammett had become the most popular of the *Black Mask* writers; most of his stories featured the first-person accounts of the private detective known only as the Continental Op, for his agency modeled on Pinkerton's. In May 1926 Hammett's second daughter, Josephine, was born, and health-service nurses required him to provide a separate residence for his daughters. Hammett needed more money, so he briefly attempted a career in advertising, but his health was too fragile, and he was forced to return to fiction for his income. In 1926 Joseph Thompson Shaw, the new editor of *Black Mask*, determined to elevate the level of fiction in the magazine and chose Hammett as the star writer in his new stable. Shaw paid Hammett more per word than he had earned before and encouraged long stories and serialized novels. Hammett responded in 1927 with his first novel, serialized in *Black Mask* as "The Cleansing of Poisonville" and published in 1929 as *Red Harvest*, and his second, serialized in 1928 and published in book form as *The Dain Curse* in 1929. On 20 March 1928 he wrote a remarkable letter to Blanche Knopf, saying "some day somebody's going to make 'literature'" from the detective story form. On 16 June 1929 he sent the typescript for *The Maltese Falcon* to Knopf with a note, saying "I am fairly confident it is the best thing I've done so far." The novel was serialized in

Black Mask from September 1929 to January 1930 and published by Knopf on Valentine's Day 1930.

Set in 1928, *The Maltese Falcon* is a complex novel about a group of crooks in search of a sixteenth-century jeweled falcon. Originally intended as a tribute from a group of Crusaders to Charles V of Spain, the falcon was stolen by pirates before it reached the king and over the next four centuries passed in disguised form from hand to hand, its value known only to an unscrupulous few. The novel opens with Samuel Spade being hired by the seductive Brigid O'Shaughnessy to shadow a man who she says has abducted her sister. Although Spade and his part-ner, Miles Archer, are suspicious of her story—it turns out that O'Shaughnessy has lied about her name and her intent—Archer volunteers to follow the man and is murdered that night. Spade is then visited by Joel Cairo, an effeminate Greek who hires him to find a black falcon statuette, and it becomes clear to Spade that Brigid is trying to use him in her own quest for the falcon. Finally, Spade comes in contact with Caspar Gutman, the man who knows the true story of the falcon and who has at various times enlisted O'Shaughnessy and Cairo to help him secure it. Gutman thinks O'Shaughnessy has stolen the falcon and enlisted Spade to protect her until she can capitalize on her coup. In the climactic scene the falcon O'Shaughnessy has stolen is shown to be a fake. Spade identifies her as the murderer of his partner and turns her over to the police, despite her pleas that she loves him.

The Maltese Falcon transcends genre fiction in its treatment of serious themes, including one's responsibility to his job and the society in which he lives, the defi-nition of moral behavior, the ambiguity of deception, and greed.

TOPICS FOR DISCUSSION AND RESEARCH

1. What did Hammett mean by writing to Blanche Knopf that he wanted to make literature of a detective novel? How does literature differ from what-ever one might call Hammett's first two novels, for example, or from other detective writing of the time? For evidence of Hammett's ideas about litera-ture, read his book reviews published in the *Saturday Review of Literature*. A selection is provided in *Discovering* The Maltese Falcon *and Sam Spade*.

2. The story of *The Maltese Falcon* is told in third-person limited narration, a form that has a long history but that was notably refined by Henry James, whose work Hammett had studied carefully. In this narrative form, the nar-rator reports only the perceptions of a single character, and thus the reader is privy to precisely the same information available to that character. Students might consider why Hammett chose this particular narrative form and what advantages it offers the author over first-person narration, which Hammett had relied on almost exclusively before. Students interested in this line of inquiry might begin by reading James's easily available essay "The Art of Fiction." Peter J. Rabinowitz's essay "'How Did You Know He Licked His Lips?': Second Person Knowledge and First Person Power in *The Maltese Falcon*" discusses narrative strategy at length.

3. In chapter VII of the novel, just after he has learned that Brigid O'Shaughnessy has lied about the other two names she gave him, Sam Spade tells her the seemingly enigmatic story about being hired to find a missing husband. The man, named Flitcraft, had left his wife and two children in Tacoma without warning one day when, walking down the street, he was nearly killed by a falling beam. He determined that he was "out of step with life" and decided the only solution was random behavior. After a couple of unpredictable years he settled in Seattle into a life much like the one he had left in Tacoma and took the name Charles Peirce. These facts are useful in interpreting the story: actuarial tables used by life-insurance salesmen to determine life expectancy of customers were published by a company called Flitcraft. More important, Charles Sanders Peirce (1839–1914) was known as the founder of the American philosophy called Pragmatism, and Peirce had a particular interest in the nature of random occurrence. He famously determined that all of the laws of science and nature are derived from the observation of habit. Write an interpretation of the Flitcraft parable. How does it relate to the novel? Why does Spade tell Brigid about Flitcraft? What significance does the anecdote have for Spade? Useful starting points for consideration of these questions is Robert I. Edenbaum's "The Poetics of the Private Eye: *The Novels of Dashiell Hammett*" and John T. Irwin's "'Unless the Threat of Death Is Behind Them': Hammett's *The Maltese Falcon*." Read Peirce if you wish to form an independent opinion; be forewarned that Peirce is difficult reading but essential to the interpretation of Flitcraft. *Charles S. Peirce: The Essential Writings,* edited by Edward C. Moore (Amherst, N.Y.: Prometheus Books, 1998) is the recommended text. Begin with chapter VI, "Pragmatism and Pragmaticism," pp. 260-299.

4. Hammett ends the novel with a one-page coda set in his office on Monday morning, the day after he has turned Brigid over to the police. Explain why Effie reacts as she does, telling Spade not to touch her. Has Effie developed as a character during the course of the novel? That scene ends with Spade going into his inner office where Iva Archer is waiting for him. Why end there? How do you explain Spade's relationship with Iva, whose risky behavior has put him in awkward positions throughout the novel. Why doesn't he rid himself of her? What does this last scene mean?

5. Critics have argued for some forty years over the question of Sam Spade's morality. Is he a hero or a villain? Why is he described as looking like a blond satan in the first paragraph of the novel? The answer to this question is complicated. It begins with a determination of the values in the novel. What does morality mean to Spade? Is his definition defensible? Do you as a reader share it? George Thompson addresses the question of Spade's values in *Hammett's Moral Vision*. That is a place to start your inquiry. See also Sinda Gregory, *Private Investigations: The Novels of Dashiell Hammett*. Keep in mind Hammett's interest in philosophy, particularly Immanuel Kant, the American Pragmatists, and the so-called pre-existentialist philosophers.

6. For as long as they have argued over Spade's morality, critics have guessed about when he first knew Brigid was guilty of Archer's murder. Edenbaum claims Spade knew as soon as he saw Archer's body. Others have argued that

Spade had doubts about Brigid's guilt until the end of the novel. What do you think and why? Remember that behavioral clues are central to Hammett's method. A related question is whether Spade loved—or might have loved—Brigid. Make a case.

7. Novelist Joe Gores, who wrote the fictional biography *Hammett* (New York: Putnam, 1975) and *Spade and Archer* (New York: Knopf, 2009), a prequel to *The Maltese Falcon*, says that *The Maltese Falcon* is really about who killed Miles Archer. Discuss Gores's statement. What is he suggesting about Spade's professionalism?

8. When Hammett submitted his novel to Knopf, he suggested that Mrs. Knopf explore adapting the novel for the stage. What does this suggestion imply about the structure of the novel? Various studies of the transformation of the novel into the 1941 movie version might be useful in answering this question. Useful essays related to this topic are included in The Maltese Falcon: *John Huston, Director*.

RESOURCES

Biography

Diane Johnson, *Dashiell Hammett: A Life* (New York: Random House, 1983).
Authorized by Hammett's possessive longtime companion, Lillian Hellman. A novelistic biography that is important for its use of previously inaccessible Hammett correspondence and interviews with late-life friends and associates.

Richard Layman, *Shadow Man: The Life of Dashiell Hammett* (New York: Harcourt Brace Jovanovich, 1981).
Carefully researched, fact-based biography with details about Hammett's writing career.

Layman and Julie M. Rivett, eds., *Selected Letters of Dashiell Hammett, 1921–1960* (Washington, D.C.: Counterpoint, 2001).
Includes biographical interchapters providing useful background information.

Joan Mellen, *Hellman and Hammett* (New York: HarperCollins, 1996).
Concentrates on Hammett's life from the time he met Hellman in November 1930. Mellen offers valuable information about the nature of his relationship with Hellman and her attempts to shape his reputation after his death.

William F. Nolan, *Hammett: A Life on the Edge* (New York: Congdon & Weed, 1983).
Written for a popular audience by one of Hammett's most devoted readers.

Criticism

Clues: A Journal of Detection, special Hammett issue, edited by Richard Layman, 23 (Winter 2005).
Includes six essays commemorating the seventy-fifth anniversary of the publication of *The Maltese Falcon*. Of particular note are "On Dashiell Hammett and Samuel Spade: A Granddaughter's Perspective," by Julie M. Rivett, and "Reading the Rara Avis: Seventy-Five Years of Maltese Falcon Criticism," by Christopher Metress.

Robert J. Edenbaum, "The Poetics of the Private Eye: The Novels of Dashiell Hammett," in *Tough Guy Writers of the Thirties,* edited by David Madden (Carbondale: Southern Illinois University Press, 1968), pp. 80–103.
Argues that *The Maltese Falcon* is the most important work in the development of the "poetics of the private-eye" because it focuses on a villainess who thrives on the sentiment of others and a hero "who has none and survives because he has none."

Sinda Gregory, *Private Investigations: The Novels of Dashiell Hammett* (Carbondale: Southern Illinois University Press, 1985).
Sets Hammett's fiction in the context of hard-boiled writing of the 1920s. Chapter five, "Ambiguity in *The Maltese Falcon,*" discusses the complex structure of the novel.

John T. Irwin, "Unless the Threat of Death is behind Them: Hammett's *The Maltese Falcon,*" *Literary Imagination,* 2, 3 (2000): 341–374.
A full discussion of the Flitcraft anecdote and its resonance throughout the novel.

Richard Layman, *The Maltese Falcon: A Study Guide* (Detroit: Gale, 2002).
A reliable student guide to the novel.

Layman and George Parker Anderson, eds., *Dictionary of Literary Biography,* volume 280: *Dashiell Hammett's* The Maltese Falcon: *A Documentary Volume* (Detroit: Gale, 2003); revised by Layman as *Discovering* The Maltese Falcon *and Sam Spade: The Evolution of Dashiell Hammett's Masterpiece, Including John Huston's Movie with Humphrey Bogart* (San Francisco: Vince Emery Productions, 2005).
Includes documentary chapters on Hammett's detective work, his pulp-fiction writing, and the publication, reception, and critical and popular reputation of the novel.

William Luhr, ed., The Maltese Falcon: *John Huston, Director* (New Brunswick: N.J.: Rutgers University Press, 1995.
The script of the 1941 movie, with a selection of reviews, commentary, and critical articles.

Peter J. Rabinowitz, "'How Did You Know He Licked His Lips?': Second Person Knowledge and First Person Power in *The Maltese Falcon,*" in *Understanding Narrative,* edited by Rabinowitz and James Phelan (Columbus: Ohio State University Press, 1994), pp. 157–177.
A careful reading of the novel that focuses on the way it "conceptualize[s] the nature of truth."

George J. Thompson, *Hammett's Moral Vision* (San Francisco: Vince Emery Productions, 2007).
A revision of Thompson's 1972 dissertation, the first full-length study of Hammett's fiction. Chapter five, "The Maltese Falcon: The Emergence of a Hero," argues that Spade is "triumphantly moral at the end of the novel."

—Richard Layman

Lillian Hellman, *The Children's Hour*
(New York: Knopf, 1934)

Lillian Hellman (1906–1984), a respected though controversial American writer, was known as much for a series of best-selling memoirs as for a handful of well-crafted, realistic, socially-conscious dramas portraying vividly drawn characters facing moral and political challenges. Some criticized her plays as too melodramatic, but her willingness to address important topics—and a taboo one in *The Children's Hour*—often won praise and commercial success. Although she was not an innovator, Hellman brought meaningful theater to the Broadway stage.

Born into a Jewish family in New Orleans, Hellman spent much of her childhood between New York City, where she attended public school, and a boardinghouse in New Orleans run by her aunts, where she lived with relatives and boarders who inspired many of the characters she created. Hellman studied at New York University (1922–1924) and Columbia University (1924), never completing a degree, before marrying the writer Arthur Kober in 1925 (they were divorced in 1932). She worked as a press agent and play reader for Broadway producer Herman Shumlin and screenplay reader for Metro-Goldwyn-Mayer. A discouraged Hellman considered giving up her attempt to succeed as a writer before Dashiell Hammett encouraged her to continue. The two met in 1931 and began a thirty-year off-and-on-again love affair. Hammett, the author of *The Maltese Falcon* (1930) and other detective novels, is believed to have used Hellman as the model for Nora Charles, the central female character in *The Thin Man* (1934); the novel is dedicated to her.

Hellman's first play, *The Children's Hour,* produced in 1934 by her old boss Shumlin, was both attacked and acclaimed for its story of a schoolgirl's defamation of two women teachers who are accused of having a lesbian relationship. Most critics heralded Hellman as a major talent and as a standout among a small group of women playwrights including Zona Gale, Susan Glaspell, Rose Franken, and Sophie Treadwell. Hellman's second play, *Days to Come* (produced 1936), was a major disappointment, closing after a week. Focused on the dissolution of the Rodman family in a small Midwestern town, the play treats the struggle between union and management when a strike is called. Critics were unsympathetic to her left-wing politics and found the play didactic. Her third drama, *The Little Foxes* (1939), was a critical and commercial success, running for 410 performances. The play offered a portrait of a predatory family of industrial entrepreneurs in the nineteenth-century American South, revealing the dark side of the pursuit for material success.

Hellman wrote two plays in response to the outbreak of World War II, *Watch on the Rhine* (1941) and *The Searching Wind* (1944), both of which championed antifascist efforts but were bluntly critical of American failures to take early stands against the aggressions of Adolf Hitler and Benito Mussolini. Following the war, Hellman's two most notable plays—*Autumn Garden* (1951) and *Toys in the Attic* (1960)—drew on her childhood memories of her aunts' New Orleans boardinghouse. After Hammett's death in 1961, she wrote only one other play:

My Mother, My Father and Me (1963), an adaptation of Burt Blechman's novel *How Much?* (1961); the play flopped. In her later years Hellman wrote four memoirs: *An Unfinished Woman: A Memoir* (1969), *Pentimento* (1973), *Scoundrel Time* (1976), and *Maybe* (1980).

Hellman as a public figure is remembered for her stance in defiance of McCarthy-era anti-Communism. In 1952 Hellman was called before the House Committee on Un-American Activities. She offered to testify about her own activities but refused to name acquaintances with Communist Party affiliations. Responding with a prepared statement, she insisted that "I cannot and will not cut my conscience to fit this year's fashions." She was blacklisted by the motion-picture industry for a decade. She won praise for her actions in some quarters, though her fractured, self-serving account of the episode in *Scoundrel Time* twenty-five years later was widely criticized. Hellman frequently battled publicly and privately with her critics, including Diana Trilling and, most famously, Mary McCarthy. The subject of the movie *Julia* (1977), based on a chapter in *Pentimento* in which Hellman falsely portrayed herself as an antifascist heroine, and plays—including Nora Ephron's *Imaginary Friends* (produced 2002), which was inspired by Hellman's feud with McCarthy—Hellman is a contentious figure in twentieth-century American cultural life.

The Children's Hour, which Hellman claimed took "a year and a half of stumbling stubbornness" to complete, set the tone for her high-profile career. The basic plot was suggested to her by Hammett, who had read about a sensational early-nineteenth-century case in Edinburgh, Scotland, in *Bad Companions* (1930), a book by William Roughead, a well-known Scottish lawyer and amateur criminologist. In a chapter titled "Closed Doors, or The Great Drumsheugh Case," Roughead describes an 1809 scandal in Edinburgh that resulted when a fourteen-year-old girl accused two headmistresses at her boarding school of having "an inordinate affection" for each other. With Hammett acting as her mentor, Hellman was able to make this true-crime material her own. Looking back on the experience in a 1952 interview collected by Jackson R. Bryer in *Conversations with Lillian Hellman* (1986), Hellman was struck by the fact that unlike most young authors who write autobiographically, she was drawn to a story she "could treat with complete impersonality." The play opened in New York City at the Maxine Elliott Theatre on 20 November 1934 and was an extraordinary success in its initial 691-performance run, but it was banned in Boston, Chicago, and London because it touched on lesbianism. It has been revived many times and continues to be a viable drama in performance.

TOPICS FOR DISCUSSION AND RESEARCH

1. Hellman took the title of her play from Henry Wadsworth Longfellow's 1860 lyric "The Children's Hour," in which an adult describes the play of three young girls. The poem reads in part, "They climb up into my turret / O'er the arms and back of my chair; / If I try to escape, they surround me; / They seem to be everywhere." Read the entire poem and consider the appropriateness of the allusion.

2. Students interested in the genesis of *The Children's Hour* are encouraged to read the chapter on the Drumsheugh case in William Roughead's *Bad Companions* and see for themselves how Hellman altered the true-crime story to suit her purposes. How did she change the facts, and what reasons do you see for the changes she made? Students may also want to read about Hammett's role in Hellman's writing process in one or more of the recommended resources.

3. The influence of the social-problem dramas of Henrik Ibsen, George Bernard Shaw, and other early modernist playwrights is significant to understanding Hellman's literate, well-crafted style in which a clearly stated sociopolitical thematic viewpoint is evident. *The Children's Hour,* however, has been attacked by critics who argued that it is not as "well made" as it might have been. Reviewer Brooks Atkinson of *The New York Times* found the suicide at the end of the play unnecessarily melodramatic. More-recent critics have found certain elements, including the ease with which Mary Tilford convinces her grandmother of the lie, implausible. The weaknesses in the play described by some critics, including Hellman's less flattering biographers, are outlined in Alice Griffin and Geraldine Thorsten's *Understanding Lillian Hellman* (1999) and many studies of Hellman's drama. Do you find the criticisms of the play just? What is meant by the phrase "well made," and how does it relate to *The Children's Hour?*

4. In retrospect, Hellman believed she made a mistake by reintroducing Mrs. Tilford at the end of the play. In a 1968 interview she was asked why she had not rewritten her ending when the play was revived in 1951. She recalled,

> When it was first written, many people thought the grandmother should not return. I felt that she should. As the years went on, I became convinced that I was wrong, that, of course, the grandmother should never have returned, the play should have ended on the suicide. When we did the revival, I was determined to rectify my mistake and went back and worked for weeks and weeks trying to take out the last eight or ten minutes of the play which sounds very easy and as if I could have done it, but I couldn't do it. It had been built into the play so long back, so far back, that I finally decided that a mistake was as much of you as a non-mistake and that I had better leave it alone before I ended up with nothing. That was my reason for not changing it.

Consider Hellman's comment carefully. Do you agree with her about the inappropriateness of the grandmother's reappearance? What problems did Hellman face in trying to revise the ending, and why do you think she found it so difficult? What changes would have to be made in the play if *you* were trying to revise it to end it with the suicide?

5. Hellman's play appeared on Broadway in an era when few works even mentioned homosexuality. Other plays that treated the topic include Edouard Bourdet's *La prisonnière* (1926; translated as *The Captive,* 1926), Mae West's *The Drag* (1927), and British writer Mordaunt Shairp's *The Green Bay Tree* (1933). Students may be able to gain insight into the era by comparing Hellman's treatment of Martha Dobie, who admits to being attracted to her partner Karen Wright, to gay characters in other plays. How are gays portrayed in these dramas written and performed between the world wars?

6. Compare the original play to either or both of the movie versions based on it: the 1936 *These Three*, for which Hellman wrote the screenplay, and the 1961 remake with the original title. What changes were made and why? In a 1976 interview Hellman said that she preferred the first movie. Do you agree? Mark W. Estrin's *Lillian Hellman, Plays, Films, Memoirs: A Reference Guide* will prove useful in locating resources regarding these films.

RESOURCES

Biography

Deborah Martinson, *Lillian Hellman: A Life with Foxes and Scoundrels* (New York: Counterpoint, 2005).

Written by one of the more admiring biographers of Hellman. Martinson covers the high points of her life and career and argues for Dashiell Hammett's importance as an editor and guide in the shaping of her dramatic output.

Joan Mellen, *Hellman and Hammett* (New York: HarperCollins, 1996).

A predominantly negative retelling of the long relationship of Hellman and Hammett. Mellen deromanticizes Hellman's accounts, while acknowledging Hammett's significance in Hellman's growth as a writer, beginning with *The Children's Hour*.

Carl Rollyson, *Lillian Hellman: Her Legend and Her Legacy* (New York: St. Martin's Press, 1988).

Describes Hellman as "America's finest radical playwright." Rollyson surveys Hellman's life with particular emphasis on her politics, sex life, and literary legacy.

Bibliography

Mark W. Estrin, *Lillian Hellman, Plays, Films, Memoirs: A Reference Guide* (Boston: G. K. Hall, 1980).

A useful general reference source on the full range of Hellman's achievement.

Mary Marguerite Riordan, *Lillian Hellman: A Bibliography, 1926–1978* (Metuchen, N.J.: Scarecrow Press, 1980).

A thorough annotated bibliography.

Criticism

Timothy D. Adams, *Telling Lies in Modern American Autobiography* (Chapel Hill: University of North Carolina Press, 1990.

Examines Hellman's writings as well as the works of several other writers—including Mary McCarthy, who in a 1980 interview on *The Dick Cavett Show* said of Hellman that "every word she writes is a lie, including *and* and *the*."

Jackson R. Bryer, ed., *Conversations with Lillian Hellman* (Jackson: University Press of Mississippi, 1986).

An essential collection of Hellman interviews spanning her career from its beginning to near the end of her life. Her many comments on *The Children's Hour* begin with her 1939 statement that "*The Children's Hour* and *The Little Foxes* were designed as dramas of morality first and last and that any one who reads too much cynicism into them is being misled."

William W. Demastes, *Realism and the American Dramatic Tradition* (Tuscaloosa: University of Alabama Press, 1996).
A wide-ranging study of Hellman's work, particularly her most noted plays, *The Children's Hour* and *The Little Foxes.*

Bernard F. Dick, *Hellman in Hollywood* (Rutherford, N.J.: Fairleigh Dickinson University Press, 1982).
A useful study of Hellman's experiences writing for the screen and the films made from her theatrical work, with particular emphasis on the problems surrounding the making of both versions of *The Children's Hour* (1936, 1961).

Mark W. Estrin, ed., *Critical Essays on Lillian Hellman* (Boston: G. K. Hall, 1989).
An eclectic collection of critical responses to Hellman's plays and productions that places particular emphasis on *The Children's Hour* and *The Little Foxes.*

Alice Griffin and Geraldine Thorsten, *Understanding Lillian Hellman* (Columbia: University of South Carolina Press, 1999).
An accessible examination of Hellman's major work as a dramatist and memoirist that is particularly useful as an introduction to her themes, characters, and style.

Barbara Lee Horn, *Lillian Hellman: A Research and Production Sourcebook* (Westport, Conn.: Greenwood Press, 1998).
A thorough and highly detailed guide to the original and adapted theater writings of Hellman; includes a bibliography.

Richard Moody, *Lillian Hellman: Playwright* (New York: Pegasus, 1972).
A general survey examining Hellman's major works for the theater, with attention paid to productions of them beginning with *The Children's Hour,* from its original Broadway production through revivals and screen versions.

—*James Fisher*

Ernest Hemingway, *The Sun Also Rises*
(New York: Scribners, 1926)

By the time he was thirty, Ernest Hemingway (1899–1961) was an acknowledged master of style and the most important influence on American writers of his generation. In 1954 he was awarded the Nobel Prize in literature "for his powerful, style-forming mastery of the art of modern narration." During the presentation ceremony it was noted that "Hemingway more than any other writer of his time in America, has given new directions to the course of story telling, new cadences in prose, particularly in dialogue" and that his central theme was "the bearing of one who is put to the test and who steels himself to meet the cold cruelty of existence." Hemingway enjoyed renown also for many self-generated public roles and his regular appearances in seemingly countless magazine articles. At the time of his death he was the most famous writer in the world.

Ernest Miller Hemingway was born in Oak Park, Illinois, on 21 July 1899 to Dr. Clarence Hemingway, a respected physician, and Grace Hall Hemingway, a music teacher and talented singer. After graduating from high school in 1917 and working briefly as a cub reporter for *The Kansas City Star,* Hemingway joined the American Red Cross in 1918 to become an ambulance driver in Italy during World War I. He was severely wounded at Fossalta on 8 July while making deliveries to frontline troops and taken to a Red Cross hospital in Milan for surgery and rehabilitation.

At home the following year, Hemingway attempted unsuccessfully to publish short fiction and worked as a freelance feature writer for *The Toronto Star.* In September 1921 he married Hadley Richardson. At the end of the year the couple moved to Paris, where Hemingway met American expatriate writers and artists who were advancing the Modernist movement. In particular, Hemingway benefited from assistance given by Ezra Pound, who mentored him and provided publishing opportunities, and Gertrude Stein, who also acted as a mentor and inspired his interest in bullfighting.

Working as a freelance journalist for *The Toronto Star,* Hemingway met Robert McAlmon and William Bird, Americans who had presses in Paris. McAlmon published Hemingway's first book, *Three Stories & Ten Poems* (1923), and Bird published his literary sketches, *in our time* (1924). Hemingway visited Spain for the first time with McAlmon and Bird in June 1923 and returned in July with Hadley for their first trip to the San Fermin Festival in Pamplona. Following a brief trip to Toronto for the birth of their son, John (Bumby), Hemingway resigned from his job with *The Toronto Star* and returned to Paris, living from proceeds of Hadley's small trust fund while serving as an unpaid assistant for Ford Madox Ford's *transatlantic review* and writing stories that appeared in his collection *In Our Time* (1925). Hemingway returned to the Pamplona festival in 1924 and 1925; the latter visit, with friends, provided the impetus for his first major novel, *The Sun Also Rises,* published by Scribners on 22 October 1926. The work launched Hemingway's literary career; five thousand copies were sold rapidly, and it was reprinted five times by February 1927.

Hemingway's marriage with Hadley was over, however, and he married Pauline Pfeiffer, whom he had met in Paris, in that city on May 1927. Two sons were born to Hemingway and Pauline: Patrick in 1928 and Gregory in 1931. In February 1928 the Hemingways moved to Key West, Florida. Aided by Pauline's family's wealth, they bought a house and took an African safari. Before his second marriage ended in 1940, Hemingway had published three story collections, *Men without Women* (1927), *Winner Take Nothing* (1933), and *The Fifth Column and First Forty-Nine Stories* (1939); a bullfight treatise, *Death in the Afternoon* (1932); a nonfiction safari book, *Green Hills of Africa* (1934); and three novels, *A Farewell to Arms* (1929), *To Have and Have Not* (1937), and *For Whom the Bell Tolls* (1940).

Hemingway married journalist and fiction writer Martha Gellhorn in 1940. The marriage lasted for five years, after which Hemingway married Mary Welsh, a journalist he met while covering World War II for *Collier's Weekly* magazine. In 1945 he embarked on an ambitious trilogy that was to be set during the decade from the mid 1930s to the mid 1940s; treat land, sea, and air war; and include the elements earth, air, water, and fire. He abandoned the project and did not publish another novel until the poorly received *Across the River and into the Trees* appeared in 1950. Critical acclaim returned, however, with the publication of *The Old Man and the Sea* in 1952. Thereafter, Hemingway worked on a safari book, *True at First Light* (posthumously published in 1999); a fictionalized memoir, *A Moveable Feast* (1964); a three-part novel set in the Caribbean, *Islands in the Stream* (1970); a novel about a doomed marriage in the south of France, *The Garden of Eden* (1986); and a nonfiction account of the "mano a mano" rivalry of bullfighters Antonio Ordóñez and Luis Dominguín, *The Dangerous Summer* (1985). Depressed and physically deteriorating following two small-airplane crashes in Africa in 1954, Hemingway took his own life at his home in Ketchum, Idaho, on 2 July 1961.

TOPICS FOR DISCUSSION AND RESEARCH

1. Arguably the most inclusive theme in *The Sun Also Rises* is the quest for authenticity, located foremost in the bullfight and in the bullfighter Pedro Romero, "the real one." What does the bullfight represent in the novel? Why does Jake feel that it is so significant? Students should consult Carlos Baker's *Ernest Hemingway: Selected Letters, 1917–1961* (1981) and read especially Hemingway's 19 July 1924 letter to Ezra Pound, supporting his preference for the authenticity of the bullfighter Maera over that of his literary friends and the significance of the plaza as the only place "where valor and art can combine for success." In "Toreo: The Moral Axis in *The Sun Also Rises*" (1986) Allen Josephs argues for the centrality of the bullfight as the "moral and spiritual dimension" of the novel. What are the values of the bullfight? How relevant are these values to life outside of the ring?

2. Although Hemingway included as an epigraph Gertrude Stein's assertion that his was "a lost generation," in a 19 November 1929 letter to the editor Maxwell Perkins he rejected Stein's "lost" label as "splendid bombast" and added that his novel was not "bitter satire" but "a tragedy." Countering Stein, he added to the novel a second epigraph, a passage from Ecclesiastes affirming the abiding earth. Students will want to read the letter, in which Hemingway proclaims the earth the hero of the novel. It represents stasis, a reference point amid chaotic transience. Nevertheless, the contention that there are both "lost" and "not-lost" characters is compelling. How would you categorize the major characters in the novel—Robert Cohn, Mike Campbell, Brett Ashley, Jake Barnes, Bill Gorton, and Pedro Romero? Consider the contrasts that arise among these characters as they search for moral and spiritual regeneration through art, nature, and religion. How does Cohn's aesthetic response to the cathedral in Bayonne compare to Bill's and Jake's feelings about the grandeur

of Notre Dame? Consider water as a pattern of imagery in the novel that has symbolic meaning, signifying regeneration and purification. How are Jake and Bill affected by their experience of trout fishing in Burguete? How does Jake respond to the salt water at San Sebastian? Why do you think Hemingway chooses to describe the taps of the tub in Cohn's room in Pamplona as being dry? What do you make of Brett's often expressed "need" for baths? Consider the attitudes of the characters toward expressions of religion. What do Jake's actions at the festival at San Fermin show about his religious feelings? How much is Brett able to share in such feelings? Students will find that Carlos Baker's chapter "The Wastelanders" in his *Hemingway: The Writer as Artist* (1972) offers support for the regeneration theme and illustrates the relevance of a mythological reading of Brett's character.

3. The theme of "the undefeated," one of Hemingway's most prevalent ideas, is seldom discussed with respect to *The Sun Also Rises*, because—with the exception of Pedro Romero—the challenges to the characters are not as tangible as those faced by Robert Jordan of *For Whom the Bell Tolls* or Santiago of *The Old Man and the Sea*. This theme was, however, in Hemingway's artistic consciousness during the gestation period of the novel and when his story "The Undefeated" appeared in the *This Quarter* Autumn–Winter 1925–1926 issue. In what scenes does Romero reveal the spirit of "the undefeated"? Can you also make a case for the spirit shown by Jake and Bill in facing a less tangible challenge, the lingering physical and psychic wounds of war? Students will find support for the novel's "undefeated" theme in Hemingway's letter to Perkins: "I've known some very wonderful people who even though they were going directly to the grave (which is what makes any story a tragedy if carried out until the end) managed to put up a fine performance en route." The "fine performance" defines "the undefeated." For Hemingway's account of a bull-fighting performance that exemplifies the "undefeated" theme and informs the novel, students should see his *Toronto Star Weekly* dispatch "Pamplona in July" in *By-Line: Ernest Hemingway* (1967).

4. In the 1920s Americans rushed to Paris not only because the American currency was strong but also because the French capital provided freedom from restricting American social conventions. In what ways does Brett Ashley signal the rejection of prewar conventional concepts of women's roles? As Hemingway's most memorable "New Woman," she is a topic of continuing debate. To gain a better understanding of Brett's place and significance in her cultural moment, students are encouraged to read Wendy Martin's "Brett Ashley as New Woman" (1987) and James Nagel's "Brett and Other Women in *The Sun Also Rises*" (1996). What makes a "New Woman" in the 1920s? Is Brett truly a paragon of the type?

5. The theme of alienation, common to Modernist literature, is apparent in Hemingway's fiction, especially as it relates to the artist. Jake Barnes notes the solitariness of consummate artist Pedro Romero, observing that although a sword handler and "three hangers-on" are present when he meets Romero, the bullfighter is "altogether by himself, alone in the room" and later, when Romero enters the ring flanked by bullfighters Marcial and Belmonte, Romero and Belmonte are "all alone." One could argue that Hemingway was often writing

about the artist and alienation even when the protagonists were bridge blowers (Robert Jordan in *For Whom the Bell Tolls*) or aging fishermen (Santiago in *The Old Man and the Sea*). What does Jake's understanding of Romero reveal to him about his own life? Students will find Michael S. Reynolds's chapter "Summer in the Sun: Summer 1925" in his *Hemingway: The Paris Years* (1989)—depicting Hemingway's growing alienation from friends and his self-imposed alienation as he entered the world of his fictional narrator—helpful in understanding the complexity of Jake's alienation in the novel.

RESOURCES

Primary Work

By-Line: Ernest Hemingway, edited by William H. White (New York: Scribners, 1967).
Collects four decades of Hemingway's journalistic reporting, treating many topics that he later transmuted into fiction.

Biography

Carlos Baker, *Ernest Hemingway: A Life Story* (New York: Scribners, 1969).
The standard one-volume Hemingway biography, notable for its meticulous documentation and highly informative notes.

Matthew J. Bruccoli, *Scott and Ernest: The Authority of Failure and the Authority of Success* (New York: Random House, 1978); revised as *Fitzgerald and Hemingway: A Dangerous Friendship* (New York: Carroll & Graf, 1994).
The most authoritative account of how F. Scott Fitzgerald's editorial advice changed the structure of *The Sun Also Rises.*

Ernest Hemingway: Selected Letters, 1917–1961, edited by Baker (New York: Scribners, 1981).
An indispensable biographical resource. It includes Hemingway's observations on the evolution of *The Sun Also Rises,* his artistic intentions in writing it, the characters of the novel, and his reactions to critics of the work.

Michael S. Reynolds, *Hemingway: The Paris Years* (Oxford & New York: Blackwell, 1989).
The second volume of a five-volume biography. Supplementing the treatment of Hemingway's Paris apprenticeship in Baker's biography, it provides extensive information about Hemingway and bullfighting, personal conflicts among Hemingway and friends in Pamplona in 1925, and Hemingway's "rediscovered Catholicity"—a point relevant to the notion of religion as regeneration in the novel.

Bibliography

Audre Hanneman, *Ernest Hemingway: A Comprehensive Bibliography* (Princeton: Princeton University Press, 1967).
The standard bibliography of works by and about Hemingway.

Hanneman, *Supplement to Ernest Hemingway: A Comprehensive Bibliography*
(Princeton: Princeton University Press, 1975).
Updates the 1967 volume.

The Hemingway Review (1981–   ).
Includes an annotated current bibliography. Articles in *The Hemingway Review*
itself are omitted, because of the immediate availability of abstracts. In 1986 a
special issue marked the sixtieth anniversary of *The Sun Also Rises*.

Kelli A. Larson, *Ernest Hemingway: A Reference Guide 1974–1989* (Boston: G. K.
Hall, 1990).
Updates the Hanneman supplement; a good annotated secondary
bibliography.

Criticism

Carlos Baker, *The Writer as Artist*, fourth edition (Princeton: Princeton University
Press, 1972).
Remains important for integrating Hemingway's life and art and credible
readings of his work. It does not treat posthumous works after *Islands in the
Stream*.

Scott Donaldson, "Hemingway's Morality of Compensation," in *Ernest Hemingway's* The Sun Also Rises, edited by Harold Bloom, Modern Critical Interpretations (New York: Chelsea House, 1987), pp. 71-90.
Argues that money is a metaphor by which the "moral responsibility" of Jake, Bill,
and Pedro is contrasted with the lack of responsibility of Mike, Brett, and Robert;
illuminates the "moral bankruptcy" component of the regeneration theme.

The Hemingway Society <http://www.hemingwaysociety.org> [accessed 24
November 2009].
Provides links to indices of *The Hemingway Review, Hemingway Notes*, and the
Hemingway collection at the Kennedy Library.

Allen Josephs, "*Toreo:* The Moral Axis in *The Sun Also Rises*," *Hemingway Review*,
6 (Fall 1986): 88–99.
Argues for the centrality of the bullfight and the quest for authenticity in
Hemingway's aesthetic.

James Nagel, "Brett and Other Women in *The Sun Also Rises*," in *The Cambridge
Companion to Hemingway*, edited by Scott Donaldson (New York: Cambridge University Press, 1996), pp. 87–108.
Comprehensive overview of the "New Woman" in American literary history that
defines Brett's role by comparing her with other women in the Paris section of
the novel.

Linda Wagner-Martin, ed., *New Essays on* The Sun Also Rises (New York: Cam-
bridge University Press, 1987).
A collection of six essays on the novel, including Wendy Martin's "Brett Ashley as
New Woman." Martin discusses the social and sexual characteristics of the "New

Woman" and draws distinctions between the Victorian ideal and Brett, who is seen to exemplify defining criteria for the new type.

—John C. Unrue

Ernest Hemingway, *A Farewell to Arms*
(New York: Scribners, 1929)

A Farewell to Arms (1929), a novel of love and war, affirmed and secured Hemingway's career, which had been launched by *The Sun Also Rises* (1926). Hemingway began writing *A Farewell to Arms* in February 1928; like most of his work, it is considerably informed by the author's personal experiences transmuted into art. Like the protagonist of the novel, Frederic Henry, Hemingway was an ambulance driver on the Italian front in World War I; was severely wounded by an Austrian mortar shell and spent time in a Milan hospital rehabilitating after surgery on his right knee; and fell in love with his nurse. Catherine Barkley, however, is a composite character, derived not only from Hemingway's nurse, Agnes Von Kurowsky, but also from his first and second wives, Hadley and Pauline; Hemingway witnessed Pauline's cesarean section during the birth of their son Patrick in Kansas City in 1928. As Hemingway would have acknowledged, however, most of the events in the novel were invented from what he knew or came to know through research. Nevertheless, few writers have ever created scenes that convey such impressions of authenticity. In fact, many readers were convinced that Hemingway actually experienced events of the war that occurred before his arrival in Italy; biographer Michael Reynolds attests that Italian critics who had been in the Caporetto retreat were certain that Hemingway had been there, as well. To comprehend the extent to which Hemingway's research into war influenced the composition of *A Farewell to Arms,* students should see Reynolds's *Hemingway's First War: The Writing of* A Farewell to Arms. *A Farewell to Arms* was published on 27 September 1929, and most reviewers praised it effusively, observing that Hemingway was already a major influence on other writers and the direction of American literature. In less than three weeks the novel sold more than twenty-eight thousand copies, and by November it was a best seller.

TOPICS FOR DISCUSSION AND RESEARCH

1. Disparate readings of Catherine Barkley's character have dominated the scholarly discourse since the appearance of *A Farewell to Arms.* Edmund Wilson saw Catherine, like Maria in *For Whom the Bell Tolls,* as Hemingway's "youthful erotic dream," an idealized woman that Rudyard Kipling might have conceived. In a letter to Carlos Baker, Malcolm Cowley wrote that he found Catherine "only a woman at the beginning of the book, in her near madness."

For a rebuttal of the Wilson and Cowley positions, see Baker's "The Mountain and the Plain" in his *Hemingway: The Writer as Artist* (1972). Many feminist critics concur with Wilson's reading of Catherine's character. Bernice Kert argues that Catherine is idealized and submissive but points to the resilience common to Hemingway's wives and lovers. Students will find that Kert's *The Hemingway Women* (1983) provides helpful insights into the complex relationships between Hemingway and women. Biographer Michael S. Reynolds joins Baker in arguing the case for Catherine's strength, finding her "far more heroic than Frederic." What is your reading of Catherine Barkley's character? Do you find her submissive at the cost of her own identity, or do you find her actually showing confidence and courage and functioning, as many readers believe, as a mentor to Frederic?

2. Before he settled on *A Farewell to Arms*—which he is believed to have taken from a poem by the sixteenth-century dramatist and poet George Peele—Hemingway considered other possible titles. Many of them seem to indicate his desire to have his protagonist more clearly seen as advancing through the narrative on a process of discovery and increasing awareness, as they include words such as "tour," "education," "experience," "progress," "wisdom," "causes," and "journey." Students should consult Bernard Oldsey's *Hemingway's Hidden Craft: The Writing of* A Farewell to Arms (1979) for a list of all known titles under consideration by Hemingway. Those wishing to trace the path of Frederic Henry's journey will find that his earliest conversation with Catherine Barkley (Book I, chapter IV), touching on the subject of causality, initiates his journey and one of the major themes of the novel, "a search for reason." A close reading of the description of the Caporetto retreat (Book III, chapters XXVII–XXXII), a pivotal point in the novel, is also important for understanding Frederic's developing perspective on reason or causality. For an analysis of this memorable episode students should read an excerpt from Charles M. Bakewell's *The American Red Cross in Italy* (1920) that is included in *Ernest Hemingway's* A Farewell to Arms: *A Documentary Volume* (2005), edited by Charles M. Oliver. They will benefit also from reading carefully Catherine Barkley's friend Fergy's response to Frederic Henry's arrival in Stresa (Book IV, chapter XXXIV) and Frederic's questions concerning Catherine's dying (Book V, chapter XLI). Is *A Farewell to Arms* best read as a bildungsroman, or do you think that such a reading is too restrictive?

3. World War I (1914–1918) was the defining event for American Modernism and for Modernist writers who advanced the new literary movement and rejected previous traditions concerning the art and culture of much of the Western world. Reacting to the devastation, disillusionment, and sense of a fragmented culture that were among the results of the war, they sought new forms and styles that reflected the loss, despair, and alienation they and others had experienced. They also rejected the social, religious, and moral "certainties" of the generation they deemed responsible for bringing about the war. The protagonist of *A Farewell to Arms* also rejects many "certainties" and comes to doubt that there is any effective help to prevent impending doom. The priest, the man of God, and Rinaldi,

the godless man, whose perspectives and counsel are carefully juxtaposed by Hemingway (Book I, chapters X and XI and again in chapters XXV and XXVI), are both ultimately evaluated by Frederic. Although readers usually concur that the counsel of Rinaldi, who apparently contracts syphilis, proves to offer no adequate support, there remain varying opinions regarding Frederic Henry's final conclusions about the efficacy of the solace provided by the priest or religion. Some readers contend that Frederic rejects faith and becomes nihilistic, embracing the nada or nothingness that is invoked in Hemingway's story "A Clean Well-Lighted Place." Students will find support for this reading in Bernard Oldsey's *Hemingway's Hidden Craft*. Others prefer the more positive reading of Carlos Baker, who concurs with Ludwig Lewisohn's contention that the fact that Hemingway "transcended moral nihilism" is evident in Frederic Henry's intense feelings for love contrasted to war. How do you read the conclusion of *A Farewell to Arms*? Do you find Frederic nihilistic, stoic, or religious, or would you choose another label for him? Do you find any possibility for affirmation at the end of the novel?

4. Abruzzi, the home of the priest, is a cold, clear, dry place that becomes associated in *A Farewell to Arms* with spiritual harmony and peace. In chapter II the priest encourages Frederic to go to Abruzzi when he has leave from his duties, but Frederic does not do so; instead, he chooses what Rinaldi calls "beautiful adventures" with women in Italian cities. Cleanth Brooks, R. W. B. Lewis, and Robert Penn Warren's *American Literature: The Makers and the Making* (1973) includes a helpful reading of *A Farewell to Arms,* suggesting that when Frederic and Catherine arrive in Switzerland, their illusions cause them to mistake a "false Abruzzi" for the real one. The rain, the novel's most portentous image of doom, is not ominous for Frederic and Catherine; it is "fine" rain, such as "they . . . never had in Italy," and they also experience a "false spring." Later, in the hospital, the illusions persist, preventing them from recognizing the false assurances of the doctor ("everything is going well") until the gas that masks Catherine's pain also loses its promise, and all illusions surrender to reality. Can you find other illusions in earlier sections of the novel? Who seems more vulnerable to illusions, Catherine or Frederic, and what are the implications of your conclusion?

5. Hemingway considered *A Farewell to Arms* a tragic book, his Romeo and Juliet; he wrote in the introduction to the 1948 edition: "The fact that the book was a tragic one did not make me unhappy since I believed that life was a tragedy and knew it could only have one end." Students will find support for a reading of *A Farewell to Arms* as tragedy in Robert Merrill's "Tragic Form in *A Farewell to Arms*" (1974). Brooks, Lewis, and Warren also commented on the tragic elements of the novel, suggesting that Catherine's calling death simply "a dirty trick" was a primitively courageous "assertion of self at the moment of annihilation" and the catharsis of the novel. Hemingway did not evoke Aristotle in his letters to his editor, Maxwell Perkins, to affirm tragic elements of his novel while the book was in production; in a note of irony, however, he wrote Perkins on 3 October 1929, complaining that a blurb had misspelled Catherine's name "Katherine (as in Katharsis)." Do you regard *A Farewell to Arms* as a tragic book? Do you see

Frederic Henry as a tragic hero? Or is Frederic a modern hero, who—having rejected all illusions and false hopes, all possibility of intervening support—recognizes that he must face his fate alone?

RESOURCES

Biography

Matthew J. Bruccoli and Robert W. Trogdon, eds., *The Only Thing that Counts: The Ernest Hemingway / Maxwell Perkins Correspondence 1925–1947* (New York: Scribners, 1996).

A convenient and invaluable source of letters between Hemingway and his editor during the most important years of Hemingway's development as a major writer.

Criticism

Carlos Baker, *Hemingway: The Writer as Artist,* fourth edition (Princeton, N.J.: Princeton University Press, 1972).

Includes the chapter "The Mountain and the Plain," in which Baker defends Hemingway's characterization of Catherine and rejects the nihilistic reading of the ending of *A Farewell to Arms.*

Cleanth Brooks, R. W. B. Lewis, and Robert Penn Warren, eds., *American Literature: The Makers and the Making,* volume 2: *1861 to the Present* (New York: St. Martin's Press, 1973), pp. 22–64.

Offers a most convincing reading of A Farewell to Arms, illustrating how the five books of the novel reflect logical stages of thematic development underscoring Frederic Henry's evolution as a hero—"the modern man" who "is able at last to confront his fate in nature."

Bernice Kert, *The Hemingway Women* (New York: Norton, 1983).

The most comprehensive study of Hemingway's complex relationships with women.

Ludwig Lewisohn, *Expression in America* (New York: Harper, 1932), p. 519.

Contends that "all sound art" is "moral in its inherent nature" and that with *A Farewell to Arms* Hemingway liberated himself from mere expression of despair for life, choosing affirmation over denial.

Robert Merrill, "Tragic Form in *A Farewell to Arms,*" *American Literature,* 45 (January 1974): 571–579.

Refutes critics who refuse to acknowledge *A Farewell to Arms* as an American tragedy because of a too rigorous application of criteria gleaned from Aristotle.

Bernard Oldsey, *Hemingway's Hidden Craft: The Writing of* A Farewell to Arms (University Park: University of Pennsylvania Press, 1979).

Builds on earlier studies of the composition of *A Farewell to Arms* by Michael S. Reynolds and Carlos Baker. Oldsey provides persuasive analyses of the process by which Hemingway selected his title and how he chose his conclusion from variant endings, including "The Nada Ending."

Charles M. Oliver, ed., *Dictionary of Literary Biography*, volume 308: *A Farewell to Arms: A Documentary Volume* (Detroit: Bruccoli Clark Layman/Gale, 2005).
An excellent and comprehensive resource for major articles on background, composition, publication, and critical reception of *A Farewell to Arms.*

Michael S. Reynolds, *Hemingway's First War: The Making of* A Farewell to Arms (Princeton: Princeton University Press, 1976).
The most thorough study of Hemingway's research into the events of The Great War. Reynolds illuminates the ways in which Hemingway transmuted historical records into the art of *A Farewell to Arms.*

Edmund Wilson, "Ernest Hemingway: Bourdon Gauge of Morale," *Atlantic Monthly*, 164 (July 1939): 36–46; republished in *Ernest Hemingway, The Man and His Work*, edited by J. K. M. McCaffery (New York: Avon, 1950), pp. 236–257.
An overview of Hemingway's work from *In Our Time* to *For Whom the Bell Tolls.* Wilson argues that Hemingway shares attitudes toward submissive women with Rudyard Kipling and that the conclusion of *A Farewell to Arms* echoes Kipling's "Without Benefit of Clergy."

—John C. Unrue

Langston Hughes, *The Ways of White Folks*
(New York: Knopf, 1934)

Langston Hughes (1902–1967) was among the most prolific and diverse writers to emerge from the Harlem Renaissance, a cultural movement of international significance that generated an outpouring of African American art, literature, and music. Although this important black arts movement was relatively brief, spanning the 1920s and early 1930s, it was formative for Hughes. The magnetic pull of Harlem, which he considered the greatest Negro city in the world, together with the intellectual and artistic sustenance of men and women such as W. E. B. Du Bois, Jessie Fauset, Zora Neale Hurston, and Alain Locke, encouraged Hughes's commitment to a writing career that lasted nearly five decades. Dismissed by a critic as the "Poet Low-Rate of Harlem" but regarded by admirers as the "Dean of Black Letters," Hughes contributed a powerful voice to American literature through novels, short stories, autobiographies, essays, journalistic prose, and poems that expressed the dreams, frustrations, and experiences of working-class black people. By 1967, the year of his death, Hughes could reflect proudly on a career distinguished by fellowships from the Guggenheim Foundation and the Rosenwald Fund, first prizes in literary competitions sponsored by *Opportu-*

nity magazine and the Poetry Society of America, the Spingarn Medal from the National Association for the Advancement of Colored People (NAACP), and honorary doctorates from Lincoln, Howard, and Western Reserve Universities. More important, he could look back on a life dedicated to the ideals of democracy and committed to activism and social reform.

Born in Joplin, Missouri, James Langston Hughes spent most of his childhood living with his maternal grandmother, who rejected the idea of second-class status based on race and provided her grandson with an inspirational grounding in black history and culture. The strong sense of African American identity conveyed by his grandmother is evident throughout Hughes's writings, as is his commitment to giving a voice to the oppressed throughout the world. His early books of poems, *The Weary Blues* (1926) and *Fine Clothes to the Jew* (1927), were recognized as outstanding achievements for their blend of traditional poetic forms and African American vernacular, and his stories of the fictional Jesse B. Semple (known as "Simple"), collected in books such as *Simple Speaks His Mind* (1950) and *Simple Takes a Wifes* (1953), were highly regarded for their humorous, ironic, philosophically astute renderings of African American working-class culture. Hughes wrote more than fifty books in his lifetime, but none better presented the complex relationships between blacks and whites during the long era of racial segregation in the United States than his first collection of short stories, *The Ways of White Folks* (1934).

The stock-market crash in October 1929 and the beginning of the Great Depression curbed much of the excitement surrounding the intellectual and artistic activities of the Harlem Renaissance; and as the nation struggled with economic collapse, Hughes began an artistic shift away from the jazz- and blues-influenced writings that characterized the first period of his career and toward a more socially conscious, radical aesthetic. The short stories in *The Ways of White Folks* show his concern for increasing racial tensions both in the United States and abroad. Hughes was especially interested, for example, in the plight of the Scottsboro Boys, nine African American youths who in 1931 were wrongly accused of raping two white women in Alabama. He makes reference to the Scottsboro trials in *The Ways of White Folks* as a means of conveying to readers the social and cultural complexities that affect the lives and actions of his fictional characters.

The Scottsboro trials—in which eight of the nine defendants, ranging in age from thirteen to nineteen, were initially sentenced to death, and all served time in prison—strengthened Hughes's increasing commitment to radical leftist politics, as did his trip in 1932 to the Soviet Union. He traveled throughout Soviet Central Asia and wrote about his impressions for a Soviet newspaper. In 1933 he left the Soviet Union; visited Korea, China, and Japan; and returned to the United States. Taking up temporary residence in Carmel, California, he worked steadily on the stories for *The Ways of White Folks* and attended meetings of the radical John Reed Club to show his support for workers engaged in the International Longshoremen's Association strike. Hughes's travels and political activities fueled his imagination, providing the social and historical contexts for the stories that made *The Ways of White Folks* such an important and powerful book.

The publication of *The Ways of White Folks* marked Hughes's debut in the genre of the thematically cohesive short-story collection. "Cora Unashamed," the first of the fourteen stories in the book—and probably the best known, after its film-version premiere in October 2000 on the Public Broadcasting Service's *Masterpiece Theatre*—sets the general thematic focus of the collection in its representation of the conflicted relationship between a young black housekeeper in the Depression-era Midwest and the white family that employs her. Hughes is particularly interested in exploring unexamined assumptions about race and how those assumptions affect the psyches of his characters. In "Slave on the Block," "Poor Little Black Fellow," and "The Blues I'm Playing," for example, he exposes through irony that white patronage toward blacks can be a thin facade masking deeply rooted racist attitudes. Hughes also shows that the psychological effects of racial assumptions often manifest themselves in physical violence—as when, for example, the gentle, talented black musician in "Home" is wrongly assumed to have nefarious intentions toward a white female music teacher and is beaten and hanged by a white mob, or when the innocent black son of a white man is lynched by whites in "Father and Son" merely to prove a point of racial supremacy. Hughes casts a critical eye on blacks, as well, in *The Ways of White Folks*, demonstrating in "Passing," for example, how a light-skinned black man has so internalized the idea of black abjection that he is willing to abandon his family for the sake of white privilege. Throughout the collection Hughes reveals humanity in all of its complexities: its tragedies, its small triumphs, its pathos, and its humor.

Reviewers of *The Ways of White Folks* noted Hughes's nuanced treatment of race relations, his lack of sentimentality even when representing the most heart-wrenching of situations, his skilled use of irony and satire, and his attention to details of time and place that lend a sense of authenticity and realism to his stories. To classify *The Ways of White Folks* solely as an example of Realism, however, is to miss the Modernist techniques that also distinguish many of his stories. The stream-of-consciousness voice of the racist white man at the center of "Red-Headed Baby," for example, allows Hughes to explore the complexities of miscegenation in a way that a more traditional first- or third-person point of view could not. In his 1934 review of the book for the Communist newspaper *Daily Worker* the poet and journalist Edwin Rolfe noted that while *The Ways of White Folks* is largely concerned with the condescending, racist, and often violent treatment of blacks by whites, the book does not, finally, engage in mere racial propaganda: Hughes shows the differences between white workers and white landowners and between whites profiting from and those suffering under capitalism, just as he differentiates between black laborers and the black middle class. Hughes's ability to represent various classes of people in conflict with each other, with themselves, and with their sociohistorical realities distinguishes *The Ways of White Folks* from other fiction concerned with race relations.

TOPICS FOR DISCUSSION AND RESEARCH

1. A careful analysis of the social and historical contexts that Hughes evokes in his stories is perhaps the most important starting point for further inquiries. Hughes is never specific about the time in which the stories are set, but stu-

dents can look for references to actual events to place the stories in their historical contexts. For example, "Father and Son," the longest story in the book, is at first evocative of the plantation culture of the old South. Hughes's mention of the Scottsboro trials of the 1930s, however, alerts the reader to the fact that the racial conflicts born of slavery are still very much a part of the modern South. Familiarity with the social and political stakes of the Scottsboro trials can aid in the understanding of this story. Similarly, some knowledge of the Harlem Renaissance, a period in which, as Hughes once stated, "the Negro was in vogue," helps to explain the tendency of whites to fetishize race in "Rejuvenation through Joy," a satire of a cult based on African American singing and dancing. Steven C. Tracy's *A Historical Guide to Langston Hughes* (2004) is an excellent starting point for inquiries about social and historical contexts in Hughes's writings.

2. Geography is also a key element in *The Ways of White Folks*. Asking why Hughes chose the setting he did for each story is always worthwhile. "Cora Unashamed," the initial story in the book, for example, concerns a black family that resides in a mostly white, rural town in the Midwest. Why didn't Hughes choose to set the story in the Deep South? Hughes, in fact, explores issues of race in many places, from Paris ("The Blues I'm Playing") to Harlem ("Home" and "A Good Job Gone") and from New England ("Poor Little Black Fellow") to Florida ("Red-Headed Baby"). Hughes is quite specific at times concerning place: for example, Central Park at Fifty-ninth Street ("Rejuvenation through Joy") or Gay Street west of Washington Square ("The Blues I'm Playing"), both in New York City. James de Jong's "The Poet Speaks of Places," included in Tracy's *A Historical Guide to Langston Hughes,* is an excellent source for inquiries about geography in Hughes's works.

3. While Hughes believed that "race" as an idea was a social construct rather than a biological fact, he was also aware of how profoundly notions of race affected people in the depths of their hearts and psyches. Examination of Hughes's depictions of interracial relationships and miscegenation in *The Ways of White Folks* can be especially rewarding. What does Hughes's use of these themes reveal about notions of race, nationality, and identity? Readers might begin such an examination with Kate Baldwin's article "The Russian Connection: Interracialism as Queer Alliance in *The Ways of White Folks*" (2007).

4. The theme of hypocrisy can be profitably explored in many of the fourteen stories, particularly in regard to philanthropy. The first volume of Arnold Rampersad's biography (1986) is a particularly good source of information on Hughes's personal experiences with philanthropy and how they shaped some of his writings. Why is hypocrisy such a focus in the collection?

5. *The Ways of White Folks* is, finally, intimately concerned with the ways of black folks. While racial conflict is central to many of the stories, so, too, are themes of survival, dignity, pride, and the richness of African American culture. Students might want to discuss the African American characters. To what extent does Hughes present his characters as being active participants in life rather than being victims of a racist culture?

RESOURCES

Biography

Faith Berry, *Langston Hughes: Before and beyond Harlem* (Westport, Conn.: Lawrence Hill, 1983).
A good supplement to Arnold Rampersad's biography. Berry's book connects Hughes's own experiences with white patronage to the story "The Blues I'm Playing."

Langston Hughes, *The Big Sea: An Autobiography* (New York: Knopf, 1940).
The first volume of the author's autobiography, documenting his life and career to the end of the Harlem Renaissance. The work is an excellent source of information on some of the social and historical contexts of Hughes's stories.

Hughes, *I Wonder as I Wander: An Autobiographical Journey* (New York: Rinehart, 1956).
The second volume of the author's autobiography, providing useful information about his life and career after the Harlem Renaissance.

Arnold Rampersad, *The Life of Langston Hughes*, volume 1, *1902–1940: I, Too, Sing America* (New York: Oxford University Press, 1986); volume 2, *1941–1967: I Dream a World* (New York: Oxford University Press, 1988).
The most extensive biography of the author. Rampersad's book should be consulted at the beginning of any study of Hughes's life and writings.

Criticism

Kate Baldwin, "The Russian Connection: Interracialism as Queer Alliance in *The Ways of White Folks*," in *Montage of a Dream: The Art and Life of Langston Hughes*, edited by John Edgar Tidwell and Cheryl R. Ragar (Columbia: University of Missouri Press, 2007), pp. 209–234.
An important article that explores Hughes's travels in the Soviet Union and how they influenced his representations of interracial relationships.

Sandra Y. Govan, "The Paradox of Modernism," in *Montage of a Dream: The Art and Life of Langston Hughes*, edited by Tidwell and Ragar (Columbia: University of Missouri Press, 2007), pp. 147–165.
A useful article that suggests that Hughes was both a practitioner of Modernist techniques and a satirist of Modernist aesthetics.

David Michael Nifong, "Narrative Technique and Theory in *The Ways of White Folks*," *Black American Literature Forum*, 15 (Fall 1981): 93–96.
Offers a helpful close reading of the book to demonstrate Hughes's experimentation with narrative technique.

Hans A. Ostrom, *Langston Hughes: A Study of the Short Fiction* (New York: Twayne, 1993).
The only study devoted entirely to Hughes's short fiction.

Steven C. Tracy, ed., *A Historical Guide to Langston Hughes* (New York: Oxford University Press, 2004).
A useful collection of essays that includes Dolan Hubbard's "Langston Hughes: A Bibliographic Essay," an excellent source for secondary bibliography.

—*Christopher C. De Santis*

Zora Neale Hurston, *Their Eyes Were Watching God*
(New York: Lippincott, 1937)

Zora Neale Hurston (1891–1960), one of the most innovative and accomplished writers of her time, was an anthropologist, folklorist, and author of fiction and non-fiction. She was also was a canny, ambitious self-promoter who mythologized or fabricated parts of her life and consciously set out to remake her own identity when she arrived in New York in 1925 and joined the writers, artists, and social activists who defined what is now known as the Harlem Renaissance. She was older and more experienced than she wished to seem, so she simply made herself younger. She provided so many variants on her birth date, in fact, that it took determined scholarship to track down the actual year she was born. Hurston's reverence for folk traditions, her upbringing in an all-black town, her training as an anthropologist and collector of folk stories—all were factors in her uncompromising desire to depict the ordinary lives of black people, unfiltered through the sociopolitical lenses of the day. A flamboyant, complex woman, Hurston was artistically at odds with some of her notable male peers. *Their Eyes Were Watching God,* now hailed as an American masterpiece, was dismissed initially by some critics as being either slight, quaint or, worse, politically damaging to the interests of the "New Negro." Both writer Richard Wright and philosopher Alain Locke—who had been Hurston's professor at Howard University—saw the work as catering to white "minstrel show" images of black "folk," though Wright in his review was unabashedly scathing while Locke recognized the lyricism and power of the writing.

At the time of her birth Hurston's father was a sharecropper in Alabama, but the family moved to Eatonville, Florida, soon afterward. Incorporated in 1887, Eatonville was the first all-black town in the nation. There John Hurston thrived, after his earlier years of hardship, as a minister and pastor of the Macedonia Baptist Church, and he eventually became the town's mayor. In both her autobiography, *Dust Tracks on a Road* (1942), and her fiction, notably her early autobiographical novel, *Jonah's Gourd Vine* (1934), Hurston presents an almost idyllic portrait of her early years in Eatonville, where the fruit was lush, her home was large, hardworking people earned their due, and amicable race relations prevailed with the neighboring whites. One of eight children, she locked horns with her formidable father, who she believed wanted to break her spirit, but revered her mother, Lucy Ann Hurston, who supported her headstrong daughter. "Mama exhorted her children at every opportunity to 'jump at de sun.' We might not land on the sun, but at least we would get off the ground," she writes in *Dust Tracks on a Road*.

Zora was thirteen when her mother died, and details of her life thereafter are sketchy. She says in her autobiography that after her father remarried, she left home and lived with various siblings in Florida, Memphis, and Baltimore. She was in her mid twenties when she finished high school in Baltimore, though in *Dust Tracks on a Road* she claims that she was much younger. She worked as a domestic and as a maid in a traveling theater troupe, then attended Howard University, where she began writing stories set in Eatonville. "Spunk" won second prize in a literary contest sponsored by the National Urban League's *Opportunity* magazine, which was edited by the influential Charles S. Johnson, who encouraged her to come to New York. The story, which effectively launched her literary career, was published in 1925 both in *Opportunity* and in Alain Locke's landmark anthology, *The New Negro*, in the section titled "Negro Youth Speaks." She transferred to Barnard College in New York, where she studied anthropology with the eminent Franz Boas and received a B.A. in 1928. She began her folklore collecting expeditions to the South, notably Florida and New Orleans and, later, Jamaica and Haiti; she was awarded a Guggenheim Fellowship in 1936 to study West Indian *Obeah* (magic and sorcery) practices.

Hurston wrote prolifically—plays, stories, essays, and field studies—and was an undeniable force within the collection of artists and intellectuals that instigated the Harlem Renaissance. She published her short story "Sweat" in the single published issue of the magazine *Fire!!*, which she founded in 1926 with Langston Hughes and Wallace Thurman. The story of the long-suffering Delia's triumph over her vicious husband, Sykes, presages Hurston's preoccupation with relationships between men and women and women's struggles for self-actualization and power—a major theme in *Their Eyes Were Watching God*. She received favorable reviews and awards, but her ever-present need for money led her to seek, like Hughes and others, the patronage of Charlotte Osgood Mason, a white benefactor whose condescension and restrictions she resented but accepted. *Jonah's Gourd Vine*, her first novel, was a Book-of-the-Month Club selection. It was followed by two folklore collections: *Mules and Men* (1935), about New Orleans hoodoo culture; and *Tell My Horse* (1938), about West Indian voodoo. She wrote *Their Eyes Were Watching God* in seven weeks in 1937 while in Haiti. Another novel, *Moses, Man of the Mountain*, was published in 1939, the year of her second marriage, to Albert Price III (they were divorced 1943; a short-lived first marriage to Herbert Sheen had ended in divorce in 1931).

In 1948, the same year she published her final novel, *Seraph on the Suwanee*, Hurston was accused of molesting a ten-year-old boy. Though the charges were dropped when she was able to prove that she was out of the country at the time of the alleged incident, she felt humiliated, violated by the press, and abandoned by her peers. She spent her last years in Florida, working variously as a domestic, a librarian, a teacher, and a reporter for a local weekly. She died of heart disease in poverty and obscurity in the St. Lucie County Welfare Home, where she was buried in an unmarked grave. Writer Alice Walker rediscovered Hurston's work and made what is now a famous literary pilgrimage to find and mark Hurston's grave. Walker's publication of the story of her search in *Ms.* magazine in 1975 sparked a reevaluation of Hurston's work and secured her place in literary history as a significant American writer.

TOPICS FOR DISCUSSION AND RESEARCH

1. Critics often discuss Janie Crawford Killicks Starks Woods's quest for self-determination and self-awareness as the main theme of the novel. Mary Helen Washington calls her "one of the few—certainly the earliest—heroic black women in the Afro-American literary tradition." What obstacles does Janie overcome? What does she learn about herself and her world? Students should in particular consider the role played by Nanny, the victim of the most vicious sexism and racism, in her granddaughter's development. How does Nanny's example—her pronouncement, "De nigger woman is de mule of de world so fur as Ah can see," coupled with her belief in "whut a woman ought be and to do"—ultimately affect Janie? Students who want to explore this theme are encouraged to read Washington's essay as well as the articles by SallyAnn Ferguson and Missy Dehn Kubitschek.

2. Janie's story is told within the larger framework of the African American community, particularly its women. Her story is rooted in Nanny's story, and these individual stories suggest the shared heritage of African American women. The creativity of African American culture is revealed in Hurston's use of folkways and folk idioms, in richly evocative language, and in the important role storytelling plays in the community. Why is story telling so important? Does storytelling perform different functions for women and men? How is the act of telling a story shown to affect the teller, the listener, and the community? Useful sources to investigate this topic include Valerie Boyd's biography, Klaus Benesch's article, and Hazel Carby's "The Politics of Fiction, Anthropology, and the Folk: Zora Neale Hurston" in Michael Awkward's collection of essays.

3. An essential theme of this book, evidenced through Janie's relationships with her three husbands, is the unequal power relationships between men and women, and women's bid for autonomy and power. At the end of the novel Janie tells Phoeby: "Two things everybody's got tuh do fuh themselves. They got tuh go tuh God, and they got tuh find out about livin' fuh theyselves." What does Janie "find out about livin'" through her relationships with men? See Rachel Blau DuPlessis' essay "Power, Judgment, and Narrative in a Work of Zora Neale Hurston: Feminist Cultural Studies" in Michael Awkward's collection and SallyAnn Ferguson's "Folkloric Men and Female Growth in *Their Eyes Were Watching God.*"

4. Richard Wright and other contemporary critics who derided Hurston's use of folk language and implied that she was not sufficiently cognizant of the fight for equalized race relations seemingly ignored Nanny's harrowing story, which infuses the tale with a grim awareness of the brutalities of the slave system. Janie's light skin is the result of egregious racial oppression. How do Janie's white features, including the "great rope of black hair swinging to her waist," affect her and influence others' reactions to her? What is the function of Mrs. Turner in the

narrative and the significance of her response to Janie? What do you think the
novel says about the delicate issue of color distinctions within the black community? See Claire Crabtree's "The Confluence of Folklore, Feminism and Black
Self-Determination in Zora Neale Hurston's *Their Eyes Were Watching God.*"

5. Hurston's sophisticated use of language, her artistic employment of vernacular speech, as well as the way she integrates "standard" English third-person
narration and exposition to frame Janie's story, is one of the most remarkable
features of *Their Eyes Were Watching God.* In his essay "Zora Neale Hurston: 'A
Negro Way of Saying,'" the afterword in the Harper Perennial edition of the
novel, Henry Louis Gates Jr. writes: "Hurston moves in and out of these distinct
voices effortlessly, seamlessly. . . . It is this usage of a *divided* voice, a double voice
unreconciled, that strikes me as her great achievement, a verbal analogue of her
double experiences as a woman in a male-dominated world and as a black person
in a nonblack world, a woman writer's revision of W. E. B. Du Bois's metaphor
of 'double-consciousness' for the hyphenated African-American." On close
inspection, can you identify the "seams" between the two voices? Do you
agree with Gates that the use of the two voices is central to the effectiveness
of the novel? What would be lost and gained if Hurston had decided to tell
the story as a first-person narrative? Students interested in the richness of
Hurston's language might want to explore how she drew on her work as a
folklorist in *Mules and Men* and *Tell My Horse.*

RESOURCES

Primary Works

*Folklore, Memoirs, and Other Writings: Mules and Men, Tell My Horse, Dust Tracks
on a Road, Selected Articles,* edited by Cheryl Wall (New York: Library of
America, 1995).
A collection of Hurston's nonfiction work that includes her 1928 article "How it
Feels to Be Colored Me."

*Novels and Stories: Jonah's Gourd Vine, Their Eyes Were Watching God, Moses, Man
of the Mountain, Seraph on the Suwanee, Selected Stories,* edited by Wall (New
York: Library of America, 1995).
An accessible and reliable edition of Hurston's fiction that includes a useful chronology of her life and work.

Their Eyes Were Watching God (New York: HarperCollins, 1990).
Includes a foreword by Mary Helen Washington and an afterword by Henry
Louis Gates Jr., a bibliography, and a chronology.

Biography

Valerie Boyd, *Wrapped in Rainbows: The Life of Zora Neale Hurston* (New York:
Scribner, 2003).
A critically acclaimed study of Hurston's life and art.

Carla Kaplan, *Zora Neale Hurston: A Life in Letters* (New York: Doubleday, 2002).
A compendium of Hurston's correspondence to literary friends, publishers, and patrons; includes an especially helpful introduction to Hurston's life and career.

Criticism

Michael Awkward, ed., *New Essays on* Their Eyes Were Watching God (Cambridge, England & New York: Cambridge University Press, 1990).
Important essays by well-known Hurston scholars: biographer Robert Hemenway, Nellie McKay, Hazel Carby, and Rachel Blau DuPlessis. Awkward's introduction provides historic context about the novel's negative contemporary reception by the influential Alain Locke and Richard Wright and the subsequent "devaluation" of her work.

Klaus Benesch, "Oral Narrative and Literary Text: Afro-American Folklore in *Their Eyes Were Watching God*," *Callaloo*, 36 (Summer 1988): 627–635.
An explication of the novel, focusing on Hurston's "merging of literary and oral style."

Harold Bloom, ed., *Zora Neal Hurston's Their Eyes Were Watching God* (New York: Chelsea House, 1987).
Collects eight essays on the novel's structure, voice, and use of oral tradition by such leading scholars as Barbara Johnson, Houston Baker, Robert B. Stepto, and Henry Louis Gates Jr., with an introduction by the prolific literary critic and Modern Critical Interpretations series editor Bloom. The volume is a good introduction to Hurston scholarship.

Claire Crabtree, "The Confluence of Folklore, Feminism and Black Self-Determination in Zora Neale Hurston's *Their Eyes Were Watching God*," *Southern Literary Journal*, 17 (Spring 1985): 54–66.
An analysis of Hurston's use of folk materials in shaping the structure and themes of her novel. Crabtree reevaluates what has often been considered the weak, problematic ending of the novel in terms of its relation to Hurston's deliberate authorial intention and her vision of authentic black life.

SallyAnn H. Ferguson, "Folkloric Men and Female Growth in *Their Eyes Were Watching God*," *Black American Literature Forum*, 21 (Spring–Summer 1987): 185-197.
Considers the specific use and reconfiguration of recognizable folklore types in Hurston's construction of Janie's three husbands. Ferguson argues that Janie's quest for self-definition is reflected in Hurston's deviating from the standard folkloric types: the foolish marriage of an old man and a young girl (Logan Killicks), Jody the Grinder (Jody Starks), and Stagolee (Tea Cake). According to Ferguson, Janie's responses to these men demonstrate her self-development.

Jennifer Jordan, "Feminist Fantasies: Zora Neale Hurston's *Their Eyes Were Watching God*," *Tulsa Studies in Women's Literature*, 7 (Spring 1988): 105–117.

Examines feminist critical perspectives and the complex characterization of Janie, considered an ambiguous feminist heroine.

Missy Dehn Kubitschek, "'Tuh De Horizon and Back'": The Female Quest in *Their Eyes Were Watching God," Black American Literature Forum,* 17 (Autumn 1983): 109–115.
Sees the quest motif as structuring the novel and the storytelling Janie as a type of artist, whose relationship to the community embodies Hurston's own vision of an artist's "responsibility to, and dependence, on the larger community."

Alice Walker, "Looking for Zora," in *In Search of Our Mother's Gardens: Womanist Prose* (New York: Harcourt Brace Jovanovich, 1983), pp. 93–116.
An indispensable text for the student of Hurston. Walker writes movingly of her artistic kinship to her literary predecessor and her quest to discover Hurston's unmarked grave.

Mary Helen Washington, "Zora Neale Hurston: A Woman Half in Shadow," in *I Love Myself When I'm Laughing . . . And Then Again When I Am Looking Mean and Impressive: A Zora Neale Hurston Reader,* edited by Walker (Old Westbury, N.Y.: Feminist Press, 1979), pp. 7–25.
A clear-eyed, appreciative reappraisal of Hurston's life and art. Washington maintains that the dialect in "Eyes" "that has been laughed at, denied, ignored, or 'improved' so that white folks and educated black folks can understand it, is simply beautiful. There is enough self-love in that one book—love of community, culture, traditions—to restore a world. Or create a new one."

Richard Wright, "Between Laughter and Tears," *New Masses,* 25 (5 October 1937): 22, 25.
Well-known negative contemporary review of Hurston's book in which Wright accuses Hurston of pandering to a white audience with her "facile sensuality" and use of the "minstrel technique." The keynotes of the essay, along with an excerpt from Alain Locke's 1938 *Opportunity* review can be found online at Stephen Railton's "Relations of Race" course at the University of Virginia <http://people. virginia.edu/~sfr/enam358/wrightrev.html> [accessed 12 November 2009].

—Kate Falvey

Ring Lardner, *How to Write Short Stories [with Samples]*
(New York: Scribners, 1924)

Ringgold (Ring) Wilmer Lardner (1885–1933), who had few pretensions as a literary artist, came to his reputation as a short-story writer with a gift for vernacular humor after establishing himself as a sportswriter. Born in Niles, Michigan, Ring Lardner was the youngest of Henry and Lena Phillips Lardner's six surviving children. His wealthy parents provided him with opportunities for academic and artistic development. Lardner developed a perfect musical pitch (which critics link to his keen ear for speech patterns) as his mother taught him to play the piano. Lena Lardner, who educated her children at home until they went to high school, encouraged them to write songs and perform plays, sparking Larder's lifelong love of theater. Despite having been born with a deformed foot, Lardner was drawn to sports and learned to play baseball with the aid of a leg brace that he wore until age eleven.

Lardner's graduation from high school in 1901 coincided with a severe financial setback for the family, a result of failed mortgage investments. At the urging of his father, he enrolled in engineering at the Armour Institute of Chicago but failed all subjects except rhetoric and was expelled after his first year. Returning to Niles, Lardner worked odd jobs while he performed with the "American Minstrels" group, for whom he wrote his first published work, the two-act play *Zanzibar*. He got his start as a sportswriter when he talked his way into a job with the *South Bend Times*. He was twenty and utterly inexperienced in journalism; nevertheless, it soon became clear that he had found his vocation.

In 1907 Lardner moved to Chicago, where he wrote for the *Inter-Ocean* and then covered the White Sox for the *Chicago Examiner*. The latter position led to several other sportswriting jobs, among them a long-term position with the *Chicago Tribune*, for whom he followed the Cubs. While traveling with the teams, he courted Ellis Abbott, a bright Smith College student, through correspondence. Married in 1911, the couple had their first son, John Abbott, in 1912. The next year, Lardner took over the *Chicago Tribune* humor column, "In the Wake of the News," featuring quirky baseball anecdotes. In 1914 his stories about the clueless, boorish ballplayer Jack Keefe began appearing in *The Saturday Evening Post* to popular acclaim. Lardner's broadening reputation as a writer was fortunately timed, for over the next two years he had two more mouths to feed: sons James Phillip and Ringgold (Bill) Wilmer Jr.

In 1916 Bobbs-Merrill published a collection of the Jack Keefe stories titled *You Know Me Al*. The experiences of Keefe, a "busher" (minor-league player) who joins the major-league White Sox, are documented through his semiliterate letters to his friend Al back home. Keefe was also featured in two subsequent collections, *Treat 'Em Rough* (1918) and *The Real Dope* (1919), and the Bell Syndicate later commissioned Lardner to write copy for a comic strip based on the character. Lardner continued to branch out as a short-story writer, and in collections such as *Gullible's Travels* (1917) and *Own Your Own Home* (1919) he introduced his frequently appearing "wise boob" character, the middle-class rube who strains to associate him- or herself with upper-crust society. It was not a coincidence that Lardner veered away from writing exclusively about sports during this period. He had grown increasingly disenchanted with American hero-worship of ballplayers and disapproved of developments such as the "rabbit ball," which made it easier to hit home runs. The "Black Sox" scandal of 1919, in which eight White Sox players accepted bribes to throw the World Series to the Cincinnati Reds, permanently damaged his faith in the integrity of the game.

In 1921 the Lardners moved to Great Neck, Long Island. By this time they had a fourth son, David Ellis, born in 1919, and the pressure to provide for his family kept Lardner writing prolifically. In *Symptoms of Being 35* (1921), a humorous collection of personal reflections on aging, he reveals the toll this constant work exacted on him. In 1922 F. Scott and Zelda Fitzgerald moved to Great Neck, and Lardner and Fitzgerald became close friends, though Lardner was eleven years older and far more reserved than Fitzgerald. The two often stayed up all night drinking and discussing writing. Lardner had been a heavy drinker for years, and during this period the habit finally began to endanger his health. Still obligated to write two syndicated columns alongside his fiction, he slept little and struggled to stay focused amid the distractions of the Long Island social scene.

The height of Lardner's reputation as a versatile fiction writer might never have been reached without Fitzgerald, who insisted upon introducing Lardner's work to editor Maxwell Perkins at Charles Scribner's Sons. With Fitzgerald's encouragement, Lardner planned a collection of selected stories in which his preface and headnotes—wholly unrelated to the stories they introduce—parodied the popular how-to books of the time. The ten stories included in *How to Write Short Stories [with Samples]*—"The Facts," "Some Like Them Cold," "Alibi Ike," "The Golden Honeymoon," "Champion," "My Roomy," "A Caddy's Diary," "A Frame-Up," "Harmony," and "Horseshoes"—mainly treat sports, and most are told through first-person vernacular narration. Lardner had not even saved copies of his stories—published over the span of ten years in magazines such as *The Saturday Evening Post* and *Metropolitan*—and to put the collection together Perkins was forced to find many of them in the public library. The book was a critical as well as a popular success, establishing Lardner as an important short-story writer and launching his productive relationship with Scribners. Over the next three years Scribners published the collections *What of It?* (1925) and *The Love Nest and Other Stories* (1926), as well as the mock autobiography *The Story of a Wonder Man* (1927).

In 1927 Lardner was diagnosed with tuberculosis. Aware that he was spreading himself too thin, he ceased contributing his "Weekly Letter" to the Bell Syndicate, which he had done for nine years, and decided to dedicate more time to writing for the theater. In between hospitalizations he mixed theatrical writing with columns for the *City Morning Telegraph*, which kept his family afloat financially. His most successful play was *June Moon*, which he coauthored with George S. Kaufman in 1929. He continued to work as much as his health allowed, sleep-deprived and sometimes suicidal. His last work was the baseball collection *Lose with a Smile* (1933). He died of a heart attack at age forty-eight. His four sons had careers as writers: James was a newspaperman; David wrote for *The New Yorker*; John was a sportswriter; and Ring Jr. was an Academy Award–winning screenwriter.

How best to understand Ring Lardner's legacy has been debated since his death. Lauded as a master of dialect and malaprops, he is frequently compared to Mark Twain. His refusal to include obscenities in his dialogue famously frustrated Ernest Hemingway, and his lack of motivation to write a novel irked Fitzgerald, who wrote in a eulogy that Lardner never reached his full potential because he had spent his formative years among "a few dozen illiterates playing a boy's game." In contrast, Virginia Woolf asserted that Lardner "writes the best prose that has come our way" because of his complete lack of self-consciousness. Lardner himself showed little interest in his legacy; writing to him was always just a job.

TOPICS FOR DISCUSSION AND RESEARCH

1. The preface to *How to Write Short Stories [with Samples]* and the headnotes for the stories are worth discussing for the questions they raise concerning Lardner's attitude toward his craft. Why does he mock the idea of a primer on writing and adopt an uneducated persona in his preface? Although the stories included are some of his most celebrated—"Champion," "The Golden Honeymoon," "My Roomy," and "Some Like Them Cold"—it is clear that Lardner has no interest in presenting his work as samples that can serve as literary models. The headnote for his first story, "The Facts," for example, explains, "This story was written on top of a Fifth Avenue bus, and some of the sheets blew away, which may account for the apparent scarcity of interesting situations." Is Lardner just trying to be humorous in the frame he provides for his stories? Or does he have something serious to say about writing? In entertaining these questions, students might want to think about Douglas Robinson's essay on Lardner's "dual audience," or "hoi polloi/intelligentsia divide."

2. Various forms of competition—including checkers, bridge, horseshoes, and roque—are featured in "The Golden Honeymoon," in which an elderly man recounts his and his wife's fiftieth-wedding-anniversary vacation. Lardner biographer Donald Elder describes the range of critical reactions to this story, one of Lardner's best known. While critic Gilbert Seldes found the characterization of the old man endearing, most critics agree with Clifton Fadiman's assessment that the story "is one of the most smashing indictments of 'a happy marriage' ever written." Students might consider the role of the competitions between the narrator and his rival Frank Hartsell, between their wives, and between the couples. Do the rituals of competition bring together or separate the participants? What does the need to triumph show about the characters? The compulsion to win is also a theme in "A Caddy's Diary," in which a teenage caddy witnesses firsthand the dishonesty of a wide range of clientele who bribe him to fudge their golf scores even though they play merely for leisure. Students may want to read Elizabeth Evans on the theme of deceit in the stories.

3. Most of the stories in the collection treat professional athletes, many of whom are quite eccentric. Students who are interested in examining Lardner's view of the world of sports are encouraged to read Otto Friedrich's essay and discuss how the darkness of the author's humor is evident in the stories. A particularly dark portrayal of sport is provided in "Champion." How does Lardner's use of a third-person narration rather than a first-person account affect your reading of the story? Students may also want to compare the 1949 movie *Champion*, starring Kirk Douglas, to the original story. What do the changes made suggest about a broader audience's view of sport?

4. Popular music is a central focus of "Some Like Them Cold," the story of a man who moves from Chicago to New York City to become rich as a songwriter.

In "Harmony" a ballplayer shows more interest in maintaining a quartet on his team than on choosing players who can win games. Elder notes that this story, with its focus on music rather than sport, presents a less-jaded outlook on the game than the others: "these were ball players as Ring liked them." In other stories music is more of an undercurrent, such as in "My Roomy" when the roommate describes his wish to travel the vaudeville circuit singing with his wife-to-be. Songs and singing are often described as vehicles for diversion and release. Elizabeth Evans discusses Lardner's relationship to music over the course of his life.

5. In "Ring," his memorial essay about Lardner, F. Scott Fitzgerald remarks that Lardner failed to be a great writer because of his subject matter: "However deeply Ring might cut into it, his cake had the diameter of Frank Chance's diamond." Frank Chance, called "the Peerless Leader," was the player-manager for the Chicago Cubs from 1905 to 1912, when Lardner covered the team. What did Fitzgerald mean by that comment? Was it something more than that Lardner wrote too often about baseball? Jonathan Yardley and Elder both address this topic in their biographies, and Elder provides a counterpoint, arguing that sports provide ample material for the full range of human experience. Read Fitzgerald's essay and respond to these divergent views, using examples from Lardner's stories to support your argument.

RESOURCES

Biography

Clifford M. Caruthers, ed., *Ring around Max: The Correspondence of Ring Lardner and Max Perkins* (De Kalb: Northern Illinois University Press, 1973).
Annotated correspondence between Lardner and Perkins over the span of their professional relationship. The letters show the extent to which Perkins (through Fitzgerald) propelled Lardner's career as a fiction writer. The volume begins with the first letter Perkins wrote to Lardner, at Fitzgerald's urging, regarding *How to Write Short Stories [with Samples]*.

Donald Elder, *Ring Lardner* (New York: Doubleday, 1956).
The first biography of Lardner; along with Yardley's, generally considered authoritative. The volume includes many excerpts from Lardner's letters and columns. Elder offers an analysis of each story in *How to Write Short Stories [with Samples]*.

Ring Lardner Jr. *The Lardners: My Family Remembered* (New York: Harper & Row, 1976).
Memoir by Lardner's son.

Jonathan Yardley, *Ring: A Biography of Ring Lardner* (New York: Random House, 1977).
Takes Fitzgerald's essay "Ring" as his point of departure. "A note on sources" offers a useful selected bibliography.

Criticism

Elizabeth Evans, *Ring Lardner* (New York: Ungar, 1979).
A brief analysis of the main themes in Lardner's work. The chapter "Players, Cheats, and Spoil Sports" discusses Lardner's increasingly dark outlook on sports.

F. Scott Fitzgerald, "Ring" (1933), in his *The Crack-Up, with Other Uncollected Pieces, Note-Books and Unpublished Letters. Together with Letters to Fitzgerald from Gertrude Stein, Edith Wharton, T. S. Eliot, Thomas Wolfe and John Dos Passos and Essays and Poems by Paul Rosenfeld, Glenway Wescott, John Dos Passos, John P. Bishop and Edmund Wilson,* edited by Edmund Wilson (New York: New Directions, 1945).
Fitzgerald's tribute to Lardner following the latter's death. Fitzgerald expounds on Lardner's views on writing and why he was not motivated to be a "great writer."

Otto Friedrich, *Ring Lardner,* Pamphlets on American Writers, no. 40 (Minneapolis: University of Minnesota Press, 1965).
Concise and insightful overview of Lardner's contributions to American letters. Friedrich discusses, in particular, the darkness of Lardner's humor.

Lardnermania: An Appreciation of Ring W. Lardner and His Work <http://www.tridget.com/lardnermania/index.htm> [accessed 5 November 2009].
Offers a selection of personal and scholarly reflections on Lardner, as well as full-text versions of many of his works.

Douglas Robinson, "Ring Lardner's Dual Audience and the Capitalist Double Bind," *American Literary History,* 4 (Summer 1992): 264–287.
Discusses Lardner's appeal to both intellectual and anti-intellectual readers and provides a rhetorical analysis of the psychological processes behind both responses.

Howard W. Webb Jr., "The Meaning of Ring Lardner's Fiction: A Re-Evaluation," *American Literature,* 31 (January 1960): 434–445.
Brief essay presenting Lardner as sympathetic to, rather than critical of, human foibles.

—*Emily Dings*

Sinclair Lewis, *Main Street*

(New York: Harcourt, Brace & Howe, 1920)

During the 1920s Sinclair Lewis (1885–1951) was considered the foremost literary chronicler of the American character, a reputation he cemented with the publication of his seventh novel, *Main Street* (1920). *Main Street* was a sensation, the best-selling novel of the first half of the decade. The critic Ludwig Lewisohn wrote that "perhaps no novel since 'Uncle Tom's Cabin' had struck so deep over so wide a surface of the national life." An indictment of the stifling mediocrity and intellectual barrenness of small towns, *Main Street* was hailed by critics and avidly read around the country with a pained sense of self-recognition, as Lewis described in an autobiographical sketch he wrote in 1930 for the Nobel Prize Committee: "Some hundreds of thousands read the book with the same masochistic pleasure that one has in sucking an aching tooth."

The model for Gopher Prairie, Minnesota, the setting of *Main Street*, was Lewis's hometown of Sauk Centre in that state. Lewis was an awkward boy whose intellectual pretensions alienated his schoolmates. His home life was also unhappy; he had a contentious relationship with his strict disciplinarian father, a doctor (like Will Kennicott in *Main Street*). At thirteen he attempted to run away from home and become an army drummer in the Spanish-American War. He left home for good to further his education, first at Oberlin College and then at Yale. His first novel, a boys' adventure story titled *Hike and the Aeroplane*, was published in 1912, four years after he finished his Yale degree.

Lewis's idea for *Main Street* had been germinating since 1905, the year he first made reference in his diaries to the "village virus," the "disease" of small-mindedness that lawyer Guy Pollock cites in the novel as the reason for Gopher Prairie's stubborn mediocrity. *Main Street* took shape in the author's mind over an extended period, culminating when he returned to the Midwest in 1917 with his wife, Gracie, and infant son in tow. Once he began in earnest, he wrote the novel quickly over an eight-month period in 1919.

After the success of *Main Street*, Lewis published four more novels during the 1920s that highlight other aspects of the American character and form the core of his literary reputation: *Babbitt* (1922), another satire, about a social-climbing real-estate agent who rejects middle-class conformity for a while but then embraces it again; *Arrowsmith* (1925), in which an idealistic doctor loses and then rediscovers his core values; *Elmer Gantry* (1927), perhaps Lewis's most controversial novel, about a greedy and fraudulent evangelist; and *Dodsworth* (1929), about a couple whose marriage collapses during their grand tour of Europe. Lewis's career reached its zenith in 1930, when he was the first American writer to win the Nobel Prize in literature.

Lewis published nine more novels in the 1930s and 1940s, though none of them had the cultural impact of his novels of the 1920s. After divorcing his second wife, newspaper columnist Dorothy Thompson, in 1942, he lived an essentially lonely life, succumbing increasingly to chronic alcoholism. He died in 1951 and was buried in Sauk Centre, which, despite his portrayal of it in *Main Street*, had come to accept him as a prodigal son.

Main Street follows episodes in the life of Carol Mitford, an idealistic young woman who moves to Gopher Prairie after marrying Will Kennicott, one of the town's two doctors. Carol is immediately taken aback by the shabby, uncultured town, and even more so by the people there, who are initially congenial to her but soon demonstrate themselves to be drearily provincial and set in their ways. Carol's attempts to introduce progressive ideas and broader perspectives to the town are met with incomprehension and sometimes outright hostility. She finds a few kindred spirits, but they are either victims of the "Village Virus," an inertia that dulls the ambitions of small-town inhabitants, or are compelled to leave Gopher Prairie when they step outside of the town's narrow conventions and public opinion turns against them.

As Carol's disillusionment grows, so does her disenchantment with her home life. She feels hemmed in after the birth of a son and after disapproving in-laws move to Gopher Prairie. Although she comes to appreciate her husband's skills as a physician and dedication to helping people, she also feels a widening gap between her and Will, who shares none of Carol's enthusiasms for culture and civic improvement. Carol nearly gives in to adulterous temptation with Erik Valborg, a local farmer's son, and eventually she leaves Will to live for a time in Washington, D.C. There she finds the cultural opportunities she has long missed; yet, when Will comes to court her anew, she responds to his devotion and feels her resentment of Gopher Prairie dissipating. After several more months of life on her own, she realizes that she is pregnant again and returns home to find the town and her marriage mostly unchanged. Carol, it seems, will continue to pursue quixotic plans for Gopher Prairie, make compromises, and anticipate a better future for her newborn daughter.

TOPICS FOR DISCUSSION AND RESEARCH

1. *Main Street* is a meticulous depiction of small-town life in the United States in the early twentieth century. Although Lewis drew from his youth in Minnesota for much of the regional detail he attributed to Gopher Prairie, he also intended for it to be representative of small towns around the nation, as his brief preface to the novel makes explicit: "The story would be the same in Ohio or Montana, in Kansas or Kentucky or Illinois, and not very differently would it be told Up York State or in the Carolina hills." Critics have debated whether or not Lewis's portrayal is as universal as he professed—Maxwell Geismar wrote that "the 'common American past' may not be quite so common as Lewis implies"—and have tried to determine why, specifically, the work appealed to such a broad geographic range of readership. George J. Becker notes that *Main Street* was published at a particular moment in the transformation of American life when the village was "reduced to impotence . . . sapped of its youth by the automobile and the factory, sterilized in its culture by the movies and the radio"—a transformation that homogenized American culture but also rendered much of the novel's satiric thrust "meaningless." Do you agree with that assessment? Do you agree with Lewis that the events of *Main Street* would have played out more or less the same in any other region of the country? What social trends does Lewis portray in the novel that emphasize the national culture of America rather than its regional differences? What are some details about the setting and characters that situate the novel clearly in the Midwest?

2. The "Village Virus"—its effects on the inhabitants of Gopher Prairie and Carol's attempts to resist it—is the primary subject of *Main Street*. The concept is introduced in the novel by the effete lawyer Guy Pollock, one of Carol's only confidants in town, who explains that he himself suffers from this spiritual

malaise. For Lewis, the Village Virus was a metaphorical response to the idealized portrayal of the American village that was popular in the late nineteenth and early twentieth centuries: small-town America, in this view, was the source of the health of the nation—its vitality, its freedom, and its democratic virtues. In *Main Street* the unconventional characters that do not succumb to the virus, such as radical handyman Miles Bjornstam or schoolteacher Fern Mullins, are driven out of town by public disapproval. Carol herself feels the weight of the scrutiny of her fellow townspeople at various times in the novel—the pressure to conform to convention is the means by which the Village Virus spreads. Not all critics, however, share this view. Barry Gross argues that *Main Street* is not the blanket indictment of small-town life that most readers take it to be. He notes that Will Kennicott, a true son of Gopher Prairie, is the most admirable character of the novel—perhaps not coincidentally, it is a stolid doctor who is contrasted to ineffectual sufferers of the Village Virus like Pollock. Has Carol succumbed to the Village Virus by the end of the novel? Does Lewis suggest any cures for this "illness"?

3. At the heart of *Main Street* is the marriage of Carol and Will. While in college Carol believes that marrying will get in the way of her plans to "do things": "I don't understand myself but I want—everything in the world!" Yet, by the start of chapter three she is married to Kennicott, whose outlook on the world has little in common with hers. "Carol and Will remain virtual strangers," Clare Virginia Eby writes, "thrown together by the practically compulsory institution of marriage." Despite her desire to buck conventional ideas, Carol seems to give in with little resistance to the convention that a woman, particularly, must marry. Although she is the protagonist of the novel, Lewis did not necessarily intend for her to be a more sympathetic character than her husband. As Brooke Allen writes, "What is brilliant about Lewis's treatment of the Kennicott marriage is that he reverses our expectations by making the frequently lumpish Will both the more powerful personality of the two and, very often, the more sympathetic." In what ways do Will and Carol each disappoint their spouse? What are the strengths each of them bring to the relationship? Considering the Kennicotts' reconciliation at the end of the novel, what might one say the author's ultimate statement on marriage is in *Main Street*?

4. One major satiric thrust of *Main Street* concerns the role that culture and art has (or does not have) in the lives of the people of Gopher Prairie. Carol, a college graduate trained as a librarian, believes in the power of art and literature to broaden the minds of their audiences. However, her every attempt to bring culture to her adopted hometown meets with disappointment. When she organizes a drama club, the assembled group decides to mount a production of *The Girl from Kankakee*, a silly melodrama that gets performed incompetently, despite Carol's best efforts to direct. Similarly, her plans to prod the ladies' literary study group, Thanatopsis, into a more thoughtful appreciation of literature are met with indifference. These passages, and others in which the artistic tastes of the people of Gopher Prairie are revealed, are the satiric highlights of the novel. Yet, one might expect Lewis, a novelist, to share his protagonist's faith in the power of art. Carol's faith in art, though, is

not tempered by realism; she is, Howell Daniels argues, "an absolutist of the imagination": she has "an aesthetic rather than a moral attitude towards life." This life of the mind, untempered by reality, is not seen by Lewis as a virtue: many critics—for example, Daniel R. Brown—have commented on a strain of anti-intellectualism that runs through his work. What evidence is there in the novel that Lewis is not sympathetic to Carol's cultural projects?

5. In *Main Street* Lewis mixes satire and realism—two generic approaches that are not always entirely compatible. Satire overemphasizes some details of what it depicts and leaves others out entirely, exaggerating comically in order to ridicule a particular social failing or foible. The realist writer approaches his or her subject with the objectivity of a journalist, attempting to depict a full picture through an accumulation of concrete detail. A famous example of Lewis's realism in the novel is the narration of Carol's first walk down Gopher Prairie's Main Street, which Sheldon Norman Grebstein likens to a "newsreel documentary": "The slow relentless movement of the lens misses nothing but pauses to note details of special significance. The narrator, his voice presumably objective, speaks what the camera sees, hammering home point after point, remarking ugliness after ugliness." But if the narrator's descriptions of Gopher Prairie are mostly realist, the novel's satire comes when Lewis gives voice to the town's inhabitants, as Martin Light notes: "At every thrust from Carol, a villager exposes his own foolishness or hypocrisy about education, economics, politics, religion." Brown questions the effectiveness of Lewis's satire in the novel, however. "Carol Kennicott's plans for a better Gopher Prairie are formless, since she is naive, and no one in the book serves the author's answer." Do the passages of realistic description in *Main Street* serve the author's satiric purposes or work against them? What evidence is there in the novel that Lewis is satirizing Carol's attitudes as well as those of the people of Gopher Prairie?

RESOURCES

Biography

Richard Lingeman, *Sinclair Lewis: Rebel from Main Street* (New York: Random House, 2002).
The most authoritative biography to date and a useful corrective to Schorer's less-than-sympathetic treatment.

Mark Schorer, *Sinclair Lewis: An American Life* (New York: McGraw-Hill, 1961).
The first full-length biography of Lewis, published ten years after his death. Schorer has been faulted for his negative judgments of the author's life and significance.

Criticism

Brooke Allen, introduction to *Main Street* (New York: Barnes & Noble, 2003).
A useful succinct summary of Lewis's life and career and of the significance of *Main Street* as what Lewis called "contemporary history."

George J. Becker, "Sinclair Lewis: Apostle to the Philistines," in *Critical Essays on Sinclair Lewis*, edited by Martin Bucco (Boston: G. K. Hall, 1986), pp. 104–111.

Considers the satiric targets of Lewis's best-known novels, observing that there are four principal targets in *Main Street:* moral and religious inhibition; crude materialism; a desire for world domination; and a cultural tendency toward "glossy mediocrity."

Lydia Blanchard, "'Gray Darkness and Shadowy Trees': Carol Kennicott and the Good Fight *Now*," in *Sinclair Lewis at 100: Papers Presented at a Centennial Conference*, edited by Michael Connaughton (St. Cloud, Minn.: St. Cloud State University, 1985), pp. 125–133.

Disputes the notion that Carol's return to Gopher Prairie at the end of the novel is a capitulation to the repressive conventions of the town. Blanchard argues that Carol has come "to recognize the relationship between freedom of choice, responsibility, and empowerment."

Daniel R. Brown, "Lewis's Satire—A Negative Emphasis," in *Sinclair Lewis*, edited by Harold Bloom (New York: Chelsea House, 1987), pp. 51–62.

Evaluates Lewis's strengths and weaknesses as a satirist, arguing that in *Main Street* the author's ambivalence with respect to his protagonist, Carol, makes the satire in the novel "watery and tepid."

Martin Bucco, *"Main Street": The Revolt of Carol Kennicott* (New York: Twayne, 1993).

Follows the evolution of Carol's character through a series of personas, including Prairie Princess, Village Intellectual, American Bovary, and, ultimately, Passionate Pilgrim.

Rick Cypert, "Intellectuals, Introverts, and Cranks: What the Misfits Tell Us about Small Town Life," *Markham Review*, 16 (1986): 3–7.

Drawing from *Main Street*, William Faulkner's *Absalom! Absalom!*, and Sherwood Anderson's *Winesburg, Ohio*, considers what determines whether someone is an outcast or is accepted into small-town life.

Howell Daniels, "Sinclair Lewis and the Drama of Disassociation," in *Modern Critical Views: Sinclair Lewis*, edited by Bloom, Modern Critical Views (New York: Chelsea House, 1987), pp. 83–102.

Discusses the recurring pattern in Lewis's novels in which his protagonists retreat into fantasy in order to come to terms with or escape from society.

Clare Virginia Eby, "'Extremely Married': Marriage as Experience and Institution in *The Job, Main Street*, and *Babbitt*," in *Sinclair Lewis: New Essays in Criticism*, edited by James M. Hutchisson (Troy, N.Y.: Whitson, 1997), pp. 38–51.

Considers marriage in three of Lewis's novels. While Carol believes that the institution of marriage "may be her enemy," Eby argues, she ultimately realizes that "Will is not."

Sheldon Norman Grebstein, *Sinclair Lewis* (New York: Twayne, 1962).
An early full-length critical treatment of Lewis's body of work. Grebstein sought to recuperate Lewis's literary achievement at a time when it was neglected. He considers *Main Street* in terms of Carol's "education in disillusionment."

Barry Gross, "The Revolt That Wasn't: The Legacies of Critical Myopia," *CEA Critic*, 39 (January 1977): 4–8.
Argues that *Main Street* is not an example of "the revolt from the village," as it is conventionally considered, but, rather, an elegy for a simpler time. Gross contends that Will Kennicott, the most admirable character in the novel, is also the one who epitomizes Gopher Prairie.

Martin Light, *The Quixotic Vision of Sinclair Lewis* (West Lafayette, Ind.: Purdue University Press, 1975).
Considers Carol a quixotic figure who "embodies both foolishness and idealism": "She is more honest and more deceived than anyone around her, and thereby both more trapped and more alive."

The Sinclair Lewis Society <http://english.illinoisstate.edu/separry/sinclairlewis/> [accessed 1 December 2009].
A website with useful links for studying Lewis and *Main Street*.

—*Charles Brower*

John O'Hara, *Appointment in Samarra*
(New York: Harcourt, Brace, 1934)

John O'Hara (1905–1970) was born in Pottsville, Pennsylvania, at the office of his father, a doctor, at 125 Mahantongo Street—the well-to-do avenue he wrote about as Lantenengo Street in his stories and novels set in the fictitious Gibbsville. Just as William Faulkner is associated with Yoknapatawpha County, the "postage stamp" of fictional territory based on the Mississippi county where Faulkner grew up, O'Hara was best known for depicting his "Pennsylvania protectorate"—the land, people, and towns of the anthracite coal fields in the eastern part of the state that local people called "The Region." But O'Hara, a thoroughgoing Realist, was a vastly different writer from Faulkner. He did not deal in myths or in figurative language but wrote in a plain style, using an acute ear for speech and a mastery of the art of dialogue to create believable characters in a world made real to his readers through accurate detail. O'Hara defined his mission as a writer in his foreword to *Sermons and Soda Water* (1960):

> I want to get it all down on paper while I can. I am now fifty-five years old and I have lived with as well as in the Twentieth Century from its earliest days. The United States in this century is what I know, and it is my

business to write about it to the best of my ability, with the sometimes special knowledge I have. The Twenties, the Thirties, and the Forties are already history, but I cannot be content to leave their story in the hands of the historians and the editors of picture books. I want to record the way people talked and thought and felt and to do it with complete honesty and variety.

The eldest of eight children, John Henry O'Hara was raised in the expectation that he would follow Dr. Patrick O'Hara into medicine. In his boyhood, the author recalled in a 1961 letter to *New Yorker* editor William Maxwell, "death was a commonplace. . . . 'He died on the table,' was a sentence I heard a hundred times—at the dinner table. Also, I saw the dying in hospitals, and once I held a brakeman's hand as he died after my father had amputated both his legs." His father's profession afforded an affluent life for the family, though their Catholicism and Irish ethnicity may have made O'Hara something of an outsider in a small city in which the social elite were Protestant English and Welsh. In the 1962 article "Don't Say It Never Happened," however, O'Hara makes it clear that he did not feel excluded from Pottsville society and did not get "the country club atmosphere for my first novel" from "pressing my nose against the club windows from the outside, or burying the same beak in the society pages of the *Pottsville Journal*." The family's financial footing fell away with the death of his father in 1925. In the article O'Hara remembers, "I went from professional class security to near poverty almost literally overnight." The reversal ended his long-held dream of attending Yale University.

At the time of his father's death O'Hara was a cub reporter for *The Pottsville Journal*. In a 1950 article O'Hara wrote that he learned on this job "to respect A Fact, and to spell names correctly," as well as "condensation (and padding, too)" and "a working cynicism about everything and everybody." He soon left Pottsville for New York. With the help of Franklin P. Adams (F.P.A.), who had been publishing O'Hara submissions in his column, "The Conning Tower," in the *World* since March 1927, he was hired by the *Herald Tribune;* it was the first of a series of newspaper and publicity jobs he found in the city. He began placing short stories with *The New Yorker,* where most of his stories were first published until he broke with the magazine in 1949. His lightly plotted, character-driven works shaped the *New Yorker*-style story, which contrasted sharply with the heavily plotted commercial stories of the time. O'Hara seldom returned to Pottsville in person, but his memories of growing up there provided most of the material for his fiction set in Gibbsville (named for Wolcott Gibbs, his closest friend at *The New Yorker*).

With the publication of his first book, *Appointment in Samarra* (1934), O'Hara initiated a prolific career that included some 13 novels and 402 short stories and novellas. Although he was often associated with his "Pennsylvania protectorate" and upper-middle-class or wealthy characters, most of O'Hara's fiction was not set in Gibbsville, and it treated people from all economic levels. His most notable novels include *A Rage to Live* (1949); *Ten North Frederick* (1955); the one he believed was his greatest achievement, *From the Terrace* (1958); and *The Lockwood Concern* (1966). Although his novels were consistently popular, O'Hara was denigrated by critics who considered Realism passé. Not a man to suffer criticism silently, O'Hara often lashed out at reviewers and critics—his irascibility further alienating the critical establishment.

O'Hara prided himself on being a professional, as well as an artist. He believed in "pre-paper discipline," an approach to writing he attributed to his training as a journalist: he composed at the typewriter, knew where he wanted to go before he struck the keys, and did little revising. In a letter to his brother Thomas written on 12 February 1934, nearly two months before he completed *Appointment in Samarra,* he explained that after showing Harcourt, Brace the beginning of his unfinished novel and outlining his plans for development, he had secured a contract that paid "$50 a week for eight weeks" to continue his work uninterrupted. He went on:

> The locale of the novel is Pottsville, called Gibbsville in the novel. . . . The plot of the novel, which is quite slight, is rather hard to tell, but it concerns a young man and his wife, members of the club set, and how the young man starts off the Christmas 1930 holidays by throwing a drink in the face of a man who has aided him financially. From then on I show how fear of retribution and the kind of life the young man has led and other things contribute to his demise. There are quite a few other characters, some drawn from life, others imaginary, who figure in the novel, but the story is essentially the story of a young married couple and their breakdown in the first year of the depression.

Because the setting of *Appointment in Samarra* was so clearly based on Pottsville, there was considerable speculation as to the model for Julian English. O'Hara finally answered the question in a 1962 letter to Gerald Murphy, who had served as a partial model for Dick Diver in F. Scott Fitzgerald's *Tender Is the Night* (1934):

> Long, long before I start writing a novel I have learned all I can about the principal characters. I have determined, to my own satisfaction, what they would do in any and all circumstances. And I am pretty generally right. Why? Because they are real people, people who are living or have lived. I use the psychological pattern of the real people, then I put them in different locations and times, and cover them up with superficial characteristics, etc.
>
> In the case of Julian English, the guy in real life was a fellow named Richards, who was definitely not country-club, but had charm and a certain kind of native intelligence, and who, when the chips were down, shot himself. I took his life, his psychological pattern, and covered him up with Brooks shirts and a Cadillac dealership and so on, and the reason the story rings so true is that it is God's truth, out of life.

Published on 16 August, a date O'Hara thereafter always considered lucky, *Appointment in Samarra* was dedicated "to F. P. A."

TOPICS FOR DISCUSSION AND RESEARCH

1. O'Hara has been called a Naturalist, as well as a novelist of manners. Do you think one or the other or both descriptions are appropriate for *Appointment in Samarra*? Is the main focus of the novel Julian English and his self-destruction or

the structure and operation of Gibbsville society? What reasons and examples can you cite to support your view? Some of the essays in Phillip B. Eppard's 1994 collection speak to these questions.

2. In a 1960 letter, to a producer who was considering making a movie of *Appointment in Samarra*, O'Hara argued that "it must be done in the period, and with the suicide ending":

> There is not even another form of suicide, such as poison or shooting. This man has got to die by motor car, by Cadillac motor car. It is equally true that this whole thing must take place in 1930. I would sooner update WUTHERING HEIGHTS than APPOINTMENT IN SAMARRA. Both are firmly fixed in their periods. Remember that in 1930 there was not yet an FDR to revive hope; the nation was stunned by the first blows of the depression, with other blows yet to come. . . . APPOINTMENT IN SAMARRA is not satirical; it is, literally, deadly serious. It is not a sarcastic comment on the time; it is *of* the time—and should be done as a motion picture, with every last detail correct.

O'Hara was a social historian who prided himself on getting details right. One of the chief difficulties for modern readers in coming to terms with O'Hara's fiction is the interpretation of those details. The make of car a man drove or the brand of cigarettes a woman smoked suggested meaningful associations for O'Hara and his contemporary readers; such associations are lost on readers who were not part of the culture. *Appointment in Samarra* and O'Hara's other books provide a means not only of entering the world the author describes but also of gaining a new perspective on our own time. As you read O'Hara's novel, make a list of details and social attitudes that separate its world from ours. Are the two worlds fundamentally the same or different?

3. In the 22 August 1934 issue of *The Nation* R. P. Blackmur begins his review by assigning *Appointment in Samarra* to "the most popular of present schools of the novel," connecting the work to Ernest Hemingway "more or less complete" and James M. Cain's *The Postman Always Rings Twice* (1934). He later considers "Julian's private and inexplicable explosion":

> It is characteristic of this school of writing that its crucial gesture is inexplicable. The man kills himself without having once, before that day, thought of death as a solution, and without ever having felt death's lag or its magnetism. We are told only, early in the book, that his grandfather killed himself after having embezzled considerably. Julian is in debt, but not, with his family resources, inextricably. He kills himself, apparently, because his wife does not immediately forgive his drunken stupidity. He kills himself, so far as I can see, either pointlessly or out of back-handed good-will, out of gruff, tough, sentimental loyalty to a code itself pointless.

Do you agree with Blackmur? Do you think the comparison of O'Hara to Hemingway or Cain is warranted? Is Julian's action inexplicable? More-recent critics who take up the question of Julian's motivation include Jesse Bier, Scott

Donaldson, and Charles W. Bassett; their essays can be found in the collection edited by Eppard.

4. Frank MacShane asserts that O'Hara was "especially courageous" in writing about sex and that "no modern American male writer understood or created women more convincingly than O'Hara." Do you agree with MacShane's assessment? Is Carolyn English a particularly credible character?

5. In a 1964 letter to James Gould Cozzens, another author whose work had been attacked by critics, O'Hara wrote,

> They, the reviewers, are not us. We tend to overlook that fact when we get intelligent, understanding reviews; but they are still not us. They and we are as different as touch football and the genuine article. No training, no tackling, no risk of any kind, and no enduring skill. And, to continue the analogy a little further, no hope of ever getting a varsity letter. But they sure as hell talk big.

Because a theme of O'Hara's career was his ongoing battle with book reviewers—whose attitudes toward his writing were established early and were often reiterated as new works appeared—it is particularly appropriate to consider the justice and appropriateness of early criticisms of *Appointment in Samarra*. Read the reviews included in *John O'Hara: A Documentary Volume* (2006), edited by Matthew J. Bruccoli, and any other reviews of the novel you can find. What are the main criticisms of the novel? What aspects are praised? Critique the critics.

RESOURCES

Primary Work

Gibbsville, Pa.: The Classic Stories, edited by Matthew J. Bruccoli (New York: Carroll & Graf, 1992; revised, 2004).
Stories arranged chronologically by date of first publication. The first edition includes fifty-three stories; the revised edition comprises forty-two stories.

Biography

Matthew J. Bruccoli, *The O'Hara Concern: A Biography of John O'Hara* (New York: Random House, 1975; revised and enlarged edition, Pittsburgh & London: University of Pittsburgh Press, 1995).
A fact-filled biography driven by Bruccoli's "conviction that John O'Hara was a major writer who was underrated by the critical-academic axis sometimes called The Literary Establishment. We never have so many great writers that we can discard one because his aims and standards are unfashionable."

Frank MacShane, *The Life of John O'Hara* (New York: Dutton, 1980).
Ranks O'Hara as "one of the half-dozen most important writers of his time." MacShane lists what he considers the author's best work: "thirty or forty short stories and novellas, for their artistic delicacy and a psychological acuteness unsurpassed in American literature; *Appointment in Samarra*, for its youthful vitality and honesty; *From the Terrace*, for its ambition, thoroughness, and

immense readability; and *The Lockwood Concern,* for confronting most completely the values that tormented him through his life."

Selected Letters of John O'Hara, edited by Matthew J. Bruccoli (New York: Random House, 1978).
A collection assembled by the editor during his work on *The O'Hara Concern.* Bruccoli notes that "O'Hara was not a saver" and that many letters and important correspondents, including Robert Benchley and Dorothy Parker, are missing from this record.

Bibliography
Matthew J. Bruccoli, *John O'Hara: A Descriptive Bibliography* (Pittsburgh: University of Pittsburgh Press, 1978).
Publication information on O'Hara's many novels and short-story collections, with illustrations of dust jackets.

Criticism
Matthew J. Bruccoli, ed., *Dictionary of Literary Biography,* volume 324: *John O'Hara: A Documentary Volume* (Detroit: Bruccoli Clark Layman/Thompson Gale, 2006).
Includes two lengthy chapters—"Pottsville/Gibbsville" and "The Thirties: *The New Yorker* and *Appointment in Samarra*"—particularly relevant to O'Hara's first novel.

Philip B. Eppard, ed., *Critical Essays on John O'Hara* (New York: G. K. Hall, 1994).
Includes contemporary reviews of *Appointment in Samarra* by William Soskin, R. P. Blackmur, and Dorothy Canfield Fisher, as well as worthwhile critical essays on the novel by Jesse Bier, Scott Donaldson, and Charles W. Bassett.

Sheldon Norman Grebstein, *John O'Hara* (New York: Twayne, 1966).
First book-length treatment of O'Hara's career.

Robert Emmet Long, *John O'Hara* (New York: Ungar, 1983).
Includes a full chapter on *Appointment in Samarra,* which Long contends "is O'Hara's most nearly perfect novel."

—George Parker Anderson

Eugene O'Neill, *Desire Under the Elms*
(New York: Boni & Liveright, 1925)

Eugene O'Neill (1888–1953) is the first great American playwright, a dominant figure in modernist drama between the two world wars. Author of more than sixty one-act and full-length plays, O'Neill was the recipient of four Pulitzer Prizes in drama (one posthumous) and remains the only U.S. dramatist awarded the Nobel Prize in literature (1936).

O'Neill had theatrical roots. Because his Irish-born father, James O'Neill, was a celebrated actor of the late-nineteenth-century melodramatic stage, O'Neill led a nomadic life as a child, often traveling with his father, mother, and elder brother on lengthy tours of his father's popular vehicle, *The Count of Monte Cristo*. The tribulations of his childhood were mixed with family tragedy: a brother died in infancy, and O'Neill's mother became addicted to morphine. The revelation of her addiction during O'Neill's adolescence proved a shattering experience for him and figures prominently in the semiautobiographical *Long Day's Journey into Night*, the play widely regarded as his masterpiece, which was not performed until three years after O'Neill's death.

O'Neill's career divides into three distinct phases. The first encompasses his earliest one-act works, beginning around 1912 and extending to starkly realistic dramas depicting the lives of the men he had encountered at sea in the previous decade, including *Bound East for Cardiff* (1916), *In the Zone* (1917), *The Long Voyage Home* (1917), and *The Moon of the Caribbees* (1918). The second period begins with O'Neill's first full-length play, *Beyond the Horizon* (1920), and continues through a diverse range of dramas marked by realistic character studies, as in *Anna Christie* (1921). It includes bold stylistic experiments in a variety of modes: Expressionism in *The Emperor Jones* (1920) and *The Hairy Ape* (1922), masks in *The Great God Brown* (1926), and spoken asides in *Strange Interlude* (1928). Other plays from the second period, such as *Desire Under the Elms* (1924) and *Mourning Becomes Electra* (1931), were inspired by classical tragedy. O'Neill also experimented with popular comedy in *Ah, Wilderness!* (1933). Following the critical failure of *Days Without End* (1934), O'Neill withdrew from the workaday theater. During the final phase he wrote his finest works—deeply personal, psychologically complex dramas devoid of overt experimentation. In the late 1930s O'Neill completed *The Iceman Cometh* (1946); his acknowledged masterpiece, *Long Day's Journey into Night* (1956); and *A Moon for the Misbegotten* (1947), an elegiac drama based on the end of his alcoholic brother's life.

Whether setting his characters in epic spectacles or in smaller naturalistic environments, and regardless of specific themes in any single work, O'Neill's plays probe the psychological turmoil of his characters. Working from a foundation of Modernist European philosophy exemplified by such thinkers as Friedrich Nietzsche, Sigmund Freud, and Charles Darwin, and inspired by the intense Modernist dramas of Henrik Ibsen and August Strindberg, O'Neill aimed for and often achieved a lofty tragic vision, as in the case of *Desire Under the Elms*. He also emphasized the Ibsen-inspired device of "saving lies"—or "pipe dreams," as O'Neill called them in *The Iceman Cometh*—the necessary self-deceptions required to survive life's vicissitudes. Drawing on a conception of tragedy manifest in the classical tradition, as well as on Ibsen's social-problem dramas, O'Neill depicts the suffering of individuals who are either self-deluded or untrue to their destinies, and his plays gain intensity through a slow stripping away of a character's mask to reveal a core psychic identity.

No single play from the work of a dramatist as prolific and experimental as O'Neill can capture the range of his themes and stylistic choices, but *Desire Under the Elms* is one of his richest works, blending his interest in classical tragedy with the raw realism and character development typical of his late plays. Inspired by the Hippolytus-Phaedra story of ancient Greek theater, *Desire Under the Elms* is set in 1850 on a New England farm owned by Ephraim Cabot, a flinty farmer obsessively devoted to hard work and the farm he inherited from his second wife. Self-delusion is a central theme in the three-part drama, as Ephraim, a man in his seventies, marries Abigail Putnam, a sensual young widow seeking security. When Abbie becomes pregnant, Ephraim is rejuvenated by the thought that he is the father; he is unaware of the unhappy Abbie's illicit relationship with his resentful son, Eben.

The play opened on 11 November 1924 at Greenwich Village Theatre in New York. Civic authorities, including the district attorney, attempted to close it because of its steamy subject matter, which included frank treatment of sexuality, incest, and violence (the play was also banned in England until 1940); but *Desire Under the Elms* won acclaim from critics and audiences and ran for 208 performances. The fine 1958 film adaptation, starring Anthony Perkins, Sophia Loren, and Burl Ives, contains significant elements of O'Neill's play, but much is changed as well. No other screen versions exist, but the play had short-lived Broadway revivals in 1952 and 2009, with Karl Malden and Brian Dennehy, respectively, in the role of Ephraim.

TOPICS FOR DISCUSSION AND RESEARCH

1. *Desire Under the Elms* explores recurring O'Neill themes, most notably dysfunctional family relationships. What are the contributing factors for the tensions that exist between Eben and Ephraim? Why is Eben emotionally estranged from his father? Who is most to blame for this dysfunctional relationship? The character of Eben encompasses many of O'Neill's own emotional and spiritual struggles, from his conflicted relationship with his own parents and brother to his intense feelings of isolation. Students who want to explore the biographical foundation for the character should delve into O'Neill's correspondence. While no complete collection exists, *Selected Letters of Eugene O'Neill* (1988), edited by Jackson R. Bryer and Travis Bogard, includes significant letters to his closest correspondents, including two of his wives, Agnes Boulton and Carlotta Monterey, and his children. O'Neill biographers, most notably Arthur and Barbara Gelb and Louis Sheaffer, further probe into O'Neill's troubled relationships with his parents and brother. Students may also want to explore and compare father-son conflicts and similarly isolated characters in other O'Neill works, including *Long Day's Journey into Night* and the lighthearted comedy *Ah, Wilderness!* Richard Eaton and Madeline Smith's *Eugene O'Neill: An Annotated Bibliography* (1988) describes essays that treat such comparisons. Most studies of O'Neill's oeuvre explore the isolation of O'Neill's protagonists, but Bogard's *Contour in Time: The Plays of Eugene O'Neill* (1972) is particularly illuminating in this respect.
2. Many of the resentments evident between son and father in *Desire Under the Elms* are driven by reasons both characters well understand, but much of the

emotional undercurrent seemingly has a primal force born of deep-seated unconscious drives. What are the psychological reasons for Eben's attraction to Abbie? What evidence is there that he is drawn to her for reasons other than her attractiveness? Why is it so important to Ephraim to have a new child at his age? O'Neill's exploration of the subconscious in his plays, which was inspired by his study of Freud's theories, is an important aspect of his presentation of human nature and well worthy of study. Most studies of O'Neill's drama, beginning with Doris V. Falk's *Eugene O'Neill and the Tragic Tension: An Interpretive Study of the Plays* (1958), treat the influence of Freud. Some critics, particularly since the early 1990s, have suggested the importance to O'Neill of Carl Jung's theories and Asian philosophy, an aspect of his work explored in James A. Robinson's *Eugene O'Neill and Oriental Thought: A Divided Vision* (1982).

3. In his dramas throughout the 1920s and early 1930s O'Neill often portrayed the isolation of the individual in an increasingly materialistic or technological world. To what extent is the psychic battle between Ephraim and Eben rooted in materialism? What does the farm mean to each man? How much is Abbie's motivation guided by her desire for possessions? What is the psychological effect of the pursuit of things upon each character? In his groundbreaking study *Eugene O'Neill's America: Desire Under Democracy* (2007) John Patrick Diggins examines O'Neill as a cultural critic of American society, and most O'Neill scholars, including Alexander, Bogard, and Falk, address these themes to a greater or lesser degree.

4. O'Neill's depiction of women raises important questions, particularly so in his presentation of Abbie, the sole female character in *Desire Under the Elms*. Mother, wife, girlfriend, and whore, or some combination of these descriptions, are the traditional roles in which O'Neill envisions women, as examined in Charu Mathur's study *Women in the Plays of Eugene O'Neill and Tennessee Williams* (2002). What roles does Abbie fill? To what extent does she consciously and/or unconsciously manipulate the men for her own ends? How culpable is Abbie in the ultimate tragedy of the play? Is she less responsible than the men?

5. The roots of *Desire Under the Elms* in Greek drama become evident with the birth of Abbie's child and the resultant confrontation between father and son over the child's parentage. Is the inevitable catastrophe more the result of the old man's hubris or his son's desire for revenge? Students interested in exploring the classical roots of *Desire Under the Elms,* and many of O'Neill's other plays, will find sources in various studies, including those by Falk, Alexander, and Bogard. Does O'Neill's invocation of the tragic flaws of Greek drama on the modern stage make for compelling tragedy or unconvincing melodrama?

RESOURCES

Biography

Jackson R. Bryer and Travis Bogard, eds., *Selected Letters of Eugene O'Neill* (New Haven, Conn.: Yale University Press, 1988).

Sheds light on O'Neill's professional collaborations and his troubled personal life, featuring letters to and about his wives, Agnes Boulton and Carlotta Monterey, and his children. Students will find the reflections on family relationships useful in studying O'Neill's domestic dramas, including *Desire Under the Elms*.

Arthur Gelb and Barbara Gelb, *O'Neill* (New York & Evanston, Ill.: Harper, 1962; enlarged edition, New York: Harper & Row, 1973).
The first important biography of O'Neill. This lengthy, copiously detailed work is essential to appreciating autobiographical elements in O'Neill's work, his personal history, and the events and people involved in his life and work.

Louis Sheaffer, *O'Neill: Son and Playwright* (Boston: Little, Brown, 1968).
Sheaffer, *O'Neill: Son and Artist* (Boston: Little, Brown, 1973).
Two biographical studies that, taken in tandem, are the equivalent of the biography by Arthur and Barbara Gelb. Sheaffer emphasizes O'Neill's family life, particularly his relationship with his parents and brother, as essential to his achievement as an artist.

Bibliography

Richard Eaton and Madeline Smith, eds., *Eugene O'Neill: An Annotated Bibliography* (New York: Garland, 1988).
A detailed resource providing a listing of critical examinations of O'Neill's work up to its date of publication, including dozens of references to essays on varied aspects of *Desire Under the Elms*, from comparative analyses with other O'Neill plays and the works of other authors inspired by ancient tragedy to examinations of his presentation of early American life and familial strife.

Criticism

Doris Alexander, *The Tempering of Eugene O'Neill* (New York: Harcourt, Brace & World, 1962).
A good if somewhat general early study of the influences on O'Neill's development as a dramatist, with *Desire Under the Elms* examined for its relation to O'Neill's themes of broken families and for its inspirations in classical tragedy and American naturalism.

Travis Bogard, *Contour in Time: The Plays of Eugene O'Neill* (New York: Oxford University Press, 1972).
At the time of its publication perhaps the most thorough examination of O'Neill's major works, treating recurrent themes as well as literary, historical, and aesthetic influences on O'Neill's evolution as a playwright. The author, who was widely regarded as a leading scholar on O'Neill's achievement, ranks *Desire Under the Elms* among O'Neill's finest work.

John Patrick Diggins, *Eugene O'Neill's America: Desire Under Democracy* (Chicago: University of Chicago Press, 2007).
A study of O'Neill's dramas that focuses on the playwright's belief that the American values of materialism and conformity were preventing the country from achieving its idealistic goals. O'Neill, as Diggins sees it, was in many of his

plays examining a kind of national self-deceit in which democracy and freedom were destroyed by arrogance and greed.

eoneill.com: An Electronic Eugene O'Neill Archive <www.eoneill.com> [accessed 2 December 2009].

An electronic archive offering a library of complete plays, scholarly studies, and the *Eugene O'Neill Newsletter,* as well as an audio archive, reference catalogue, production archive, study companion, an international listing of current and future productions of O'Neill's work, and links to various museums and projects emphasizing O'Neill's achievement.

Eugene O'Neill National Historic Site <www.nps.gov/euon> [accessed 2 December 2009].

Supported by the National Park Service. The site focuses on Tao House, O'Neill's California home, but also features information and links on many aspects of his life and work.

Doris V. Falk, *Eugene O'Neill and the Tragic Tension: An Interpretive Study of the Plays* (New Brunswick, N.J.: Rutgers University Press, 1958).

The first major examination of O'Neill's plays following his death. The author interprets O'Neill plays, *Desire Under the Elms* central among them, as exemplars of a modern form of tragedy.

Linda L. Herr, "Stillborn Future: Dead and Dying Infants and Children as a Secondary Image in the Plays of Eugene O'Neill. An Analysis of the Image in *Desire Under the Elms,*" in *Art, Glitter, and Glitz: Mainstream Playwrights and Popular Theatre in 1920s America,* edited by Arthur Gewirtz and James J. Kolb (Westport, Conn.: Praeger, 2004), pp. 11–17.

Focuses on the imagery of dead and dying children employed by O'Neill in the depiction of Eben and Abbie's illegitimate son in *Desire Under the Elms,* while also referencing such O'Neill plays as *Bound East for Cardiff, Beyond the Horizon* (1920), *The Web* (written in 1913; unproduced), and *Long Day's Journey Into Night.*

Charu Mathur, *Women in the Plays of Eugene O'Neill and Tennessee Williams* (Jaipur, India: Rawat, 2002).

Examines and compares the psyches of the major heroines of both playwrights.

Margaret Loftus Ranald, *The Eugene O'Neill Companion* (Westport, Conn.: Greenwood Press, 1984).

An essential encyclopedic compendium of all matters related to O'Neill's life and work, including synopses of the plays and production details for *Desire Under the Elms* and all of O'Neill's known works, analyses of all but the most minor characters, actors associated with productions of O'Neill's work, film and television productions, family members, friends, and collaborators, etc.

James A. Robinson, *Eugene O'Neill and Oriental Thought: A Divided Vision* (Carbondale: Southern Illinois University Press, 1982).

Argues that Hinduism, Buddhism, and Taoism influenced O'Neill throughout his career.

Ronald H. Wainscott, *Staging O'Neill: The Experimental Years, 1920–1934* (New Haven, Conn.: Yale University Press, 1988).
A useful critical analysis of the experimental nature of O'Neill's work during the second phase of his playwriting career, with attention paid to the major works written and produced between O'Neill's first full-length play, *Beyond the Horizon*, and the failure of *Days Without End*, with considerable attention paid to *Desire Under the Elms*.

—James Fisher

Katherine Anne Porter, The Miranda Cycle

in *The Collected Stories of Katherine Anne Porter*
(New York: Harcourt Brace, 1965)

In the 1920s Katherine Anne Porter began to imagine a long novel constructed around an autobiographical character she called "Miranda." It was to be divided into three parts: "Legend and Memory," exploring Miranda's family history and family legends; "Midway of This Mortal Life," tracing Miranda's transition from childhood to adulthood; and "The Present Day," following Miranda into contemporary political and social experiences that would continue her intellectual and spiritual growth. That novel, the working title of which was "Many Redeemers," never materialized as Porter originally conceived it. But pieces of the first two parts were published between 1935 and 1941 as short stories and short novels.

The seven stories and two short novels that make up what is now known as the Miranda cycle were written in the 1930s and early 1940s; the novels were collected in *Pale Horse, Pale Rider: Three Short Novels* (1939), and six of the stories were included in *The Leaning Tower and Other Stories* (1944), but the entire cycle was not gathered into a single volume until the publication of *The Collected Stories of Katherine Anne Porter* in 1965. (Detailed publication information is provided in Darlene Harbour Unrue's *Katherine Anne Porter: The Life of an Artist* [2005].) In *Collected Stories* Porter arranged seven short stories to constitute a short novel titled "The Old Order," which both initiates and concludes the saga of Miranda Gay; the short novels "Old Mortality" and "Pale Horse, Pale Rider" provide crucial intervening experiences. The best way to experience Miranda's development is to read "The Old Order" first, followed by "Old Mortality," and then "Pale Horse, Pale Rider." Porter often said that the Miranda stories and short novels were "not autobiographical," hoping to discourage readers from regarding them as "mere reportage" and ignoring their art. She preferred to call Miranda her "representative" and her authorial "observer." But the correlation between Porter's life and Miranda's experiences as delineated in the stories and short novels is apparent, and Porter's earliest notes for those works reveal both their autobiographical components and the stages of Porter's artistic transformation of them.

At her birth on 15 May 1890 in Indian Creek, Texas, Porter was named Callie Russell Porter by her parents, Harrison Boone Porter and Mary Alice Jones Porter. When her mother died in 1892, Callie went with her father, brother, and two sisters to live with her grandmother Catharine Ann Skaggs Porter in Hays County, Texas. After the grandmother died in 1901, Callie sporadically attended convent schools in Texas and Louisiana before spending a full academic year in San Antonio at the Thomas School, where she informally changed her name to "Katherine" and intensified the avid reading that constituted her lifelong self-education. In 1906 she married John Henry Koontz, the son of a prosperous Texas rancher.

During her marriage to Koontz, a heavy drinker who routinely beat her, she continued to read widely and to write stories and poems. She finally fled from the marriage in 1914 and went to Chicago, where she worked briefly in the movies. She returned to Texas and divorced Koontz in 1915, asking that her name be legally changed from "Katherine Koontz" to "Katherine Porter" in the decree. Soon she began giving her name as "Katherine Anne Porter," confirming her identification with her paternal grandmother. During the next four years she survived near-fatal influenza and life-threatening tuberculosis, married and divorced twice, and served a journalistic apprenticeship at Texas newspapers and *The Rocky Mountain News* in Denver. In 1919 she moved to New York City to join other serious writers.

Porter was in New York only a year before she decided to go to Mexico, where a social revolution was taking place. She quickly became acquainted with revolutionaries, expatriates, and Mexican artists and intellectuals. Between 1920 and 1923 she was in Mexico three times. Her first mature story, "María Concepción," appeared in 1922. By 1930 she had published a total of nine stories, and Harcourt, Brace collected six of them in a limited edition titled *Flowering Judas.* The volume was so enthusiastically praised by reviewers that Porter's position in American letters was established.

Porter was in Mexico again from the spring of 1930 until the summer of 1931, when she sailed to Europe with Eugene Pressly and settled in Paris for four years. By the time she moved back to the United States, she had married Pressly and published, among other works, three stories in the Miranda cycle. She enhanced her already stellar reputation with the publication in 1939 of *Pale Horse, Pale Rider: Three Short Novels,* which included *Old Mortality* and *Noon Wine.* By 1941 she had divorced Pressly, moved to Louisiana, and married Albert Russel Erskine Jr. Over the course of the next twenty years she sporadically accepted the patronage of the Yaddo artists colony, divorced Erskine, worked as a screenwriter in Hollywood, fulfilled speaking engagements and academic appointments at colleges and universities, undertook a Fulbright assignment in Belgium, and published segments of her novel-in-progress and "The Fig Tree," a Miranda story that had been drafted in the 1920s and misplaced. When *Ship of Fools* was published in 1962, reviews ranged from Mark Schorer's laudatory assessment in *The New York Times* to scathing attacks in *Commentary* and several German newspapers. Although the novel, a satire in the spirit of Jonathan Swift and Erasmus, ran counter to 1960s literary aesthetics, its popular success led to an award-winning 1965 film and brought Porter substantial wealth.

From 1962 until 1980, with the exception of a yearlong sojourn in Europe, Porter lived in Washington, D.C., and Maryland, publishing only works that she had written earlier. She continued to receive the awards and honorary degrees she had begun gathering in the 1940s, and in 1966 she received both the Pulitzer Prize and the National Book Award for *The Collected Stories of Katherine Anne Porter.* When Porter died on 18 September 1980, she left behind a body of Modernist work that many consider unsurpassed in the purity of its classical style and its deep insight into the human condition.

TOPICS FOR DISCUSSION AND RESEARCH

1. The coda to "The Grave," the final story of the seven in "The Old Order," leaps ahead "almost twenty years," when Miranda is nearly thirty, thereby providing the final view of Miranda in the saga that includes the events of "Old Mortality" and "Pale Horse, Pale Rider." The overarching theme of the Miranda cycle is that of initiation. What does Miranda learn about herself and her world? What does she see is worth preserving of the old social order? Placing the Miranda cycle in the context of other changing-of-order works, such as Alfred Tennyson's *Idylls of the King* (1859), Anton Chekhov's *The Cherry Orchard* (1904), and William Faulkner's *Absalom, Absalom!* (1936), and applying to Miranda's chronicle Robert L. Perry's thesis in "Porter's 'Hacienda' and the Theme of Change" (1965) yields insights into the central meaning of one of the most important passageways in Miranda's transition from innocence to experience.

2. By the time Miranda is seen in the coda of "The Grave," she has acquired knowledge of life, death, and love. But those fragments of knowledge have been hard-won, and Miranda has also learned that truth is elusive and often subjective—the premise of Unrue's *Truth and Vision in Katherine Anne Porter's Fiction* (1985). In notes Porter made on "Old Mortality" a decade after its publication she said that "the legend [of Amy and Gabriel] was true as the one who loved it told it [e.g., Miranda's father, Harry], true as Miss Honey, who hated it, told it, and true as Eva told it. And over and above all that was the whole truth which no one could get at." Porter's concept of subjective truth is centered in "Old Mortality." How does the distinction Miranda learns to make between the truths of the "everyday world" and the symbolic truth in the "world of poetry" help her? Why do you think Porter later identified the photograph as the most important symbol in the short novel? Fruitful conclusions about Porter's concept of subjective truth can emerge from an analysis of Porter's use of photography in the Miranda stories, especially "Old Mortality," as Sari Edelstein proves in "'Pretty as Pictures': Family Photography and Southern Postmemory in Porter's 'Old Mortality'" (2008).

3. Why does Miranda reject the standards of female behavior represented by her grandmother's and father's generations? How fulfilling an identity do you think she creates for herself? Gary Ciuba in *Desire, Violence & Divinity in Modern Southern Fiction: Katherine Anne Porter, Flannery O'Connor, Cormac McCarthy, Walker Percy* (2007) examines Miranda's decision not to imitate a model but to find her own way. Jane Krouse DeMouy in *Katherine Anne Porter's Women: The Eye of Her Fiction* (1983) defines the "feminine psychology" of Miranda as her

conflict between a desire for freedom from the constraints of the past and a desire for the comfort of traditional female roles of wife and mother. Do you see Miranda coping well with this conflict, or not being able to resolve it? Mary Ann Wimsatt in "The Old Order Undermined: Daughters, Mothers, and Grandmothers in Katherine Anne Porter's Miranda Tales" (1999) traces Miranda's evolution to a reconciliation of the conflict. Further examination of Miranda's differing desires and contrasting models, with special attention to Miranda's insights into the issue of slavery (dealt with in "The Witness" and obliquely in the middle section of "Old Mortality"), can reveal the complexity of her dilemma, which Janis Stout addresses in the chapter "Among the Agrarians" in her *Katherine Anne Porter: A Sense of the Times* (1995).

4. The recognition of the past as the foundation of the present is an important principle of modernists such as James Joyce, Ezra Pound, William Faulkner, and T. S. Eliot; in his essay "'Ulysses,' Order, and Myth" (1923) Eliot argued for "manipulating a continuous parallel between contemporaneity and antiquity." How effective is Porter in creating this parallel in the Miranda cycle? Is her evocation of the literary past burdensome or seamlessly elegant? To begin an examination of the traditions Porter explored in writing her cycle, read Sara Youngblood's and George Cheatham's essays.

5. Within the knowledge Miranda acquires is an awareness of possible sources for answers to questions about life's meaning. Porter insisted that such answers might be found in art, religion, and sometimes science. She also believed that deep truth about oneself can be found in dreams. Consider the ways dreams are used in the cycle. What does Miranda learn from dreams? Do dreams always lead to truth? A good essay to read when exploring these questions is Thomas F. Walsh's "The Dream Self in 'Pale Horse, Pale Rider'" (1979). Examining the roles of science, religion, art, and dreams throughout the Miranda stories can contribute to a more complete understanding of Miranda's cumulative knowledge.

RESOURCES

Biography

Joan Givner, *Katherine Anne Porter: A Life* (New York: Simon & Schuster, 1982; revised edition, Athens: University of Georgia Press, 1991).

The first comprehensive Porter biography; contains errors and omissions but is particularly useful in accounts of Porter's Thomas School education and details of Porter's first marriage, subjects relevant to the evolution of Miranda Gay.

Janis Stout, *Katherine Anne Porter: A Sense of the Times* (Charlottesville: University Press of Virginia, 1995).

An intellectual biography that analyzes Porter's artistry in the context of her historical moment.

Darlene Harbour Unrue, *Katherine Anne Porter: The Life of an Artist* (Jackson: University Press of Mississippi, 2005).

Traces Porter's evolution as an artist and links elements in her personal experience to core ideas in her fiction.

Bibliography

Ruth M. Alvarez and Kathryn Hilt, *Katherine Anne Porter: An Annotated Bibliography* (New York: Garland, 1990).
Complete through 1988; to be supplemented with the annotated bibliographies in the annual *Newsletter of the Katherine Anne Porter Society* (1994–), online at <http://www.lib.umd.edu/Guests/KAP/pubs.html>, and the bibliographies in the *MLA International Bibliography*.

Criticism

George Cheatham, "Fall and Redemption in 'Pale Horse, Pale Rider,'" *Renascence*, 39 (Spring 1987): 396–405.
Explains the "Christian truth" of humanity's fall, suffering, and redemption as the "informing myth" of the structure and details of the short novel.

Gary M. Ciuba, *Desire, Violence & Divinity in Modern Southern Fiction: Katherine Anne Porter, Flannery O'Connor, Cormac McCarthy, Walker Percy* (Baton Rouge: Louisiana State University Press, 2007).
Includes chapter 2, "'Given Only Me for Model': Porter's 'Miranda' Stories and the Dilemmas of Mimetic Desire," which takes its point of departure from the theory of mimetic violence proposed by critic René Girard.

Jane Krouse DeMouy, *Katherine Anne Porter's Women: The Eye of Her Fiction* (Austin: University of Texas Press, 1983).
Includes an analysis of Miranda's "feminine psychology": the internal conflict between the desire "for the independence and freedom to pursue art or principle regardless of social convention" and "the desire for the love and security inherent in the traditional roles of wife and mother."

Sari Edelstein, "'Pretty as Pictures': Family Photography and Southern Post-memory in Porter's 'Old Mortality,'" *Southern Literary Journal*, 40 (Spring 2008): 151–165.
Compares Porter's use of photographs with Faulkner's in *Absalom, Absalom!* and, using premises of postmodern theory, draws conclusions about photographs as a means of reconstructing history.

Robert L. Perry, "Porter's 'Hacienda' and the Theme of Change," *Midwest Quarterly*, 6 (Summer 1965): 403–415.
Compares and contrasts elements of social change with constant human traits and reveals that some perceived change is only illusion.

Darlene Harbour Unrue, *Truth and Vision in Katherine Anne Porter's Fiction* (Athens: University of Georgia Press, 1985).
Analyzes Porter's canonical theme as the arduous search for truth by categorizing the obstacles in the quest.

Thomas F. Walsh, "The Dream Self in 'Pale Horse, Pale Rider,'" *Wascana Review*, 14 (Fall 1979): 61–79.

A demonstration that the five dreams in the story reveal Miranda to the reader but not to herself.

Mary Ann Wimsatt, "The Old Order Undermined: Daughters, Mothers, and Grandmothers in Katherine Anne Porter's Miranda Tales," in *Southern Mothers: Fact and Fictions in Southern Women's Writing*, edited by Nagueyalti Warren and Sally Wolff (Baton Rouge: Louisiana State University Press, 1999), pp. 81–99.
Examines Miranda's evolution as she reconciles the conflict between what her society tells her she should be and the constraints she must break through to forge her own identity.

Sarah Youngblood, "Structure and Imagery in Katherine Anne Porter's 'Pale Horse, Pale Rider,'" *Modern Fiction Studies*, 5 (Winter 1959–1960): 344–352.
Locates a tripartite structure in the narrative and explains the dream sequence as Miranda's progress toward reality and reunification with the physical world.

—Darlene Harbour Unrue

John Steinbeck, *Of Mice and Men*
(New York: Covici-Friede, 1937)

John Steinbeck (1902–1968) is best known for his poignant depictions of the hardships faced by Americans dispossessed by the Great Depression. His early years as a struggling writer kept him only a few steps removed from the fate of migrant workers whose lives he shadowed first as a fellow laborer and later as a sympathetic observer and author. Born in Salinas, California, to former school-teacher Olive Hamilton and flour mill manager (and later Monterey County treasurer) John Ernst Steinbeck, he spent summers exploring nearby Pacific Grove with his uncle Sam Hamilton (on whom the character of the same name in *East of Eden* [1952] is based), developing an early interest in the topography of the coast that later figured into much of his fiction.

Between 1919 and 1925 Steinbeck studied intermittently at Stanford University, where he took literature courses and published his first stories in the *Stanford Spectator*. When not in school, he worked on area ranches and estates as a laborer or caretaker, settling into whatever situation interested him and gathering stories from fellow workers. On graduating, he moved briefly to New York in hopes of publishing his writing; but he was unsuccessful and returned, as he often did during difficult periods, to California.

Steinbeck was supported by intellectually stimulating people throughout his life. His first wife, Carol Henning, acted as his editor. In 1930 the couple settled in Steinbeck's family cottage in Pacific Grove. There Steinbeck met marine biologist Edward F. Ricketts, owner of the Pacific Biological Laboratory, who became his best friend and greatest intellectual influence. Studying with Ricketts, Steinbeck became a scientist in his own right and developed a philosophy based on biological principles that guided his writing. Ricketts also introduced the Steinbecks to a dazzling circle of writers and thinkers with whom they discussed ideas, among them Joseph Campbell and Henry Miller. In 1933 Henning began work with the Emergency Relief Organization, an aid agency for migrant families. Struck by Henning's accounts of the lives of the people she encountered, Steinbeck began to incorporate many of their stories into his writing.

Although Steinbeck achieved his first commercial success with *Tortilla Flat* (1935), it was his late-1930s works, beginning with *Of Mice and Men* (1937), that made him famous. Although vulgar language in the novella resulted in an immediate outcry—it was banned and even burned in areas throughout the country—it nevertheless became the Book-of-the-Month Club selection in March 1937 and enjoyed tremendous sales. Based on Steinbeck's own experiences as a farm laborer, the book became equally popular that same year as a stage adaptation. The spare, compelling story of the relationship between two bindle stiffs, the shrewd George Milton and the hapless Lennie Small, captivated audiences with its simple expression of human yearnings for self-sufficiency and companionship. Critic Harry Hensen called the work "the finest bit of prose fiction of this decade."

Steinbeck's distaste for his new fame following *Of Mice and Men* increased alongside his awareness of the miserable living conditions in migrant camps, which he investigated through journalistic assignments for the *San Francisco News*. Despite his fear that he would no longer be able to immerse himself unobserved in the daily struggles of everyday people, he used his celebrity to promote awareness of the plight of the migrants after a profoundly upsetting trip to Visalia, where he had been sent to document the lives of workers in a flood zone. In 1938 he completed the manuscript for *The Grapes of Wrath* (1939), the epic story of the Joad family's struggle for survival as "Okies" during the Great Depression. The book was a best seller and the movie (filmed that same year) an Academy Award nominee for Best Picture, but Steinbeck's work was again dogged by controversy. The book shocked audiences with its bleak portrayal of migrant life and was denounced by Congress and by the Associated Farmworkers of California as communist propaganda (although it was called an accurate depiction of conditions by First Lady Eleanor Roosevelt) and for its provocative final scene. Despite being banned in many areas, the book was awarded the Pulitzer Prize in 1940.

In 1941 Steinbeck separated from his wife and began living in New York with the actress Gwendolyn Conger, with whom he had been having an affair for several years. In 1942 he was made a special consultant to the secretary of war and asked to write a book about the training of bomber crews, which became the propaganda novel *Bombs Away: The Story of a Bomber Team* (1942). Still happiest when able to blend in rather than observe from a distance, he fought successfully for clearance to be embedded with an Army regiment as a war correspondent for the *New York Herald Tribune* in 1943. That year he was divorced from his first wife and married Conger. The couple had two children, Thom in 1944 and John in 1946, but the marriage deteriorated. In 1948 Steinbeck endured dual blows: Ricketts died in a car crash, and his wife left him, resentful of the sacrifices she had made for his career. The next year Steinbeck met the former stage manager Elaine Scott; they were married in 1930.

In 1962 Steinbeck was awarded the Nobel Prize in literature for his life's work, an honor that surprised many critics. Despite the success of *Cannery Row* (1944), *East of Eden,* and *The Winter of Our Discontent* (1961), Steinbeck had by the 1960s been dismissed by many as a simplistic, sentimental writer—a lesser artist than contemporaries such as Ernest Hemingway and F. Scott Fitzgerald—whose best work was three decades behind him. Popular audiences in the United States and international critics, however, continued to revere Steinbeck's work and to consider him a beloved and influential figure in American letters. As evidence of this reputation, President Lyndon Johnson awarded Steinbeck the Presidential Medal of Freedom in 1964, four years before the author's death in Sag Harbor, New York.

TOPICS FOR DISCUSSION AND RESEARCH

1. The popularity of *Of Mice and Men* may be partially attributed to the fact that it was the least political of Steinbeck's Great Depression works. *In Dubious Battle* (1936) and *The Grapes of Wrath* were often labeled Marxist or Communist, though Steinbeck, a New Deal Democrat, intended *In Dubious Battle* to be a detached account of a labor strike and wrote *The Grapes of Wrath* as an impassioned call to end a national disaster. *Of Mice and Men* fell somewhere between these two extremes, featuring sympathetic, well-developed characters but invoking a sense of inevitability about their tragic outcome. Nevertheless, insofar as it depicted the catastrophic effect of large-scale farming on the western U.S. poor, some critics attacked the novella as "antibusiness." An additional claim stated that it endorsed euthanasia. Still others reacted most strongly to its vulgar language. For whatever combination of these reasons, the novella has remained on the American Library Association's "Most Challenged Books" list well into the twenty-first century and has been banned in schools as recently as 2003. Tracing the objections to Steinbeck's novella can be a revealing study of American culture and politics. Barbara Heavilin's *John Steinbeck's* Of Mice and Men: *A Reference Guide* (2005) catalogs the various responses. Morris Dickstein's essay "Steinbeck and the Great Depression" (2004) follows the trajectory of the author's changing reactions to the events of the Depression through his three major works during the 1930s. Students might consult this essay, along with Nancy Steinbeck and Robert Wallsten's *Steinbeck: A Life in Letters* (1975), to explore the tension between popular and critical reactions and Steinbeck's own interpretations of his works.

2. For most people familiar with the novella, the title *Of Mice and Men* immediately conjures the childlike Lennie's stated wish to "live off the fatta the lan'" and "tend the rabbits." This simple desire, echoed through the years in numerous popular-culture references, including Warner Brothers cartoons, crystallizes the modest vision of the American Dream sought by George and Lennie: all the two men want is to have a homestead they can farm, to

be free of the whims of a cruel boss, and to not have to keep running when Lennie unwittingly harms animals and people because of his obsession with touching soft things. Even though Candy, another laborer, offers to join them and contribute his wages, they cannot collect enough money to make the dream a reality before Lennie accidentally kills Curley's wife. Students might consider the positive and negative effects of the American Dream on the novella's characters. Whereas their fixation on the goal of landowning sets them up for eventual disappointment, it also provides a communion among them that is otherwise impossible. In *Steinbeck's Re-Vision of America* (1985) Louis Owens sees this human connection as Steinbeck's expression of a positive alternative to the American Dream. It is also productive to consider the character of Lennie as an embodiment of the American Dream. Heavilin posits that the reader's recognition of this embodiment gives the character a dimension he would otherwise lack.

3. George and Lennie's dream of a homestead is ripe with Edenic imagery, and Curley's wife, the pretty, seductive lone woman on the ranch, can easily be seen as the biblical temptress. Early in the novella she represents trouble for the male workers. George's irritation with her flirtatiousness underscores his frequently negative response to sexual temptation. Further, Lennie's fascination with her concerns George, who fears that Lennie will eventually harm her. Referring to her only as "Curley's wife," Steinbeck claimed he did not give the character a name because he did not perceive her as a full character but only as a foil for the male characters. Thus, when Lennie accidentally kills her when stroking her hair, the men's dream of having their own land disappears, and the woman's role in the drama has been fulfilled. When writing the script for the 1937 stage adaptation, Steinbeck made subtle changes to her role in the plot based on a suggestion by adviser George S. Kaufmann to make her a more central part of the confrontation between George and Lennie. When Clare Boothe Luce, who played Curley's wife, protested that she had mixed feelings about the character, Steinbeck's view of her came into greater focus: she was "really a good person," he wrote in the stage instructions, "and you would end up loving her." Lewis Milestone, director of the 1939 film, developed her character further along these lines, giving her the name "Mae" and writing in a new scene showing her interactions with Curley and his father so that the viewer would be more empathetic toward her. Charlotte Cook Hadella's Of Mice and Men: *A Kinship of Powerlessness* (1995) offers a comprehensive analysis of critical views on Curley's wife. Students might fruitfully consider her as a representation of the loneliness of the human condition. It is also worth comparing Steinbeck's development of this character to that of female characters in his other works.

4. Despite frequent criticism that the novella is overly sentimental, Steinbeck in fact attempted to tell the story of the two ranch hands without manipulating readers' reactions in any particular direction. Proof of this perspective can be seen in the working title of the book: "Something That Happened." This detached approach stems from the influence of Ed Ricketts, who

enlightened Steinbeck to "non-teleological" or "is" thinking, in which one observes a situation as it is without considering how it evolved. Thus, Steinbeck conceived of the plot as though he were observing a tidal pool with Ricketts. The book's tragic ending seems inevitable, foreshadowed by the scene in which the team boss, Curley, orders that Candy's dog be shot because he no longer considers the animal useful. Lennie, whose strength is harmless only when applied to manual labor, is only alive because George protects him when he innocently injures animals and people. One day, the reader perceives, George and Lennie's plans to settle down on a small plot of land will go "a-gley" (awry), as in the Robert Burns poem "To a Mouse" (1785) for which the work was finally named. Richard Astro's *John Steinbeck and Edward F. Ricketts: The Shaping of a Novelist* (1973) offers a thorough analysis of how Steinbeck's work was affected by his relationship with Ricketts. Becoming familiar with the scientific principles that guided *Of Mice and Men* will help students place in critical context arguments regarding the sentimentality of the novella. Heavilin charts a range of critical responses to the claim of sentimentality, foregrounding Harold Bloom's famously dismissive reaction that Steinbeck's work "fell into bathos" and Jill Karson's contrasting response that the novella "strikes a timeless, universal chord." Heavilin also provides analysis of how the Burns poem relates to the novella. Students might consider whether the change in title indicates a less detached approach by Steinbeck.

5. Nearly all of the characters in *Of Mice and Men*—which is set in the town of Soledad (solitude)—experience a profound sense of isolation. Whereas several of Steinbeck's novels, including *The Grapes of Wrath* and *East of Eden*, are family sagas, *Of Mice and Men* is based on a group of misfits who have been brought together by dismal economic circumstances and who at times simulate a family. Lennie and George are isolated because they are always on the run; Candy because of his age and missing hand; Curley because he had to abandon his profession as a boxer; his wife because she is the only woman on the ranch and believes that she has missed out on a chance to be a famous actress; and Crooks because he is the only African American ranch hand and because he is disabled. Early in the novella, Slim, the jerkline skinner respected by all on the ranch, confronts George about why he has been taking care of Lennie. George replies that Lennie's companionship, although burdensome, is preferable to solitude: "I ain't got no people. . . . I seen the guys that go around on the ranches alone. They ain't no good. They don't have no fun. After a long time they get mean. They get wantin' to fight all the time." Students might investigate how moments of communion among the characters are alternately positive and destructive; a good starting point is Hadella's study. Another inquiry might be whether such moments of communion are authentically positive among such disparate individuals; Stephen George's *Moral Philosophy of John Steinbeck* considers sexism and racism as key isolating factors among the characters. Owens argues that loneliness is the primary theme of the novella.

RESOURCES

Biography

Richard Astro, *John Steinbeck and Edward F. Ricketts: The Shaping of a Novelist* (Minneapolis: University of Minnesota Press, 1973).
Devoted exclusively to the fruitful intellectual connection between the two men; presents Steinbeck as a true scientist rather than a dilettante.

Jackson J. Benson, *The True Adventures of John Steinbeck, Writer* (New York: Viking, 1984).
A detailed account more focused on setting straight misconceptions about Steinbeck's life than on delving deeply into the critical fray about his works. Benson spent fifteen years writing this authoritative volume.

Jay Parini, *John Steinbeck: A Biography* (New York: Holt, 1995).
Considered a formidable supplement to Benson's volume. Parini's biography is largely based on interviews with individuals such as the author's third wife, Elaine, and focuses on Steinbeck's writing process and his place in American letters.

Elaine Steinbeck and Robert Wallsten, eds., *Steinbeck: A Life in Letters* (New York: Viking, 1975).
An intimate portrait drawn from letters between 1923 and 1968, revealing Steinbeck's own views about his writing and critical reception.

Bibliography

Barbara Heavilin, *John Steinbeck's* Of Mice and Men: *A Reference Guide* (Westport, Conn.: Praeger, 2005).
A useful guide to all aspects of the work. The concluding bibliographical essay gives insights into the range of critical reactions.

Michael J. Meyer, *The John Steinbeck Bibliography, 1996–2006* (Lanham, Md.: Scarecrow Press, 2008).
The most current and complete source for primary and secondary bibliography. Meyer was mentored in Steinbeck bibliography by Tetsumaro Hayashi, who compiled three previous bibliographies.

Criticism

Morris Dickstein, "Steinbeck and the Great Depression," *South Atlantic Quarterly*, 103 (Winter 2004): 111–131.
Offers a useful overview of Steinbeck's changing literary reaction to the Depression in his 1930s works.

Stephen K. George, ed., *The Moral Philosophy of John Steinbeck* (Lanham, Md.: Scarecrow Press, 2005).
Based on the editor's conviction that Steinbeck's interest in moral philosophy separates him from his contemporaries. The collection includes an essay by Richard E. Hart on the moral dimension of *Of Mice and Men*.

Charlotte Cook Hadella, *Of Mice and Men: A Kinship of Powerlessness* (New York: Twayne, 1995).
A general guide to the work that includes a particularly useful section on symbol and myth.

Martha Heasley Cox Center for Steinbeck Research <www.steinbeck.sjsu.edu/home/index.jsp> [accessed 2 December 2009].
Includes a tremendous amount of information on Steinbeck's life and works, as well as a searchable bibliography of secondary materials.

Louis Owens, *Steinbeck's Re-Vision of America* (Athens: University of Georgia Press, 1985).
Discusses Steinbeck's connection to California.

—Emily Dings

John Steinbeck, *The Grapes of Wrath*
(New York: Viking, 1939)

The Grapes of Wrath (1930), John Steinbeck's eighth novel, established him as one of the most significant writers of the twentieth century. A best seller with sales of three hundred thousand copies in 1939, it was denounced on the floor of the U.S. House of Representatives; banned and burned in Kern County, California, where the fictional Joads end up in the novel; defended by First Lady Eleanor Roosevelt, who said that it accurately portrayed the injustices done to migrant workers; and awarded the Pulitzer Prize in fiction. Having written sympathetically about conditions among migrant workers—notably, in *In Dubious Battle* (1936)—Steinbeck was asked in 1936 by the *San Francisco News* to write a series of seven articles describing the plight of farmers driven to California from the southern Great Plains states of Colorado, Kansas, Oklahoma, and Texas by the decade-long drought that finally caused the land to be so dry that the spring winds kicked up choking storms of dust. It was estimated that in the early 1930s one hundred million acres of land lost their topsoil to the wind, destroying farms and lives in the process.

Moved by the tragedy of the farmers and frustrated by the lack of response on the part of the government, Steinbeck determined to act himself. He performed his own research, traveling to the Farm Security Administration migrant camps in California's Central Valley and working among the displaced farmers. He wrote an angry novel about the migrants, which he discarded as too inflammatory. Then he undertook *The Grapes of Wrath*, with the intention of informing readers about the horrendous effects of what was called the Dust Bowl, promoting understanding of its human toll, and moving readers to respond to the tragedy. He took his title from Julia Ward Howe's "The Battle Hymn of the Republic" (1862):

Mine eyes have seen the glory of the coming of the Lord:
He is trampling out the vintage where the grapes of wrath are stored;
He hath loosed the fateful lightning of His terrible swift sword:
His truth is marching on.

He decided on a structure that offers two perspectives. The focus of the story is the Joad family, Okies who migrate to workers' camps in California after their livelihood is blown away in the dust storms and they are ravaged by starvation. In alternate chapters Steinbeck provides a broader view, describing the political forces that affected families like the Joads and identifying the Joads as victims who typify the migrants of the time. Steinbeck relates the resentment of workers at the government camps, the frustration and anger of desperate migrant families, the instigation of revolutionaries toward mobilization, and, finally, the indomitable human spirit of brotherhood. The novel ends with Rose of Sharon, the eldest of the Joad children, her breasts filled with milk after her child is stillborn, suckling a starving man.

While Steinbeck does not romanticize the Joads, he humanizes them, portraying the social and economic conditions that affect them and their understandable anger at the social injustice they suffer in the wake of being victimized by forces of nature. Students interested in studying *The Grapes of Wrath* would do well to begin with Jackson Benson's biography, *The True Adventures of John Steinbeck, Writer* (1984). Steinbeck studies are greatly enhanced by the significant collections of the author's correspondence, in which he talks in detail about his work, his literary intentions, and his influences. His wife, Elaine, edited *Steinbeck: A Life in Letters* (1975), and his letters to his friend and editor Pascal Covici have been collected by Thomas Fensch in *Steinbeck and Covici: The Story of a Friendship* (1979). Use the index to these volumes to find Steinbeck's comments about specific works. Key interviews have been collected by Fensch in *Conversations with John Steinbeck* (1988). It is important to get a sense of social context for the novel. A quick overview of the Dust Bowl with firsthand accounts can be found in the "Farming in the 1930s" section of the W*essels Living History Farm* website at <http://www.livinghistoryfarm.org/farminginthe30s/water_02.html> [accessed 10 December 2009]. Timothy Egan's *The Worst Hard Time: The Untold Story of Those Who Survived the Great American Dust Bowl* (Boston: Houghton Mifflin, 2006) is an excellent account for students who seek more than superficial treatment of the subject.

After getting a good sense of Steinbeck's feelings about the book and its social context, criticism will be useful. Good collections of essays are edited by Warren French, John Ditsky, David Wyatt, and Harold Bloom. If those collections do not provide the information you are seeking, consult Robert B. Harman's bibliography.

TOPICS FOR DISCUSSION AND RESEARCH

1. In a 1939 review in *The New Republic* Malcom Cowley argues that *The Grapes of Wrath* does not rank with the best modern fiction of Ernest

Hemingway, F. Scott Fitzgerald, and John Dos Passos, but that it does rank among the great angry books, such as Harriet Beecher Stowe's *Uncle Tom's Cabin* (1852) that "roused a people to fight against intolerable wrongs." Discuss Cowley's conclusion. Do you agree? If so, what is lacking in *The Grapes of Wrath* that keeps it from being ranked with the works of the great writers between the world wars? Does "angry" fiction always belong in a second rank of literature? For a discussion of the literary merits of the novel, see Donald Pizer's essay.

2. After reading about the Dust Bowl, including accounts of people who experienced it, consider the impact of *The Grapes of Wrath* on the audience of 1939 and how the effect might be different on readers today. For help in addressing this topic, see Walter Fuller Taylor's essay, keeping in mind that it was written in 1959. If asked to expand the essay to cover an additional fifty years after Taylor wrote, what would you add?

3. Much has been made by critics of biblical imagery in *The Grapes of Wrath*, particularly with regard to Rose of Sharon's act at the end of the novel. James D. Brasch finds allusions to both the Old and New Testaments. Before reading any criticism, make your own survey of biblical allusions and consider how they work within the novel. Are they overly obtrusive, or are they integral to the story? Then read Brasch's piece; Harry T. Moore's pioneering essay in *The Novels of John Steinbeck* (1939); and other essays on the topic you might locate and revise your assessment. See Lorelei Cederstrom's "The 'Great Mother' in *The Grapes of Wrath*," in *Steinbeck and the Environment: Interdisciplinary Approaches* (1997), edited by Susan F. Beegel and others, for a counterargument.

4. Before Steinbeck wrote *The Grapes of Wrath*, he wrote newspaper articles about the Dust Bowl, interviewed social scientists who were studying the migrant population in California, and surveyed documentary evidence related to the topic. How did this research affect the novel? Is the work made better by the fact that Steinbeck was so well versed, or was he too close to his material to view it objectively? See William Howarth's "The Mother of Literature: Journalism and *The Grapes of Wrath*," in *New Essays on* The Grapes of Wrath (1990) edited by David Wyatt.

5. A hazard of writing a novel such as *The Grapes of Wrath* is sentimentality, or the exaggeration of emotion to distort the characters and the manner in which they are portrayed. Steinbeck recognized that danger, and said in an interview in *The Paris Review* that a writer should keep his emotions at arm's length in his work. Do you think he succeeded in doing so in *The Grapes of Wrath*? Are the misfortunes of the Joad family exaggerated? Are Jim Casy's speeches believable? Is the scene in which Rose of Sharon feeds a starving man overly dramatic? Louis Owens's "The Culpable Joads: Desentimentalizing *The Grapes of Wrath*" in the Ditsky collection provides useful ideas about approaching this topic.

RESOURCES

Bibliography

Robert B. Harmon and John F. Early, The Grapes of Wrath: *A Fifty Year Bibliographic Survey* (San Jose, Cal.: Steinbeck Research Center of San Jose State University, 1990).
The most reliable secondary bibliography of works on the novel.

Biography

Thomas Fensch, ed., *Conversations with John Steinbeck* (Jackson: University of Mississippi Press, 1988).
A collection of interviews with Steinbeck throughout his career.

Fensch, ed., *Steinbeck and Covici: The History of a Friendship* (Middlebury, Vt.: P. S. Eriksson, 1979).
Steinbeck's letters to his dear friend and editor at Viking Press.

Criticism

Susan F. Beegel, Susan Shillinglaw, and Wesley N. Tiffney Jr., eds., *Steinbeck and the Environment* (Tuscaloosa: University of Alabama Press, 1997).
A collection of essays gathered collaboratively by two literary scholars and a scientist.

Harold Bloom, ed., *John Steinbeck's* The Grapes of Wrath (New York: Chelsea House, 1998);
Bloom, ed., *John Steinbeck's* The Grapes of Wrath (Philadelphia: Chelsea House, 2005).
Two books, comprising completely different essays. Students should consult both volumes.

James D. Brasch, "*The Grapes of Wrath* and Old Testament Skepticism," *San Jose Studies*, 3 (May 1977): 16–27.
Essay that argues that "a careful reading of *The Grapes of Wrath* demonstrates that John Steinbeck was not the great celebrant of American values and assumptions articulated by Emerson and Whitman."

John Ditsky, ed., *Critical Essays on Steinbeck's* The Grapes of Wrath (Boston: G. K. Hall, 1989).
A good general collection of essays.

Warren G. French, *A Companion to* The Grapes of Wrath (New York: Viking, 1963).
A readable, thematic approach to the novel.

Harry T. Moore, *The Novels of John Steinbeck* (Chicago: Normandie House, 1939).
An interesting early study of Steinbeck's work by a respected scholar and critic.

Louis Owens, The Grapes of Wrath: *Trouble in the Promised Land* (Boston: Twayne, 1989).
A useful reference work in Twayne's Masterwork series.

Donald Pizer, "John Steinbeck: *The Grapes of Wrath*," in his *Twentieth-Century Literary Naturalism: An Interpretation* (Carbondale: Southern Illinois University Press, 1982), pp. 65–81.
Argument by a leading authority on literary Naturalism that *The Grapes of Wrath* is "naturalism suffering the inevitable consequences of its soft thinking and its blatant catering to popular interests."

Walter Fuller Taylor, "*The Grapes of Wrath* Reconsidered: Some Observations on John Steinbeck and the 'Religion' of Secularism," *Mississippi Quarterly,* 12 (Summer 1959): 136–144.
Argues that "the 'meaning' of a book is not absolute or unalterable."

David Wyatt, ed., *New Essays on* The Grapes of Wrath (New York & Cambridge, England: Cambridge University Press, 1990).
A collection of newly commissioned essays on the novel in the Cambridge New Essays series.

—George Parker Anderson

Wallace Stevens, *Harmonium*

(New York: Knopf, 1923; revised and enlarged, 1931)

In appearance and in reality, Wallace Stevens was a successful lawyer and business executive. "Wally! Poetry?" exclaimed a business associate when he was told that Stevens was an important poet and that his correspondence was likely valuable. Stevens kept his work at the office largely separated from his life at home. Throughout his literary career Stevens meditated on the interrelationship between imagination and reality. In his work the reader encounters a poet who creates orders of words that, more than religion or any other means, answer his search for meaning. "Blanche McCarthy"— the poem that editor Holly Stevens presents as her father's earliest surviving work in *The Palm at the End of the Mind* (1971)—begins with an injunction that suggests this search: "Look in the terrible mirror of the sky / And not in this dead glass, which can reflect / Only the surfaces—the bending arm, / The leaning shoulder and the searching eye." In "Of Mere Being," the latest poem included in the collection, the poet provides a last metaphor for the strangeness of human existence in the image of "The Palm at the end of the mind, / Beyond the last thought": "A gold-feathered bird / Sings in the palm, without human meaning, / Without human feeling, a foreign song."

Stevens was born in Reading, Pennsylvania, on 2 October 1879. He grew up with a brother two years older, another brother a year younger, and two much younger sisters. His mother had also been born in Reading, where she taught school before she married; his father was an attorney and a businessman. Both parents were of Dutch and German ancestry, which Stevens later studied, in part to involve himself more personally in American history. In a 15 June 1953 letter he wrote of his satisfaction in "being one of these hard-working and faithful people." In his journal Stevens remembered how his mother "always read a chapter from the Bible every night" to her children when they were ready for bed.

From 1897 to 1900 Stevens attended Harvard, where he pursued an interest in composition and literature—French and German, as well as English. Although he did not take a course with George Santayana, he was influenced by the philosopher's thought, especially Santayana's *Interpretations of Poetry and Religion* (1900). He became president of the *Harvard Advocate,* contributing poems that were mostly imitative of existing Romantic and Victorian models. He wrote in conventional forms such as the quatrain and sonnet, showing technical control of meter and rhyme but little of the originality that characterizes his mature work.

After a brief stint as a journalist for the *New York Tribune,* Stevens studied to become an attorney, graduating from New York Law School in 1903. He then pursued a career in insurance law. In 1909 he married Elsie Kachel Moll and in the next few years lost both of his parents. The poems he was then writing began to show Stevens's mature voice. Four of his poems appeared in a special issue of *Poetry* in 1914 and were praised by Hart Crane. In 1916 Stevens started working for Hartford Accident and Indemnity Company, where he stayed until his death, becoming vice president in 1934. He was deeply affected by the death of his youngest sister, May Katherine, in 1919. In 1923, the year he turned forty-four, he published his first volume of poems, *Harmonium* (1923). The next year the Stevenses' only child, Holly, was born.

After a new and enlarged edition of *Harmonium* was published in 1931, Stevens began to publish poetry regularly: *Ideas of Order* (1935; enlarged, 1936), *The Man with the Blue Guitar & Other Poems* (1937), *Parts of a World* (1942), and the long philosophical poem *Notes Toward a Supreme Fiction* (1942). He was awarded the Bollingen Prize in Poetry by the Yale University Library in 1949 and won a National Book Award for *The Auroras of Autumn* (1950), a long poem that incorporates memories of his mother, which he wrote when he had reached the age at which she died, sixty-four. *The Necessary Angel* (1951), a book of essays, was followed by his last work, *The Collected Poems of Wallace Stevens* (1954), which received a National Book Award and a Pulitzer Prize. Stevens died on 2 August 1955. Throughout his career as a poet he worked full-time at the insurance company. References that students will want to consult to learn more about Stevens's life and career include the biographies by Holly Stevens, Peter Brazeau, and Joan Richardson and the descriptive primary bibliography by J. M. Edelstein.

In *The Comic Spirit of Wallace Stevens* (1963) Daniel Fuchs writes of Stevens's development: "He does, of course change, but his changes are different ways of exploring the same themes, themes which are sufficiently complex to justify a lifetime's meditation. Though they are all present in *Harmonium,* these themes achieve expression, some of them fullest expression, well after *Harmonium.*" The collection thus provides a good way of entering into Stevens's world as well as being a watershed in his development as a poet. Including many of Stevens's most famous poems, *Harmonium* is particularly interesting because it is the only collection that the poet actually arranged—in all of his later collections the poems are presented in roughly chronological order of composition. *Harmonium* is also Stevens's only collection that has a dedication. He dedicated the first edition "To MY WIFE"; the enlarged 1931 edition was dedicated "to MY WIFE AND HOLLY."

The 1923 edition of *Harmonium* comprises seventy-four poems; almost all had been published from 1915 to 1922 in periodicals, including *Poetry: A Magazine of Verse, Others, The Little Review,* and *The Dial.* For the 1931 edition Stevens omitted three poems—"The Silver Plough-Boy," "Exposition of the Contents of a Cab," and "Architecture"—and added fourteen more, which he had inserted in a specified order before the final two poems that close both editions, "Tea" and "To the Roaring Wind." *The Collected Poems of Wallace Stevens* (1954), published to mark Stevens's seventy-fifth birthday, reprints the 1931 edition of *Harmonium.* The Library of America's *Wallace Stevens: Collected Poetry and Prose* (1997) presents all the poems from the 1923 edition followed by a section titled "Poems added to Harmonium (1931)."

TOPICS FOR DISCUSSION AND RESEARCH

1. In *A Reader's Guide to Wallace Stevens* (2007) Eleanor Cook considers the reasons Stevens may have had for settling on *Harmonium* as a title. She explains that a harmonium was a keyboard instrument, "a kind of reed-organ," which, she contends, is a good trope for poetry: "The word is derived from Greek and Latin *harmonia,* so that it also suggests questions of harmony, including the older idea of the harmony of the universe, as it moves in accordance with the unheard heavenly music of the spheres." Stevens's poems are often difficult to understand, all the more so at times because of his unusual diction, which occasionally includes words from foreign languages. As you read and think about a poem by Stevens, pick out words to study, looking up those that you do not know or that strike you as odd in the context in which they are used. Why do you think Stevens chose the word? Might he have selected it as much as for its sound or rhythm as for its meaning? Is there a denotation, etymological meaning, or connotation that you discover in the *Oxford English Dictionary* that seems relevant to understanding the poem? You might want to consult Cook's guide, in which she discusses difficult passages in Stevens's poems, as well as the poet's letters, in which he sometimes comments on his choice of words, and Thomas F. Walsh's *Concordance to the Poetry of Wallace Stevens* (1963).

2. In a 6 January 1933 letter to William Rose Benét, who was planning an anthology of poets' favorite poems, Stevens wrote, "I think I should select from my poems as my favorite the Emperor Of Ice Cream. This wears a deliberately commonplace costume, and yet seems to me to contain something of the essential gaudiness of poetry; that is the reason why I like it." In a follow-up 24 January letter Stevens wrote, "I dislike niggling, and like letting myself

go. This poem is an instance of letting myself go. Poems of this sort are the pleasantest on which to look back, because they seem to remain fresher than others. This represented what was in my mind at the moment, with the least possible manipulation." Discussing a French translation of the poem in a 1 June 1939 letter, Stevens made specific assertions about his intentions: "In the second verse of THE EMPEROR, the word fantails does not mean fans, but fantail pigeons.... Going back to the first verse, the true sense of Let be be the finale of seem is let being become the conclusion or denouement of appearing to be: in short, icecream is an absolute good. The poem is obviously not about icecream, but about being as distinguished from seeming to be." In a 16 May 1945 letter he discussed the poem at some length, asserting that "the point of that poem is not its meaning" and going on to comment on his diction: "The words 'concupiscent curds' have no genealogy; they are merely expressive: at least, I hope they are expressive. They express the concupiscence of life, but, by contrast with the things in relation to them in the poem, they express or accentuate life's destitution, and it is this that gives them something more than a cheap luster." How much weight should Stevens's opinions of his poem carry? Should his explanation of how he wrote the poem or his intention in choosing certain words determine how the poem is read? Read the critics—Helen Vendler, Kia Penso, Milton J. Bates, and Kenneth Lincoln—who comment on "The Emperor of Ice Cream" at the Modern American Poetry website on Wallace Stevens. Which of them, if any, help you to appreciate the poem? Are their opinions of the poem more or less illuminating than Stevens's?

3. As Stevens's comments on "The Emperor of Ice Cream" in his letters show, he sometimes had a great deal to say about a poem in a variety of circumstances over a long period of time. Such comments open a window not only on the poems of *Harmonium* but also on Stevens's view of himself as a poet, his attitudes about the role of a poet vis-à-vis his or her work and the public, and his evolving sense of his own development and themes. Many rewarding research projects might arise from a close study of a poem or a group of poems in conjunction with his comments on them in *Letters of Wallace Stevens*. As you investigate and try to draw conclusions from Stevens's comments in his letters, remember to consider the circumstances in which he is writing and his relationship with his correspondent, as sometimes a seeming inconsistency may be explained by differing situations. For example, Stevens was definite about his intentions when he discussed the French translation of "The Emperor of Ice Cream," even stating forthrightly what his poem was about. Six years later, in his 16 May 1945 letter, he writes that "the point of the poem is not its meaning." Is this a contradiction? Is it important? Be sure to have several points for support when you try to draw a conclusion about Stevens's views of his art.

4. The reader can easily be overwhelmed by the variety of the eighty-eight poems that Stevens included in the two editions of *Harmonium*. One way of studying the volume is to narrow your examination by focusing on a group of poems that are related in some way. For example, the first poem in the collection is "Earthly Anecdote." Looking at the table of contents for the volume,

you will notice that there are four other poems that have the word *anecdote* in the title: "Anecdote of Men by the Thousand," "Anecdote of Canna," "Anecdote of the Prince of Peacocks," and "Anecdote of the Jar." Are these poems connected in other ways? Another striking detail of "Earthly Anecdote" is its setting: Oklahoma. Many other poems in the collection invoke the names of states or regions, such as "In the Carolinas," "Fabliau of Florida," "O, Florida, Venereal Soil," and "New England Verses." In other poems he uses state names in the poem, including Oklahoma in "Life is Motion," Tennessee in "Anecdote of a Jar," and Florida in "Nomad Exquisite." Why and how does Stevens use the idea of states? Is Oklahoma really Oklahoma? Is Florida really Florida? What other connections between poems can you make from the table of contents? Or how might you group his poems based on formal considerations, such as his use of particular stanza types, meters, or sound effects such as rhyme or alliteration? "The Snow Man," one of Stevens's most famous works, is one of several poems in the collection that are written as a single sentence.

5. "The Comedian as the Letter C," the longest poem in *Harmonium* and one of the most difficult, is often commented on by critics. Before turning to critical views of the poem, try to come up with your own observations. What can you say about the subject of the poem, Crispen? What seems to be the attitude expressed toward him in the poem? Critics you might want to read include Richard Allen Blessing, Harold Bloom, and Helen Vendler.

RESOURCES

Primary Works

The Palm at the End of the Mind: Selected Poems and a Play, edited by Holly Stevens (New York: Knopf, 1971).

A chronological presentation of Stevens's poems edited by his daughter. Although a good introduction to the whole of Stevens's career, it does not include all the poems of *Harmonium*.

The Collected Poems of Wallace Stevens (New York: Vintage, 1990).

A widely available paperback edition that reprints the contents of the collection originally published by Knopf in 1954, including the enlarged 1931 edition of *Harmonium*.

Wallace Stevens: Collected Poetry and Prose, edited by Frank Kermode and Joan Richardson (New York: Library of America, 1997).

A useful edition that includes all of the poems in both the 1923 and 1931 editions of *Harmonium*.

Bibliography

J. M. Edelstein, *Wallace Stevens: A Descriptive Bibliography* (Pittsburgh, Pa.: University of Pittsburgh Press, 1973).

Provides a detailed physical description of all of Stevens's works.

The Wallace Stevens Journal <www.wallacestevens.com> [accessed 2 December 2009].
Includes a bibliography listing all the essays published in the journal since its inception in 1977.

Biography

Peter Brazeau, *Parts of a World: Wallace Stevens Remembered. An Oral Biography* (New York: Random House, 1983).
Based on interviews of those who knew Stevens—"more than 150 writers, scholars, business associates, neighbors, friends and members of Stevens' family"—divided into three parts: I. "The Insurance Man," II. "The Man of Letters," and III. "The Family Man."

Letters of Wallace Stevens, edited by Holly Stevens (Berkeley, Los Angeles & London: University of California Press, 1996).
Offers valuable insight into the poet and his work. A comprehensive index makes it easy to find the poet's remarks on specific poems.

Criticism

William W. Bevis, "The Arrangement of *Harmonium*," *ELH: English Literary History*, 37 (September 1970): 456–473.
Argues that Stevens, in his "delightfully perverse book," placed "his most dissimilar poems side by side." He contends that "adjacent poems are usually contrasted in some single specific way."

Richard Allen Blessing, *Wallace Stevens' "Whole Harmonium"* (Syracuse, N.Y.: Syracuse University Press, 1970).
An early study of *The Collected Poems of Wallace Stevens*. Describing Stevens as "among the greatest of all the American poets," Blessing provides accessible readings of such poems as "Sunday Morning," "The Snow Man," "The Comedian as the Letter C," and "Thirteen Ways of Looking at a Blackbird."

Harold Bloom, *Wallace Stevens: The Poems of Our Climate* (Ithaca, N.Y.: Cornell University Press, 1977).
Follows the ordering and dating of *The Palm at the End of the Mind* in offering "a full commentary" on Stevens's poems. Bloom treats *Harmonium* in three chapters, giving particular attention to such poems as "Sunday Morning" and "The Comedian as the Letter C." He argues that "The Man Whose Pharynx Was Bad," "The Snow Man," and "Tea at the Palaz of Hoon" are key to understanding Stevens's aesthetic: "The reader who masters the interrelationships of these three brief texts . . . has reached the center of Stevens' poetic and human anxieties and of his resources for meeting those anxieties."

Edward Brunner, John Timberman Newcomb, and Cary Nelson, *Modern American Poetry: Wallace Stevens (1879–1955)* <http://www.english.illinois.edu/ maps/poets/s_z/stevens/stevens.htm> [accessed 2 December 2009].

A useful site that presents excerpts from a variety of critical views on twelve poems in *Harmonium:* "Sea Surface Full of Clouds," "Thirteen Ways of Looking at a Blackbird," "Floral Decorations for Bananas," "Tea at the Palaz of Hoon," "A High-Toned Old Christian Woman," "Anecdote of the Jar," "Disillusionment of 10 O'Clock," "The Snow Man," "The Emperor of Ice Cream," "Peter Quince at the Clavier," "Sunday Morning," and "The Death of a Soldier."

Robert Buttel, *Wallace Stevens: The Making of* Harmonium (Princeton: Princeton University Press, 1967).
A close examination of Stevens's apprenticeship.

Eleanor Cook, *A Reader's Guide to Wallace Stevens* (Princeton & Oxford: Princeton University Press, 2007).
A valuable study that includes a biographical essay and glosses on all of Stevens's poems.

Charles Doyle, ed., *Wallace Stevens: The Critical Heritage* (London & Boston: Routledge & Kegan Paul, 1985).
Includes twenty reviews of the two editions of *Harmonium* by contemporaries such as Marianne Moore, Harriet Monroe, and Edmund Wilson, and a lengthy review by R. P. Blackmur.

Daniel Fuchs, *The Comic Spirit of Wallace Stevens* (Durham, N.C.: Duke University Press, 1963).
A thematic approach to Stevens's poetry that devotes a chapter to "The Comedian as the Letter C." Fuchs argues that without an appreciation of the poet's comic sense "there is no true understanding of Stevens."

George F. Lensing, *Wallace Stevens: A Poet's Growth* (Baton Rouge: Louisiana State University Press, 1986).
A study in three parts tracing Stevens's growth "from apprenticeship, to full engagement as a practicing poet, and to presenting and promoting his poems among publishers and readers." Although not an introductory study, Lensing's account of Stevens's development leading to *Harmonium* provides valuable background for understanding the poet's work.

Helen Vendler, *On Extended Wings: Wallace Stevens's Longer Poems* (Cambridge, Mass.: Harvard University Press, 1969).
Includes discussions of "The Comedian as the Letter C," "Le Monocle de Mon Oncle," "Sunday Morning," and "Thirteen Ways of Looking at a Blackbird."

Thomas F. Walsh, *Concordance to the Poetry of Wallace Stevens* (University Park: Pennsylvania State University Press, 1963).
A valuable resource for studying Stevens's diction, mainly based on *The Collected Poems of Wallace Stevens* but also covering poems from *The Necessary Angel* (1951) and *Opus Posthumous* (1957).

—George Parker Anderson

Jean Toomer, *Cane*
(New York: Boni & Liveright, 1923)

Jean Toomer (1894–1967) was an innovative writer, thinker, and religious seeker whose best-known work, *Cane* (1923), is one of the most illustrious works of the Harlem Renaissance. Toomer, who disdained being defined by race and promoted the concept of a new "American" race that melded black and white, spent his post-*Cane* life in relative obscurity, searching for a congenial spiritual community heedless of racial distinctions. He was, therefore, an unlikely representative of African American letters.

Nathan Eugene Toomer was raised primarily by his maternal grandparents in Washington, D.C. His grandfather, Pinckney Benton Stewart Pinchback—the son of a white plantation owner and a former slave who lived openly as husband and wife—was the first African American to serve as a state governor. Pinchback's legacy as a newspaper publisher, lawyer, founder of Southern University, and public servant loomed large in Toomer's life. Toomer, however, also romanticized Nathan Toomer, the father who had abandoned him and his mother, as the dashing aristocratic son of a Georgia plantation owner who had swept Nina Pinchback into marriage and freed her from her controlling father.

Toomer's privileged upper-middle-class upbringing, his mixed racial lineage, his attendance at schools that were both all-black (in D.C.) and all-white (in New Rochelle, New York, after his mother's remarriage), as well as the general sense of rootlessness caused by his father's desertion and his mother's death when Toomer was fifteen—all contributed to his unconventional racial attitudes and prompted what his biographers, Cynthia Earl Kerman and Richard Eldridge, term his "hunger for wholeness." His questing began early as he roamed from college to college, trying new courses and majors, studying agriculture at the University of Wisconsin, premed at the University of Chicago, and sociology, history, literature, and psychology at New York University and City College of New York.

Although Toomer never completed a degree, he became a serious student of literature and philosophy. He began calling himself "Jean" and decided to become a writer. In New York he met established authors, including the novelist and social historian Waldo Frank. Frank, who became Toomer's friend, envisioned America as a historically unique country in which true social change and spiritual renewal were possible. Frank believed that artists—especially minority artists—could help forge a new American identity.

In 1921 Toomer spent two months as interim principal of the Sparta Agricultural and Industrial Institute in Sparta, Georgia. There, in an area near where his father had lived and exposed to the spiritualizing solace of song and story in a fertile folk culture, he was inspired to compose the work that established his literary reputation. *Cane* can be read as a kind of swan song to the vanishing rural life of blacks in the South and as a critique of postwar moral barrenness. Published in 1923, the novel was a critical, if not popular, sensation, lauded as a signal work in the New Negro Renaissance and as an original, progressive expression of literary modernism. In "The New Negro in American Literature," published in Alain Locke's seminal anthology, *The New Negro* (1925), African American critic William Stanley Braithwaite's glowing praise of *Cane* reveals something of the fevered temper of the times: "*Cane* is a book of gold and bronze, of dusk and flame, of ecstasy and pain, and Jean Toomer is a bright morning star of a new day of the race in literature."

In the 1920s Toomer studied Eastern philosophy and became a follower of the mystic George Ivanovitch Gurdjieff; he eventually became a leader of the Gurdjieff movement in the United States. In his unpublished book "Portage Potential" Toomer documented a "Cottage Experiment" in which a group of unmarried men and women shared a farmland home in Wisconsin to practice Gurdjieff-inspired harmonious living, scandalizing their neighbors in the process. The writer Margery Latimer, a participant in the experiment, became his first wife, sparking a public backlash against miscegenation. Toomer chronicled their lives in an artists' colony in Carmel, California, and the hostility to their mixed-race marriage in his unpublished novel "Caromb." Latimer died in 1932 giving birth to their daughter, Margery. Toomer's second marriage, to Marjorie Content—who was, like his first wife, white—lasted until his death and also ignited public outrage.

In 1936 Toomer and his wife moved to Doylestown, Pennsylvania, where Toomer studied and wrote about Quakerism; he eventually joined the Society of Friends. He wrote prolifically but published sporadically, alienating some of those in the African American literary world because of his complex ideologies of race and racial identity. He was rediscovered in the 1960s and 1970s, when his unorthodox stance on race seemed more like forward thinking than a betrayal of New Negro politics. He died in Doylestown after several years of incapacitating illness. His literary reputation rests securely but not solely on the remarkable achievement of *Cane*. Some of his other works of note are the long poem "The Blue Meridian" (1936); *Essentials* (1931), a collection of sayings and poems; and the dramas *Natalie Mann* and *The Sacred Factory*, which were written in the 1920s but remained unpublished in his lifetime. Darwin T. Turner has brought together many of these works in *The Wayward and the Seeking: A Collection of Writings by Jean Toomer* (1980). Toomer's papers are held by the Beinecke Rare Book and Manuscript Library at Yale University.

TOPICS FOR DISCUSSION AND RESEARCH

1. Critics have differed on what to call and how to interpret Toomer's impressionistic blend of poetry, narrative, and drama. The disparate components of *Cane* are clearly thematically linked—to such an extent that some critics consider it a novel. Others have suggested that it is a story cycle, similar to Sherwood Anderson's *Winesburg, Ohio* (1919). Darwin Turner, who calls the work a "montage," asserts that Toomer never conceived of *Cane* as a novel but as a kind of evocative song, an attempt to conjure the dying spirit of the Southern backcountry. The first section, set in the South, is composed of six stories focused on women and twelve richly descriptive poems about the land and workers on that land, including the often-anthologized "Georgia Dusk."

The second section consists of vignettes set in Chicago and Washington, interspersed with poems such as "Harvest Song" that suggest the broken connection with the land and a lack of spiritual grounding in the urban world of money and violent struggle. The final dramatic section, "Kabnis," is again set in the South, where the Northern-reared African American man of the title finds little solace. Mary Battenfield, while recognizing the violence and grievous loss described, considers the saving power of Toomer's language. One of the many ways to approach *Cane* is to consider, as Battenfield does, how the rendering of community spirit in these multiple genres, places, and stories sounds a collective voice that demands recognition and active change. Another way to study the work is to consider the shaping force of the third-person narration. William Dow sees the "self-reflective" narrative voice as expressing Toomer's sense of social and spiritual interconnectedness. Studying individual poems and the links between poems or between poems and stories can also be fruitful. Students might consult Nellie Y. McKay's essay in the Norton Critical Edition of *Cane* (1989) for detailed analyses of the language and structure of *Cane,* Michael Krasny's essay "Aesthetic Structure" in the same volume, and the edition of Toomer's poems (1988) edited by Robert B. Jones and Margery Toomer Latimer.

2. Toomer's sojourn in rural Georgia deepened his identification with his African ancestry and led directly to the composition of *Cane*. One of the signal themes in American literature is the search for self, and Toomer's sketches are often about the conflicts and failures of psychological and social integration. A worthwhile avenue of study would be to consider the portraits of Southern and Northern blacks in *Cane* as explorations of Toomer's complex attitudes about identity and race. Charles Scruggs and Lee Van Van Demarr consider the tensions within Toomer's "new American race" philosophy and set his ideas within contemporary social and political contexts. Students might also read Toomer's own writings on race, race relations, and "passing," such as "The Negro Emergent" (1924) and "The Crock of Problems" (1928), collected in Robert B. Jones's edition of Toomer's essays (1996). In "Race Problems and Modern Society" (1929) Toomer accuses blacks and whites of sharing "the same stupidity" and implicates both races in exacerbating "the very attitudes which entrapped them." He claims that "the dominant white is just as much a victim of his form as is the Negro of his."

3. Though the status of *Cane* as a celebrated text of the Harlem Renaissance is assured, the work transcends categorization as an African American classic. Toomer has been compared with such Jazz Age writers as Eugene O'Neill, William Faulkner, Sinclair Lewis, John Steinbeck, and Edgar Lee Masters in terms of his language experiments and his central preoccupation with the spiritual and moral bankruptcy of modern, postwar, materialist life. Modernist authors often criticize and defy the bleak, dispiriting forces of outmoded religious and social authorities while they assert the autonomy of the individual. Their characters are frequently isolated from each other and disconnected from a sustained sense of life's meaning. The vexed issues of race and identity, thematically central to *Cane,* can be viewed through Modernist lens. Toomer

posits no easy solutions for wholesale societal change, but inherent in his portraits of struggling, fear-ridden, or deluded people is the sense that life is violent and threatening, that meaning is elusive, and that conventional values are insufficient or distorted. Students might make a comparative study of characters from the North such as Rhobert, Avey, Bona and Paul, and Muriel and Dan in "Box Seat" with characters from the South such as Louisa and Tom in the harrowing "Blood Burning Moon," focusing on the causes of their psychosocial conflicts. Werner Sollors's "Jean Toomer's *Cane:* Modernism and Race in Interwar America," in Genevieve Fabre and Michel Feith's collection of critical essays (2000), is a good source for understanding *Cane* within contemporary cultural conditions.

4. The lives of women figure prominently in *Cane.* The first section, in particular, is devoted to a series of impressionistic sketches of women who defy societal expectations and who are misunderstood, vulnerable, strong, and associated through the land with the fertility of the Southern past and the passing of its way of life. These women are erotic and mystical forces, representations of history, and expressions of passion and suffering. Karintha, whose "soul . . . ripened too soon"; Becky, "the white woman who had two Negro sons"; Carma, "strong as any man"; and Fern, who "became a virgin," are individual portraits that meld, through the poetic bridges that interconnect the stories, into the body of meaning that is the text itself. Students might consider analyzing images of women in *Cane,* comparing the portraits in the "Southern" section with women such as Avey and Muriel in the stories set in the North. Janet M. Whyde considers the symbolic resonance of the women characters and Toomer's poetic use of language.

5. Toomer's sensual descriptions of the land and the people make use of folk idioms, dialect, work songs, spirituals, and the blues. *Cane* evokes the beauty and bounty of the natural world and shows the soul-killing effects of separation from nature and its potential for harmonizing body, mind, and spirit. The Northern city streets contrast sharply with the lush, imagistic depictions of the Southern countryside. Darwin Turner asserts that Toomer's presentation of rural Georgia life is no mere paean to the pastoral or "primitive" but is multitextured and complex. In his introduction to the 1975 Liveright edition of *Cane,* Turner cites Toomer's own explanation of the Sparta experience he wove into the work: "The folk-spirit was walking in to die on the modern desert. That spirit was so beautiful. Its death was so tragic. Just this seemed to sum life for me. And this was the feeling I put into *Cane.*" The oppositions and tensions between spirit and materialism, country and city, past and present, black and white, and South and North are part of the dynamic movement of the text. Just as generic distinctions are smoothed away and poetry and prose are absorbed into each other, it is also possible to find intimations of harmony in the aching beauty of the natural world. Physical nature, then, is also symbolic of spiritual richness and becomes a place where social constructs and oppositions lose their meaning. A student might do an analysis of how individual poems such as "The Reapers," "November Cotton Flower," or "Georgia Dusk" help to illuminate the prose pieces with which they are interspersed. Helpful

sources are McKay's "Structure, Theme, and Imagery in *Cane*," Bernard W. Bell's "The Poems of *Cane*," and Lucinda H. MacKethan's "Jean Toomer's *Cane:* A Pastoral Problem," all of which can be found in Turner's Norton Critical Edition.

RESOURCES

Primary Works

The Collected Poems of Jean Toomer, edited by Robert B. Jones and Margery Toomer Latimer (Chapel Hill: University of North Carolina Press, 1988).
Collects fifty-five poems spanning the breadth and varied phases of Toomer's career, displaying his formative thinking and artistic innovations.

Selected Essays and Literary Criticism, edited by Jones (Knoxville: University of Tennessee Press, 1996).
Collects Toomer's cultural and literary criticism and autobiographical writings, notably his analyses of race problems in America and his explanations of his religious affiliations.

Cane: An Authoritative Text, Backgrounds, Criticism, edited by Darwin T. Turner (New York: Norton, 1988).
The Norton Critical Edition. Turner collects important essays on Toomer's life and work by such Harlem Renaissance notables as W. E. B. Dubois and Arna Bontemps; Toomer's correspondence with literary figures such as Waldo Frank, Sherwood Anderson, and Allen Tate; and selected criticism on the themes, structures, and symbols in *Cane* by such scholars as Nellie Y. McKay, Patricia Watkins, and Michael Krasny ("Aesthetic Structure").

The Wayward and the Seeking: A Collection of Writings by Jean Toomer, edited by Turner (Washington, D.C.: Howard University Press, 1980).
An indispensable source for autobiographical writings, poetry, and plays, most of which were unpublished during Toomer's lifetime.

Biography

Cynthia Earl Kerman and Richard Eldridge, *The Lives of Jean Toomer: A Hunger for Wholeness* (Baton Rouge: Louisiana State University Press, 1987).
Treats Toomer's spiritual quest for wholeness within contemporary political and aesthetic movements, drawing on interviews with family members and associates as well as archival material.

Criticism

Mary Battenfield, "'Been Shapin Words T Fit M Soul': *Cane*, Language, and Social Change," *Callaloo*, 25 (Fall 2002): 1238–1249.
Focuses on the "Kabnis" section of *Cane* and Toomer's complex vision of social change and its relationship to language.

William Stanley Braithwaite, "The New Negro in American Literature," in *The New Negro: An Interpretation,* edited by Alain Locke (New York: A. & C. Boni, 1925), pp. 29–44.
An overview of African American literature that concludes with a tribute to *Cane,* praising Toomer's uncompromising artistic vision.

William Dow, "'Always Your Heart': The 'Great Design' of Toomer's *Cane,*" *MELUS,* 27 (Winter 2002): 59–88.
A study of the narrative strategies in *Cane* and the relationship of the narrative voices to Toomer's conceptions of race and identity.

Genevieve Fabre and Michel Feith, eds., *Jean Toomer and the Harlem Renaissance* (New Brunswick, N.J.: Rutgers University Press, 2000).
Collects twelve essays from a 1998 Paris conference on the Harlem Renaissance that detail critical debates about Toomer's relationships with literary Modernism and the Harlem Renaissance and the symbolism and narrative structure of *Cane.*

Barbara Foley, "'In the Land of Cotton': Economics and Violence in Jean Toomer's *Cane,*" *African American Review,* 32 (Summer 1998): 181–198.
An analysis of Toomer's depiction of social and economic realities of rural Georgia life in the lyrically symbolic vignettes in *Cane.* Foley argues that though Toomer only partially connects racial violence with Georgia's political economy, his "mythifying imagination" ultimately cannot distort the savagery of that violence.

Robert B. Jones, *Jean Toomer and the Prison-House of Thought: A Phenomenology of the Spirit* (Amherst: University of Massachusetts Press, 1993).
Analyzes Toomer's sense of social and psychological alienation as a driving force in his life and work, which Jones divides into aesthetic, ethical, and religious "spheres."

Nellie Y. McKay, *Jean Toomer, Artist: A Study of His Literary Life and Work, 1894–1936* (Chapel Hill: University of North Carolina Press, 1984).
An analysis of Toomer's desire to transcend racial identity, his adherence to Gurdjieff's teachings on wholeness and harmony, and his pioneering experiments with language. McKay provides an extended treatment of tonal nuance and the interplay between prose and poetry in *Cane.*

Therman O'Daniel, ed., *Jean Toomer: A Critical Evaluation* (Washington, D.C.: Howard University Press, 1988).
Collects forty-six essays on Toomer's life and work, providing a student-friendly historical overview of critical trends and contexts.

Charles Scruggs and Lee VanDemarr, *Jean Toomer and the Terrors of American History* (Philadelphia: University of Pennsylvania Press, 1998).
Provides context for Toomer's literary and philosophical development within the cultural politics of his times. Scruggs and VanDemarr read Toomer's early work, letters, and autobiographical writings as evidence of his conflicts about race and identity.

Darwin T. Turner, "Introduction," in *Cane* (New York: Liveright, 1975), pp. ix–xxv.
A reliable overview of Toomer's life and times, discussing the importance of *Cane* as "a harbinger of [the Harlem] Renaissance and as an illumination of 'a significant psychological and moral concerns of the early 1920's.'"

Janet M. Whyde, "Mediating Forms: Narrating the Body in Jean Toomer's *Cane*," *Southern Literary Journal*, 26 (Fall 1993): 42–53.
Explores *Cane* as a literary "body" and Toomer's attempt to integrate in his narrative a fragmented racial and human identity. Whyde analyzes the representation of women in the text as symbolic expressions of the African American past: women's bodies link to song, oral tradition, and the land.

—*Kate Falvey*

Eudora Welty, *A Curtain of Green*
(Garden City, N.Y.: Doubleday, Doran, 1941)

Eudora Alice Welty (1909–2001), the oldest of three surviving children of Christian and Chestina Andrews Welty, lived nearly all of her life in Jackson, Mississippi. Her parents' love of learning and her passion for reading supplemented her public-school education. Her early poems, sketches, and stories appeared in *St. Nicholas* magazine, her high-school newspaper, and the campus publications of Mississippi State College for Women, which she attended for two years, and the University of Wisconsin, where she graduated in 1929 with a B.A. in English.

Welty's mother supported her desire to become a writer, but her father encouraged her to learn practical job skills, so she spent a year at Columbia University Graduate School of Business in New York. The Depression had dried up the job market, and she returned to Jackson in 1931; her father died of leukemia the same year. For the next few years she held a variety of part-time jobs, writing for a local radio station, contributing to local newspapers, and serving as society correspondent for the Memphis *Commercial Appeal*. In 1936 her first full-time job as a junior publicity agent for the Works Progress Administration (WPA) took her all over Mississippi—interviewing, writing, photographing, becoming more familiar with the people and places of her home state, and stocking her imagination with impressions that filled her fiction throughout the years ahead.

Taking snapshots taught Welty the importance of capturing transient moments, a skill she applied in writing fiction. Her photographs were exhibited in two gallery shows in the mid 1930s, but she was unable to sell "Black Saturday," a manuscript that combined her photographs, short stories, and nonfiction sketches. Several collections of her photographs were published much later, including *One Time, One Place* (1971) and *Photographs* (1989).

In mid 1936 Welty's first story outside campus publications, "Death of a Traveling Salesman," was published in *Manuscript*, a small magazine that did not pay but that brought wider exposure to her work. Publishers began to send inquiries, but they were interested in novels, as the market for short-story collections was small. Robert Penn Warren and Cleanth Brooks published several of her stories in the influential *Southern Review*, and Katherine Anne Porter began to encourage and promote Welty. In 1940 Welty signed with literary agent Diarmuid Russell, who did not push her to write a novel but worked to build her reputation through publishing stories in major national magazines. "Powerhouse" and "A Worn Path"—now widely anthologized—were rejected by more than a dozen editors before being accepted by *The Atlantic Monthly* in December 1940.

Doubleday, Doran published Welty's first book, *A Curtain of Green*, in November 1941. It comprised seventeen stories: "Lily Daw and the Three Ladies," "A Piece of News," "Petrified Man," "The Key," "Keela, the Outcast Indian Maiden," "Why I Live at the P.O.," "The Whistle," "The Hitch-Hikers," "A Memory," "Clytie," "Old Mr. Marblehall," "Flowers for Marjorie," "A Curtain of Green," "A Visit of Charity," "Death of a Traveling Salesman," "Powerhouse," and "A Worn Path." The attack on Pearl Harbor a month later distracted readers, but initial reviews were generally favorable. Led by Katherine Anne Porter's influential introduction to the volume, as well as the stereotypes of Southern fiction based on the works of Erskine Caldwell, William Faulkner, and others, many reviewers focused on the abnormal, "grotesque" elements of the stories.

Welty's first book was quickly followed by a novella, *The Robber Bridegroom* (1942), and another collection, *The Wide Net* (1943), both set on the Natchez Trace. With *The Wide Net* she followed her editor, John Woodburn, from Doubleday to Harcourt, Brace. Her first novel, *Delta Wedding* (1946), was criticized for not addressing political issues; in her 1965 essay "Must the Novelist Crusade?" she explained her refusal to let social activism dominate fiction. She traveled through Europe on a Guggenheim Fellowship in 1949–1950 and made several more trips to Europe over the next four decades. Her masterful collection of interrelated modernist short stories, *The Golden Apples*, was published in 1949, followed by a humorous novella, *The Ponder Heart* (1954)—which was dramatized on Broadway in 1956—and another story collection, *The Bride of the Innisfallen and Other Stories* (1955).

Welty spent much of the 1950s and 1960s caring for her ill mother. Her brother Walter died in 1959; then in a single week in January 1966, both her mother and her brother Edward died. Throughout the 1960s, Diarmuid Russell became increasingly concerned about the direction Harcourt Brace was taking under the leadership of William Jovanovich. When a Harcourt editor suggested substantial cuts and editing of Welty's longest novel, *Losing Battles*, Welty moved to Random House to work with editor Albert Erskine, whom she had known since her early days of being published by the *Southern Review*. *Losing Battles* (1970) was her first book on the best-seller lists, and her somewhat autobiographical novel, *The Optimist's Daughter* (1972), won the Pulitzer Prize. Her memoir, *One Writer's Beginnings*, was published in 1984.

In Welty's later years collections of her essays, reviews, photographs, and stories were published. She was the only living writer to be included in the Library of America series, and she amassed honorary degrees and awards, including election to the National Institute of Arts and Letters, the William Dean Howells Medal, election to the American Academy of Arts and Letters, the National Medal of Literature, the Presidential Medal of Freedom, the National Medal of Arts, and the French Legion of Honor. Biographer Suzanne Marrs notes that she "also became a cultural icon."

Welty died of cardiopulmonary failure on 23 July 2001 and was buried in Greenwood Cemetery—which she had often photographed—within sight of her childhood home.

TOPICS FOR DISCUSSION AND RESEARCH

1. Welty has often been identified—even belittled—as a regional writer. In her essay "Place in Fiction," collected in *The Eye of the Story: Selected Essays and Reviews* (1978), she explores the significance of place and the limitations of the term "regional": "When I speak of writing from where you have put down roots, it may be said that what I urge is 'regional' writing. 'Regional,' I think, is a careless term, as well as a condescending one, because what it does is fail to differentiate between the localized raw material of life and its outcome as art. 'Regional' is an outsider's term; it has no meaning for the insider who is doing the writing, because as far as he knows, he is simply writing about life." Read "Place in Fiction" and assess Welty's use of place in *A Curtain of Green*. Can you find examples in which the evocation of place and specific descriptions are important to her creation of character?

2. In *One Writer's Beginnings* Welty noted that writing "Death of a Traveling Salesman" opened her eyes to her "real subject: human relationships." In her introduction to *One Time, One Place,* she identified her passion as "not to point the finger in judgment but to part a curtain, that invisible shadow that falls between people, the veil of indifference to each other's presence, each other's wonder, each other's human plight." Robert Penn Warren identified "the fact of isolation" as "the basic situation" of her fiction. Explore the tension between isolation and relationship in Welty's stories. What story in *A Curtain of Green* best reveals the "invisible shadow" of which Welty writes? In which story do you think "the fact of isolation" is most profoundly present?

3. Katherine Anne Porter expressed a preference for Welty's stories "where external act and internal voiceless life of the human imagination almost meet and mingle on the mysterious threshold between dream and waking." In her chapter "The Mysteries of Eudora Welty" Ruth Vande Kieft explores the interweaving of fact and fantasy, dream and reality in Welty's early writings. In *Understanding Eudora Welty* (1999) Michael Kreyling notes that this type of story tends to be nonchronological, focuses on psychological rather than physical aspects of character, and brings "allusion, reference, controlled patterns of imagery, and other aesthetic aspects of the *work* into play." How do the stories in *A Curtain of Green*—especially "A Memory," "The Key," "The Hitch-Hikers," and "Death of a Traveling Salesman"—exhibit these characteristics?

4. In *One Writer's Imagination: The Fiction of Eudora Welty* (2002) Suzanne Marrs argues that in *A Curtain of Green* Welty suggests that although poverty and

racism "may wound or destroy the imagination," "imagination can provide moments of connection and communication" despite the challenges of life. For example, in "The Whistle," when sharecroppers Jason and Sara Morton burn their kitchen table in desperation to keep warm, the fire "seemed wonderful to them—as if what they had never said, and what could not be, had its life, too, after all." Peter Schmidt, on the other hand, sees Welty's early stories as "an attempt to confront her own anxieties about how to validate her imaginative activity as a writer." Marrs emphasizes Welty's joy in the power of imagination, while Schmidt argues for a darker feminist interpretation that focuses on "issues of imprisonment and release" and an "either/or choice between conformity and madness." For example, Schmidt argues that Clytie is doomed by her imagination, while Marrs argues that Clytie's "inability to use her imagination"—which Welty intensified during revision—was the real problem. Evaluate Marrs's and Schmidt's chapters on *A Curtain of Green*. Which approach leads to a better understanding of the stories?

5. Welty writes in her introduction to *One Time, One Place* that photography taught her "a story-writer's truth: the thing to wait on, to reach there in time for, is the moment in which people reveal themselves. . . . Every feeling waits upon its gesture." In his chapter on *A Curtain of Green* in *Eudora Welty's Achievement of Order* (1980) Michael Kreyling suggests that the "photographic metaphor for the artist's vision" may be the best way to understand Welty's early stories. In chapter 2 of her *The Welty Collection* (1988) Suzanne Marrs discusses the connections between Welty's photographs and fiction, emphasizing the selective scope of the photograph and the short story. Read Kreyling's and Marrs's chapters, as well as Welty's interview about photography in *More Conversations with Eudora Welty*. What revealing moments and gestures do you find in Welty's stories? What passages or images seem to you to show the influence of Welty's experience as a photographer?

RESOURCES

Primary Works

The Eye of the Story: Selected Essays and Reviews (New York: Random House, 1978).
Collects Welty's essays on writers and writing, book reviews, and personal and occasional pieces. The essays on writing are particularly helpful in understanding her fiction.

One Time, One Place: Mississippi in the Depression: A Snapshot Album (New York: Random House, 1971).
Includes a selection of Welty's photographs from the 1930s, as well as a preface in which she describes what she learned from photography.

One Writer's Beginnings (Cambridge, Mass.: Harvard University Press, 1984).
Based on a series of autobiographical lectures Welty gave at Harvard University in 1983, despite her often-repeated contention that fiction should stand on its own

without information about the author's life. She explores the influences of her childhood, youth, and early adulthood that led her to become a writer.

Bibliography

Suzanne Marrs, *The Welty Collection* (Jackson: University Press of Mississippi, 1988).
Annotated guide to Welty's manuscripts, documents, and photographs at the Mississippi Department of Archives and History.

Pearl Amelia McHaney, "A Eudora Welty Checklist, 1973–1986," in *Welty: A Life in Literature*, edited by Albert J. Devlin (Jackson: University Press of Mississippi, 1988), pp. 266–302.
Primary bibliography and selective checklist of secondary materials, arranged by the Welty publications they explore. The book includes four pages of studies of *A Curtain of Green and Other Stories*.

Noel K. Polk, *Eudora Welty: A Bibliography of Her Work* (Jackson: University Press of Mississippi, 1994).
Comprehensive primary descriptive bibliography.

Polk, "A Eudora Welty Checklist, 1936–1972," in *Welty: A Life in Literature*, edited by Albert J. Devlin (Jackson: University Press of Mississippi, 1988), pp. 238–265.
Primary bibliography and selective checklist of secondary materials, arranged by the Welty publications they explore. Polk includes three pages of studies of *A Curtain of Green and Other Stories*.

Victor H. Thompson, *Eudora Welty: A Reference Guide* (Boston: G. K. Hall, 1976).
Annotated secondary bibliography, arranged chronologically, covering 1936–1975. Topical index entries such as "place" and "the grotesque" identify recurring patterns in Welty criticism.

Biography

Michael Kreyling, *Author and Agent: Eudora Welty and Diarmuid Russell* (New York: Farrar, Straus & Giroux, 1991).
Draws on and quotes from Welty's correspondence with her agent, Diarmuid Russell, who became her trusted advisor and close friend. Explores Welty's development as a writer and her publishing career and reputation.

Suzanne Marrs, *Eudora Welty: A Biography* (Orlando, Fla.: Harcourt, 2005).
Intended to counteract "misleading public images of Eudora." Marrs's warm biography is informed by her friendship with Welty and her unprecedented access to unpublished correspondence, manuscripts, photographs, date books, and scrapbooks.

Criticism

Eudora Welty Society <http://eudoraweltysociety.org/> [accessed 2 December 2009].
Provides a wide variety of resources for the study of Welty, including links to checklists of scholarship, the Eudora Welty Foundation, the Welty House Museum, the Mississippi Department of Archives and History, and the *Eudora Welty Newsletter*.

Michael Kreyling, *Eudora Welty's Achievement of Order* (Baton Rouge: Louisiana State University Press, 1980).
A formalist approach that emphasizes the literary influences on Welty's writing and argues that it is not primarily regional, as it is often characterized by reviewers and critics.

Kreyling, *Understanding Eudora Welty* (Columbia: University of South Carolina Press, 1999).
Explores the history and significance of Welty criticism—including New Critical formalist analysis and more recent feminist interpretations—and offers close readings of Welty's fiction and memoir.

Suzanne Marrs, *One Writer's Imagination: The Fiction of Eudora Welty* (Baton Rouge: Louisiana State University Press, 2002).
Draws on conversations and friendship with Welty to explore the relationships between her life and work and examines textual revisions to illuminate Welty's creative process.

Katherine Anne Porter, "Introduction," in Welty's *A Curtain of Green* (Garden City, N.Y.: Doubleday, Doran, 1941), pp. ix–xix; republished as "A Curtain of Green," in *Eudora Welty*, edited by Harold Bloom (New York: Chelsea House, 1986), pp. 11–17.
Downplays Welty's art while praising her as a "born writer." This influential introduction established Welty's frequent identification as primarily or merely a regional writer in the Southern grotesque tradition.

Peggy Whitman Prenshaw, ed., *Conversations with Eudora Welty* (Jackson: University Press of Mississippi, 1984).
Twenty-six interviews that enhance understanding of Welty's life and fiction. Interviewers include Alice Walker, William F. Buckley Jr., and Reynolds Price.

Prenshaw, ed., *More Conversations with Eudora Welty* (Jackson: University Press of Mississippi, 1996).
Twenty-six additional interviews. The volume includes interviews by Louis D. Rubin Jr., Anne Tyler, and Cleanth Brooks, as well as Welty's discussion of photography with Hunter Cole and Seetha Srinivasan, reprinted from *Photographs* (1989).

Peter Schmidt, *The Heart of the Story: Eudora Welty's Short Fiction* (Jackson: University Press of Mississippi, 1991).

Uses feminist and new historicist techniques to evaluate earlier formalist and archetypal assumptions in Welty criticism and offer new interpretations of her short stories.

Ruth M. Vande Kieft, *Eudora Welty,* revised edition (Boston: Twayne, 1987).
Revised from the influential 1962 first edition, the first book-length study of Welty's fiction. Vande Kieft focuses on close readings to examine the "inner life" of Welty's fiction and explores the variety and patterns in her writings.

Robert Penn Warren, "The Love and Separateness in Miss Welty," *Kenyon Review,* 6 (Spring 1944): 246–259; republished as "Love and Separateness in Eudora Welty," in *Eudora Welty,* edited by Harold Bloom (New York: Chelsea House, 1986), pp. 19–28.
Explores *A Curtain of Green and Other Stories* and *The Wide Net* with a focus on the isolation of the characters and the theme of innocence and experience.

—*Mary Jo Tate*

Nathanael West, *The Day of the Locust*
(New York: Random House, 1939)

The literary career of Nathanael West (1903–1940) was cut short by his death in an automobile accident, but West's small body of work, particularly the novella *Miss Lonelyhearts* (1933) and the corrosive Hollywood satire *The Day of the Locust* (1939), has continued to interest readers and scholars. Born Nathan Weinstein to Lithuanian Jewish parents in New York City, West was an indifferent student who used forged transcripts to scam his way first into Tufts University and then into Brown. He changed his name after finishing college, apparently inspired, as Jonathan Lethem notes, by Horace Greeley's famous exhortation, "Go West, young man!"

West finished his first novel while working the night desk in a hotel in Manhattan, where he made the acquaintance of writers such as Lillian Hellman, Dashiell Hammett, and William Carlos Williams. *The Dream Life of Balso Snell* (1931) is a satiric fantasy set almost entirely within a vast Trojan horse. Two years later, West published *Miss Lonelyhearts;* his best-known work aside from *The Day of the Locust,* it is a black comedy about a newspaper journalist driven to despair and madness when he takes over the writing of an advice column. In 1933 West landed a screenwriting contract in Hollywood. His third novel, *A Cool Million,* was published in 1934; a parody of Horatio Alger's rags-to-riches novels, it is like its two predecessors a savagely satirical dissection of the American character. For most of the rest of the 1930s West wrote scripts with little success. His observations from the periphery of the movie business and from living on Hollywood Boulevard, however, provide much of the inspiration for *The Day of the Locust.*

The characters in *The Day of the Locust* are further out in the margins of Hollywood than West was. A grotesque assortment of dreamers, has-beens, and freaks, they exploit one another for professional opportunities and sexual conquest or to assuage their lonely desperation. Tod Hackett, a scenery painter with pretensions of being an artist, falls in with neighbors Faye Greener, a movie extra and part-time prostitute, and her father, Harry, a former vaudevillian who peddles door-to-door a "silver polish" that he makes in his bathroom sink. Only Homer Simpson, a lonely bookkeeper who becomes smitten with Faye and unwisely gives her a home after Harry dies, has no ambitions to make it in show business. He has come to Los Angeles for his health (another local preoccupation), which makes his fate at the end of the novel bitterly ironic.

The Day of the Locust evolved significantly between the time West began the novel in the mid 1930s and its publication in spring 1939. As Robert Emmet Long relates, West originally conceived of a "ship of fools" plot, with his cast of grotesques on a debauched pleasure cruise. He considered and discarded several protagonists, including Harry Greener and screenwriter Claude Estee, before settling on Hackett. West drew from his experiences in Hollywood to create the characters, incidents, and settings of the novel: the apartment building on Hollywood Boulevard in which he lived during his time there became the building in which Tod and the Greeners live, for example, and a dwarf who sold newspapers on a nearby street corner was the inspiration for Abe Kusich; the illegal cockfights he attended provided the many details of bird fighting and training in the novel. According to Long, West considered several titles for the novel, including "The Cheated," a reference to the hopeful masses who come to Hollywood only to find failure and disillusionment—as Tod notes about the crowd at the movie premiere, "They have been cheated and betrayed"—and "The Wroth to Come," a title that, like *The Day of the Locust*, suggests a plague of biblical proportions.

The novel proceeds more as a series of episodes than a coherent narrative. Contemporary reviewers considered its loose structure a failing, but commentators such as Alistair Wisker have tended to view it as a conscious design on West's part. They see in the episodic nature of *The Day of the Locust* ironic echoes of popular entertainment, comic strips, and movies—exactly the sort of mass culture that West is satirizing. By this way of thinking, the form of the novel mirrors its garish, absurdist incidents and cartoonish characters. The erratic quality of the narrative corresponds to the unstable lives it depicts and to life in general in Hollywood, with its fakery and pastiche. This undercurrent of instability makes it inevitable that the novel should end in a total collapse of order.

The publication of *The Day of the Locust* was met with mostly negative reviews and was largely unnoticed by the reading public. After his death the following year, West became something of a cult figure who was remembered mainly through the memoirs of his literary acquaintances. The publication of his collected novels in 1957 by Farrar, Straus and Cudahy prompted a reevaluation of reputation. *The Day of the Locust* is now recognized as one of the most trenchant novels about Hollywood and the American love-hate relationship with movies and celebrity, a touchstone work in that particular subgenre of fiction and film.

TOPICS FOR DISCUSSION AND RESEARCH

1. The Hollywood setting is key to a proper understanding of *The Day of the Locust*. An important theme is the essential unreality of Hollywood, home to the industry that peddles dreams of a more romantic life to the rest of the nation. In the mid 1930s, when West was writing the novel, unemployment and poverty afflicted many Americans, and so the disparity between the movies' fantasies of happiness and material comfort and the grim facts of life outside the theater was particularly sharp. How does Hollywood as a "dream factory" affect those it attracts? How do the characters, all from somewhere other than Hollywood, react when faced with the reality of the city? Is the ending of the novel appropriate given the intensity of the dreams Hollywood inspires? To begin to place *The Day of the Locust* in the context of other novels about Hollywood, see particularly Chip Rhodes's *Politics, Desire, and the Hollywood Novel*.

2. Critics have generally described the characters with which West populates his vision of Hollywood as pure grotesques, defined entirely by isolated, exaggerated features—Homer Simpson's hands, for example, and Faye's platinum blond hair and "swordlike" legs. Stanley Edgar Hyman argues that they are essentially "symbolic abstractions . . . with some loss of human reality." Whether such characterization hinders the effectiveness of the novel has been the subject of ongoing critical debate. Tod's character is also a problem for some readers: Kingsley Widmer, for example, finds him underdeveloped and uninteresting compared to Faye, Homer, and even secondary characters such as Harry Greener and Abe Kusich. Nevertheless, Tod does have an important role in the novel, as the point-of-view character and as a visionary whose painting *The Burning of Los Angeles* comments on the events of the novel and anticipates its cataclysmic ending. Did West intend his characters to be believable? Is his approach to characterization a weakness or strength in the novel?

3. Some critics have considered the crowd itself a character in the novel. "Fed . . . on lynchings, murder, sex crimes, explosions, wrecks, love nests, fires, miracles, revolutions, wars," the people at the movie premiere are described by Tod as an undifferentiated mass of the disaffected, the bitter—the "cheated," as West's original title for the novel had it. They restlessly seek stimulation, boredom being the worst fate for them. Thus, a small crowd gathers for Harry Greener's funeral, "hoping at least for one of the mourners to be led weeping hysterically from the chapel." Faced with the emptiness of the mass culture that draws them together, the cheated need little prodding to persuade them to lash out violently, as John Springer notes. They are, as Hyman calls them, West's "fantasy of American democracy, and it is terrifying and overpowering." Whether West views this roiling crowd with any sympathy, or only suspicion and contempt, is a worthwhile topic for further discussion.

4. In *The Day of the Locust* the worship of screen idols seems a kind of secular religion, while religion, as represented by the likes of the Tabernacle of the Third Coming and the Temple Moderne, is portrayed as having been contaminated by the flimflammery of show business. Critic Rita Barnard argues that the social cohesion that religion once provided has been replaced by the emptiness of mass culture, in particular the movies and tabloid journalism. West's emphasis

on sensationalism and its effects on people's dreams and desires have led critics such as Jonathan Lethem to consider him a writer ahead of his time. How do the imagery and messages of popular culture affect Faye and the other characters? What critique of mass culture does West's novel offer?

5. Sexual desire, uncomfortably intertwined with violence, is another important element of *The Day of the Locust*. Critics have considered various explanations as to what West intended to convey with his portrayal of sex in the novel. Walter Wells sees West's curdled view of male-female intimacy as integral to the novel's theme of the corruption of romantic love. In his discussion of Faye's importance to *The Day of the Locust*, Robert Emmet Long notes that men view her with sexual fear as well as desire—the fear of castration provoked by her "swordlike" legs. How does Faye affect Tod, rodeo cowboy Earle Shoop, the Mexican cockfighter Miguel, and Homer? What is her role in the novel?

RESOURCES

Biography

Jay Martin, *Nathanael West: The Art of His Life* (New York: Farrar, Straus & Giroux, 1970).

A lengthy biography that is the most authoritative source for information on West's life.

Criticism

Rita Barnard, *The Great Depression and the Politics of Abundance: Kenneth Fearing, Nathanael West, and Mass Culture in the 1930s* (New York: Cambridge University Press, 1995).

Uses the writings of West and poet Kenneth Fearing as lenses through which to view the early days of mass culture and consumerist society.

Stanley Edgar Hyman, "Nathanael West," in *Seven Modern American Novelists: An Introduction*, edited by William Van O'Connor (Minneapolis: University of Minnesota Press, 1964), pp. 226–264.

Concludes that, despite some powerful scenes, *The Day of the Locust* is ultimately an artistic failure because it lacks dramatic unity and a moral core.

Jonathan Lethem, "The American Vicarious: An Introduction to *Miss Lonelyhearts; and The Day of the Locust*," in *Miss Lonelyhearts; and The Day of the Locust* (New York: New Directions, 2009).

Describes *The Day of the Locust* as a prescient novel "of superb relevance to the future of American literature" because of its insightful dissection of the national fascination with celebrity.

James F. Light, *Nathanael West: An Interpretive Study* (Evanston, Ill.: Northwestern University Press, 1961).

Contends that in *The Day of the Locust* West presents a mythology based on "man's emotional needs, the frustration of those needs, and the need for a scapegoat to vent one's rage upon."

Robert Emmet Long, *Nathanael West* (New York: Ungar, 1985).
Discusses *The Day of the Locust* as a "parable of evil . . . comic and horrible at once." Long looks particularly at the links between sex and violence in the novel and at the characters' use of sexuality as a weapon against one another.

Irving Malin, *Nathanael West's Novels* (Carbondale: Southern Illinois University Press, 1972).
A close reading of *The Day of the Locust* arguing that Tod's lack of focus as a character is a realistic portrayal of the fate of the artist in Hollywood.

Randall Reid, *The Fiction of Nathanael West: No Redeemer, No Promised Land* (Chicago: University of Chicago Press, 1967).
Looks at *The Day of the Locust* as a novel about performers and their audiences, describing the action between the two as "compulsive and mutually degrading."

Chip Rhodes, *Politics, Desire, and the Hollywood Novel* (Iowa City: University of Iowa Press, 2008).
Focuses on the portrayal of desire and the ways in which thwarted desire leads to violence in *The Day of the Locust*. Rhodes considers West's work, along with Budd Schulberg's *What Makes Sammy Run?* (1941) and Raymond Chandler's *The Little Sister* (1949), the best novels about Hollywood written during the era of the studio system.

John Springer, "'This Is a Riot You're In': Hollywood and American Mass Culture in Nathanael West's *The Day of the Locust*," *Literature Film Quarterly*, 24 (January 1996): 439–444.
Describes how West "sets out to expose the contradictions at the center of the Hollywood myth." In his critique of Hollywood, according to Springer, West finds the "dream factory" to be a symbol of crisis and upheaval.

Walter Wells, *Tycoons and Locusts: A Regional Look at Hollywood Fiction of the 1930s* (Carbondale: Southern Illinois University Press, 1973).
Considers West a moralist and the main theme of *The Day of the Locust* to be the corruption of sex and love, as represented by Faye's relationships to the other characters of the novel.

Kingsley Widmer, *Nathanael West* (Boston: Twayne, 1982).
Describes Tod Hackett as a problematic main character, an ersatz artist and intellectual who is too much of a parasite and hack to be taken seriously as an observer and visionary.

Alistair Wisker, *The Writing of Nathanael West* (New York: St. Martin's Press, 1990).
Describes the setting of *The Day of the Locust* as "a truly monstrous world," fantastic and absurd because it accurately reflects its subject, Hollywood.

—*Charles Brower*

Edith Wharton, *The Age of Innocence*
(New York & London: Appleton, 1920)

In a writing career that spanned more than fifty years, Edith Wharton (1862–1937) not only became a popular and acclaimed author of novels and short stories but also produced poetry, autobiography, literary criticism, and books on travel, landscape gardening, Italian architectural history, and interior decorating. Enamored of European culture since her childhood, she spent much of her life abroad and was often critical of her native country. Yet, as biographer Hermione Lee notes, Wharton was at once "a great lover of France" and "an American to her marrow." She "remained an American citizen and continued, in spite of her almost thirty years of life in France, to write in English principally about American life and American character."

Edith Newbold Jones was born on 24 January 1862 into the wealthy New York world about which she would write in *The Age of Innocence* (1920). She was the third child and first daughter of George Frederic Jones, a gentleman of leisure, and Lucretia Rhinelander Jones, a society matron. Having suffered financially in the wake of the Civil War, the Joneses in 1866 rented out their townhouse in the city and their summerhouse in Newport, Rhode Island, to travel to Europe, in part to live more economically. During their six years abroad the family traveled or resided in England, France, Spain, Italy, and Germany. Young Edith was deeply affected by European culture and learned to read and speak French, German, and Italian. In her memoir *A Backward Glance* (1934) Wharton wrote that these years provided her with an enduring "background of beauty and old-established order." After "the nobility and harmony of the great European cities," the ten-year-old Edith was appalled by the ugliness of her native city when the Joneses returned in 1872. In an undated autobiographical fragment, "Life and I," she recorded that she had "never since thought or felt otherwise than as an exile in America." She sought escape from the conventions and expectations of her parents and New York society in her father's library and through early attempts at authorship. In "A Little Girl's New York," a portrait of herself written when she was seventy-five, Wharton wrote, "I have often sighed, in looking back at my childhood, to think how pitiful a provision was made for the life of the imagination behind those uniform brownstone facades."

In 1885 Edith Jones married Edward "Teddy" Wharton, with whom she shared a love of traveling but few other interests. The couple spent springs in Italy, summers in Newport, and winters in New York, England, or France. Edith Wharton began to write and publish stories in the 1890s. Her first book was *The Decoration of Houses* (1897), which she coauthored with the Boston architect Ogden Codman. In her first major novel, *The House of Mirth* (1905), she wrote sympathetically of Lily Bart, the perfect female product of aristocratic New York society. In *A Backward Glance* Wharton explains why she chose to write about "a society of irresponsible pleasure-seekers": "The answer was that a frivolous society can acquire dramatic significance only through what its frivolity destroys. Its tragic implication lies in its power of debasing people and ideals. The answer, in short, was my heroine, Lily Bart." As her relationship with her husband deterio-rated—he was eventually diagnosed as a manic depressive—Wharton continued to produce novels, most notably *Ethan Frome* (1911), which had poor sales, and *The Custom of the Country* (1913), which was a popular success.

Granted a divorce from Teddy Wharton in 1913, Edith Wharton made France her permanent home. With the start of World War I, she opened a Paris *ouvroir* (workroom) for seamstresses. As the war continued, she was instrumental in organizing the American Hostels for Refugees and the Children of Flanders Rescue Committee; she also served as the vice president of a charity that adminis-tered a program to cure French soldiers stricken with tuberculosis. In 1916 Whar-ton was made a chevalier of the Legion of Honor for her service to the country.

In *A Backward Glance* Wharton recalled writing *The Age of Innocence*, which she began in September 1919 and completed in March 1920, as a "momentary escape" from the present. In a masterful opening chapter set on "a January eve-ning" of the early 1870s during a performance of Charles Gounod's opera *Faust* (1859) at the Academy of Music in New York, Wharton in her precise, knowing narrative voice presents her main characters—Newland Archer; his fiancé, May Welland; and the woman with whom he will fall in love, Ellen Olenska, May's Europeanized cousin—and begins to invoke the intricate social world in which their triangle will play out. Archer arrives late because it is "'not the thing' to arrive early at the opera; and what was or was not 'the thing' played a part as important in Newland Archer's New York as the inscrutable totem terrors that had ruled the destinies of his forefathers thousands of years ago." Wharton goes on to reveal Newland's character and to show how he is wholly a creature of his world:

> The second reason for his delay was a personal one. He had dawdled over his cigar because he was at heart a dilettante, and thinking over a pleasure to come often gave him a subtler satisfaction than its real-ization. This was especially the case when the pleasure was a delicate one, as his pleasures mostly were; and on this occasion the moment he looked forward to was so rare and exquisite in quality that—well, if he had timed his arrival in accord with the prima donna's stage-manager he could not have entered the Academy at a more significant moment than just as she was singing: "He loves me—he loves me not—*he loves me!*" and sprinkling the falling daisy petals with notes as clear as dew.
>
> She sang, of course, "*M'ama!*" and not "he loves me," since an unalter-able and unquestioned law of the musical world required that the German text of French operas sung by Swedish artists should be translated into Italian for the clearer understanding of English-speaking audiences. This seemed as natural to Newland Archer as all the other conventions on which his life was moulded: such as the duty of using two silver-backed brushes with his monogram in blue enamel to part his hair, and of never appearing in society without a flower (preferably a gardenia) in his buttonhole.

The power of the social environment to shape and define the individual is the main theme of *The Age of Innocence* and most of her work, but Wharton here presents her carefully observed and imagined world without approval or condemnation. A reviewer for *The Nation* observed that Wharton had described the customs and rituals of Old New York "as familiarly as if she loved them and as lucidly as if she hated them."

Although she continued to be a productive, popular, and respected writer until her death on 11 August 1937, Wharton never again matched the achievement of *The Age of Innocence,* for which, in 1921, she became the first woman to be awarded the Pulitzer Prize for a novel. During her later years and especially after her death, critics lowered their estimation of Wharton's reputation. She was classified by many as a disciple of Henry James, her close friend of many years, and not seen as an original artist in her own right. Her wealth, aristocratic background, and expatriate status, as well as her educated, allusive style, were held against her by some critics. In 1975 R. W. B. Lewis's *Edith Wharton: A Biography* provided a full portrait of a different woman than critics believed they had known—a woman of deep passion, not a puritanically repressed grande dame. In the years since, Wharton has been recognized for what she was and is—a major American author.

TOPICS FOR DISCUSSION AND RESEARCH

1. Critics such as Cynthia Griffin Wolff read *The Age of Innocence* as a bildungsroman of Newland Archer. How do you view Archer? What do you make of his decision not to go up to visit Ellen at the end of the novel?
2. Wharton says that she wrote *The Age of Innocence* as an escape, and certainly the world of the New York aristocracy of the 1870s presents a view of society less subject to the disorder and violence that Wharton had recently witnessed in the war. What are we to make of that society? What are the virtues and faults of the society? Does it represent an "age of innocence," or is such a description ironic?
3. An important aspect of Wharton's style is her use of meaningful allusions, though she was careful not to overwhelm her reader with her erudition. Hermione Lee points to a characteristic example in chapter 9 of *The Age of Innocence,* during the second private meeting between Newland Archer and Ellen Olenska. Deeply drawn into the atmosphere of Ellen's "funny house," Newland hesitates to advise her about her relationship with Julius Beaufort:

> to give advice of that sort would have been like telling someone who was bargaining for attar-of-roses in Samarkand that one should always be provided with arctics for a New York winter. New York seemed much farther off than Samarkand, and if they were indeed to help each other she was rendering what might prove the first of their mutual services by making him look at his native city objectively. Viewed thus, as through the wrong end of a telescope, it looked disconcertingly small and distant; but then from Samarkand it would.

Lee suggests that the unobtrusive allusion is to James Elroy Flecker's "The Golden Journey to Samarkand," a poem that celebrates "a bold, sensual quest for knowledge and adventure—exactly what Newland Archer fails in." Read

Flecker's poem. Do you agree with Lee that Wharton had his poem in mind when she wrote this passage? Are there other connections to be drawn between the poem and the novel? In her *Edith Wharton: Art and Allusion* (1966) Helen Killoran identifies two "structural allusions" in the novel, as well as "thematic allusions that cluster into four major groups: themes of innocence, themes of living death, themes of revolt, and themes of inaccessible love." Exploring some of these allusions in depth allows a deeper understanding of Wharton's aesthetic.

4. From the Academy of Music in the opening chapter to Ellen Olenska's "funny house," Wharton—the author of *The Decoration of Houses* and *Italian Villas and Their Gardens* (1904)—is intensely aware of architecture and interior space and decoration as cultural and personal expressions. Anaylze a setting such as Ellen's house. How does Wharton use the objects with which Ellen chooses to surround herself to reveal her character?

5. After the death of Henry James in 1916, Wharton wrote that she counted his friendship as "the pride and honour" of her life. In his introduction to the collection of essays on the novel he edited (2005), Harold Bloom writes: "Wrongly regarded by many critics as a novel derived from Henry James, *The Age of Innocence* is rather a deliberate complement to *The Portrait of a Lady*, seeking and finding a perspective that James was conscious of having excluded from his masterpiece. Wharton might well have called her novel *The Portrait of a Gentleman*, since Newland Archer's very name is an allusion to Isabel Archer, a far more attractive and fascinating character than Wharton's unheroic gentleman of Old New York." In addition to the issue of the relationship of the two novels—which is addressed by Cushing Strout in the first essay in Bloom's collection—the larger question of James's influence on Wharton is worth exploring. Is it at all appropriate to call Wharton a disciple of James?

6. Comparing Wharton's novel to its adaptation by director Martin Scorsese can be a valuable experience. The book on the making of the movie includes a shooting script that will make comparisons easier and provides background information for understanding the film project. Do you think that Scorsese successfully captures the spirit of Wharton's novel? Does seeing the movie affect the way that you think about the novel?

RESOURCES

Biography

Eleanor Dwight, *Edith Wharton: An Extraordinary Life* (New York: Abrams, 1994).
A well-illustrated chronicle organized around the places that shaped the author's life: New York, Rome, Newport, Lenox, Paris, and the South of France.

Hermione Lee, *Edith Wharton* (New York: Knopf, 2007).
An acclaimed biography that the author calls "the story of an American citizen in France."

R. W. B. Lewis, *Edith Wharton: A Biography* (New York: Harper & Row, 1975).
A groundbreaking biography, the first written with full access to Wharton's letters and the archives of her unfinished fictional works. Lewis reveals new depths of character of a writer he considers "one of the most intelligent American women who ever lived."

The Letters of Edith Wharton, edited by R. W. B. Lewis and Nancy Lewis (New York: Scribners, 1988).
A selection of some four hundred letters from the more than four thousand that have survived.

Bibliography

Helen Killoran, *The Critical Reception of Edith Wharton* (Rochester, N.Y.: Camden House, 2001).
Analyzes the evolution of the critical response to Wharton's writing.

Criticism

Harold Bloom, ed., *Edith Wharton's* The Age of Innocence, Bloom's Modern Critical Interpretations (Philadelphia: Chelsea House, 2005).
A collection of eleven essays, including Cushing Strout's comparison of Wharton's novel to Henry James's *The Portrait of a Lady* (1881) and John Updike's appreciation of the work.

The Edith Wharton Society <http://www.edithwhartonsociety.org/index.html> [accessed 29 October 2009].
A reliable forum for Wharton studies that includes bibliographies and valuable links.

Katherine Joslin, "*The Age of Innocence* and the Bohemian Peril," in her *Edith Wharton,* Women Writers series (New York: St. Martin's Press, 1991), pp. 89–107.
Argues that the plot of the novel "turns on the Woman Question puzzled out by a male protagonist." Joslin sees Ellen Olenska as representing the bohemian clan that "challenges Old New York's hold on its most intelligent, imaginative, sensitive members."

Helen Killoran, *Edith Wharton: Art and Allusion* (Tuscaloosa & London: University of Alabama Press, 1996).
An analysis of how Wharton uses allusions in ten of her works. Killoran identifies a pattern of "branching thematic" allusions in *The Age of Innocence.*

Martin Scorsese and Jay Cocks, The Age of Innocence: *A Portrait of the Film based on the Novel by Edith Wharton,* edited by Robin Standerfer (New York: Newmarket Press, 1993).
Described by Cocks as a "family album" for the making of the acclaimed 1993 adaptation of Wharton's novel. The book includes the shooting script for the movie.

James W. Tuttleton, Kristin O. Lauer, and Margaret P. Murray, eds., *Edith Wharton: The Contemporary Reviews* (New York: Cambridge University Press, 1992).
Provides a chronological record of reviewers' estimations of Wharton's works.

Linda Wagner-Martin, The Age of Innocence: *A Novel of Ironic Nostalgia* (New York: Twayne, 1996).
Treats the literary and historical contexts for the novel and examines the novel from several perspectives, including those of the characters Newland Archer, Ellen Olenska, and May Welland.

Cynthia Griffin Wolff, *A Feast of Words: The Triumph of Edith Wharton* (New York: Oxford University Press, 1977).
The first critical reassessment of Wharton's career written in the wake of Lewis's biography.

Sarah Bird Wright, *Edith Wharton A to Z: The Essential Guide to the Life and Work* (New York: Facts on File, 1998).
A useful, well-illustrated reference.

—George Parker Anderson

Thornton Wilder, *Our Town*
(New York: Coward McCann, 1938)

Typical descriptions of Thornton Wilder's novels and plays as optimistic or sentimental belie the philosophical depth and theatrical sophistication of his work. His most famous play, the Pulitzer Prize–winning *Our Town* (produced 1938), is regarded as quintessentially American in espousing traditional small-town values, but Wilder led an untraditional life as a gay man who traveled extensively abroad and was deeply influenced by European literature and theatre. The enduring power of *Our Town* results from Wilder's ability to capture the American experience that speaks to universal human conditions beyond the borders of culture and time. His plays, as Jeremy McCarter stresses, "disdained kitchen-sink drama" at a time when such an approach was in critical favor. Adopting a boldly theatrical approach, Wilder found, as theatre critic Jeremy McCarter observed, "the universe in a grain of sand, then reversing the lens to view the whole cathedral of existence."

Thornton Niven Wilder was born on 17 April 1897 in Madison, Wisconsin. His early years were not spent, as one might suspect from the evidence of *Our Town*, in a small town. His father, Amos, a career diplomat, took his family to Hong Kong, but the family returned to the United States for extended periods, and Wilder found outlets in music—studying piano and violin and singing in the Episcopal Church choir—and in his passion for literature and theater. Following graduation from Yale University, Wilder studied at the American Academy in

Rome, where in 1921 he attended Luigi Pirandello's *Six Characters in Search of an Author*. The overt theatricality of Pirandello's play, especially its fracturing of the unities of time, place, and action, and blurring of reality and illusion, fascinated Wilder and, ultimately, were among the influences on *Our Town*. Wilder was further influenced by classical tragedy and epic poetry, Molière's comedies, the English philosopher Francis Bacon, the Austrian comic playwright Johann Nestroy, and James Joyce's novel *Finnegans Wake* (1939), a central inspiration for *The Skin of Our Teeth* (produced 1942).

Wilder's second novel, *The Bridge of San Luis Rey* (1927), won commercial and critical success as well as a Pulitzer Prize, permitting Wilder to spend time in Europe studying dramatic techniques in continental theatres. The experiments he made in short plays were brought to full fruition in *Our Town* and subsequent works, including *The Merchant of Yonkers* (produced 1938; revised as *The Matchmaker*, produced 1955), and *The Skin of Our Teeth*, which brought Wilder his third Pulitzer Prize. (He is the only writer to win a Pulitzer Prize in both drama and fiction.) Wilder rarely returned to playwriting after a period of military service during World War II, and he otherwise wrote novels until his death in 1975.

Our Town, which opened at the Henry Miller Theatre on Broadway on 4 February 1938, combines elements of Realism with a range of non-realistic devices to depict two neighboring families over more than a decade (1901–1913) in Grover's Corners, a fictional New Hampshire small town resistant to the encroachment of twentieth-century progress. A character identified as the Stage Manager narrates scenes of daily life, and Wilder otherwise breaks away from a linear chronological approach, utilizing flashbacks and eliminating traditional scenery (only a few ladders and chairs represent various locations as necessary). In the course of the three acts, George Gibbs and Emily Webb form a close bond in childhood that leads to marriage, which ends when Emily dies in childbirth. The ordinariness of their lives and circumstances serves, in Wilder's approach, to enhance the profundity of their joys and tragedies, reflecting on universal truths inherent in their experiences.

TOPICS FOR DISCUSSION AND RESEARCH

1. Wilder's seemingly contradictory style, his mixture of realism and theatricality, is one of the most worthwhile subjects for students to explore and discuss. David Castronovo's *Thornton Wilder* and Donald Haberman's *Plays of Thornton Wilder: A Critical Study* are among many critical studies exploring the influences on Wilder, particularly German theater and Bertolt Brecht's epic style. The Brechtian element of Wilder's work is also examined in Francis Fergusson's "Three Allegorists: Brecht, Wilder, and Eliot," included in Martin Blank's *Critical Essays on Thornton Wilder*. In *Our Town*, Wilder treats the stage as a place in which it is possible to travel to any place at any time, free of the constraints of the unities of time, place, and action, or the boundaries of realistic illusion. Does this freedom undercut the ability of the audience to accept the dramatic moments the play presents?

2. In his writings and commentary on playwriting, Wilder stresses that the stage is a place of "pretenses"—and he chooses to reveal his artifices openly rather than to submerge them beneath a surface realism. Wilder's conceptions of playwriting are most vividly expressed in his own essay, "Some Thoughts on Playwriting," but many critics, including Paul Lifton in *"Vast Encyclopedia": The Theatre of Thornton Wilder*, comment on his ideas. In writing of his stagecraft, Wilder has made it clear that that he was mocking realism throughout *Our Town* for what he regarded as its "superficial smugness," especially the notion that realism is the only theatrical approach to equate with "seriousness." Wilder aimed to shatter the "ossified conventions" of the realistic tradition in order to reveal not only emotional depth but also the fullness of his characters' experiences. Consider the intimate interactions of characters, as, for example, when Mr. Gibbs moves an adolescent George to tears with a fatherly lecture or the scene in which George and Emily realize the depth of their mutual feelings. Are these characters fully realized? Are these brief scenes emotionally satisfying?

3. The characters in *Our Town* experience the mysteries of life, love, and death, without ever fully understanding the meaning of their lives—a circumstance that is the subject of conversation for the deceased Grover's Corners citizenry in the third act of the play. Both Lincoln Konkle in *Thornton Wilder and the Puritan Narrative Tradition* and Paul Lifton in *"Vast Encyclopedia": The Theatre of Thornton Wilder* explore the critical debate on the significance and influence of Wilder's personal religious journey on his work. Wilder also addresses this topic frequently in his interviews, collected by Jackson R. Bryer in *Conversations with Thornton Wilder*. In coming to terms with Wilder's view of spirituality, students might grapple with his observation in the essay "Goethe and World Literature": "The mind of modern man has become a hold-all of flying leaves torn from some vast encyclopedia; but these leaves are not merely items of information. Each one is variously vibrant with emotion." What does this quotation suggest about the nature of human experience? Is it relevant in understanding *Our Town*?

4. The major essay collections edited by Martin Blank, Harold Bloom, and Donald Haberman each include works that examine Wilder's view of small-town America. Look closely at Wilder's depiction of the values of Grover's Corner. What are the traditional values that the play seems to endorse? What is negative in the depiction of small-town life? Would you want to live in Grover's Corner? Would Wilder?

5. The struggle to comprehend the meaning of life and death—and the unending striving for answers to questions of existence—are the wellspring of *Our Town* and much scholarship on this quintessentially American play. Many critics presume that Emily in death speaks for Wilder—"Oh, earth, you're too wonderful for anybody to realize you"—but, as critics such as Malcolm Goldstein in the Harold Bloom collection point out, her insight is hard-won as she is compelled to face the arbitrary forces of life, the randomness of experience, and the inevitable losses and suffering of existence. What do you make of Emily's insight? Is it a life-affirming comment? Is it a tacit acknowledgement that the deepest individual longings for understanding and belonging go unfulfilled?

RESOURCES

Primary Works

"Goethe and World Literature," in *"American Characteristics" and Other Essays*, edited by Donald Gallup (New York: Harper & Row, 1979).
An essay that reflects Wilder's lifelong admiration of Johann Wolfgang von Goethe.

"Some Thoughts on Playwriting," in *Thornton Wilder: Collected Plays & Writings on Theater*, edited by J. D. McClatchy (New York: Library of America, 2007).
An essential essay that describes Wilder's thinking about the process of playwriting and the purpose of drama.

Biography

Edward M. Burns and Ulla E. Dydo with William Rice, eds., *The Letters of Gertrude Stein & Thornton Wilder* (New Haven, Conn. & London: Yale University Press, 1996).
Wilder's correspondence with Stein, a close friend. The letters include his comments on his writing process, productions of his plays, and his personal life.

Donald Gallup, ed., *The Journals of Thornton Wilder, 1939–1961* (New Haven, Conn. & London: Yale University Press, 1985).
A font of information on Wilder's writing process and the issues that concerned him. Although the journals begin after the successful Broadway production of *Our Town*, there are many references to the play and its subsequent revivals.

Richard H. Goldstone, *Thornton Wilder: An Intimate Portrait* (New York: Saturday Review Press/Dutton, 1975).
A biography, published shortly after Wilder's death, that emphasizes the relationship of his life to his work and reveals personal material not previously published.

Gilbert A. Harrison, *The Enthusiast: A Life of Thornton Wilder* (New Haven, Conn.: Ticknor & Fields, 1983).
An engaging biography that emphasizes the playwright's fundamental optimism as reflected in all of his literary works, most particularly *Our Town* and *The Skin of Our Teeth*.

Linda Simon, *Thornton Wilder: His World* (Garden City, N.Y.: Doubleday, 1979).
A serviceable biography of Wilder emphasizing the cultural influences on his development as a writer, with attention paid to his dramatic work and the central significance of *Our Town*.

Robin G. Wilder and Jackson R. Bryer, eds., *The Selected Letters of Thornton Wilder* (New York: HarperCollins, 2008).
Offers glimpses of Wilder's intellectual and artistic concerns, his friendships, his process of writing, the publication and theatrical presentation of his works, and his personal life.

Bibliography

Richard H. Goldstone, *Thornton Wilder, An Annotated Bibliography of Works by and About Thornton Wilder* (New York: AMS Press, 1982).
Covers Wilder's achievement in all literary forms, but with an emphasis on his dramatic writing. Among Wilder's plays, *Our Town* has inspired the most scholarly and critical interest.

Claudette Walsh, *Thornton Wilder: A Reference Guide, 1926–1990* (New York: G. K. Hall, 1993).
Extends Goldstone's earlier bibliographic work.

Criticism

Martin Blank, ed., *Critical Essays on Thornton Wilder* (New York: G. K. Hall, 1996).
A collection in which *Our Town* receives particular attention in Malcolm Cowley's essay "The Man Who Abolished Time," Barnard Hewitt's "Thornton Wilder Says 'Yes,'" and Paul Lifton's "Symbolist Dimensions of Thornton Wilder's Dramaturgy."

Harold Bloom, ed., *Thornton Wilder* (Philadelphia: Chelsea House, 2003).
An essay collection that puts particular emphasis on *Our Town* and *The Skin of Our Teeth*. The essays on *Our Town* include explorations of deceased characters (Mary McCarthy), expressionistic elements (A. R. Fulton), family themes (Arthur Miller), simplicity (Winfield Townley Scott), avoiding clichés and sentimentality (Travis Bogard), Emily's "Good-by, World" speech (Malcolm Goldstein), time (Donald Haberman), the function of the stage manager (M. C. Kuner), critical reaction (Linda Simon), film versions (Gilbert A. Harrison), and contemporary obstacles to appreciating the play (David Castronovo).

Dalma Hunyadi Brunauer and David Garrett Izzo, eds., *Thornton Wilder: New Essays* (West Cornwall, Conn.: Locust Hill Press, 1999).
Wide-ranging collection of essays stressing thematic aspects of Wilder's works and comparative analyses with other writers. The book includes two essays specifically on *Our Town*—Nancy Bunge's "The Social Realism of *Our Town*: A Study in Misunderstanding" and Richard Londraville's "*Our Town*: An American Noh of the Ghosts"—although most essays included reference the play.

Jackson R. Bryer, ed., *Conversations with Thornton Wilder* (Jackson: University Press of Mississippi, 1992).
A collection of Wilder interviews, many of which feature his discussion of *Our Town* and the philosophical and cultural influences on it and his other dramatic works.

David Castronovo, *Thornton Wilder* (New York: Ungar, 1986).
A general survey of Wilder's life and career that includes substantial treatment of *Our Town*.

Donald Haberman, *Our Town: An American Play* (Boston: Twayne, 1989).
An introductory guide to themes, characters, and production concerns.

Haberman, *Plays of Thornton Wilder: A Critical Study* (Middletown, Conn.: Wesleyan University Press, 1967).
A scholarly analysis of Wilder's works that centrally features *Our Town*.

Lincoln Konkle, *Thornton Wilder and the Puritan Narrative Tradition* (Columbia: University of Missouri Press, 2006).
Explores the spiritual and ethical background of Wilder's literary achievement, with *Our Town* examined as it represents the "Christian dispensation" inherent in Wilder's plays and other writings.

Paul Lifton, *"Vast Encyclopedia": The Theatre of Thornton Wilder* (Westport, Conn.: Greenwood Press, 1995).
A study of Wilder's plays that emphasizes his artistic and intellectual influences; it includes considerable details on the writing and production of *Our Town*.

Jeremy McCarter, "The Genius of Grover's Corners," *New York Times,* 1 April 2007.
An appreciation of *Our Town* and the ways in which Wilder presents his timeless themes.

Thornton Wilder Society Website <www.tcnj.edu/~wilder/> [accessed 7 September 2009].
An informative website dedicated to preserving Wilder's legacy.

—*James Fisher*

Tennessee Williams, *The Glass Menagerie*
(New York: Random House, 1945)

As a prolific theatrical innovator, Tennessee Williams (1911–1983) was equaled only by his predecessor, Eugene O'Neill, in the annals of Modernist American drama. Honored twice with the Pulitzer Prize in drama, for *A Streetcar Named Desire* (1947) and *Cat on a Hot Tin Roof* (1955), Williams wrote more than forty poetic, often impressionistic, character-driven Southern Gothic plays that probed repressed tensions, madness, and sexual confusions with a frank intimacy occasionally shocking to mid-twentieth-century audiences unaccustomed to taboo subjects and to the intensity of emotion characteristic of Williams's work. His emergence as a playwright initiated a period of renewed energy and excitement in post–World War II American drama, inspiring theatrical artists with both the form and content of his plays.

Born Thomas Lanier Williams in Columbus, Mississippi, to Cornelius Coffin "C.C." Williams and Edwina Dakin Williams, he was a sickly, effeminate child who preferred books to sports. Williams's domineering mother inspired several of his most iconic characters, most particularly Amanda Wingfield of the partially autobiographical drama *The Glass Menagerie* (1944). The marriage of Williams's parents was unhappy, and their frequent arguments deeply affected Williams and his fragile, psychologically troubled sister Rose, who was also a model for various Williams characters—especially Laura Wingfield of *The Glass Menagerie*.

Steeped in modern American and European literature, Williams particularly admired D. H. Lawrence and Anton Chekhov, both of whom he frequently acknowledged as significant influences. Writing one-act plays as early as 1930, Williams attended the University of Missouri, but his education was interrupted by his father's insistence that he leave school to work as a typist at the International Shoe Company—a miserable experience that he chronicled in *The Glass Menagerie* as the dead-end job of his stage alter ego, Tom Wingfield. An even more significant trauma resulted from news of the deteriorating mental condition of his sister, who, in her teen years, began showing signs of mental disturbance. Williams was horrified when informed that his mother had allowed Rose to undergo a prefrontal lobotomy; as a result, she spent the rest of her life in institutions. Once Williams achieved financial success with the Broadway triumph of *The Glass Menagerie,* he supported his sister's care for the rest of his own life.

Despite his dreary factory job, Williams continued to write. In 1933 "Stella for Star," a short story, won him first place in the St. Louis Writers Guild contest. He spent the summer of 1935 with his grandparents in Memphis, Tennessee, where he wrote *Cairo! Shanghai! Bombay!* (1935). His plays *Candles to the Sun* and *The Fugitive Kind* were produced early in 1937 by a St. Louis community troupe, The Mummers. Williams finally completed his education at the University of Iowa in 1938, where he experimented with the "living newspaper" style pioneered by the Federal Theatre Project in *Spring Storm* (unproduced; completed in 1938) and wrote *Not About Nightingales* (1998).

Taking the first name "Tennessee," Williams moved to New York, where he studied at Erwin Piscator's Drama Workshop at the New School for Social Research and spent some time in Provincetown, Massachusetts, the setting for one of his last plays, the semiautobiographical *Something Cloudy, Something Clear* (1982). Williams's *The Battle of Angels* never made it to Broadway, closing during its out-of-town tryout in Boston in January 1941. He returned to St. Louis, where he adapted his short story "Portrait of a Girl in Glass" to dramatic form as "The Gentleman Caller." Audrey Wood, Williams's agent, secured him a $250-a-week position as a screenwriter for Metro-Goldwyn-Mayer. Unhappy with his assignments, Williams continued to polish "The Gentleman Caller" and was fired for failing to complete his assigned projects. Williams retreated to Provincetown to complete "The Gentleman Caller," which he finally titled *The Glass Menagerie*.

In addition to *A Streetcar Named Desire,* Williams's subsequent works include *Summer and Smoke* (1947) and *The Rose Tattoo* (1951). Williams's style grew more experimental over time—most evidently so in *Camino Real* (1953), a bold plunge into surreal theatrical illusionism—and in *Cat on a Hot Tin Roof, Orpheus Descending* (1957), *Suddenly Last Summer* (1958), and *Night of the Iguana* (1959), in which increasingly grotesque symbolism depicts a predatory universe. Alcoholism and drug addiction, exacerbated by the death of his longtime lover Frank Merlo, did little to slow Williams's writing, though after the early 1960s his plays won scant approval from critics. His well-known problems with alcohol and drugs, as well as his homosexuality, inform his work. He wrote poetry, short stories, novels, and screenplays, but his major contribution is to the stage, as he indelibly influenced the evolution of American drama in the twentieth century and beyond.

The Glass Menagerie stands alongside the other mid-twentieth-century classics of American drama: Thornton Wilder's *Our Town* (1938), Arthur Miller's *Death of a Salesman* (1949), and Eugene O'Neill's *Long Day's Journey into Night* (1956). It was recognized as a masterpiece from its first performance in Chicago during its tryout tour beginning on 26 December 1944; the Broadway production opened on 31 March 1945. The play has been frequently revived and has been filmed four times.

An elegiac "memory play," *The Glass Menagerie* treats themes Williams explored in various ways in subsequent work. In his production notes he describes a "memory play" as having a three-part structure in which (a) a character experiences a profound event, (b) that event creates an "arrest of time" or continual loop of time compelling (c) the character to relive the event in memory. Tom Wingfield, whom Williams permits to step in and out of the play, speaks for the author, conjuring his past in a St. Louis tenement with his mother and sister. Tom, an aspiring writer, longs to escape his domineering mother, Amanda, and fragile sister, Laura. Set in the Great Depression, the plot involves a battle of wills between Tom and Amanda over his aspirations and Laura's situation. Convinced that her deeply repressed daughter's plight is desperate, Amanda pressures Tom to bring home a "gentleman caller," believing that the security of marriage may be the only hope for Laura, insisting that "Girls that aren't cut out for business careers usually wind up married to some nice man." Amanda's hopes are dashed when the young man makes a hasty retreat after confessing his engagement to another girl. Amanda turns angrily on Tom for what she considers his blunder, and they argue bitterly—leading to the realization of Amanda's deepest fear: Tom storms out the door, never to return. As the play ends, Tom is again seen in the present, reflecting back with sadness; he explains that despite geographic distance and the intervening years, he has been unable to extinguish the memory of his sister.

TOPICS FOR DISCUSSION AND RESEARCH

1. Williams begins *The Glass Menagerie* with an epigraph: the last line from e. e. cummings's poem "somewhere I have never travelled, gladly beyond" (1931). During the performance of his play Williams has a line from François Villon's "Ballade of the Ladies of Bygone Times" (1462) projected as a legend on a screen. Read these works and consider their relevance to the play. Why did Williams choose to cite these poems? Does a fuller knowledge of these literary references add to the appreciation of the play?

2. Williams's first treatment of the material that he developed into *The Glass Menagerie* was the short story "Portrait of a Girl in Glass," which was collected in his *One Arm and Other Stories* (1948). Compare this story to the play. What differences are there between the characters and their relationships in the two works? Do you think the story or the play is more effective? Williams also

wrote of his sister, Rose, in the stories "The Resemblance between a Violin Case and a Coffin" (1950) and "Completed" (1974).

3. In an interview with the magazine *P.M.* after the opening of *The Glass Menagerie* in New York, Williams said that he was moved by human valor: "The one dominant theme in most of my writings, the most magnificent thing in all human nature, is valor—and endurance." Do you see valor in the Wingfield family? What action or character best shows valor? Whom do you consider to be the central character of the play?

4. Often Williams's most compelling and tragic characters are women who, despite their individual weaknesses and failings, are presented with sympathy. Carefully read the descriptions Williams offers of Amanda and Laura Wingfield at the beginning of *The Glass Menagerie*. Do you think Williams stays true to these descriptions through the action of the play? Is there "as much to love and pity as there is to laugh at" in Amanda? Laura is compared to "a piece of her own glass collection, too exquisitely fragile to move from the shelf." What other qualities do you see in her? A broader study of Williams's women characters beyond *The Glass Menagerie* will present the student with a varied range of sympathetic and grotesque figures, many of whom evolve from his feelings about his mother and sister, who are represented most directly in *The Glass Menagerie*. Most critical studies of Williams's work centrally respond to his women characters, most particularly in the essay collections edited by Harold Bloom, Matthew C. Roudané, and Thomas Siebold. Williams's biographers, including Lyle Leverich, probe this terrain, as well, and there is much to be discovered in various collections of Williams's published letters.

5. The "memory play" aspect of *The Glass Menagerie* is another potentially fruitful topic for students. In his essay "The Timeless World of the Play" Williams expressed fascination with the possibilities of suspending and reordering time on stage, and many of his plays feature at least a statement on this subject. In *The Glass Menagerie* Tom reflects from a "present" on selectively chosen events in the "past," thus fracturing linear time and allowing Williams to edit the experiences of the Wingfield family in the present and past. Thus, stage reality to Williams reflects the relative nature of truth, not a slavish dependence on linear cause and effect. Do you see any differences in the Tom of the present and the Tom he remembers? How might the events of the play have been presented differently if Amanda or Laura had been the narrator? What would be the appearance of the stage—a nonrealistic setting where some details are omitted and others are exaggerated according to emotional value—if it were one of the other characters remembering the past and the visit of the gentleman caller?

6. *The Glass Menagerie* demonstrates Williams's characteristic use of poetic language laced with carefully selected symbols, such as the glass figurine of a unicorn with which Laura identifies. For many, the real strength of the drama is the rich poetry of Williams's descriptions and dialogue. Williams also makes use of Epic Theatre–inspired projected titles reflecting on the content and time of each scene. Productions of *The Glass Menagerie* do not always include this device or other nonrealistic techniques Williams envisions. Consider the

function of the projected phrases and images. How necessary do you think they are to the play? Do they add to the power of the work, or are they a distraction?

7. The first movie version of *The Glass Menagerie,* the 1950 production featuring Gertrude Lawrence, Arthur Kennedy, Jane Wyman, and Kirk Douglas, is the least reliable; it changes elements of the play and eliminates much of its theatricality, reducing the drama to kitchen-sink realism. Three other screen versions are far more faithful to Williams's play: a 1966 CBS Playhouse production with Shirley Booth, Hal Holbrook, Barbara Loden, and Pat Hingle and the much-heralded 1973 ABC television film production, starring Katharine Hepburn, Sam Waterston, Joanna Miles, and Michael Moriarty, are marked by fine performances and both restored the play's "memory play" elements, as did a 1987 big-screen version starring Joanne Woodward, John Malkovich, Karen Allen, and James Naughton. Students may find an excellent topic in comparing and contrasting interpretations of the film versions.

RESOURCES

Biography

Five O'Clock Angel: Letters of Tennessee Williams to Maria St. Just, 1948–1982, edited by Maria St. Just (New York: Knopf, 1990).
A collection of Williams's letters to his longtime friend and literary executor. The correspondence is revealing of the playwright's private life and his responses to American life and theater.

Ronald Hayman, *Tennessee Williams: Everyone Else Is an Audience* (New Haven, Conn.: Yale University Press, 1993).
Stresses the relationship of Williams's life and work, especially the autobiographical inspirations of his plays. Not a sympathetic portrait of Williams, the book emphasizes his failings and theatrical failures.

Lyle Leverich, *Tom: The Unknown Tennessee Williams* (New York: Crown, 1995).
An acclaimed biography that includes much previously unknown material. Leverich covers Williams's early life from birth through the Broadway triumph of *The Glass Menagerie* and pays particular attention to the influence of Anton Chekhov on Williams. It was intended as the first of two volumes, but Leverich died before completing the second.

The Selected Letters of Tennessee Williams, volume 1: *1920–1945,* edited by Albert J. Devlin and Nancy Marie Patterson Tischler (New York: New Directions, 2000).
An annotated collection of selected Williams correspondence that begins with his childhood and continues through the writing and initial Broadway production of *The Glass Menagerie.*

Tennessee Williams' Letters to Donald Windham, 1940–1965, edited by Donald Windham (New York: Holt, Rinehart & Winston, 1977).

A collection of Williams's letters to his friend and early collaborator. It is especially interesting in regard to Williams's early work in the theater, including the period in which he wrote *The Glass Menagerie* and participated in its first production.

Dakin Williams and Shepherd Mead, *Tennessee Williams: An Intimate Biography* (New York: Arbor House, 1983).
An account of Williams's life and family by his frequently estranged brother.

Edwina Williams, as told to Lucy Freeman, *Remember Me to Tom* (New York: Putnam, 1963).
A memoir by Williams's mother, the model for Amanda Wingfield in *The Glass Menagerie*. It is a revealing, though incomplete, portrait of Williams, emphasizing his early life.

Bibliography

George W. Crandell, *Tennessee Williams: A Descriptive Bibliography* (Pittsburgh: University of Pittsburgh Press, 1995).
A well-annotated primary bibliography.

Drewey Wayne Gunn, *Tennessee Williams: A Bibliography* (Metuchen, N.J.: Scarecrow Press, 1990).
A standard bibliographic source on Williams and his work up to the late 1980s.

Philip C. Kolin, ed., *Tennessee Williams: A Guide to Research and Performance* (Westport, Conn.: Greenwood Press, 1998).
A useful guide with entries on each Williams work.

Criticism

Harold Bloom, ed., *Tennessee Williams's* The Glass Menagerie (New York: Chelsea House, 1988).
Includes essays that treat stage techniques, themes, and characters; also provides an annotated bibliography.

George W. Crandell, ed., *The Critical Response to Tennessee Williams* (Westport, Conn.: Greenwood Press, 1996).
Provides a well-chosen sampling of critical reactions to Williams's work from the beginning of his career to the early 1990s, with reviews of *The Glass Menagerie* from its first performances in Chicago in 1944 through many revivals. The book also includes an essay by Geoffrey Borny on comparisons between the acting and published editions of the play.

Albert J. Devlin, ed., *Conversations with Tennessee Williams* (Jackson: University Press of Mississippi, 1986).
A chronological collection of interviews with Williams, in which he often reflects on his plays and the relation of his life to his work. *The Glass Menagerie* is referenced in almost all of the interviews included.

Robert F. Gross, ed., *Tennessee Williams: A Casebook* (New York: Routledge, 2002).
Brings together an eclectic sampling of essays on a range of topics and plays, including *The Glass Menagerie*.

Michael Paller, *Gentlemen Callers: Tennessee Williams, Homosexuality, and Mid-Twentieth-Century Drama* (New York: Palgrave Macmillan, 2005).
A useful study of homosexual characters and themes during the golden age of American theater, emphasizing Williams's seminal importance in the depiction of gay life on stage.

Delma E. Presley, *The Glass Menagerie: An American Memory* (Boston: Twayne, 1990).
An accessible guide to *The Glass Menagerie* aimed at college students and theater buffs.

Matthew C. Roudané, ed., *The Cambridge Companion to Tennessee Williams* (New York: Cambridge University Press, 1997).
Analyses, by fourteen outstanding scholars, of Williams's plays, including *The Glass Menagerie,* in the context of American culture, critical thought, and the practice of making theater.

—James Fisher

William Carlos Williams, *Collected Poems, 1921–1931*

(New York: Objectivist Press, 1934)

William Carlos Williams, like Walt Whitman, wanted to create a distinctly American poetry, and he struggled against traditions of poetic practice and sought to define a worthwhile role for the poet in American society. He was born on 17 September 1883; his father was an English immigrant and New York businessman, and his mother was a native of San Juan, Puerto Rico, and was of French, Dutch, Spanish, and Jewish ancestry. After studying abroad for a couple of years, Williams attended Horace Mann High School in New York City. There he studied poetry and was influenced by the works of Whitman and John Keats; he also excelled in the sciences. He graduated in 1902 and went on to study medicine at the University of Pennsylvania, where he also continued to pursue his interest in poetry.

At college Williams met Ezra Pound, establishing a relationship that influenced his direction as a poet and deepened his interest in contributing to a new strain of American poetry. Through Pound, Williams met Hilda Doolittle (known as H.D.) and the painter Charles Demuth. All of them went on to become involved with the Imagist movement, an approach to poetry that emphasized, as Pound described it, the direct presentation of the "thing," or subject of the poem, rather than formal elements such as rhyme or meter. Williams's concern with the presentation of the image is evident in such early works as *The Tempers* (1913) and *Al Que Quiere!* (1917) and remained a focus throughout his career. Perhaps even more important to his development as a poet, Williams did not give himself wholly over to his interest in literature. Graduating from medical school in 1906, he was a successful pediatrician and general practitioner in his hometown of Rutherford, New Jersey, for more than forty years. He wrote whenever he could find the time, drawing inspiration from his patients and jotting lines on scraps of paper. In addition, Williams's relationships with family and friends influenced his work. He married Florence Herman in 1912, and they had two sons. His relationship with Florence, whom he called Floss, was a driving force behind much of his poetry, along with his mother and his paternal grandmother, Emily Dickenson Wellcome, who helped raise him.

In his struggle to establish himself as a poet, Williams defined himself in opposition to T. S. Eliot, whose publication in 1922 of *The Waste Land,* an influential poem written with Pound's support and encouragement, seemed to augur a poetry intended only for an intellectual audience. Williams viewed Eliot, unlike himself, to be Pound's equal in culture and cultivated taste, but he recounts in *The Autobiography* (1951) that he came to regard *The Waste Land* as a declaration of war. More so than any other poem Eliot ever wrote, almost every line of *The Waste Land* carried a learned allusion. Rather than viewing Eliot's references to the past as necessary for the representation of the fragmented modern mind, Williams saw such allusiveness as stifling to creation. The poetry Williams wrote in the next decade may be read as his response to Eliot. Students interested in Eliot's impact on Williams's work will want to read Philip Bufithis's "William Carlos Williams Writing against *The Waste Land*" (1989).

While Williams may have lacked the depth of classical learning of Pound and Eliot, he was an accomplished man of letters who produced stories, novels, plays, essays, translations, and an autobiography in addition to his poetry. His greatest work was his urban epic *Paterson,* a poem published in five volumes from 1946 to 1958. Although critical regard came slowly to Williams (the first book-length study of his work was published in 1950, whereas Eliot and Pound had received serious attention much earlier), young poets in the 1950s began to claim him as an important influence; he was a strong and willing mentor to Charles Olsen, Robert Creeley, Denise Levertov, H. H. Lewis, Robert Lowell, Theodore Roethke, and Allen Ginsberg. After a period of declining health, Williams died in his home in Rutherford on 4 March 1963. He had worked feverishly on his writing up until his death, and even in his last days had had Floss read to him for up to four hours a day. In 1963 he was posthumously awarded the Pulitzer Prize for *Pictures from Brueghel and Other Poems* (1962).

Collected Poems, 1921–1931 (1934) is made up of sixty-seven poems, divided into five sections: "Poems" (twenty-nine poems); "*Della Primavera Trasportata al Morale,*" an Italian phrase that might best be translated as "A Moral Interpretation of Springtime" (eight poems); "Spring and All," a selection from the 1923 collection of that title, slightly rearranged (twelve poems); "The Descent of Winter" (nine poems); and "The Flower" (nine poems). Despite the title of the collection, Williams had written eight of the poems in the final section before 1921; "Sicilian

Emigrant's Song" (1913) was the earliest. Because the volume was published by a small press and has not been reprinted, it is difficult to find a copy of it; students interested in studying the collection can, however, consult the table of contents for the volume provided in the appendix of *The Collected Poems of William Carlos Williams*, volume 1: *1909–1939*.

The publication of *Collected Poems, 1921–1931*, for which Wallace Stevens wrote a preface, marked the beginning of serious attention being paid to Williams's poetry. In a review in *Scribner's Magazine* Eli Siegel was "careful" in his claim that Williams's poems "belong to the history of American Poetry and therefore, Literature," but he went on to assert, "Williams is big time—any time in American Poetry." In *William Carlos Williams: A New World Naked* (1981) Paul Mariani contends that the collection, published more than a decade after *Spring and All*, reinvigorated Williams's interest in poetry. Mariani relates that Williams went to great lengths to find a publisher for the book and claimed that it was "the best collection of verse in America today." It was an important volume in Williams's career project to make poetry accessible to readers beyond the borders of academe and to change American poetry in content, diction, and form.

TOPICS FOR DISCUSSION AND RESEARCH

1. Williams often wrote about common, everyday objects. As he notes in *The Autobiography*, he wanted people to realize that "even the most trivial happenings may carry a certain weight." One of Williams's most anthologized poems, "The Red Wheelbarrow," originally published in *Spring and All* and included in *Collected Poems, 1921–1931*, provides an excellent example of the poet's focus on the ordinary. What other poems in the collection have a similar focus on seemingly unremarkable objects? Before reading what a critic has to say about a particular poem in which you are interested, carefully consider the object about which Williams has chosen to write. What meaning does the object have—in the world and for you personally? How does Williams's poem make you see the object differently? The wheelbarrow, as Barry Ahearn notes on the *Modern American Poetry website* (<http://www.english.illinois.edu/maps/poets/s_z/williams/williams.htm>), is one of the oldest machines, a simple but useful tool that could be found in any yard anywhere. Williams, though, leads the reader to see the wheelbarrow as an object of art. In accordance with Pound's formulation of Imagism, the poem shows how Williams carefully chooses his words so that each one contributes to the presentation of "a red wheel/ barrow" on which "so much depends." Williams's poems ask readers to look at the ordinary with fresh eyes and to form a new appreciation for their surroundings. For students interested in learning more about Williams's ideas about poetic content, James E. Breslin, Bram Dijkstra, and Paul Mariani provide detailed accounts of Williams's poetic development. *The Modern American Poetry website* provides extracts of the comments of these critics, as well as the insights of other critics into Williams's poetic development and theories.

2. Williams believed that if poetry was to be accessible to everyone, poets needed to abandon "poetic" diction—language that readers encountered in stilted

poems but did not hear living people use—and try to evoke and distill the patterns of ordinary speech. In the poem "This Is Just to Say," for instance, we can almost hear him speaking the words, "I have eaten / the plums / that were in / the icebox . . . forgive me." Read aloud the poems in *Collected Poems, 1921–1931* and try to find the rhythm of Williams's words with your own voice. Do you encounter any words that are not heard in ordinary speech? Identify any unusual word choice and consider how it fits into the poem. Would any other word work as well or better? Students interested in a deeper understanding of Williams's ideas about language will want to read *The Wedge* (1944), his first manifesto on poetic language; *I Wanted to Write a Poem* (1958), in which he describes his processes and philosophies; and *Paterson,* which illustrates the culmination of his ideas about the American idiom.

3. To create poetry that captures American speech, Williams believed that he had to find an appropriate poetic form. He thought that the use of rhyme schemes and traditional meters such as iambic pentameter distanced the average reader from the poem and its content; therefore, he embraced the use of free-form styles. In *Collected Poems, 1921–1931* he experiments with form in poems such as "The Attic Which Is Desire," in which he uses typography to indicate the sign he sees across the street:

from the street
by
* * *
* S *
* O *
* D *
* A *
* * *

ringed with
running lights

As you read Williams's poems, look closely at the arrangement of the words on the page. How does the arrangement lead you to read the poem? How are you led to *see* the images the poet presents? What lines strike you as particularly effective? In the 1920s and 1930s Williams was still working out his ideas about poetic form. He eventually developed what he called "the variable foot," which is rooted in the American idiom, and the stepped triadic line, a long line divided into three segments. He employed these ideas in later works such as *Paterson* and "Asphodel, That Greeny Flower" in *Pictures from Brueghel and Other Poems* (1962). Williams discusses the development of his ideas on content, diction, and form in *I Wanted to Write a Poem.*

4. Williams frequented art galleries and openings and wrote many poems focused on works of art, an interest apparent in *Collected Poems, 1921–1931.* For example, Bram Dijkstra argues that the poem "Young Sycamore" is likely based on Alfred Stieglitz's photograph *Spring Showers* (1902). Read the poem carefully and form a mental image of the scene described. Then examine Stieg-litz's photograph (the image is shown on the *Modern American Poetry website,*

<http://www.english.illinois.edu/maps/poets/s_z/williams/sycamore.htm>.
How did the image you had formed in your mind differ from the photograph?
Do you agree with Dijkstra that Williams is describing the photograph? If we
stipulate that the photograph did inspire the poem, what details did Williams
choose to leave out? As Dijkstra notes, Williams often did not indicate when
poems were based on artworks, but in his personal papers and essays there are
detailed descriptions and rough sketches of artworks that touched him. How
does seeing *Spring Showers* affect your appreciation of "Young Sycamore"? For
another poem in *Collected Poems, 1921–1931* based on an artwork, see "Portrait
of a Lady."

5. Williams believed that many of Americans' prudish opinions about sex were
the result of outdated traditional beliefs. He equated his desire for the opposite
sex with a desire to discover the feminine principle of imagination, which he
called *Kore*, thus making sexual desire inseparable from creativity. Desire and
love, though, like the seasons, have their own cycles of dearth and bounty, and
Collected Poems, 1921–1931 often explores cycles through love and rebirth.
Consider, for example, "The Botticellian Trees," a title that invokes the early
Renaissance Italian artist known as Sandro Botticelli, best known for his
painting *The Birth of Venus* (circa 1485). Would you call this work a love poem?
A poem about desire? A celebration of nature? What other poems can you
identify in which nature is paralleled with the feminine and desire? For more
discussion of *Kore* and the feminine principle, see Mariani.

RESOURCES

Primary Work

The Collected Poems of William Carlos Williams, volume 1: *1909–1939,* edited by
A. Walton Litz and Christopher MacGowan (New York: New Directions,
1986).
A chronological collection that allows the reader to trace Williams's development. The book includes the table of contents for *Collected Poems, 1921–1931* in
an appendix.

Biography

Neil Baldwin, *To All Gentleness: William Carlos Williams, the Doctor-Poet* (New
York: Atheneum, 1984).
Covers the merging of Williams's careers as doctor and poet. Baldwin catalogued
the Williams archives at Yale University and the State University of New York
at Buffalo.

Paul L. Mariani, *William Carlos Williams: A New World Naked* (New York:
McGraw-Hill, 1981).
The most extensive biography.

Pound/Williams: Selected Letters of Ezra Pound and William Carlos Williams, edited
by Hugh Witemeyer (New York: New Directions, 1996).

Provides insights into Williams and Pound's working relationship and highlights many of Williams's other important connections, poetic themes, and writing decisions.

William Carlos Williams, *The Autobiography* (New York: New Directions, 1951).
The poet's own account of his life and work. Some of the facts have been disputed; the discrepancies have been attributed to the haste with which Williams wrote the book.

Criticism

Academy of American Poets website <http://www.poets.org/poet.php/prmPID/119> [accessed 1 November 2009].
Allows students to listen to and read Williams's poetry and to read interpretations of his work. In addition, the site offers introductions to Imagism, Objectivism, and Modernism.

James E. Breslin, *William Carlos Williams: An American Artist* (New York: Oxford University Press, 1985).
Offers interpretations and criticisms of Williams' poetry and an overview of his work.

Philip Bufithis, "William Carlos Williams Writing against *The Waste Land*," *Sagetrieb*, 8, 1–2 (1989): 215–223.
Highlights the importance of T. S. Eliot's work on Williams's development of a distinctly American content and form.

Bram Dijkstra, *Cubism, Stieglitz, and the Early Poetry of William Carlos Williams* (Princeton: Princeton University Press, 1978).
Examines the early work of Williams in relation to the art of the 1920s, illustrating the impact such art had on Williams's career and poetic development.

Edith Heal, ed., *I Wanted to Write a Poem* (Boston: Beacon, 1958).
Presents five months of conversations in which Williams responds to Heal's questions about specific works.

Eli Siegel, "William Carlos Williams: *Collected Poems, 1921–1931*," *Scribner's* (April 1934) <http://www.aestheticrealism.net/reviews/Scribners_Williams_1934.htm> [accessed 1 November 2009].
Offers a brief clip of Siegel's review of Williams's collection.

Linda Welshimer Wagner, ed., *Interviews with William Carlos Williams: "Speaking Straight Ahead"* (New York: New Directions, 1976).
Conversations with Williams about the content, meaning, and themes of his work by one of the first major scholars of his prose and poetry.

Thomas R. Whitaker, *William Carlos Williams*, revised edition (Boston: Twayne, 1989).

Examines Williams's prose and poetry, with a special emphasis on language and content.

"William Carlos Williams," *Modern American Poetry website* <http://www.english. illinois.edu/maps/poets/s_z/williams/williams.htm> [accessed 1 November 2009].
Provides a biography and critical interpretations by leading scholars of several poems. In addition, the site includes a bibliography, a list of Williams's poems, and links to other sites highlighting Williams.

—*Sheri Hardee*

Thomas Wolfe, *Look Homeward, Angel*
(New York: Scribners, 1929)

Thomas Wolfe (1900–1938) was born in Asheville, North Carolina, the youngest of eight children of William Oliver Wolfe and Julia Westall. The South into which he was born was a region literally as well as metaphorically straddling two centuries, caught between past and future, and the respective occupations of Wolfe's parents can be connected to those two currents: Wolfe's father was a stone carver, an artisan of the past who primarily produced gravestones; his mother not only ran a boardinghouse but also speculated actively and successfully in real estate, benefiting from Asheville's relatively new status as a mountain resort town. Wolfe began his education and literary career in the South, entering the University of North Carolina before he turned sixteen and producing both journalism and plays during his four years there; but he subsequently moved to Cambridge to study playwriting at Harvard University with George Pierce Baker and never again lived in his native region. Wolfe moved to New York City after graduating from Harvard with an M.A.; unable to get his plays produced, he taught English as an instructor at New York University from 1924 to 1930 while continuing to pursue his writing career. He began his first novel in 1926, encouraged by Aline Bernstein, a married New York set and costume designer with whom he was vacationing in England. Nearly twenty years his senior, Bernstein became a source of emotional and financial support for Wolfe during the course of their seven-year affair. It took Wolfe nearly four years to complete his novel, first as a manuscript titled "O Lost" and then—after a period of cutting and revising, in which he worked closely with his Scribners editor Maxwell Perkins—as *Look Homeward, Angel* (1929), which he dedicated to Bernstein. For his second novel, *Of Time and the River* (1935), Wolfe again worked with Perkins to cut and revise a large manuscript. Although he remained with Scribners for the story collection *From Death to Morning* (1935) and an expanded lecture on writing, *The Story of a Novel* (1936), he broke with the publisher in 1937, in part because he was sensitive to criticism that he relied on Perkins to shape his novels. Wolfe contracted pneumonia on a western trip a year later, and died of tuberculosis of the brain in

September 1938; he left behind voluminous manuscripts that were subsequently assembled by Edward Aswell, his editor at Harper and Brothers, into two additional novels, *The Web and the Rock* (1939) and *You Can't Go Home Again* (1940), and the collection *The Hills Beyond* (1941).

Despite the some sixty-six thousand words that were cut during the editorial process, *Look Homeward, Angel* remains a big book: its more than six hundred pages cover two full decades in the life of not only its autobiographical protagonist, Eugene Gant, but also important experiences in the lives of members of his large family—especially his father Oliver, mother Eliza, and brother Ben—and, just as important, the fictional town of Altamont, North Carolina, which is clearly based on Wolfe's native Asheville. Moreover, Wolfe's verbose style, his tendency to create long sentences full of complex emotional and metaphorical imagery, demands an engaged and active reader to appreciate the interconnected themes of past and future, region and identity, family, and artistic creation.

The beginning of the novel introduces many of its themes. In his note "To the Reader" Wolfe gives his view of literary art by asserting that "all serious work in fiction is autobiographical" and addressing the real people who may find themselves represented in his novel. He claims a complex relationship between fiction and fact: "Fiction is not fact, but fiction is fact selected and understood, fiction is fact arranged and charged with purpose." But despite Wolfe's assertions that "he meditated no man's portrait" and wrote his book "without rancor or bitter intention," many Asheville natives were offended by Wolfe's revealing depictions of his fictional town and its people. Part One of the three-part novel begins with an epigraph, an excerpt of prose poetry lifted from Wolfe's original manuscript for "O Lost" that establishes a tone of longing and lament. Often echoed in the narrative, the epigraph ends with an apostrophe to a ghost:

> *O waste of loss, in the hot mazes, lost, among bright stars on this most weary unbright cinder, lost! Remembering speechlessly we seek the great forgotten language, the lost lane-end into heaven, a stone, a leaf, an unfound door. Where? When? O lost, and by the wind grieved, ghost, come back again.*

The first chapter of Part One covers the generational, geographical, and psychological prehistory of the Gant family on whom the novel focuses, beginning with an 1837 voyage from Bristol, England, to Baltimore, moving with the family's ancestors to the town of Altamont, and culminating with the engagement of Oliver Gant and Eliza Pentland, the protagonist's parents, and an invocation of the epigraph, as Oliver listens to the talk of his future in-laws: "And like a man who is perishing in the polar night, he thought of the rich meadows of his youth: the corn, the plum tree, and ripe grain. Why here? O lost!"

The next two chapters summarize the first phase of the Gants' marriage, in which six children survive their "grim and casual littering": the oldest, Steve, born in 1885; followed by Daisy; Helen; the twins, Grover and Benjamin; and Luke in 1894. The birth six years later of their last child, Eugene, at the opening of chapter 4 introduces the central lens through which history, place, and family will be viewed. Over the remainder of Part One and the subsequent two parts Wolfe continues to rotate that lens, paying extended attention to Eugene's parents and siblings, as well as to a variety of regional, national, and even international developments. But the narration and perspective remain closely connected to Eugene's own developing consciousness and voice, both as a young man and as an artist. And with Part Three the novel turns almost entirely to Eugene's final and central question about his identity and future, as framed in the final word of the penultimate chapter: "Where?" The conversation in the final chapter between Eugene and the ghost of his closest brother, Ben, one that refers back to the epigraph of Part One on multiple levels, makes clear how much the concept of home will inform Eugene's future and identity and art no matter where he travels.

Because of the close connections between Wolfe and Eugene Gant, any analysis of the novel can benefit from biographical information and contexts, and there is a wealth of material available for such research. Wolfe's own *Autobiographical Outline* can be usefully paired with John Chandler Griffin's *Memories of Thomas Wolfe: A Pictorial Companion to* Look Homeward, Angel (1996), John Lane Idol Jr.'s *A Thomas Wolfe Companion* (1987), or Ted Mitchell's *Thomas Wolfe: A Documentary Volume* (2001). John E. Bassett's *Thomas Wolfe: An Annotated Critical Bibliography* (1996) and Carol Ingalls Johnston's *Of Time and the Artist: Thomas Wolfe, His Novels, and the Critics* (1996) cover Wolfe scholarship from his initial publications through the mid 1990s; *The Thomas Wolfe Review,* published annually (since 2000; semiannually before that year) and available in full text online through the *Literary Journals Index,* is an excellent resource through which to trace more recent trends and voices in Wolfe scholarship.

TOPICS FOR DISCUSSION AND RESEARCH

1. The central focus of the novel is the character of Eugene Gant. Is he a purely autobiographical construct? How much is Wolfe's alter ego an invention? One way of focusing the analysis of the character of Eugene and the significant autobiographical parallels in the novel as well as the broader questions of the relationship between fact and fiction—and avoid simply tracing such autobiographical connections without a purpose—is to consider whether the genre of bildungsroman is sufficient to describe Wolfe's text. Richard Kennedy's essay, "Wolfe's Fiction: The Question of Genre," in the collection edited by Harold Bloom provides context for such an analysis. Because Wolfe's maturing protagonist is also a budding artist, it is also worthwhile to consider other such novels that treat artists, such as James Joyce's *A Portrait of the Artist as a Young Man,* a comparison Warren Edminster explores in his essay.

2. Because Wolfe had such difficulty in shaping his material into a form that Scribners would publish, the effectiveness of the structure of *Look Homeward, Angel* is particularly interesting to consider. What does the way that the text is structured—the three parts and the forty chapters into which they are divided—suggest about Wolfe's purposes in the novel? Does the material fit together in a unified narrative? Does Wolfe's use of the idea of home and employment of metaphorical images such as angels serve to bring cohesion? John Hagan's essay, "Structure, Theme, and Metaphor in *Look Homeward, Angel,*" in the Bloom collection focuses on Wolfe's angel imagery to argue

for a unified structure; Igina Tattoni argues instead that the novel anticipates postmodernism through its fragmented structure.

3. The evaluation of Thomas Wolfe as a novelist is complicated by editor Maxwell Perkins's extraordinary role in shaping the final text, for the question of how much Perkins influenced Wolfe to make changes he did not agree with lingers over the novel. Arlyn Bruccoli and Matthew Bruccoli have edited and published Wolfe's original manuscript, affording the opportunity to compare the work Wolfe submitted to the novel Perkins convinced him to publish. To understand how the editing process changed Wolfe's novel, begin with the articles by Michael Mills and Suzanne Stutman. Mills considers the changes on a broad level, and Stutman emphasizes the Pennsylvania sections of the manuscript that were entirely jettisoned. Did Wolfe allow Perkins to have too much influence?

4. One of the central themes of *Look Homeward, Angel* is the relationship of the past to the present and future, as Wolfe examines the issues of loss and memory—both exemplified by the recurring references to ghosts. What does the novel suggest about the usefulness of the past or of the act of looking homeward? How do Eugene and his mother and father relate to the past? In considering these questions students might want to read two critics who disagree: Morris Beja in "The Escapes of Time and Memory," included in the Bloom collection, argues for the value of the past in the novel; D. G. Kehl in "Writing the Long Desire: The Function of Sehnsucht in *The Great Gatsby* and *Look Homeward, Angel*" is much more critical of how characters turn to memory.

5. How important is the presentation of Altamont in its various aspects—a North Carolina mountain town, a resort locale on the rise, a place with extremes of wealth and poverty, its broader regional identity within the South in the generations after the Civil War and into the early twentieth century—to the success of the novel? While Wolfe is not usually considered part of the Southern Renaissance as exemplified by writers such as William Faulkner, Robert Penn Warren, and Allen Tate, his novels can certainly be read as another set of contemporaneous literary visions of the region; C. Hugh Holman's essay, "The Web of the South," in the Bloom collection introduces just such a reading. Ted Mitchell's article, on the other hand, focuses on a much more local context, the marble angels built by Wolfe's father for various North Carolina settings and their influence on Wolfe's imagery in the novel.

RESOURCES

Primary Work

O Lost: A Story of the Buried Life, edited by Arlyn Bruccoli and Matthew J. Bruccoli (Columbia: University of South Carolina Press, 2000).
Uncut version of *Look Homeward, Angel.*

Biography

Joanne Marshall Mauldin, *Thomas Wolfe: When Do the Atrocities Begin?* (Knoxville: University of Tennessee Press, 2007).

A thorough, analytical biography of the last years of Wolfe's life, including extended analysis of the novel.

Thomas Wolfe, *The Autobiographical Outline for* Look Homeward, Angel, edited by Lucy Conniff and Richard S. Kennedy (Asheville, N.C.: Thomas Wolfe Society, 1991).
Much more specific and helpful than a broad autobiography, this text collects Wolfe's notes for the interconnected presentation of autobiographical and fictional characters, places, events, and details in the novel.

Bibliography
John E. Bassett, *Thomas Wolfe: An Annotated Critical Bibliography* (Lanham, Md: Scarecrow Press, 1996).
A vital starting point for any engagement with Wolfe scholarship.

Criticism
Harold Bloom, ed., *Thomas Wolfe: Modern Critical Views* (New York: Chelsea House, 1987).
Collects eight seminal critical articles, including essays by Richard Kennedy, John Hagan, Morris Beja, and C. Hugh Holman that focus on *Look Homeward, Angel.*

Warren Edminster, "A Portrait of an American Artist: The Implied Author/ Protagonist Relationship in Wolfe's *Look Homeward, Angel,*" *Thomas Wolfe Review,* 20, 2 (Fall 1996): 37–43.
An analysis of the implications of autobiographical readings of the novel for images of artistic imagination and creation, both as performed by Eugene and as embodied in Wolfe's own modernist text (especially in relationship to James Joyce's *A Portrait of the Artist as a Young Man*).

John Chandler Griffin, *Memories of Thomas Wolfe: A Pictorial Companion to* Look Homeward, Angel (Columbia, S.C.: Summerhouse Press, 1996).
Produced with the help of Wolfe's brother Fred, includes and analyzes a variety of photographs and documents that provide important biographical contexts for the novel.

John Lane Idol Jr., *A Thomas Wolfe Companion* (New York: Greenwood Press, 1987).
Provides a wealth of information about Wolfe's life, works, and the critical responses to him, including an extended, annotated primary bibliography and excellent introductions to library and archival collections of Wolfe materials.

Carol Ingalls Johnston, *Of Time and the Artist: Thomas Wolfe, His Novels, and the Critics* (Columbia, S.C.: Camden House, 1996).
Highlights and analyzes both contemporary and later twentieth-century reviews and scholarly analyses of Wolfe's novels.

D. G. Kehl, "Writing the Long Desire: The Function of Sehnsucht in *The Great Gatsby* and *Look Homeward, Angel*," *Journal of Modern Literature*, 24 (Winter 2000–2001): 309–319.

Argues that the novel's historical vision is one of intense nostalgia, using the concept (from German Romanticism) of an addiction to longing for the past.

Aldo P. Magi and Richard Walser, eds., *Thomas Wolfe Interviewed, 1929–1938* (Baton Rouge: Louisiana State University Press, 1985).

Collects more than twenty extended interviews, almost all of which include discussion of both the novel and the relevant biographical contexts.

Michael S. Mills, "From 'O Lost' to *Look Homeward, Angel:* A Generic Shift," *Thomas Wolfe Review*, 10 (Spring 1986): 64–72.

Analyzes Wolfe's revisions to his original manuscript and examines Maxwell Perkins's editorial role and influence throughout the revising process; Mills argues that "O Lost" was significantly more satirical and broadly focused on American culture than *Look Homeward, Angel*.

Ted Mitchell, "Thomas Wolfe's Angels," *Thomas Wolfe Review*, 18 (Spring 1994): 1–18.

Highlights and analyzes some of the many marble angels constructed by Wolfe's father and their relationship to Wolfe's interest in and use of the image.

Mitchell, ed., *Dictionary of Literary Biography*, volume 229: *Thomas Wolfe: A Documentary Volume* (Detroit: Bruccoli Clark Layman/Gale, 2001); republished as *Thomas Wolfe: An Illustrated Biography* (New York: Pegasus, 2006).

Includes a wealth of relevant materials, particularly the sixty-page section on the four years comprising the novel's composition, editing, and reception.

Suzanne Stutman, "Home Again: Thomas Wolfe and Pennsylvania," *Resources for American Literary Study*, 18, 1 (1992): 44–52.

Highlights and analyzes the deleted Pennsylvania sections of the novel, as well as the editorial process through which they were cut.

Igina Tattoni, "*Look Homeward, Angel:* A Postmodern Perspective," *Unfound Door*, 46 (1992): 89–128.

Argues that the novel anticipates postmodernism, particularly through its structure and narration.

The Thomas Wolfe Society, University of North Carolina, Wilmington <http://library.uncwil.edu/Wolfe/Wolfe.html> [accessed 7 September 2009].

Excellent website devoted to Wolfe, including photographs and collections on biographical and regional contexts for the novel and tables of contents for the latest issues of *The Thomas Wolfe Review*.

—Ben Railton

Richard Wright, *Native Son*

(New York: & London: Harper, 1940)

Richard Wright (1908–1960) was born near Natchez, Mississippi, to Nathaniel Wright, a sharecropper, and Ella Wilson Wright, a schoolteacher. His parents' respective occupations suggest the central tension that defined Wright's childhood, for like his father he was circumscribed by his status—a black male in the Jim Crow South—and, yet, like his mother, he aspired to better himself and later determined to become a writer. By 1927 a series of familial and communal traumas and setbacks had made it clear to Wright that in the South his status would always weigh down his ambitions, and in December of that year he moved to Chicago. In the 1930s he pursued his career as a writer, publishing his first story in 1931, his first poems two years later, and his first book, the important short-story collection *Uncle Tom's Children,* in 1938. He also became a public activist, joining the Communist Party in 1933. These activities came to quite distinct heads in the early 1940s: in 1940 Wright published his masterpiece, the novel *Native Son;* two years later he severed all ties with the Communist Party. As was his practice, Wright publicly reflected on these important events, writing about *Native Son* in *How "Bigger" Was Born* (1940) and his political experiences in "I Tried to Be a Communist" and "The Man Who Lived Underground" (both 1944). He then published the first volume of his autobiography, *Black Boy: A Record of Childhood and Youth* (1945), which became a tremendous success. Uncomfortable in the United States because of his political history and views, Wright after World War II lived the remaining years of his life abroad. He continued to write—nonfiction as well as the novels *The Outsider* (1953), *Savage Holiday* (1954), and *The Long Dream* (1958)—but he was never again to reach such audiences as he had with his earlier works. He died of an apparent heart attack in Paris. His second autobiographical volume, *American Hunger,* was published in 1977, seventeen years after his death.

Native Son* has always led a double life of sorts. The novel was chosen as a Book-of-the-Month Club selection (the first by an African American author to be so honored), sold 250,000 copies in its first year, and was awarded the NAACP's Spingarn Medal; these commercial and critical successes made Wright an instant celebrity and his novel a national conversation piece. While popularity and even contemporary critical acclaim are no guarantee of a book's quality, *Native Son* has endured because it is a complex, unsettling novel that confronts, without offering any facile resolution, core American issues: race and gender, poverty and violence, law and politics.

Book I of *Native Son,* "Fear," narrates a hugely significant single day for the novel's protagonist, Bigger Thomas, as he moves from family life in his cramped South Side apartment and street life with his friends to a job as a chauffeur for a wealthy white family, the Daltons; a night out with the Daltons' politically radical daughter, Mary, and her Communist boyfriend, Jan Erlone, ends in tragedy when Bigger, trapped in Mary's room and fearing discovery by her blind mother, kills Mary, an act that the novel frames as both accidental and yet the culmination of Bigger's psychological and emotional trajectory as a young African American male.

Books II and III are significantly less tight in structure and focus but enrich the novel's web of characters and social themes. "Flight" parallels Bigger's botched attempt to pin Mary's murder on Communists and the subsequent manhunt for him (in both of which he is accompanied by his girlfriend, Bessie, whom he eventually murders in a much more premeditated manner than Mary) with the shifting journalistic coverage of the case, as the newspapers move from purveying Red Scare propaganda to the most stereotyped and racist portrayals of African Americans. "Fate" focuses on Bigger's trial, and especially the dueling voices of his Communist lawyer, Boris Max, who argues for the social causes of Bigger's crimes and pleads for leniency in his sentencing, and state's attorney Buckley, who successfully argues for Bigger's individual responsibility and the death penalty.

While *Native Son* stands alone in Wright's career, any analysis of it would be enriched by a reading of the early fiction that preceded it and the autobiographical and political writings from the years around it. Much of the fiction is included in the first half (*Early Works*) of the Library of America edition, along with *Native Son*; the nonfiction is not collected in any one volume, but Charles Davis's *Richard Wright: A Primary Bibliography* identifies all such texts. Hazel Rowley's excellent biography, *Richard Wright: The Life and Times*, in conjunction with Wright's own two-volume autobiography and the essential *Conversations with Richard Wright*, provide a thorough recounting of the years before and during the writing and publication of the novel.

By far the best place to begin any search of Richard Wright criticism is with Keneth Kinnamon's two bibliographic collections; similarly, his edited collection of essays on *Native Son* makes a strong starting point for work on the novel. From there, the more than ninety publications on or treating *Native Son* since 2000 (as found in an MLA Bibliography search) reveal the breadth of continuing work on Wright's text.

TOPICS FOR DISCUSSION AND RESEARCH

1. The most compelling topic for analysis in *Native Son* is Bigger's character and behavior. Why does Bigger become increasingly violent? What role does his family's poverty, his early experiences in the South and loss of his father there, and the influence of his peer group play? How determinative are psychological factors such as his desire to prove himself as a man and his sexual urges, especially his tabooed attraction to Mary? To what extent is he motivated by the differences he apprehends between his world and Mary's, his sense of an entirely limited life and future? Why does he experience a feeling of constant fear? Many critics have treated this topic; for an excellent starting point, see James A. Miller's essay, "Bigger Thomas's Quest for Voice and Audience in Richard Wright's *Native Son*," in Kinnamon's *Critical Essays on Richard Wright's* Native Son.

2. Many of the social themes in the novel are linked directly to Communism, as are all three of the most fully developed white characters: Mary Dalton, Jan Erlone,

and Boris Max. How does the novel depict communism and communists? Is communism shown to be a viable American political movement? What do the differences between the perspectives of the white communists and Bigger's own shifting views on communism show about Wright's portrayal of the Communist Party? George C. Grinnell's essay examines how Wright's contemporaries and later scholars have read the meaning of communism in the novel.

3. Wright's novel is filled with various references to the history and popular culture of the era. The most famous such reference is the movie-theater sequence from Book I, in which an actual movie, *Trader Horn,* is invoked. What is the relevance of this movie to the themes of the novel? Perhaps the most extended and complex historical parallel developed in the novel is to the Leopold and Loeb murder and trial. Is this an appropriate parallel to draw to Bigger's trial? How is it fitting? How is it not? For the role of movies in the novel, see James Smethurst's essay; for an interpretation of the importance of the Leopold and Loeb reference, read Robert Butler's essay.

4. Wright's third-person narration is well worth analysis. Some critics read the narration as entirely limited to Bigger's perspective, while others have suggested that there is significant divergence between the perspective of the implied narrator and that of his protagonist. Is the narrative limited solely to what is included in Bigger's point of view? What does Wright gain from this narrative approach? What does he lose? The John M. Reilly essay, "Giving Bigger a Voice," in Kinnamon's *New Essays on* Native Son effectively frames these issues.

5. A topic that has received much attention but perhaps not sufficient consideration is the novel's treatment of gender and sexuality. In part because of Wright's harshly critical review of Zora Neale Hurston's *Their Eyes Were Watching God* (a review that had very little to do with gender but that has been read as gendered by feminist proponents of Hurston's inclusion in the canon), Wright's novel has sometimes been read as explicitly misogynistic. How successful is Wright in portraying his female characters—Mary and Bessie, as well as Bigger's mother and sister? For two recent scholarly perspectives on femininity in the novel, see Yvonne Robinson Jones, "Sexual Diversity in Richard Wright's Characterization of Bigger Thomas," and Carol E. Henderson, "Notes from a Native Daughter," both in Ana Maria Fraile's *Richard Wright's Native Son*; for an exemplary analysis of masculinity in the text, see Jeffrey B. Leak's *Racial Myths and Masculinity in African American Literature.*

RESOURCES

Primary Works

Richard Wright, *Black Boy: A Record of Childhood and Youth* (New York: Harper, 1945).

Wright's first autobiographical volume, one of the most significant and impressive works of personal narrative in American literature.

Wright, *American Hunger* (New York: Harper & Row, 1977).

The posthumously published second volume of Wright's autobiography. More inconsistent than the first volume, it covers the years immediately before, during, and after the publication of *Native Son*.

Biography

Hazel Rowley, *Richard Wright: The Life and Times* (New York: Holt, 2001).
The definitive biography, Rowley's text is especially effective when paired with Wright's own versions of his life in the two-volume autobiography.

Bibliography

Charles Davis and Michel Fabre, *Richard Wright, a Primary Bibliography* (Boston: G. K. Hall, 1982).
Thoroughly documents Wright's writings in every genre.

Keneth Kinnamon, *A Richard Wright Bibliography: Fifty Years of Criticism and Commentary, 1933–1982* (New York: Greenwood Press, 1988).
The first of Kinnamon's two bibliographies. The two works are the best starting points for any search of Wright criticism are; they are both organized chronologically, but include excellent indexes to allow for subject-specific searches of their more than twenty-one thousand combined entries.

Kinnamon, *Richard Wright: An Annotated Bibliography of Criticism and Commentary, 1983–2003* (Jefferson, N.C.: McFarland, 2006).
Highlights the increasing breadth of topics considered by recent scholars, as well as the boom in Japanese scholarship on Wright.

Criticism

Harold Bloom, ed., *Richard Wright's* Native Son (New York: Chelsea House, 1996).
A useful collection of scholarly articles.

Robert Butler, "The Loeb and Leopold Case: A Neglected Source for Richard Wright's *Native Son*," *African American Review*, 39 (Winter 2005): 555–567.
One of the first scholars to focus on Leopold and Loeb in the novel.

Ana Maria Fraile, ed., *Richard Wright's* Native Son (Amsterdam: Rodopi, 2007).
An excellent collection of recent scholarship on the novel.

George C. Grinnell, "Exchanging Ghosts: Haunting, History, and Communism in *Native Son*," *English Studies in Canada*, 30 (September 2004): 145–174.
Analyzes both textual representations and contextual images of Communism.

Keneth Kinnamon, ed., *Critical Essays on Richard Wright's* Native Son (New York: Twayne, 1997).

A great first resource for work with the novel's scholarship. It needs to be supplemented with the Fraile collection and database searches for the subsequent dozen years.

Kinnamon, ed., *New Essays on* Native Son (Cambridge, England: Cambridge University Press, 1990).
Particularly strong as an introduction to scholarly voices and focuses from the 1980s, including narration and the blues.

Kinnamon and Michel Fabre, eds., *Conversations with Richard Wright* (Jackson: University Press of Mississippi, 1993).
Highly engaging conversations in which much of the material covered relates directly or indirectly to *Native Son* and its era in Wright's life and career.

Jeffrey B. Leak, *Racial Myths and Masculinity in African American Literature* (Knoxville: University of Tennessee Press, 2004), pp. 59–89.
Includes a chapter on *Native Son* and *A Lesson before Dying* that illustrates the complexity of masculinity in Wright's novel and mid-twentieth-century African American literature.

James Smethurst, "'You Reckon Folks Really Act Like That?': Horror Films and the Work of Popular Culture in Richard Wright's *Native Son*," in *Scandalous Fictions: The Twentieth-Century Novel in the Public Sphere*, edited by Jago Morrison and Susan Watkins (New York: Palgrave, 2006), pp. 83–98.
A good starting point for an exploration of the movie-theater section of the novel and related themes.

Andrew Warnes, *Richard Wright's* Native Son (London: Routledge, 2007).
Part of the Routledge Guides to Literature series. This volume includes a critical history and reprinted critical essays, along with excellent guides to further research in a variety of areas.

—*Ben Railton*

Part IV
Annotated Bibliography

Doris E. Abramson, *Negro Playwrights in the American Theatre, 1925–1959* (New York & London: Columbia University Press, 1969).
Examines "plays of American Negro authorship which were produced in the New York professional theatre," beginning with Garland Anderson's *Appearances,* the first play by an African American produced on Broadway. Abramson discusses works by Wallace Thurman, Hall Johnson, Frank Wilson, Rudolph Fisher, Hughes Allison, Langston Hughes, and Theodore Ward.

William G. Bailey, *Americans in Paris, 1900–1930: A Selected, Annotated Bibliography* (New York: Greenwood Press, 1989).
Designed "to provide a resource for scholars interested in the entire phenomenon of Americans in Paris," treating tourists as well as writers, musicians, and other artists.

Bert Bender, *Evolution and "The Sex Problem": American Narratives during the Eclipse of Darwinism* (Kent, Ohio: Kent State University Press, 2004).
A wide-ranging book that includes discussion of twentieth-century figures such as Theodore Dreiser, Gertrude Stein, and Willa Cather.

Shari Benstock, *Women of the Left Bank: Paris, 1900–1940* (Austin: University of Texas Press, 1986).
Examines "the contributions of some two dozen American and English expatriate women to the life of literary Paris between 1900 and 1940," including Sylvia Beach, Janet Flanner, H. D., Anaïs Nin, Gertrude Stein, and Djuna Barnes.

Sacvan Bercovitch, ed., *The Cambridge History of American Literature,* 8 volumes (New York: Cambridge University Press, 1994–2005).
Includes two volumes that are most relevant to the years 1914 to 1945: volume 5, *Poetry and Criticism, 1900–1915,* and volume 6, *Prose Writing, 1910–1950.*

Gerald M. Berkowitz, *American Drama of the Twentieth Century* (London & New York: Longman, 1992).
Includes discussion of the years 1914 to 1945 that mainly concerns Naturalism, Realism, comedy, and alternatives to Realism. Eugene O'Neill, Clifford Odets, Maxwell Anderson, Thornton Wilder, and Tennessee Williams are treated in some detail.

C. W. E. Bigsby, *A Critical Introduction to Twentieth Century American Drama,* 3 volumes (Cambridge, England: Cambridge University Press, 1982–1985).
Includes chapters on Provincetown, Eugene O'Neill, the Theatre Guild, Group Theatre and Clifford Odets, the Federal Theatre, Black drama, Thornton Wilder, and Lillian Hellman.

Sterling Brown, *The Negro in American Fiction* (Washington, D.C.: Associates in Negro Folk Education, 1937).
Includes brief discussions of many novels and stories featuring African American characters by both white and black authors.

Matthew J. Bruccoli and Robert W. Trogdon, eds., *Dictionary of Literary Biography Documentary Series,* volume 15: *American Expatriate Writers: Paris in the Twenties* (Detroit: Bruccoli Clark Layman/Gale, 1997).
A well-illustrated chronicle that documents the lives of a dozen expatriates, as well as the important little magazines *The Little Review, The Transatlantic Review, This Quarter,* and *transition.*

Humphrey Carpenter, *Geniuses Together: American Writers in Paris in the 1920s* (Boston: Houghton Mifflin, 1988).
Tells "the story of the longest-ever literary party, which went on in Montparnasse, on the Left Bank, throughout the 1920s."

John J. Conder, *Naturalism in American Fiction: The Classic Phase* (Lexington: University Press of Kentucky, 1984).
Argues that free choice can exist within the determinism of Naturalism. Conder discusses such twentieth-century writers as Theodore Dreiser, John Dos Passos, William Faulkner, and John Steinbeck.

Peter Conn, *The American 1930s: A Literary History* (Cambridge, England: Cambridge University Press, 2009).
A wide-ranging account of the decade that makes connections between historical events and literature. The book includes discussions of historical novels, plays and poems, biographies and autobiographies, as well as factual and imaginary works of history.

Stanley Cooperman, *World War I and the American Novel* (Baltimore: Johns Hopkins University Press, 1967).
A thematic study that aims to "re-experience" a literary period that was "in a vital sense" created by war. Cooperman discusses Willa Cather, John Dos Passos, Eliot Paul, William Faulkner, Thomas Boyd, e. e. cummings, and Ernest Hemingway.

Stanley Corkin, *Realism and the Birth of the Modern United States: Cinema, Literature, and Culture* (Athens: University of Georgia Press, 1996).
Discusses Dreiser's *Sister Carrie* and Edwin S. Porter's movies, as well as Ernest Hemingway's *In Our Time* and D. W. Griffith's *The Birth of a Nation.*

Malcolm Cowley, *Exile's Return: A Literary Odyssey of the 1920s,* third edition, edited by Donald W. Faulkner (New York: Penguin, 1994).
Tells the story of how the Lost Generation "earned its name (and tried to live up to it) and then how it ceased to be lost, how, in a sense, it found itself."

Emory Elliott, ed., *Columbia Literary History of the United States* (New York: Columbia University Press, 1988).
Treats the years 1910 to 1945 in part 4, which comprises four sections: I. Contexts and Backgrounds, II. Regionalism, Ethnicity, and Gender, III. Fiction, and IV. Poetry and Criticism.

Albert Gelpi, *A Coherent Splendor: The American Poetic Renaissance, 1910–1950* (Cambridge, England: Cambridge University Press, 1987).

Focuses on the poetry of Robert Frost, John Crowe Ransom, T. S. Eliot, Ezra Pound, H.D., William Carlos Williams, Allen Tate, Hart Crane, and Robinson Jeffers.

Horace Gregory and Marya Zaturenska, *A History of American Poetry, 1900–1940* (New York: Harcourt, Brace, 1942).
A contemporary history that treats many poets still considered major, as well as others such as John Gould Fletcher, John Wheelwright, and Dudley Fits.

Trudier Harris, ed., *Dictionary of Literary Biography*, volume 51: *Afro-American Writers from the Harlem Renaissance to 1940* (Detroit: Bruccoli Clark Layman/Gale, 1987).
Essays on the biographies and careers of major and minor figures.

Susan Hegeman, *Patterns for America: Modernism and the Concept of Culture* (Princeton: Princeton University Press, 1999).
A "book about the idea of culture as it was understood and deployed in early-twentieth-century United States" that considers the contributions of such writers and thinkers as Franz Boas, Van Wyck Brooks, Edward Sapir, Ruth Benedict, Waldo Frank, James Agee, Sherwood Anderson, T. S. Eliot, and Nathanael West.

Anthony Channell Hilfer, *The Revolt from the Village 1915–1930* (Chapel Hill: University of North Carolina Press, 1969).
Includes discussions of Willa Cather, Van Wyck Brooks, H. L. Mencken, Zona Gale, Edgar Lee Masters, Sherwood Anderson, Sinclair Lewis, Thomas Wolfe, and T. S. Stribling.

Gregory S. Jay, ed., *Dictionary of Literary Biography*, volume 63: *Modern American Critics, 1920–1955* (Detroit: Bruccoli Clark Layman/Gale, 1988).
Treats the critics who participated in the rise of modern criticism after World War I.

Hugh Kenner, *The Pound Era* (Berkeley: University of California Press, 1971).
A blend of biography, history, and analysis that treats Ezra Pound, a poet who was at the center of the vortex of literary modernism.

Bobby Ellen Kimbel, ed., *Dictionary of Literary Biography*, volume 86: *American Short-Story Writers, 1910–1945, First Series* (Detroit: Bruccoli Clark Layman/Gale, 1989).
Includes an introduction that provides context and background for the essays on Sherwood Anderson, Kay Boyle, Roark Bradford, Louis Bromfield, Maxwell Struthers Burt, and twenty more writers.

Kimbel, ed., *Dictionary of Literary Biography*, volume 102: *American Short-Story Writers, 1910–1945, Second Series* (Detroit: Bruccoli Clark Layman/Gale, 1991).
Builds on *American Short-Story Writers, 1910–1945, First Series*. Entries on Conrad Aiken, Stephen Vincent Benét, Pearl S. Buck, John Cheever, Robert M. Coates, and thirty-two more writers are included.

Donald Pizer, *American Expatriate Writing and the Paris Moment: Modernism and Place* (Baton Rouge & London: Louisiana State University Press, 1996).
Focuses on "the fiction and autobiography that derives from and depicts" the expatriate experience in 1920s Paris, discussing Ernest Hemingway's *A Moveable Feast* and *The Sun Also Rises*, Gertrude Stein's *The Autobiography of Alice B. Toklas*, Anaïs Nin's diary, John Dos Passos's *Nineteen Nineteen*, F. Scott Fitzgerald's *Tender Is the Night*, and Henry Miller's *Tropic of Cancer*.

Karen Lane Rood, ed., *Dictionary of Literary Biography*, volume 4: *American Writers in Paris, 1920–1939* (Detroit: Bruccoli Clark/Gale, 1980).
Includes nearly one hundred biographical essays and an appendix listing selected little magazines and newspapers.

Edmund Wilson, *Classics and Commercials: A Literary Chronicle of the Forties* (New York: Farrar, Straus, 1950).
A selection of literary articles Wilson wrote during the 1940s, including "The Boys in the Back Room," which treats James M. Cain, John O'Hara, and John Steinbeck.

Wilson, *The Shores of Light: A Literary Chronicle of the Twenties and Thirties* (New York: Farrar, Straus & Young, 1952).
A more-varied volume than the earlier *Classics and Commercials* that presents "a kind of panorama of the books and ideas, the movements and the literary life of a lively era." In addition to essays and reviews, Wilson includes dialogues, short sketches, and even personal letters.

Part V
Glossary

Agrarians   A group of twelve Southern writers—Allen Tate, John Crowe Ransom, Robert Penn Warren, Donald Davidson, Frank Lawrence Owsley, John Gould Fletcher, Lyle H. Lanier, Andrew Lytle, Herman Clarence Nixon, John Donald Wade, Henry Blue Kline, and Stark Young—whose essays in *I'll Take My Stand: The South and the Agrarian Tradition* (1930) were critical of Northern industrial society and praised the more humane agrarian life of the South. Most of these writers were also associated with the Fugitives.

anarchism   A political philosophy that holds that government is inherently evil and urges individuals to form voluntary associations; many anarchists also oppose capitalism. Anarchists were involved in the 1919 bombings that sparked the Red Scare and the Palmer Raids. Nicola Sacco and Bartolomeo Vanzetti, who were at the center of a celebrated trial, were anarchists who, many believe, were innocent of the robbery and murders with which they were charged and were executed for their political beliefs.

avant-garde   A French military term for the vanguard of an army; it serves as a metaphorical description of artists and writers leading the way to the future through experiment and rebellion against tradition. Ezra Pound suggested that "Artists are the antennae of the race."

bildungsroman   A German term meaning "formation-novel." It refers to a novel that follows the protagonist through a passage from innocence to experience or from ignorance to knowledge.

blank verse   A flexible verse form of unrhymed iambic pentameter lines. Robert Frost and Wallace Stevens were admired for their mastery of the form.

existentialism   A current in philosophy, developed in Europe, that holds that human beings are "abandoned" in a universe that has no intrinsic meaning or value and must create their own meaning and value through the choices that they make. Some French critics considered several American hard-boiled writers, including James M. Cain and Horace McCoy, to be existentialist authors.

expatriate   One who resides permanently or temporarily in a country other than his or her birthplace. The experience of expatriatism, especially in Paris in the 1920s, was central to the development of American literature, especially Modernism.

Expressionism   A literary mode opposed to Realism and Naturalism in that it presents a world shaped by intense personal moods, ideas, and emotions. In the American context Expressionism is chiefly found in the theater; Eugene O'Neill's *The Emperor Jones* (1920) and *The Hairy Ape* (1922) and Elmer Rice's *The Adding Machine* (1923), for example, use nonrealistic effects to suggest the emotional worlds of the characters.

feminism   The activist pursuit of equal rights for women, including suffrage (the right to vote). The latter was won with the Nineteenth Amendment to the Constitution, ratified on 18 August 1920.

free verse, or vers libre   A poetic form that self-consciously refuses to observe strict metrical arrangement or rhyme schemes. Many Modernist poets wrote sometimes or often in free verse.

The Fugitives   A group of poets and critics centered in Nashville, Tennessee, particularly at Vanderbilt University, who began discussing poetry and modern trends in the 1920s. They published *The Fugitive* (1922–1925), a little magazine that served as a forum for traditional and Modernist verse. Notable members included John Crowe Ransom, Donald Davidson, Allen Tate, Robert Penn Warren, and Laura Riding.

Imagism   A poetry movement led by Ezra Pound, who defined it by means of three principles: 1. to treat the "thing," whether subjective or objective, directly; 2. to use absolutely no word that does not contribute to the presentation; and 3. as regarding rhythm, to compose in the sequence of the musical phrase, not in the sequence of a metronome.

Naturalism   A literary movement primarily associated with the French novelist Émile Zola that emphasized a deterministic philosophy in which human beings are more acted on by natural forces and the social environment that they are actors. Theodore Dreiser's *An American Tragedy* (1925) is considered the highpoint of American Naturalism in the years between the world wars.

novel of manners   A novel that examines relationships of individuals within and between classes of society. Writers as different as Edith Wharton and F. Scott Fitzgerald have been considered novelists of manners.

Prohibition   The period from 17 January 1920 until 5 December 1933, when "the manufacture, sale, or transportation of intoxicating liquors" were illegal in the United States. The law was intended to remedy social ills caused by drinking, such as worker absenteeism and spousal abuse, but it was widely flouted and resulted in bootlegging, speakeasies, police corruption, and the rise of powerful organized-crime syndicates.

proletarian literature   Novels, poems, and drama that focus on the exploitation of the workers in a capitalist system.

revolt from the village   A phrase coined by Carl Van Doren in 1920 to designate writers who showed the faults of life in small-town America. Works that have been so categorized include Edgar Lee Masters's *Spoon River Anthology* (1915; enlarged, 1916), Sherwood Anderson's *Winesburg, Ohio* (1919), and Sinclair Lewis's *Main Street* (1920).

stream of consciousness   A literary technique in which the flow of an individual's sense perceptions, thoughts, feelings, and memories is represented in an "unedited" fashion. One of the most famous examples is the opening section of William Faulkner's *The Sound and the Fury* (1929); it is narrated by Benji Compson, a mentally challenged man whose understanding of the world is limited.

Index